Abdellah Taïa's Queer Migrations

After the Empire: The Francophone World and Postcolonial France

Recent Titles

Global Revolutionary Aesthetics and Politics after Paris '68, by Martin Munro, William Cloonan, Barry Falk, and Christian Weber

Francophone African Narratives and the Anglo-American Book Market: Ferment on the Fringes, by Vivan I. Steemers

Ethnic Minority Women's Writing in France: Publishing Practices and Identity Formation (1998-2005), by Claire Mouflard

Theory, Aesthetics, and Politics in the Francophone World: Filiations Past and Future, by Rajeshwari S. Vallury

Refiguring Les Années Noires: Literary Representations of the Nazi Occupation, by Kathy Comfort

Paris and the Marginalized Author: Treachery, Alienation, Queerness, and Exile, by Valérie K. Orlando and Pamela A. Pears

French Orientalist Literature in Algeria, 1845–1882: Colonial Hauntings, by Sage Goellner

Corporeal Archipelagos: Writing the Body in Francophone Oceanian Women's Literature, by Julia Frengs

Spaces of Creation: Transculturality and Feminine Expression in Francophone Literature, by Allison Connolly

Women Writers of Gabon: Literature and Herstory, by Cheryl Toman

Backwoodsmen as Ecocritical Motif in French Canadian Literature: Connecting Worlds in the Wilds, by Anne Rehill

Intertextual Weaving in the Work of Linda Lê: Imagining the Ideal Reader, by Alexandra Kurmann

Front Cover Iconography and Algerian Women's Writing: Heuristic Implications of the Recto-Verso Effect, by Pamela A. Pears

The Algerian War in French-Language Comics: Postcolonial Memory, History, and Subjectivity, by Jennifer Howell

Abdellah Taïa's Queer Migrations

Non-places, Affect, and Temporalities

Edited by
Denis M. Provencher and Siham Bouamer

LEXINGTON BOOKS
Lanham • Boulder • New York • London

Published by Lexington Books
An imprint of The Rowman & Littlefield Publishing Group, Inc.
4501 Forbes Boulevard, Suite 200, Lanham, Maryland 20706
www.rowman.com

6 Tinworth Street, London SE11 5AL, United Kingdom

British Library Cataloguing in Publication Information Available

Library of Congress Cataloging-in-Publication Data

Names: Bouamer, Siham, editor.
Title: Abdellah Taïa's queer migrations : non-places, affect, and temporalities / edited by Denis M. Provencher and Siham Bouamer.
Description: Lanham : Lexington Books, 2021. | Series: After the empire: the Francophone world and postcolonial France | Includes bibliographical references and index. | Summary: "The book is the first edited collection in English on Moroccan author Abdellah Taïa and frames the distinctiveness of his migration by considering current scholarship in French and Francophone studies, post-colonial studies, affect theory, queer theory, and language and sexuality"—Provided by publisher.
Identifiers: LCCN 2021018546 (print) | LCCN 2021018547 (ebook) | ISBN 9781793644862 (cloth) | ISBN 9781793644879 (ebook)
Subjects: LCSH: Taïa, Abdellah, 1973—Criticism and interpretation. | Homosexuality in literature. | Disillusion (Philosophy) in literature. | Race in literature. | Immigrants in literature.
Classification: LCC PQ3989.2.T27 Z55 2021 (print) | LCC PQ3989.2.T27 (ebook) | DDC 843/.92—dc23
LC record available at https://lccn.loc.gov/2021018546
LC ebook record available at https://lccn.loc.gov/2021018547

Contents

Acknowledgments

This book began modestly as a paper session on "Queer Maghrebi French" organized by the LLC Francophone Executive Committee of the *Modern Language Association*, which took place in Chicago, Illinois in January 2019. Subsequently, several panelists reconvened for a paper session on "Cruel Optimism, Queerness, and Postcolonial Shame," specific to Abdellah Taïa's work, which took place at the *Contemporary French Civilizations* conference in Tucson, Arizona in August 2019. It was during these events where we discussed the possibility of assembling the first book-length study published in English on the work of Abdellah Taïa. Several additional scholars in French and Francophone studies who were already working on Taïa's oeuvre at the time also willingly agreed to join us on the project and we are very happy to have now brought this project to fruition. Indeed, we could not have done this without their hard work and generous contributions, and we want to extend a very warm thanks to all of them. We would like to extend a special thank you to Abdellah Taïa for agreeing to participate in this project by submitting an original short story in French for the volume and to let us also publish an English-language translation of his text. Moreover, without Abdellah's friendship, courage, determination, creativity, and talent, none of our own scholarly work would have been possible.

We would like to thank our commissioning editor Holly Buchanan at Lexington Books for her initial interest in our project and her care in guiding us through the proposal process and book production. We are also grateful to Valérie Orlando, editor of the series *After the Empire*, who has always remained enthusiastic about the book project. *Un grand merci!*

Siham would also like to thank Denis Provencher, an extraordinary and thoughtful interlocutor, for the invitation to co-edit this volume. His dedication, knowledge, and support have made the process both intellectually stimulating and personally enriching. She is also grateful for the support of her friend Ervin Malakaj and their continuous discussions on the work of the "feminist killjoys" that often appear in this volume. Siham is also forever indebted to her parents and their sacrifices. Their courage and resilience, through their own story of immigration from Morocco to France, will always be an inspiration for her work.

Denis would also like to thank the College of Humanities, the School of International Languages, Literatures, and Cultures, and the Department of French and Italian at the University of Arizona for their generous support. He is also grateful to his co-editor Siham, whose creativity, intellect, and ambition remind him of why he first got into this profession; it's been an absolute pleasure to work alongside her. As always, Denis wants to thank his husband Stephen, whose love, support, compassion, and laughter strengthen and guide him every day.

Introduction

Reconsidering Abdellah Taïa's Queer Migration

Denis M. Provencher and Siham Bouamer

Abdellah Taïa is a Moroccan-born author who grew up in a large working-class family in the small town of Salé on the outskirts of Rabat. As a young child, he would sit for hours in the Bibliothèque générale de Rabat while his father worked in the building as a *chaouche* [civil servant]. In fact, it is thanks in large part to his father and eldest brother that Taïa developed a love respectively for books and cinema and dreamed of becoming an author and director one day. He attended public school and university in his home country of Morocco and then eventually moved to Europe to pursue higher education in Switzerland and France.

Abdellah Taïa's well-known letter "L'homosexualité expliquée à ma mère" [Homosexuality explained to my mother] was published in Morocco's well-circulated *Tel Quel*, and many scholars have read this essay as a "coming-out" letter and its author as the first or one of the first "openly gay" or "openly queer" Moroccan writers.[1] Indeed, it was his "queer migration" (discussed in detail later in this chapter) to Geneva in 1998 and Paris in 1999 where he began to pursue his dreams. This has led, however, to an overly rehearsed interpretation, in the scholarship at times, of Taïa's path to Europe as a migration of a gay man and a modern influence by Western values of urban life, commercialism, conspicuous consumption, "pride," and liberation, and reverse sexual tourism. Moreover, in the Preface to the English-language version of Taïa's third novel, *Salvation Army* (2009), queer American critic Edmund White emphasizes Taïa as a young Moroccan boy who left his small hometown of Salé to become educated in the French tradition, and who eventually moved to the big gay city to live out his life as a "French intellectual, a Parisian."[2] However, many recent critics, among whom the two editors of the volume (Provencher and Bouamer), have questioned White's and others' typification by nuancing Taïa's contributions.

For example, Ralph Heyndels has written extensively in French on Taïa's oeuvre, which he analyzes through a theoretical lens of European literary criticism coupled with postcolonial studies. Heyndels situates the author's work alongside that of his contemporaries like Rachid O. and compares their work to Jean Genet and other canonical French and Francophone authors. Heyndels has devoted a decade to the study of Taïa's work and has published extensively on themes in Taïa's writing such as gender, sexuality and desire, prostitution in public space, the influence of Arabic and French, reinventing Islam, and "trans" as a new identity category for the queer author. Throughout, he has often implicitly deconstructed the teleology mentioned above of Taïa's ultimate "arrival in the city" and satisfaction with his life in Paris. More recently Heyndels and Zidouh have published *Around/Autour d'Abdellah Taïa* (2020) that assembles a set of papers that emerged from a conference in 2015 hosted at the University of Miami.[3] This volume includes an important set of chapters that explore such important topics in French and English as migration and borders, decolonial trajectories, reverse sexual tourism, subaltern and ambivalent mothers, as well as poetics and revolution, among others. Interestingly, Heyndels and Zidouh decided for this particular volume not to include an introduction or conclusion that would situate the papers in terms of themes, which to some extent, helps us to further nuance Taïa's migratory path and integration (or not) in Europe. Instead, they open the volume with a letter from Abdellah Taïa to James Baldwin (dated June 2020) written at the height of the coronavirus and the Black Lives Matter movement prompted by the death of George Floyd at the hands of the police. Indeed, this frames the volume, and rightly so, with a sense of solidarity across cultures, to be read in a particularly urgent light. The volume concludes in a similar way with another chapter with an original short story by Taïa, "Un jardin, en attendant . . ." [A garden, while waiting . . .], which leaves the reader in an ambiguously open space where the protagonist and other characters who are different from him are all able to find a common space of belonging.

Jean-Pierre Boulé published, in spring of 2020, the first book-length study of Taïa's work in French, with an emphasis on the themes of melancholia, mourning, nostalgia, and reparation among others.[4] He provides the reader a close textual analysis of Taïa's oeuvre and situates it in conversation with the author's public interviews and public media presence/public persona. Boulé has also nuanced the teleology of "arrival in the city" by arguing for an author and figure who is not completely welcomed in his host countries of Switzerland and France and who longs through his treatment of the aforementioned various themes in his writings for his homeland and ties to Morocco.

Expanding notions of identity, place, time, and mobility, Siham Bouamer dismantles narrative expectations grounded in what José Estaban Muñoz identifies as "straight time"[5] and migrant self-exploration paradigms of belonging in Abdellah Taïa's work. Focusing on *Infidèles* [*Infidels*] (2012), Bouamer argues for a transmedial and transtemporal reading of the text to highlight the author's initiatory journey not as a transcultural success story of "gay arrival" and return, but rather as one that ultimately leads to death. If death can be seen as a state of departure, Bouamer highlights that in the case of Abdellah Taïa, it also signifies revival; hence, showing a constant cyclic movement in the author's self-exploratory narrative.[6]

Denis M. Provencher has directly and systematically deconstructed White's supposed teleology of the poor Moroccan boy who must flee to the postcolonial metropolis where he can be saved by France and its model of citizenship based on republican universalism and integration.[7] Taïa may very well have become an intellectual living in Paris, however, twenty-first century France remains largely unsympathetic to communities of difference, that is, queer, Muslim, or otherwise. In fact, Provencher illustrates how Taïa and his characters' wanderings represent a set of "comings and goings" that rely on multiple temporalities in Morocco, Egypt, Switzerland, France, and other sites to make sense of their own belonging.[8]

At the same time, Taïa does not always completely feel at home in France even when he relies on these multiple spaces. Like other interlocutors Provencher has interviewed, Taïa has to work through the "cruel optimism"[9] sold by the West to its migrants, which often leaves them running on empty. For example, Farid, a queer French-speaking migrant from Algeria whom Provencher interviewed speaks of his "impossible" life and living situation in Paris, four years after moving to France. Farid finds it difficult to pay his bills, meet men of substance, and feel a sense of accomplishment.[10] He expresses this most saliently when he states: "Il y a une date d'expiration pour ma vie . . . J'ai l'impression que j'ai joué toutes mes cartes . . . J'ai le sentiment quand tu arrives à la fin de quelque chose" [There's an expiration date on my life . . . I have the impression I've played my whole hand . . . I have the feeling like when you arrive at the end of something].[11] For this and many other reasons, Farid is left in an impossible situation where saying "I" in the gay metropolis in a satisfying way never happens.

Unlike Farid however, Abdellah Taïa emphasizes the use of "I" in his autofiction—sometimes more successfully than others—to work through his own cruel optimism and situation as a queer migrant. Indeed, throughout his migrations, the author acquires a "flexible accumulation of language"[12] or an accrual of lexical items and scripts, which finds its way into his writing. These speech acts draw on a transnational repertoire of signifying practices that help him and his characters remain less bound to one specific site of meaning making.[13] Moreover, and as mentioned above, Taïa's sense of belonging does not come from a new-found form of belonging and citizenship in France through its form of republican universalism that touts integration. In contrast, a queer migrant like Taïa who "comes and goes" across cultures, languages, and spatial-temporalities, acquires a form of transgressive filiation or "transfiliation" according to Provencher (2017) that transcends national borders in order to create new forms of transgressive association with individuals and communities that have otherwise seemed mutually exclusive.

Indeed, we aim to bring into conversation the previous scholarship mentioned above with the essays published in our current volume. Overall, the volume aims to examine the evolution of Taïa's work from his earliest to latest texts. While all contributors to this volume may cite Taïa's earlier novels—*Mon Maroc* [*My Morocco*] (2000), *Le rouge du tarbouche* [*The Red of the Fez*] (2004), *L'armée du salut* [*Salvation Army*] (2006), *Une mélancolie arabe* [*An Arab Melancholia*] (2008), and *Le jour du Roi* [*The Day of the King*] (2010)—many of them also turn to his later work—*Infidèles* [*Infidels*] (2012), *L'armée du salut* (his 2013 film based on his 2006 novel), *Un pays pour mourir* [*A Country For Dying*] (2015), *La vie lente* [*The Slow Life*] (2017), and *Celui qui est digne d'être aimé* [*The One Who is Worthy of Love*] (2019). In particular, we and the authors in this volume aim to explore the theme of (queer) migration beyond geographical displacement with an emphasis on non-places, affective economies, and postcolonial temporalities.

FRAMING QUEER MIGRATION AND DIASPORA FOR THIS VOLUME

Since 2000, much scholarship has been conducted on the themes of queer migration and diaspora. Some salient examples include Cantú (2009), Cashman (2017), Cruz-Malavé and Manalansan (2002), Decena (2011), Gaudio (2009), Gray and Baynham (2020), Manalansan (2003; 2006), Mole (2018), Patton and Sánchez-Eppler (2000), and Zheng (2015) where scholars examine, to varying degrees, queer migration from the village to the city (in-country migration); from one city to another (in-country or trans-country); and sexual asylum from the global South to the global North. Most of this scholarship, however, has overlooked the Francophone regions of the world. In fact, it is really only within the past several years that scholarship in French and Francophone Studies, which draws on scholarship in queer migration and diaspora, has expanded with examinations of the work of authors, artists, directors, and everyday speakers from the French-speaking world.[14]

In the case of Abdellah Taïa, this involves both the migration from a small town of Salé to a city, first to Rabat, and then a non-named sexual asylum from the global South of Morocco to the global North of Switzerland and France. Within those different movements, we first consider Abdellah Taïa as un "homme dépaysé" [man out of place, literally "out of his country"].

Despite the fact that Todorov does not engage with queer subjectivities, his concept of "homme dépaysé"[15] allows for an analysis of the different implications of Taïa's exploration of identity and mobility, whether in some of his specific works or in the evolution of his oeuvre. As the different translations of the term foreground, "dépaysé" entails notions of loss of national ties, dis(orientation), and displacement from/to different centers/margins and social beliefs. As it is the case in Todorov's experiences of exile, Taïa's *dépaysement* is the result of intertwined dynamics involved in the author's self-definition, which the different contributors of the volume explore. More recently, Gray and Baynham identify similar complexities and argue that often an "in-country migration can be a prelude to subsequent cross-border migration"[16] and this is indeed the case for the author who is the focus of our edited volume. Gray and Baynham also suggest that "linguistic approaches can bring much to the interdisciplinary investigation of queer migration by providing close attention to the materiality of talk, to questions of voice, and to the construction of subjectivity and identity positions through language."[17] They continue: "Whether within borders or across them, queer migration is clearly a complex phenomenon in which the intersections of sexuality, gender identity, desire, affect, abjection, economic necessity, social class, politics, and fear for one's one life (along with doubtlessly unnamed other aspects of human experience) combine in ways that are unique in the lives of individual migrants" (online). Indeed, as we will see in the collection of essays in this volume, authors explore the construction of identity in Taïa's oeuvre and each one, to varying degrees, points to the materiality of talk that is allotted to queer Maghrebi French speakers.

Ultimately, our approach aims to frame the uniqueness of Abdellah Taïa's migration by considering current queer theory. Several recent studies call for a reexamination of migrancy through queer subjectivities. Drawing on Nacira Guénif's (2014) and Fatima El-Tayeb's (2011) scholarship on queering the European space, James S. Williams, in the specific case of film, regrets the lack of scholarship on the cinematic representations of queer migration and attributes this gap to the conflation with broad themes of "immigration and the post-migrant experience of integration, assimilation, and diasporic identity."[18] Instead of an analysis of the condition of the queer migrant within national identities, he proposes to "queer the migrant [. . .] beyond borders"[19] which entails a "celebrat[ion] [of queer migrants] as global *shifters* in a continuous, transcultural process with important ethical and political, aesthetic and philosophical implications."[20] While we recognize the importance of considering Taïa's work within the possibilities of global and transcultural mobility, to which we should add transfiliation, transtemporality, and transmodality,[21] it is our contention, however, that such dynamics are and should not be seen as celebratory. Indeed, Taïa's stories are as unique as any in this regard and they help us to better understand, as we will see, the material conditions concerning migration and, most importantly, the impossibility for many queer migrants living in the diaspora to access citizenship in their new homeland or a successful return to their home country.

Our refusal to read Taïa's works as successful stories of migration is firmly grounded in queer theory's assessment and redefinition of success for the queer subject.[22] As Taïa himself explains in an interview, "The dream [. . .] is to be the darkest possible."[23] Our volume favors the recognition of failure in migrancy and dismantles expectations of a utopic reconciliation between home, host country, and queer subjectivities. Our analysis of Taïa's work, for that reason, aims to explore queer migrancy not only beyond geographical borders, but also beyond the bounds imposed by fixed socio-historical spaces. The chapters in this volume expand on exploration of migrant identities as defined by cultural and geographical attachments and dwell with entanglements of national identity, place, emotions, sexual orientation, and the colonial past in the author's search of belonging. The chapters highlight, among others, different paradigms that constitute or affect queer migrancy. We divided the volume into three thematic parts: Part I (On Place and Non-Place); Part II (Affective Migration); and Part III (Postcolonial Temporalities).

PART I: ON PLACE AND NON-PLACE

In Part I, Ralph Heyndels, Olivier Le Blond, and Dan Maroun allow us to first question traditional attachments to place(s) in processes of migration. The three chapters explore what Sara Ahmed (2006) calls "migrant orientation," to describe "how bodies arrive and how they get directed in this way or that way as a condition of arrival, which in turn is about how the 'in place' gets placed."[24] Much scholarship in border studies explores transit spaces, but often neglects their value as non-places. Studies instead highlight movements from one point to another, from home to host-sites or host-countries. For example, in *Open Roads, Closed Borders: The Contemporary French-Language Road Movie* (2013), Michael Gott and Thibaut Schilt articulate the importance of examining and identifying two subcategories of road movies, namely the ones depicting "voyages to or through France" and the "ones involv[ing] movement in the opposite direction."[25] However, they also begin to reconsider the rigid directionality involved in both movements. Indeed, their analysis of both movements in dialogue aims to show that "culture is a process in motion, linked to the constant melding of both local and global traditions" while at the same time dismantling "France and French identity [. . .] [as] rigidly defined, clichéd spaces."[26] Considering Abdellah Taïa's fondness for film references, his own endeavor in the genre, and his cinematic eye in his novels, the contributions in this section seek to observe similar dynamism in his "road narratives." They divest the notion of migrant identity of fixed markers defined by geographical arrivals or departures and introduce the concepts of the nowhere (Heyndels), geographical fluidity (Le Blond), and mobile borderland (Maroun).

In chapter 1, Ralph Heyndels contextualizes Taïa's novel as a reaction to what Pierre Tevanian and Saïd Bouamama call "un racisme post-colonial" [a postcolonial racism] and "un passé qui ne passe pas" [a past that does not pass] by focusing on a decolonial reading of Taïa's *Celui qui est digne d'être aimé*, and drawing from works by Abdelalli Hajjat, Catherine Withol de Wenden, Nacira Guénif-Souilamas, and Françoise Vergès, among several others. Heyndels also examines this topic from the viewpoint of what Bourdieu in *On the State* defines as "alienating integration as a condition of domination, submission, of depossession"[27] based on an ethno-centered notion of "Western civilization" superiority. He specifically looks at the use of language in Taïa's *Celui qui est digne d'être aimé*, in which the French-Arabic interface plays a significant role while the protagonist Ahmed proclaims his intention to exit French and what he has realized to be its very coloniality.

Olivier Le Blond focuses in chapter 2 on Taïa's novel *L'armée du salut*, in which the author tells the story of Abdellah's journey to Geneva to pursue his graduate studies and the struggles he encounters during his first few days in this city along with that of happier times in Morocco. Through the lens of queer theory, Le Blond argues that movement, whether it be through the author's writing, the temporal movement between the present of the novel and the flashbacks in Morocco or the geographical movement, contributes to the creation of a queer Moroccan identity. He first proposes to look at the theme of movement in the novel and how the changes in pronouns in each of the three sections of the novel are an integral part in the creation of this queer identity. Next, Le Blond looks at the chronological movement with the incessant back and forth between the present of the novel, the chapters in Geneva, and the past, represented by the chapters in Morocco, and how this temporal movement participates in the creation of the protagonist Abdellah's queer identity. Le Blond concludes that the geographical movement also informs this queer identity. Indeed, a great deal of attention is brought to the description and importance of the different places in *L'armée du salut* where Abdellah moves and interacts with other characters.

In chapter 3, Daniel Maroun examines how Taïa constructs his narratives of queer masculinity across his greater corpus of texts. This scholar argues that the evolution of queer Moroccan masculinity in Taïa's works is embedded in Muñoz's process of "disidentification" where queer performativity collides with heteronormative ideologies pushing performativity to the periphery. Maroun divides his analysis in two parts by first exploring how Taïa's works negotiate with and undermine Moroccan patriarchy, and then looking at how these queer, sexually non-normative performativities uniquely occur in liminal spaces. The works reviewed in this chapter include *L'armée du salut* (2006), *Une mélancolie arabe* (2008), *Lettres à un jeune marocain* [*Letters to a Young Moroccan*] (2009), and *Le jour du Roi* (2010); texts Maroun argues are narratively reflective. These are works whose aim is to recount to the audience how the protagonist of the novel came to "today," the present reading of the text. This structure is later opposed in Taïa's more recent novels, *Celui qui est digne d'être aimé* (2017) and *La vie lente* (2019), that highlight a continual presence of queerness. The division follows how Taïa begins to nuance his character's engagement with social expectations of sexuality and the clandestine sexual underbelly of homosexuality in Moroccan society. Maroun argues that these performances of queer Moroccan masculinity find their true expression on the border, in a place that is traversed instead of being inhabited.

PART II: AFFECTIVE MIGRATION

Part II further dismantles the question of place by considering the "affective economies," to borrow Sara Ahmed's words, at play in processes of migration and national belonging.[28] In*The Cultural Politics of Emotions* (2004), Ahmed reflects on the effects of linguistic, bodily, and affective expressions in the shaping of western narratives of nationhood. In a phenomenological tradition, she explores how emotions are materialized through bodies and languages, and how such physicality leads to the constitution of communities, a process through which individuals are included or excluded. In particular, Siham Bouamer, Ryan Schroth, and Jean-Pierre Boulé consider "how emotions work to shape the 'surfaces' of individual and collective bodies"[29] in Abdellah Taïa's work. They argue that Taïa's narratives are not only part of a story of queer migrants who move to other places. His writings are also part of *queering* the migration process, which Gray and Baynham refer to as the "pulling away of the migration story from neoliberal accounts."[30] Indeed, the contributors aim to underscore how Taïa's use of language moves us away from stories of successful migration toward conversations about affective migration, through the lens of cruel optimism (Bouamer), shame (Schroth), and melancholy (Boulé).

Siham Bouamer proposes in chapter 4 to examine Abdellah Taïa's film *L'armée du salut* (2013) through the lens of Lauren Berlant's notion of "cruel optimism." In an interview, Taïa explains that he does not understand the optimism imposed on his work. He further explains that for him, "The dream [. . .] is to be the darkest possible," but he regrets failing every time and does not "know where that hope comes from."[31] Bouamer argues that this hope stems from what Berlant has coined as "cruel optimism" to describe "the relation of attachment to compromised conditions of possibility."[32] This notion provides a way to dismantle the affective structure imposed on Taïa's work. Bouamer explores how Taïa destroys possibilities of "forever love" for protagonist Abdellah, to which Berlant prefers the expression "durable intimacy."[33] In particular, Bouamer analyzes the importance of his failed relationships with his father Mohammed, his brother Slimane, and the Swiss professor, Jean. She shows how the negotiations of intimacy with the three characters lead to Abdellah's gradual detachment from cruel optimism and expectations of durable intimacy at different stages of his life, articulated through the multiple repetitions in the film of Abdel Halim Hafez's song "*Ana Laka 3ala Toul*" [I am yours forever].

In chapter 5, Ryan K. Schroth examines the letter form in Taïa's writing, an element of his work that is often overlooked by critics. Schroth studies a different selection of Taïa's letters: his personal open letter destined to his mother, "L'homosexualité expliquée à ma mère" [Homosexuality explained to my mother]; a letter to his nephew published in Taïa's *Lettres à un jeune marocain*; and two letters from his epistolary novel, *Celui qui est digne d'être aimé*. Schroth demonstrates the importance Taïa gives to the letter form and its implications of circulation, exchange, and connection. Interrogating the question of shared origins and the lived experiences of shame related in these letters, Schroth traces the emergence of a queer Arab shame that is not predicated on the post-Stonewall binary politics of "pride" and "shame." In this way, shame becomes less the opposite of pride and more a productive experience of queer existence. Identifying several reception paradigms (e.g., between author and mother, author and nephew, etc.), Schroth focuses on the ways in which Taïa structures the relationship between author and reader, arguing that Taïa's epistolarity ultimately serves to connect author and reader through common experiences of shame, while fortifying queer Arab shame and its specificities to queer Arab communities.

In chapter 6, Jean-Pierre Boulé focuses on Taïa's penultimate novel to date *Celui qui est digne d'être aimé* (2017), composed of four letters written by three different narrators, spanning four time periods. Through an analysis of the letters, Boulé demonstrates that the novel is a work of mourning, supported by Melanie Klein's pyscho-ananalytic theories. Starting with the first letter, Boulé examines the first stage: anger. Feeling abandoned by the death of his mother, the narrator Ahmed displays anger, when the letter was supposed to be a homage to her. Boulé shows that despite the fact that the father is seen as the "good internal object," the narrator identifies with the mother and turns his anger against himself. Then, Boulé attributes to the second letter the task of castigating Ahmed as it is written from the point of view of his French lover Vincent whom Ahmed abandoned. Next, Boulé turns to the fourth letter, written from the point of view of Ahmed's "older brother" Lahbib, in which he warns Ahmed against sexual exploitation by rich Westerners, in his own case Gérard. Boulé contrasts Lahbib and Ahmed's experiences: while the former accepted Gérard's mother's love and has an open heart, which will lead to his suicide, the latter has a closed heart, which allows him, like his mother, to survive. Boulé concludes with the third letter, written by Ahmed for his French lover, Emmanuel. Describing the letter as the most political one, Boulé analyzes Ahmed's process of reconciliation. In particular, Boulé examines how Ahmed, first, dwells with the colonial and neocolonial attitude of Emmanuel and his relationship to the French language, and second, wants to reconcile himself with his mother and his sisters.

PART III: POSTCOLONIAL TEMPORALITIES

In Part III, Thomas Muzart, Philippe Panizzon, and Denis M. Provencher further deconstruct neoliberal accounts of Abdellah Taïa's work by considering neocolonial structures involved in the processes of queer migrancy. While the chapters do not specifically deal with emotionality as a foundation of queer experiences within the discursive building of nationhood, the authors engage with a similar framework to the previous section and question definitions of "the legitimate subject of the nation."[34] Recognizing that Taïa's portrayal of migrant experiences constitutes, to borrow Ahmed's words, a "contact [that] is shaped by past histories of contact," the contributions in this section dismantle the "alignment of family, history, and race [. . .] that recognises all non-white others as strangers, as bodies *out of place*."[35] Ultimately, the chapters explore how Taïa displaces discourses of belonging and otherness to create spaces where the queer migrant is allowed to offer a counter-history to one of white and heteronormative nationhood.

For example, in chapter 7, Thomas Muzart aims to determine how sexual marginality can play a role in postcolonial struggles such as the Arab Spring in 2011 by focusing on the influence of Taïa's migration on his relations to others both in Europe and in the Arabo-Muslim World. Muzart begins by considering the geographical displacements depicted in Taïa's autofictional work as attempts to develop what Foucault calls an aesthetic of existence, which allows the individual to occupy in the community a specific and proper place.[36] Using Ahmed's concept of the "melancholic migrant," Muzart also shows the difficulties encountered by Taïa to bind the hybrid self that he elaborates to any national ideal. By keeping attachment to his culture and traditions through literature, Muzart argues nonetheless that Taïa shows that he aspires to a return to his origins through a new form of belonging shaped by his experience as a migrant. Next, Muzart shows that the recognition of his marginality is not an end-goal but the position through which he can belong to what Michael Hardt and Antonio Negri call "the multitude," that is, a resistance collective in which individuals as singularities can develop new circuits of collaboration that contribute to the development of a sense of commonality. Muzart concludes that writing constitutes, in Taïa's case, a performative return to his homeland that overcomes the melancholia of migration and opens a path for the Arabo-Muslim world to become more inclusive of marginal voices, especially in light of the Arab Spring.

In chapter 8, Philippe Panizzon explores the power relations at play in cultural and sexual liaisons between the Moroccan protagonists and Frenchmen in Taïa's fiction. He argues that the encounters between the protagonists in Taïa's fictions occur, except in a few cases, according to pre-written scripts informed by old paradigms of colonial violence or by French policy concerning sexuality and race at the turn of the twentieth-first century. Furthermore, he offers a fresh perspective on the place of the homosexual ethnic Other in France today, given ongoing political debates around race, sex, and sexualities. He demonstrates that whereas France incorporates those queer white subjects living according to the homonormative model in the nation state, other "orientalized" bodies remain actively excluded.

In chapter 9, Denis M. Provencher briefly lays out the recent work in postcolonial mythologies and postcolonial realms of memory where scholars like Etienne Achille, Charles Forsdick, and Lydie Moudileno examine the postcolonial sites of memory and mythmaking both in and beyond the Hexagon that continues to erase the memory making for communities of color in France.[37] For example, through an analysis of French public space, popular culture, literature, media, the world of sports, consumer products, among other realms, Achille and Moudileno aim to expose the underlying racial stereotypes and blind spots that still undergird many institutions and cultural phenomena in contemporary France. In contrast to this work, Provencher illustrates through an analysis of Taïa's writings that while queer Maghrebi French speakers may be initially drawn to the French Republic and its associated cultural mythologies and realms of memory first discovered through films and books—like Jean Genet or Isabelle Adjani among others—they will sooner or later decolonize them and propose new "non-white" and Arabicized models of belonging in the postcolonial, the French, and the transnational contexts because of their sense of disconnection and disidentification.[38] While Taïa is not a postcolonial French subject creating a new set of cultural myths or realms of memory for all citizens of the Hexagon, he does assemble from a distance to the French metropole a different set of signifiers that are not necessarily always and already linked to colonial memory. In contrast then to the myths that Achille and Moudileno examine, for example, that emerge in specifically French contexts of the Hexagon and the departments and territories of the *Outre-Mer*—where a tension exists between the two poles of mythmaking—"de l'occultation d'une part, et de l'exploitation racialisante de l'autre" [the concealing on the one hand and the racializing exploitation on the other][39]—Provencher illustrates that Taïa moves beyond this binary and proposes new transfilial paths forward to a more understanding space of belonging for queers of color in the Francosphere and beyond. Indeed, Taïa's work involves global bodies and transfilial signifiers, mainly U.S. based in this particular case study, like Marilyn Monroe and James Baldwin, which is largely due to the desire among queer migratory individuals to seek new forms of queer and neoliberal belonging on a global scale but also to combat forms of isolation, unrealized dreams and cruel optimism as well as impossible citizenship.[40]

PART IV: NEW DIRECTIONS AND CONCLUSION

In this final section, Antoine Idier addresses a letter to author and friend Abdellah Taïa where he suggests how "it may be time" for the author "to return to the Arabic language," citing Taïa's own words to prompt further discussion on an established topic.[41] Idier underscores that "returning" is one of the fundamental concerns of Taïa and his characters, and like Heyndels (in this volume), he raises again the important question, "but how and where to return?" Idier then clarifies that Taïa's work involves what could be called an "impossible reappropriation" or, at least, draws a return that is not a destination, but a path and a cartography that are eternally moving, displaced in the course of attempts to return, in the course of the words and voices that are expressed therein. Indeed, Idier closes his letter with a sentiment of desire, indeed shared by many of Taïa's readers, wondering about Taïa's next project and where the author will take all of us in his next installment, always indicative of his own continued migratory path.

As we near the end of the volume, in chapter 11, Abdellah Taïa contributes an original short story titled "Three Tired Men," which has not been previously published. Taïa's novella offers a fresh and surprising perspective on all three themes explored in this volume (non-places, affect, and temporalities) and invites the reader to walk with him as he thinks through where he belongs and does not belong. In chapter 12, Denis M. Provencher provides an English translation of Taïa's new text. Finally, Denis M. Provencher and Siham Bouamer, conclude the volume in chapter 13 with an analysis of the novella along the three themes of the volume and then point us on the road to new directions in the scholarship on queer migration and diaspora studies and on authors like Taïa specifically.

NOTES

1. Tina Dransfeldt Christensen, "Writing the Self as Narrative of Resistance: *L'Armée du salut* by Abdellah Taïa," *The Journal of North African Studies* 21, no. 5 (2016): 857–876; Tina Dransfeldt Christensen, "Breaking the Silence: Between Literary Representation and LGBT Activism. Abdellah Taïa as Author and Activist," *Expressions maghrébines* 16, no. 1 (2017): 107–125; Antoine Idier, "'Sortir de la peur'. Construire une identité homosexuelle arabe dans un monde post-colonial" (Entretien avec Abdellah Taïa), *Revue critique de fixxion française contemporaine* 12 (2016): 197–207; Daniel N. Maroun, "Comment échapper à la honte du *zamel*: Vers la construction de la masculinité maghrébine queer," *Revue Analyse* 11, no. 3 (2016): 135–154; Ryan K. Schroth, "Le Sacrifice de l'écrivain homosexuel: entretien avec Abdellah Taia," *The French Review* 89, no. 3 (2016): 175–183; Ryan K. Schroth, "Queer Shame: Affect, Resistance, and Colonial Critique in Abdellah Taïa's *Celui qui est digne d'être aimé*," *The Journal of North African Studies* 26, no. 1 (2021): 138–162. Published online October 22, 2019: DOI: 10.1080/13629387.2019.1683449.

2. Abdellah Taïa, *Salvation Army,* translated by Frank Stock (Los Angeles: Semiotext(e), 2009), 9.

3. Ralph Heyndels and Amine Zidouh, *Autour d'Abdellah Taïa: Poétique et politique du désir engagé /Around Abdellah Taïa: Poetics and Politics of Engaged Desire* (Caen: Editions Passage(s), 2020).

4. Jean-Pierre Boulé, *Abdellah Taïa: La mélancolie et le cri* (Lyon: Presses universitaires de Lyon, 2020).

5. José Estaban Muñoz, *Cruising Utopia: The Then and There of Queer Futurity* (New York: New York University Press, 2009).

6. Siham Bouamer, "De 'River of no Return' à 'Trouble of the World,': Parcours initiatique musical dans *Infidèles* (2012) d'Abdellah Taïa," *Expressions maghrébines* 19, no. 1 (2020): 107–124.

7. Denis M. Provencher, *Queer French: Globalization, Language, and Sexual Citizenship in France* (Burlington/Aldershot: Ashgate Publishing, 2007).

8. Denis M. Provencher, *Queer Maghrebi French: Language, Temporalities, Transfiliations* (Liverpool: Liverpool University Press, 2017).

9. Lauren Berlant, *Cruel Optimism* (Durham: Duke University Press, 2011).

10. Provencher, *Queer Maghrebi French,* 267–280.

11. Provencher, *Queer Maghrebi French,* 267.

12. William L. Leap, "Language and Gendered Modernity," in *The Handbook of Language and Gender*, edited by Janet Holmes and Miriam Meyerhoff (Oxford: Blackwell, 2003), 401–422; Provencher, *Queer Maghrebi French.*

13. Provencher, *Queer Maghrebi French.*

14. Jarrod Hayes, *Queer Nation: Marginal Sexualities in the Maghreb* (Chicago, IL: U of Chicago P, 2000); Provencher, *Queer Maghrebi French*; Mehammed Amadeus Mack, *Sexagon: Muslims, France, and the Sexualization of National* (New York: Fordham University Press, 2017); Valérie Orlando, and Pam Pears, eds., *Paris and the Marginalized Author: Treachery, Alienation, Queerness, and*

Exile (Lanham: Lexington Books, 2019); Bouamer, "De 'River of no Return' à 'Trouble of the World,': Parcours initiatique musical dans *Infidèles* (2012) d'Abdellah Taïa."

15. Tzvetan Todorov, *L'Homme dépaysé* (Paris: Seuil, 1996).

16. John Gray, and Mike Banham, "Narratives of Queer Migration," in *The Oxford Handbook of Language and Sexuality*, edited by Kira Hall and Rusty Barrett (Oxford: Oxford University Press, 2020), online.

17. Gray and Banham, "Narratives of Queer Migration," online.

18. James S. Williams, *Queering the Migrant in European Cinema* (New York: Routledge, 2020), 18.

19. Williams, *Queering the Migrant*, 5.

20. Williams, *Queering the Migrant*, 31.

21. Provencher, *Queer Maghrebi French*; Bouamer, "De 'River of no Return' à 'Trouble of the World': Parcours initiatique musical dans *Infidèles* (2012) d'Abdellah Taïa."

22. José Esteban Muñoz, *Disidentifications: Queers of Color and the Performance of Politics* (Minneapolis: University of Minnesota Press, 1999); Jack Halberstam, *The Queer Art of Failure* (Durham: Duke University Press, 2011); Sara Ahmed, *The Promise of Happiness* (Durham: Duke University Press, 2010).

23. Abdellah Taïa, "Our Monsters Are Like Us: An Interview with Abdellah Taïa," Interview with Sam Metz, *Los Angeles Review of Books*, 9 January 2017, https://blog.lareviewofbooks.org/interviews/monsters-like-us-interview-abdellah-taia/. Accessed 10 Dec. 2018.

24. Sara Ahmed, *Queer Phenomenology: Orientations, Objects, Others* (Durham: Duke University Press, 2006), 10.

25. Michael Gott and Thibaut Schilt, editors, *Open Roads, Closed Borders: The Contemporary French-Language Road Movie* (Bristol: Intellect, 2013), 5.

26. Gott and Schilt, editors, *Open Roads, Closed Borders*, 6.

27. Pierre Bourdieu, *On the State: Lectures at the Collège de France, 1989–1992*, Trans. Patrick Champagne (United Kingdom: Wiley, 2014), 222.

28. Sara Ahmed, *Cultural Politics of Emotions* (Durham: Duke University Press, 2004), 8.

29. Ahmed, *Cultural Politics of Emotions*, 1.

30. Gray and Banham, "Narratives of Queer Migration," online.

31. Taïa, "Our Monsters Are Like Us."

32. Berlant, *Cruel Optimism*, 24.

33. Berlant, *Cruel Optimism*, 3.

34. Ahmed, *Cultural Politics of Emotions*, 2.

35. Ahmed, *Cultural Politics of Emotions*, 7.

36. Michel Foucault, "L'éthique du souci de soi comme pratique de la liberté," in *Dites et Ecrits, II 1976–1988* (Paris: Gallimard, 2001), 1534.

37. Etienne Achille, Charles Forsdick, and Lydie Moudileno, eds, *Postcolonial Realms of Memory: Sites and Symbols in Modern France* (Liverpool: Liverpool University Press, 2020); Etienne Achille and Lydie Moudileno, *Mythologies postcoloniales: Pour une décolonisation du quotidien* (Paris: Honoré Champion, 2018).

38. Muñoz, *Disidentifications*.
39. Achille and Moudileno, *Mythologies postcoloniales*, 21.
40. See Siham Bouamer (in this volume) and Provencher, *Queer Maghrebi French*. For more on these concepts, please see Denis M. Provencher, "Transnational approaches to language and sexuality," in *Transnational French Studies,* edited by Charles Forsdick and Claire Launchbury (Liverpool: Liverpool University Press, forthcoming).
41. Abdellah Taïa, "Écrire sans mots," in *Voix d'auteurs du Maroc*, edited by Abdellah Baïda, Mamoun Lahbabi, and Jean Zaganiaris (Rabat: Éditions Marsam, 2016), 141–144.

BIBLIOGRAPHY

Achille, Etienne, Charles Forsdick, and Lydie Moudileno, eds. *Postcolonial Realms of Memory: Sites and Symbols in Modern France.* Liverpool: Liverpool University Press, 2020.

Achille, Etienne, and Lydie Moudileno. *Mythologies postcoloniales: Pour une décolonisation du quotidien.* Paris: Honoré Champion, 2018.

Ahmed, Sara. *The Promise of Happiness.* Durham: Duke University Press, 2010.

———. *Queer Phenomenology: Orientations, Objects, Others.* Durham: Duke University Press, 2006.

———. *The Cultural Politics of Emotion.* Edinburgh: Edinburgh University Press, 2004.

Berlant, Lauren. *Cruel Optimism.* Durham: Duke University Press, 2011.

Bouamer, Siham. "De 'River of no Return' à 'Trouble of the World,': Parcours initiatique musical dans *Infidèles* (2012) d'Abdellah Taïa." *Expressions maghrébines* 19, no. 1 (2020): 107–124.

Boulé, Jean-Pierre. *Abdellah Taïa: La mélancolie et le cri.* Lyon: Presses universitaires de Lyon, 2020.

Bourdieu, Pierre. *On the State: Lectures at the Collège de France, 1989–1992.* Trans. Patrick Champagne. United Kingdom: Wiley, 2014.

Cantú, Lionel. *The Sexuality of Migration: Border Crossings and Mexican Immigrant Men.* New York: New York University Press, 2009.

Cashman, Holly. *Queer, Latinx, and Bilingual: Narrative Resources in the Negotiation of Identities.* New York: Routledge, 2017.

Christensen, Tina Dransfeldt. "Writing the Self as Narrative of Resistance: *L'Armée du salut* by Abdellah Taïa." *The Journal of North African Studies* 21, no. 5 (2016): 857–876.

———. "Breaking the Silence: Between Literary Representation and LGBT Activism. Abdellah Taïa as Author and Activist." *Expressions maghrébines* 16, no. 1 (2017): 107–125.

Cruz-Malavé, Arnaldo, and Martin F. Manalansan IV, eds. *Queer Globalizations: Citizenship and the Afterlife of Colonialism.* New York: New York UP, 2002.

Decena, Carlos Ulises. *Tacit Subjects: Belonging and Same-Sex Desire among Dominican Immigrant Men*. Durham: Duke University Press, 2011.

El-Tayeb, Fatima. *European Others: Queering Ethnicity in Postnational Europe*. Minneapolis: U of Minnesota P, 2011.

Foucault, Michel. "L'éthique du souci de soi comme pratique de la liberté." In *Dites et Ecrits, II 1976–1988*, 1526–1535. Paris: Gallimard, 2001.

Gaudio, Rudolf Pell. *Allah Made Us: Sexual Outlaws in an Islamic African City*. New York: Wiley Blackwell, 2009.

Gott, Michael, and Thibaut Schilt, eds. *Open Roads, Closed Borders: The Contemporary French-Language Road Movie*. Bristol: Intellect, 2013.

Gray, John, and Mike Baynham. "Narratives of Queer Migration." In *The Oxford Handbook of Language and Sexuality*, edited by Kira Hall and Rusty Barrett, online. Oxford: Oxford University Press, 2020.

Guénif, Nacira. "Straight Migrants Queering European Man." In *What's Queer about Europe? Productive Encounters and Re-enchanting Paradigms*, edited by Mireille Rosello, 69–78. New York: Fordham University Press, 2014.

Halberstam, Jack. *The Queer Art of Failure*. Durham: Duke University Press, 2011.

Hayes, Jarrod. *Queer Nation: Marginal Sexualities in the Maghreb*. Chicago, IL: U of Chicago P, 2000.

Heyndels, Ralph, and Amine Zidouh. *Autour d'Abdellah Taïa: Poétique et politique du désir engagé /Around Abdellah Taïa: Poetics and Politics of Engaged Desire*. Caen: Editions Passage(s), 2020.

Idier, Antoine. "'Sortir de la peur'. Construire une identité homosexuelle arabe dans un monde post-colonial" (Entretien avec Abdellah Taïa). *Revue critique de fixxion française contemporaine* 12 (2016): 197–207.

Leap, William L. "Language and Gendered Modernity." In *The Handbook of Language and Gender*, edited by Janet Holmes and Miriam Meyerhoff, 401–422. Oxford: Blackwell, 2003.

Mack, Mehammed Amadeus. *Sexagon: Muslims, France, and the Sexualization of National Culture*. New York: Fordham University Press, 2017.

Manalansan, Martin F. *Global Divas: Filipino Gay Men in the Diaspora*. Durham: Duke University Press, 2003.

———. "Queer Intersections: Sexuality and Gender in Migration Studies." *International Migration Review* 40, no. 1 (2006): 224–249.

Maroun, Daniel. "Comment échapper à la honte du *zamel*: Vers la construction de la masculinité maghrébine queer." *Revue Analyse* 11, no. 3 (2016): 135–154.

Mole, Richard C. M. "Identity, Belonging, and Solidarity in the Russian-Speaking Queer Diaspora in Berlin." *Slavic Review* 77, no. 1 (2018): 77–98.

Muñoz, José Esteban. *Disidentifications: Queers of Color and the Performance of Politics*. Minneapolis: University of Minnesota Press, 1999.

———. *Cruising Utopia: The Then and There of Queer Futurity*. New York: New York University Press, 2009.

Orlando, Valérie, and Pam Pears, eds. *Paris and the Marginalized Author: Treachery, Alienation, Queerness, and Exile*. Lanham: Lexington Books, 2019.

Patton, Cindy, and Benigno Sánchez-Eppler, eds. *Queer Diasporas*. Durham: Duke UP, 2000.

Provencher, Denis M. *Queer Maghrebi French: Language, Temporalities, Transfiliations*. Liverpool: Liverpool University Press, 2017.
———. *Queer French: Globalization, Language, and Sexual Citizenship in France*. Burlington/Aldershot: Ashgate Publishing, 2007.
———. "“*Je suis terroriste, pédé et le fils de Marilyn Monroe*”: Cinematic Stars and Transfiliaton in Abdellah Taïa's *Infidèles*." In *Paris and the Marginalized Author: Treachery, Alienation, Queerness, and Exile*, edited by Valerie K. Orlando and Pamela A. Pears, 153–166. Lanham: Lexington Books, 2019.
———. "Transnational Approaches to Language and Sexuality." In *Transnational French Studies,* edited by Charles Forsdick and Claire Launchbury. Liverpool: Liverpool University Press, forthcoming.
Schroth, Ryan K. "Queer Shame: Affect, Resistance, and Colonial Critique in Abdellah Taïa's *Celui qui est digne d'être aimé*." *The Journal of North African Studies* 26, no. 1 (2021): 138–162. Published online October 22, 2019: DOI: 10.1080/13629387.2019.1683449.
———. "Le Sacrifice de l'écrivain homosexuel: entretien avec Abdellah Taia." *The French Review* 89, no. 3 (2016): 175–183.
Taïa, Abdellah. *Mon Maroc*. Biarritz: Séguier, 2000.
———. *Le rouge du tarbouche*. Biarritz: Séguier, 2004.
———. *L'armée du salut*. Paris: Seuil, 2006.
———. *Salvation Army*. Translated by Frank Stock. Los Angeles: Semiotext(e), 2009.
———. *Une mélancolie arabe*. Paris: Seuil, 2008.
———. *Le jour du Roi*. Paris: Seuil, 2010.
———. *Infidèles*. Paris: Seuil, 2012.
———. *Un pays pour mourir*. Paris: Seuil, 2015.
———. *Celui qui est digne d'être aimé*. Paris: Seuil, 2017.
———. *La vie lente*. Paris: Seuil, 2019.
———. "Our Monsters Are Like Us: An Interview with Abdellah Taïa." Interview with Sam Metz. *Los Angeles Review of Books*. 9 Jan. 2017, https://blog.lareviewofbooks.org/interviews/monsters-like-us-interview-abdellah-taia/. Accessed 10 Dec. 2018.
———. "Écrire sans mots." In *Voix d'auteurs du Maroc*, edited by Abdellah Baïda, Mamoun Lahbabi, and Jean Zaganiaris, 141–144. Rabat: Éditions Marsam, 2016.
———, director. *L'Armée du salut*. Les Films de Pierre, Les Films Pelleas, Rita Production, Ali N'Films, 7 May 2014.
Taïa, Abdellah, ed. *Lettres à un jeune marocain*. Paris: Seuil, 2009.
Todorov, Tzvetan. *L'Homme dépaysé*. Paris: Seuil, 1996.
Williams, James S. *Queering the Migrant in European Cinema*. New York: Routledge, 2020.
Zheng, Tiantial. *Tongzhi Living: Men Attracted to Men in Postsocialist China*. Minneapolis: University of Minnesota Press, 2015.

Part I

ON PLACE AND NON-PLACE

Chapter 1

"Sortir de tous les territoires"

To Be a Racialized and Colonized Subject within France Today. Is There for Abdellah Taïa a There *Where to Go and to* Exist?

Ralph Heyndels

In *La vie lente* [*The Slow Life*] (2019), Abdellah Taïa's latest novel to date, the main character, Mounir, who is its narrator-vector, has exited "la zone de confort et d'inconfort" [the zone of comfort and discomfort] of the "Marocain faux" [false Moroccan] he has become.[1] He has started feeling "un lien" [a link], a solidarity, even a kind of togetherness, with the "Français arabes, africains, nés ici mais que la France voyait toujours comme des immigrés" [Arab and African French, born here but whom France still saw as immigrants].[2] He also asks himself what is perhaps (and I want to propose: very probably) for the writer today *the* cardinal question, existential, poetical, and political: "*Où aller*? Où aller de nouveau reproduire *la stratégie de la fuite*? Où, dans ce Paris indifférent, reprendre la course solitaire?" [*Where to go?* Where to go to newly reproduce *the escape strategy?* Where in this indifferent Paris, to take up again this solitary race[3] (my emphasis). The allusion to the *escape strategy* haunts Taïa's oeuvre from its very inception. In *Le rouge du tarbouche* [*The Red of the Fez*] (2004) for instance, the author directs the query "Fuir le Maroc?" [Flee Morocco?] to himself. And in "Terminus des anges," one of the novellas collected in that book, his self-reflective character Ahmed somehow responds: "Je n'ai rien ici, aucune chance, aucun avenir" [I have nothing here, no chance, no future] as he has "une seule préoccupation: foutre le camp" [one sole preoccupation: get the hell out].[4] But such a problematic is actually now displaced and relocated *within France* and could be encapsulated in the following formulation: *Fuir Paris, fuir la France?* [Flee Paris, flee France?] Indeed, the answer to the question *where to go?* in *La vie lente* is assuredly *not* to go to the predominantly *white*, historical, cultural, and literary center of the mythical French capital. The latter was the *dreamed of* site of all the ego-centered illusions, hopes, and ambitions of the young narrator of *L'armée du salut* [*Salvation Army*] (2006)—the "intellectuel"-to-be the author wanted so enthusiastically to become.[5] *That* Paris had already been sarcastically deconstructed, to say the least, in *Un pays pour mourir* [*A Country for Dying*] (published four years before the 2019 novel), and the place where (maybe?) to move to *now*—in the imaginary/poetical/political sense, maybe even the physical/corporeal one—is, as will be further developed, the capital's deprived periphery: "Je n'ai pas l'intention de quitter la France. J'irai peut-être vivre en banlieue. (. . .) je prends cette décision: *quitter Paris*. Aller en banlieue" [I don't plan to leave France. I will perhaps go live in the suburbs. (. . .) I make this decision: *to leave Paris.* To go into the suburbs] (my emphasis).[6]

In *La vie lente*, in a more advanced way than in the immediately anterior *Celui qui est digne d'être aimé* [*The One Worthy of Being Loved*] (2017), all fascination for the Paris "légendaire" [legendary][7] has undeniably been shattered. A new *sub/peri urban*[8] socio-geography of "the othered Paris," "stigmatized and neglected,"[9] emerges in Taïa's work for the first time, an area whose topography includes Nanterre or Cergy[10] and which is overwhelmingly populated by racialized non-white people who have no "droit à la ville" [right to the city].[11] Mounir realizes the "erreur" [error], which is also the "faute politique" [political mistake][12] he made by bringing *there* a Franco-French police inspector whom he is momentarily fond of but who is "un Français blanc qui ne comprendrait jamais rien, à qui il faudrait toujours tout expliquer, notre histoire, notre imaginaire, notre peau" [a white Frenchman who would never understand anything, to whom you'd always have to explain everything, our history, our imaginary, our skin].[13]

Even more symptomatic is the conjunction between the objective realization by Mounir—in whom, as it is very often the case in the author's (meta) auto-fictional works, Taïa is present while having also somehow *disappeared* to his reader and himself[14]—of that "lien" [link/bond] with the Arab and African subjects of the contemporary French state's coloniality with the vertiginously subjective interrogation of "where to go?" It should be noted here that in "Premier retour," an auto-biographical short story that ends *Le rouge du tarbouche* (published fifteen years before *La vie lente*), the writer, who is on a bus on his way back to Morocco, confesses that he had, until that moment, never really frequented the Moroccan immigrants in Paris, those who could be among the parents of the French Maghrebi youth born in France and were probably living in the underprivileged outskirts—in the "cités des banlieues" [high-rise slums of the suburbs]—of the capital (and all the big French cities): *Ces gens, je ne les avais jamais croisés à Paris, je ne savais pas où ils se cachaient en France.* C'était comme s'ils étaient encore au Maroc. (. . .) Ils étaient visiblement heureux, ils faisaient semblant d'être heureux. (. . .) Ils connaissaient très bien le rituel du "Retour estival de nos émigrés" (. . .) [*These folks, I never crossed paths with them in Paris, I didn't know where they were hiding in France*. It was as if they were still in Morocco (. . .) They were visibly happy, they pretended to be happy. (. . .) They knew very well the ritual of "Summer return of our emigrants"][15] (my emphasis).

By contrast, in *La vie lente*, there is evidently a declared concomitance with those whom Olivier Le Cour Grandmaison calls the "colonisés-immigrés" [colonised-immigrants] of a country structured by "un racisme d'Etat" [a racism of the State][16]—already denounced as such decades ago by Foucault and Bourdieu,[17] and pointed at, even explicitly alluded to, for *what it is* in Taïa's three last works.[18] Moreover, the possible eventuality of that recently self-discovered *vivre avec* [to live with], such existential and political togetherness, is lived by Mounir as a form of *salvation* from the existential "perte de sens" [loss of senses] from which he is emerging. The term "salvation" matters as it echoes the title of Taïa's 2006 first novel in which a relative and cautious attraction toward the West is already self-questioned, and will soon be thoroughly disassembled in what I have called elsewhere the poetical/political *decolonial laboratory* of the writer's *écriture*.[19] In that regard, the passage of *La vie lente*, which is referred to here appears to be simultaneously in a kind of syntony and a striking divergence with the introspective epilogue of *L'armée du salut*[20]:

> Pour sortir de ma zone de confort et d'inconfort, j'avais décidé enfin d'aller explorer la banlieue, d'aller à la rencontre de ces Français arabes, africains, nés ici mais que la France voyait toujours comme des immigrés. C'est-à-dire pas vraiment à la hauteur de ce pays. Presque indignes de ce pays.
>
> Je voyais soudain le lien entre eux et moi. Clairement. Très clairement. Et, terrifié, je me rendais compte que depuis mon installation en France je les avais pareillement négligés, ignorés, maltraités, peut-être même méprisés.
>
> Il a fallu que j'arrive à ce point précis de ma vie, à cet âge, pour que je me tourne vers eux, que je reconnaisse leur humanité, leur histoire, et que, avec une curiosité bienveillante et une humilité sincère, *j'aille à côté d'eux réapprendre la vie*. Les voir dans les ghettos de France. Les aimer. De près. De loin. Les enregistrer en moi. Leur donner je ne sais quoi de moi. *Construire un pont entre nous. Et surtout ceci: par ce mouvement, espérer être sauvé de cette perte de sens que je traversais* (. . .)[21] (my emphasis)
>
> [To come out of my zone of comfort and discomfort, I decided finally to go explore the *banlieue*, to go meet these French Arabs, Africans, born here but

whom France always saw as immigrants. Meaning not really up to snuff for this country. Almost unworthy of this country.

I suddenly saw a link between them and me. Clearly. Very clearly. And terrified, I realized that since my move to France I had also neglected, ignored, mistreated, maybe even scorned them.

It was necessary for me to arrive at this exact point in my life, at this age, for me to turn toward them, to recognize their humanity, their history, and to, with a benevolent curiosity and sincere humility, *go to their side to relearn life.* To see them in the ghettos of France. To love them. From close up. From afar. To record them in me. To give them I don't know what of myself. *To build a bridge between us. And above all this: by this maneuver, hoping to be saved by this loss of feeling I was experiencing* (. . .)]

J'allais évoluer longtemps encore dans le noir. Il me faudrait très vite prendre des décisions radicales et immédiates, choisir mon camp, m'éloigner de plus en plus des gens que j'aimais, arrêter une fois pour toutes de pleurer, gérer les crises de panique. Oublier le repos. Réapprendre à aimer. (. . .) Me construire dans le doute. Avancer seul. (. . .) Constituer enfin, le matin d'un jour gris et de grand froid, *une armée pour mon salut.* Cela ne se ferait pas du jour au lendemain. Au début de la Grande Bataille, les anges fidèles (musulmans?) seraient là, de mon côté. Puis ils m'abandonneraient lâchement. Entre-temps, je serais devenu plus fort, mais plus maigre, *et mon rêve d'être un intellectuel à Paris* serait peut-être une réalité.[22] (my emphasis)

[I was going to evolve for a long time still in the dark. I would be required to quickly make radical and immediate decisions, to choose my camp, to distance myself more and more from the people I loved, to stop once and for all from crying, managing panic attacks. To forget rest. To relearn to love. (. . .) To construct myself in doubt. To progress alone. (. . .) To build finally, on the morning of a gray and very cold day, *an army for my salvation.* It wouldn't be made overnight. At the beginning of the Great Battle, the faithful angels (Muslims?) would be there, by my side. Then, they would abandon me cowardly. In the meantime, I would become stronger, but thinner, *and my dream to be an intellectual in Paris* would maybe be a reality.]

The aforementioned quotation from *L'armée du salut* should be contrastively cross-read with what Mounir/Taïa declares about thirteen years later in *La vie lente*, having abandoned his illusions or having been abandoned by them, and having definitely forgone to believe, even minimally, in a nation-state arrogantly defining itself as the homeland *par excellence* of human rights, ethical values, and intellectual preeminence:

> Après quinze ans de vie à Paris, je n'étais plus satisfait d'être au cœur du mythe intellectuel froid construit autour de cette ville. Vivre de la cité légendaire ne me suffisait plus. La réalité simple de la vie pauvre, comme au Maroc, la réalité quotidienne, triviale même, me manquait terriblement.[23]
>
> J'étais en apparence si libre à Paris, si maître de moi, si réfléchi, si indépendant. (. . .) Je pouvais passer des jours et des jours sans parler à personne. *Que moi à moi. Dans trop de moi.*
>
> J'étais moi. Et c'est tout. Après avoir tout détruit pour être *soi-disant libre*, je me rendais compte que *je ne construisais plus rien avec les autres, avec le monde.* J'avançais. Oui. J'évoluais. Oui. *Mais dans la déconnexion*, la solitude. *Une autre forme de solitude.*
>
> [After 15 years of life in Paris, I was no longer satisfied being at the heart of this cold intellectual myth constructed around this city. Living on/off the legendary city was no longer enough. The simple reality of the poor life, like in Morocco, the daily reality, even trivial, I missed it terribly.
>
> I appeared so free in Paris, so much my own master, so reflective, so independent. (. . .) I could spend days and days without talking to anyone. *Only me for myself. Too much into myself.*
>
> I was me. And that's all. After destroying everything to be *supposedly free*, I realized that *I was no longer building anything with others, with the world.* I was progressing. Yes. I was evolving. Yes. But in disconnection, in solitude. *Another form of solitude.*][24] (my emphasis)

Engulfed in a profound "abattement" [despondency],[25] Mounir knows *where not to live anymore* while the Abdellah of *L'armée du salut* was convinced that Paris was the place where he wanted to go. "Où vivras-tu à ton retour d'Istanbul?" [Where will you live upon your return from Istanbul?] (where he is planning a trip), asks Mounir's neighbor, Madame Marty.[26] Is there still a *there* where to go and to *exist* for somebody who, as a young gay Moroccan, came to France and has "sauvé [sa] peau" [saved his skin],[27] but who has also realized, like Ahmed in *Celui qui est digne d'être aimé*[28]—another scriptural embodiment of Taïa who did the same voyage into exile—how deeply he, the "immigré arabe qui parlait si bien la langue française et maîtrisait parfaitement la littérature française" [Arab immigrant who spoke the French language so well and perfectly mastered French literature][29] is actually a colonized subject (Memmi) even if apparently a privileged one, being "l'étranger, le colonisé, l'immigré (. . .) en position d'infériorité éternelle"[the stranger, the colonized, the immigrant (. . .) in an eternal position of inferiority],[30] "[b]ien élevé, [b]ien éduqué, [d]ocile (. . .)" [well raised, well educated, docile],[31] playing the "gentil Arabe" [nice Arab],[32] the "bon immigré bien intégré (. . .) qui ne demande qu'à jouer le soumis devant le patron, les maîtres" [good immigrant well integrated (. . .) who only asks to play the submissive one in front of the boss, the masters],[33] and who, while he has no intention to leave France thinks about going "vivre en banlieue" [to live in the suburbs][34] and regrets having traded his studio apartment on rue de Belleville—a highly immigrant populated neighborhood located within the inner borders of the French capital—for the all-white and upscale district of the "rue de Turenne," a "territoire" [territory] where he does not feel well at all.[35]

Moreover, Mounir is well aware of the racialized way Arab and African immigrants (himself included) are treated in France, as one can see when speaking of Antoine, the white French policeman with whom he has had an affair. He describes the latter as "[u]n policier français qui défend bien sa belle patrie aux belles valeurs universelles, qui protège les siens, ses concitoyens, et qui arrête sans aucun problème dans les rues les types arabes *comme moi* (. . .)" [a French police officer who bravely defends his beautiful homeland with its beautiful universal values, who protects his own, his fellow citizens, and who stops without any problem in the streets the Arab types *like me*][36] (my emphasis). Simone Marty, the old and poor lady with whom he enters in a complex relationship, tells him, in what could be listened to as Taïa's own words but uttered from the perspective of a Franco-French subaltern subject[37] who "vivait dans les mêmes conditions que certains immigrés logés dans les cages qu'on appelle foyers"[38]: "Je sais ce que peuvent vivre les Arabes en France. J'ai des yeux: je vois ce qu'on leur fait, aux immigrés, comment on les traite, comment on parle d'eux" [lived in the same conditions that certain immigrants housed in cages that they called *foyers*: I know what Arabs in France can live like. I have two eyes: I see what they've done to them, to the immigrants, how they treat them, how they speak about them].[39] What his eccentric neighbor tells Mounir is actually already somehow thematized toward the beginning of *Celui qui est digne d'être aimé*, in the context of the ideological French homo-nationalism[40] supposedly "liberating" Maghrebi queer people from their hegemonic heterosexist societies:

> Ceux qui sont comme moi aujourd'hui, je les croise ici à Paris depuis mon arrivée. Ils viennent eux-aussi du Maroc ou des pays d'à côté. Ils sont homosexuels. Ils ont désormais presque 60 ans et ils disent que la France les a sauvés. Cela me fait rire chaque fois que je les entends parler ainsi de la France qui émancipe et donne les clefs indispensables à la liberté. Les pédés arabes qui cherchent un abri en France sont traités de la même façon que les autres émigrés.

Une case préparée pour eux depuis plusieurs décennies, plusieurs siècles, les y attend, les y enferme. (. . .) Ils sont intégrés. Ils sont acceptés. Ils sont libres. Ils le disent et le redisent. Ils peuvent tromper les autres, les Français, avec ces affirmations. Pas moi (. . .).

[Those who are like me today, I cross paths with them here in Paris since I arrived. They also come from Morocco or from nearby countries. They are homosexuals. They are now nearly sixty years old and they say that France has saved them. It makes me laugh each time I hear them talk like that about France that frees and gives the necessary keys of freedom. The Arab faggots that search for a shelter in France are treated in the same way as the other emigrants. *A shack prepared for them for several decades, several centuries, awaits them there, encloses them there, (. . .) They are integrated. They are accepted. They are free. They say it and resay it. They can fool others, the French, with these affirmations. Not me (. . .).*][41] (my emphasis)

Ahmed, in *Celui qui est digne d'être aimé*, after having broken up with his French lover of thirteen years and gone through an intersectional process of *racial/class consciousness*[42] similar to Mounir's in *La vie lente* and described in details, does not know what to do with himself—just that he wants "[a]ller ailleurs" [to go elsewhere], "[e]n banlieue [in the suburbs].[43] A Gennevillier. A Clichy" and that he has "trouvé un autre travail" [found another job].[44] But Mounir, in *La vie lente*, who like the young Abdellah of *L'armée du salut*, *wanted also to be writer*, will radically change his life and start teaching alienated Arab and African kids, as he has signed a contract to become "professeur de français dans un lycée de Drancy" [a French teacher in a high-school in Drancy], a Parisian banlieue which will be for him "le miracle final" [the final miracle] he has lately been hoping for: "La banlieue et ses habitants dévalorisés, *c'était cela l'espoir*. Entrer dans leurs richesses" [The suburbs and their devalued inhabitants, *that was hope*. To enter into their riches][45] (my emphasis). It is *there*, as Simone Marty tells him—and this could very well be the writer addressing himself—that he will finally have "l'occasion de *sortir complètement de [lui]-même et des illusions de notre monde qui [l']a fait rêver, qui [l']a décu, qui [l']a rejeté et continue de rejeter les gens comme [lui]*" [the opportunity to completely come out of himself and of the illusions of our world that made you dream, deceived you, rejected you and continued to reject the folks like you][46] (my emphasis). She adds: "*Tu dois vivre encore, Mounir*" [You have to live again][47] (my emphasis). The latter injunction, which could also be proffered by the author to himself, is a reminder of Ahmed saying to his ex-lover to be, Emmanuel—an *intellectuel "de gauche"* [intellectual of the political left] who incarnates the so-called universal values of the French republic without questioning the neo-colonialist ideology and racialized oppression they implicitly camouflage: "Je me suis réveillé maintenant, Emmanuel. *J'ai encore une chance de trouver loin de toi un autre sens à la vie, à ma vie*" [I am awake now, Emmanuel. I still have a chance to find far from you another meaning to life, to my life].[48]

Abdellah Taïa has been living in Paris since 1998. His first book, published in France in 2000, is entitled *Mon Maroc* [*My Morocco*]. In a succession of short-stories he narrates his childhood, and also, in "A la gare" [At the Station], his departure from his country "pour l'étranger, le lointain" [to go abroad, the far away],[49] actually inaugurating what will become a *self-anthropological viatic writing*[50] which will cross his entire work until nowadays. In *L'armée du salut*, the self-reflective narrator expresses his enthusiasm for being for the first time in "une terre étrangère" [a foreign land][51] and his desire to move from Geneva, where he first landed and stayed in a fast degrading relationship with the Swiss professor he had seduced in Rabat, to Paris.[52] But his excitement is already tempered by doubts, which are recurrently and subtly, often implicitly, disposed through the work.[53] Interestingly enough, in the 2013 released film bearing the same title as the novel, but which in numerous ways is strikingly different (even divergent) from the latter, Paris, that in the written version is referred to as the city "qui depuis toujours [le] fascinait et où [il] rêvai[t] d'habiter un jour (. . .)"[that since always fascinated [him] and where [he] dreamed of living one day],[54] is not even mentioned anymore, and the movie, actually much more somber and cryptic than the narrative published seven years before, ends in a totally enigmatic tone. The writer/film director has described his cinematographic enterprise, which is absolutely not an adaptation but is actually a kind of self-critical interpretation or revisiting and even a deconstruction of the novel, as the "remains of the book, the ruins of the book."[55] I would actually propose that *Un pays pour mourir*, *Celui qui est digne d'être aimé*, and *La vie lente* are also all written within the ruins of Taïa's first novel.

The memory of Morocco, embodied not only in poverty, alienation, suffering, but also in ecstatic moments of ravishment and bliss, is reiterative in the author's entire work, which also includes texts related to photographic renderings of his native country.[56] In a superbly written short text recently published in *The Art Newspaper* under the title "Regarder tout au fond du monde" [Look at the ends of the Earth], he writes, comparing his youth of "pauvreté et dénuement" [poverty and destitution], "misère" [misery], and "abandon" to a kind of subjectively dreamed paradise[57]:

> Il y a le paradis. Il existe. Il existe vraiment. Je l'ai connu. Dans la pauvreté et le dénuement. Dans les cris et les disputes. Dans la misère et l'abandon. Mais c'était le paradis quand même. Avant le monde et ses nombreuses et terrifiantes chutes, j'ai été au paradis. En noir et blanc.

[There's paradise. It exists. It truly exists. I have known it. In poverty and destitution. In the cries and the disputes. In misery and abandon. But it was paradise all the same. Before the world and its numerous and terrifying falls, I have been in paradise. In black and white.][58]

But Taïa's faithfulness is to the poor people of his native country and certainly not to the latter's ruling class social arrogance, political authoritarianism, state sponsored and regulated Islamism, and "appareils idéologiques d'Etat" [ideological apparatuses of the State]—to use Althusser's terminology (1976)[59]—which the author adamantly criticizes, particularly in *Le jour du Roi* [*The Day of the King*] (2010) and *Infidèles* [*Infidels*] (2012).[60] Such memorial loyalty is thus embedded into a denunciation of the Moroccan state apparatus, which is often assimilated to a betrayal by those who oppose the writer's literary and political positioning. By the way, such dialectics of loyalty and treason lay at the core of Taïa's poetical ethics, but in a totally *reworked* way.[61] When Omar in *Le jour du Roi* asks "Qui suis-je, si je ne suis plus Marocain?" [Who am I, if I am not longer Moroccan?], it is both an inquiry the author directs to himself and a critique of the nationalistic reification and ideological manipulation operated by the power in place (represented in this case by Hassan II). Slima, who in *Infidèles* has fled Morocco, where she had been tortured and raped by the king's secret police, for Egypt, burns her Moroccan passport, makes an assertion the writer himself is obviously endorsing: "*Le Maroc? C'est quoi, le Maroc? Un pays? Une idée? Un sentiment?* (. . .) On ne peut pas réussir au Maroc. On fait tout pour vous arrêter, vous contrôler, vous maintenir petit" [*Morocco? What's Morocco? A country? An idea? A feeling?* (. . .) You cannot succeed in Morocco. They do everything to stop you, to control you, to keep you down] (my emphasis). [62]

Almost all of Taïa's main characters, who are always to some extent literary mediations of himself, need to leave Morocco (with the exception of those of *Le jour du Roi,* whose narrative is entirely framed within the Cherifian nation). Such an existential requirement is well summed up by Zineb in *Un pays pour mourir*:

– Qu'est-ce qu'il a fait pour moi, le Maroc?
– A toi de me le dire.
– Rien
(. . .)
Il fallait que je parte plus loin, que je m'éloigne du Maroc. Quelque part ailleurs, un autre destin m'attendait. Une autre vie. (. . .).

[– What has Morocco done for me?
– It's up to you to tell me.

– Nothing
(. . .)
I had to go far away, to distance myself from Morocco. Someplace else, another destiny was waiting for me. Another life. (. . .)][63] (my emphasis)

Evoked in ways sometimes lyrical, sometimes tragic, and often both, Morocco, as a land and a people distinct from the nation-state bearing that name, traverses almost the entirety of Taïa's oeuvre and it is still present in the author's last novel, for instance when Mounir, poetically remembers Rabat and Salé:

> Ce lieu magique est important *pour nous*. Ce lieu où deux mondes se rencontrent. Le fleuve Bouregreg les partage, les lie. Et l'océan Atlantique les accueille et ne cesse de les envahir. Deux villes. Rabat qui regarde vers Salé. Salé qui défie Rabat. Et la casbah des Oudayas là-haut, sur une petite colline rien qu'à elle, à l'embouchure du fleuve, comme un rêve. Un beau mirage. Jardin et prison à la fois. Palais et forteresse d'un temps ancien.
>
> [This magical place is important for us. This place where two worlds meet. The Bouregreg river shares them, links them. And the Atlantic Ocean welcomes them and never ceases to invade them. Two cities. Rabat that looks toward Salé. Salé that defies Rabat. And the casbah of the Oudayas upon high, on a small hill all to herself, at the mouth of the river like a dream. A beautiful mirage. Garden and prison at the same time. Palace and fortress from an ancient time.][64] (my emphasis)

In that sense, Morocco is the primal (both individual and collective—"*pour nous*" [for us]) but also the always and forever productive matrix of meaning for Mounir, as it is for Taïa, simultaneously marked by precarity, danger, violence, oppression—social, political, sexual—, and rebellion, while intimately mixed with humanity, desire, sex, and love. This is for instance perceptible in the following passage—somehow reminiscent of the opening section of *Une mélancolie arabe* [*An Arab Melancholia*] (2008), which I have analyzed elsewhere[65]—in which Mounir/Taïa remembers his past of wild street kid in a phallocentric sexual socio-culture and a country dominated by the authoritarian and hegemonic regime of "toutes les dictatures" [all the dictators][66]:

> De ces batailles quotidiennes au Maroc, la petite chose folle et efféminée que j'étais sortait *à la fois* traumatisée et excitée. Il ne fallait jamais baisser la garde. Tout, le lendemain, la semaine dernière, le mois d'après, recommencerait. Les guerres. Les affrontements. Les cris. Les insultes. Les règles. L'intensité folle.[67] *Et étrangement au coeur de tout cela*, il y avait

de l'humanité, de la séduction, de la transgression, du sexe volé, de l'amour malmené et sans cesse redéfini.

[Of these daily battles in Morocco, that small crazy and effeminate thing that I was, going out both traumatized and excited. You could never lower your guard. All, the next day, last week, the month after, would start again. The Wars. The assaults. The cries. The insults. The rules. The crazy intensity. *And strangely at the heart of it all,* there was humanity, seduction, transgression, stolen sex, rough sex and endelessly redefined.][68] (my emphasis)

The *dislocation* (geographic, socio-mental, and linguistic)[69] from his native country and the distance it produces has generated in the author's literary enterprise, from its very beginning, the effects of a *retro-projected* self-ethnological representation,[70] as illustrated in *Mon Maroc.*

Bizarrement, (. . .) mon esprit (. . .) commença à m'imposer ceci: *penser continuellement au Maroc.* Le Maroc me revenait, me sollicitait en permanence. Bien plus: *il me suivait dans mes déplacements.* Ainsi, au fur et à mesure que je rencontrais cet objet, toute une réflexion se développait dans ma tête, à mon insu presque, concernant mon pays d'origine. Cette dualité me passionnait me passionne toujours. Elle me cause un sentiment étrange, difficile à décrire: je perds tous mes repères et dans les grandes villes d'Europe, je suis paumé, désaxé (. . .). Je dirais plutôt que je vis dans l'entre-deux: chacune des deux cultures me tire de son côté (il y a donc une bataille en moi, dans mon corps). Cela pourrait être enrichissant—et ça l'est—mais aussi très déstabilisant.

[Bizarrely, (. . .) my mind/spirit (. . .) started to impose this: *to think continually of Morocco.* Morocco came back to me, solicited me permanently. Even more: *it followed me in my displacements.* Thus, slowly but surely, that I would recognize this object, a whole reflection developed in my head, without me knowing almost, concerning my country of origin. This duality fascinated me and still fascinates me. It causes me to have a strange feeling, difficult to describe: I lose all my bearings and in the big cities of Europe, I am lost, unhinged (. . .) I would say more that I live between the two: each of the two cultures pulls me to its side (there is hence a battle in me, in my body). It could be enriching—and it is that—but it's also very destabilizing.][71]

Taïa's connection with his native country, which he visits often for usually brief sojourns and where he directed the entire Moroccan segment of his film *L'armée du salut,* is not only emotional. It has a strong political component and has allowed him to insert himself into the Moroccan social, political and socio-sexual debates, issues, and polemics of the past twenty years. He has also edited and participated in a collective book entitled *Lettres ouvertes à un jeune Marocain* [*Open Letters to a Young Morrocan*] (2009). In the presentation of this volume, published in France but also largely distributed in Morocco (for free, thanks to the sponsorship of the Saint-Laurent Foundation and the local magazine *Tel Quel*), he writes:

> Le Maroc bouge. Le Maroc attend. Le Maroc recule. Ses jeunes sont toujours ignorés, écartés. Qui leur parle directement? Qui les comprend? Qui les inspire? Qui les aide à s'affirmer, à être eux-mêmes et libres? A ne plus se sentir abandonnés, isolés? A prendre leur vie en main?
>
> [Morocco moves. Morocco waits. Morocco pulls back. Its youth are always ignored, set aside. Who speaks directly to them? Who understands them? Who inspires them? Who helps them to assert themselves, to be themselves and free? To no longer feel abandoned, isolated? To take life into their own hands?] [72]

But the idea of returning to live in Morocco, while the latter occupies a major dimension of his imaginary and his identity[73] is repeatedly projected by the author through the voice of his characters as a *non-starter*[74] -- as it is the case for Ahmed, and for Mounir:

> Je n'étais pas aveuglé par la nostalgie. Je savais parfaitement les raisons qui m'avaient poussé à partir du Maroc, à m'exiler. La pauvreté principalement. Je n'oubliais rien des atrocités que j'avais vécues là-bas. Le silence assourdissant au milieu du vacarme de la foule. Cela avait failli me tuer. J'avais survécu.
>
> [I wasn't blinded by nostalgia. I knew perfectly the reasons that had pushed me to leave Morocco. To exile myself. Poverty primarily. I haven't forgotten the atrocities that I had lived there. The deafening silence in the middle of the clamor of the crowd. It had nearly killed me. I had survived.][75]

What Mounir relates is actually similar to the recounting by the writer of his Moroccan youth in a 2015 interview published by *Urbain Tanger*:

> Pendant longtemps j'ai pensé qu'au Maroc je ne pourrais pas survivre. J'étais trop seul et je ne savais pas où trouver mon propre salut (. . .) De mon côté, j'avais plein de rêves, d'aspirations artistiques, mais nous étions très pauvres et je ne voyais pas comment accéder à un monde qui semblait très éloigné. D'autre part, je me savais homosexuel, et même si j'ai gommé cela pendant des années, même si je ne l'ai pas montré au monde d'une manière affirmée, je me rendais bien compte que j'allais un jour être dans l'obligation d'affronter cette chose

en moi... Je comprenais que mon salut en aucune façon n'était au Maroc, que j'allais être obligé de fuir, que *je ne voulais pas de ce pays pour mourir* (. . .)

[For a long time I thought I would not be able to survive in Morocco. I was too lonely and I didn't know where to find my own salvation (. . .) From my perspective, I had plenty of dreams, artistic aspirations, but we were very poor and I didn't see how I could access a world that seemed so far away. On the other hand, I knew I was homosexual and even if I erased it for years, even if I had not shown it to the world in an asserting manner, I realized that one day I was going to be forced to confront this thing in me . . . I understood that my salvation in no way was in Morocco, that I was going to be forced to flee, that *I didn't want of this country for dying* (. . .)]

France, however, whose "ancêtres ont inventé les droits de l'homme (. . .) [et] se gargarisent de mots trop grands pour dire leur liberté" [ancestors invented human rights (. . .) gargle words that are too big to name their freedom] becomes increasingly *unqualified* as a host nation, and its capital, whose socio-cultural prestige is reduced into shambles, is inhospitable "pour les hommes arabes et musulmans (. . .) usés par cette ville qui les maltraite sans remords et par des patrons français blancs qui les exploitent au noir sans éprouver la moindre culpabilité" [for Arab and Muslim men (. . .) worn out by this city that mistreats them without remorse and by white French bosses that exploit them on the black market without feeling the least amount of guilt].[76] Moreover, it is literally contaminated by ever-growing arabophobia and islamophobia, which have actually been part of its entire modern history and have become hysterical in the recent decade, as it is also institutionally and socio-mentally structured by a coloniality that permeates even the self-affirmed intellectuals of the "left" like Emmanuel—who, says the narrator, does not have any "scrupule à reproduire sur moi, dans mon corps, *tout ce que la France refuse de voir*: *du néo-colonialisme*" [scruples to reproduce for me, in my body, *all that France refuses to see: neo-colonialism*].[77] (my emphasis). Almost consequently, Mounir declares in *La vie lente*: "Moi-même je vais partir. Je vais abandonner tout ce que je possède et partir. Parfois, il faut pouvoir faire des sacrifices pour de vrai" [I'm myself going to leave. I'm going to abandon all I possess and leave. Sometimes, you must be able to make sacrifices for real].[78] Departing, but for where? For Ahmed, for Mounir, for Taïa, Paris, or more broadly France as a nation-state, is not *a where* to *exist*, while the ideologically and politically repressive Maghreb countries are excluded for an array of reasons.[79] As Mounir formulates it:

Ni l'avenir en France. Ni l'avenir au Maroc. Et encore moins l'avenir de l'adulte désarmé, domestiqué, que j'étais devenu depuis que j'avais choisi l'émigration.

> [Neither the future in France. Nor the future in Morocco. And even less the future of the disarmed, domesticated adult, who I had become since I had chosen emigration.][80]

And Aziz, in *Un pays pour mourir* (as somebody this time caught between France and Algeria): *Des deux côtés, c'est du pareil au même* [On both sides, it's the same all the same].[81] The writer himself is taken between "l'exil," [exile] "l'attente du retour," [the wait of the return], and "l'impossible retour," [the impossible return] as he delineates in "Regarder tout au fond du monde."[82]

The characters of *Un pays pour mourir* are all undergoing the same condition, would it be in different modalities. In the aforementioned interview in *Urbain Tanger*, Taïa specifies what Paris could have or should have been for them, while it is absolutely not *that*.[83] Just by returning to *L'armée du salut*, one can read through the 2015 novel the author's own destroyed dreams and his decolonial awareness—even if he is very conscious of his apparent and actually very relative privileged status, as well of the latter's limitations, as he is a kind of "guest-member" of the French literary and cultural scene. In the *Urbain Tanger* intervention, the writer adds:

> Paris aurait pu être l'espace physique du *salut* des trois personnages de mon roman "Un pays pour mourir". Ils en ont tous rêvé. Ils ont tous été attirés par une vision sensuelle de cette ville. Mais, une fois arrivés dans la capitale, ils se rendent compte qu'ils sont dans l'obligation de devenir Français tels que la France décide qu'ils doivent l'être. Ce n'est plus eux, ces idées sur eux qu'on leur impose en permanence. D'où qu'ils viennent dans le monde, on exige d'eux cette impossibilité. La France est dans un tel nombrilisme, dans de telles certitudes par rapport à son histoire et ses valeurs, qu'elle ne prendra jamais le temps d'écouter des gens aussi peu visibles que mes personnages. Or, ces gens participent aussi à la vie, à l'économie, à la culture, à la sexualité de ce pays.
>
> [Paris could have been the physical space of salvation of the three characters in my novel. "A Country For Dying." They all dreamed about it. They had all been attracted by a sensual vision of this city. But once they had arrived in the capital, they realize that they are forced to become French in just the way France decides they should become so. It's no longer them, these ideas on them that are permanently imposed. No matter where they come from in the world, they require this impossibility of them. France is so completely wrapped up in itself, in such certainties about its history and its values, that it will take the time to listen to people with so little visibility as my characters. And yet, these people participate also in the life, the economy, the culture, the sexuality of this country]

All the protagonists of the novel are domiciled in the heavily immigrant populated neighborhood of Barbès (the very quartier where the author occupies a tiny studio) and actually never venture outside of it, but for prostituting themselves in Clichy. Here is how one of them, Zahira, in *Un pays pour mourir*, describes the Jardin du Luxembourg, where she accompanies at his request a gay Iranian political and sexual refugee for whom Paris is only a place of transit on his voyage to Stockholm.[84] We can guess that her experience of alienation is that of thousands of poor Maghrebi immigrants when arriving in or passing by areas in which they are objectively *persona non grata*—something also experienced by those who are confined to the "cités" [low-income highrises] of the impoverished periphery, *de facto* relegated to the status of "les étrangers de l'intérieur" [strangers of the interior] and "assignés à résidence" [under house arrest] in their designated areas like the "indigènes" [indigenous] were in the colonies of the French empire[85]:

> Ce jardin était un territoire étranger. Mon corps a été traversé durant cinq très longues minutes d'une crise de panique monumentale. J'ai réussi à l'étouffer sans savoir où j'ai puisé l'énergie nécessaire pour le faire. (. . .) Je ne suis jamais venue ici, dans ce quartier, dans ce monde. (. . .) Je reconnaissais certains bâtiments qui font l'histoire de ce pays, mais seulement à travers des souvenirs lointains. Des images vieilles de Paris vues à la télévision marocaine, avec mon père quelque temps avant sa mort. Elles étaient destinées à nous faire rêver. A nous écraser aussi un petit peu. "Ce monde-là n'est pas pour vous. Regardez mais seulement de loin, à travers l'écran. Ne venez pas. Restez où vous êtes. Ce n'est pas pour vous."
>
> [This garden was a foreign territory. My body had been overcome the last five long minutes with a monumental panic attack. I was able to stifle it without knowing where I found the necessary energy to do so. (. . .) I had never come here, in this neighborhood, in this world. (. . .) I recognized certain buildings that make up the history of this country, but only through memories from long ago. Old images of Paris seen on Moroccan television, with my father some time before his death. They were destined to make us dream. To crush us also little by little. "That world is not for you. Look but only from a distance, through the screen. Don't come. Stay where you are. It's not for you."] [86]

The Algerian Aziz—to become Zanouba after having been operated—has decided to stay in Paris, which he calls "ce trou qu'on ose encore appeler la plus belle ville du monde" [this whole that they still dare to call the most beautiful city in the world].[87] He speaks of it as a place "qui va [le] tuer" [that will kill him] and is "devenu froid, sourd, triste, insensible. Raciste" [become cold, deaf, sad, insensitive. Racist].[88] He is obviously without any illusion left about the *hospitalité française* [French hospitality].[89] For him, there is no choice to be possibly made between his native country—where he was regularly raped "gratis"—and France where he became a cheap, orientalist, "sauvage" [savage][90] libidinal fantasy-object of French white guys "affamés du sexe" [starved for sex].[91] The Moroccan Zahira, who is also a sex worker—prostitution is a recurrent *not "judgmental"* topic in Taïa's work[92]—led her "statut de femme soumise" [submissive status of woman] in Morocco and feels, in that sense, "libre" [free] in Paris,[93] a city she declares loving in a type of dream-like attachment as she has made it *hers*—"[sa] cité, [son] royaume, [son] chemin" [her city, her kingdom, her path]—but where she is condemned to stay within the shadow of society because she does not have "les papiers français" [French papers].[94] Moreover, her real motivation for having resorted to remain in Paris has actually nothing to do with any of the connotations supposed to be encapsulated in the mythical capital. If she is *there* it is out of affection for a little boy named Antoine, her "petit oiseau français charmant" [little, charming French bird],[95] and because she loves Iqbal, an immigrant from Sri Lanka.[96] Naima, an older Moroccan woman retired from up-scale prostitution, after having been baby-sitter "chez les affreux bourgeois du XVIème arrondissement, (. . .) est devenue barmaid dans un bar pour vieux Arabes pas encore remis du choc d'avoir donné leur jeunesse, leur force, leur âme, pour la France, pays plus qu'ingrat avec eux et que, pourtant, ils n'arrivent pas à quitter" [at the home of the awful bourgeois of the 16th district, (. . .) became a barmaid in a bar for old Arabs who had not yet recovered from the shock of having given their youth, their strength, their soul, for France, the country more than ungrateful to them and that, yet, they are unable to leave].[97]

"Aujourd'hui je sais que dans nos vies tout est politique" [Today, I know that in our lives, everything is political].[98] Taïa's writing is directly or mediately auto-fictional,[99] Muslim-queer,[100] transgendered and even transsexual,[101] and dealing with the intricacies of transfiliation,[102] loss and mourning,[103] love, desire, and sex.[104] It is also eminently political,[105] but in a very subjective perspective, which differentiates it from "la littérature engagée"[engaged literature] as its specific poetics of engagement combines the political with the existential and the corporeal—like it is the case in the works of Rimbaud or Genet.[106] The latter, whom Taïa refers to as *Un saint marocain* [A Moroccan saint] (2010), has actually exercised a profound, but also somehow complicated, influence on him.[107] The writer incorporates in his work what he has denounced as "la peur des maîtres" [the fear of the masters] and "le cœur noir du Maroc" [the black heart of Morocco],[108] and he excoriates his native country where he was "rien" [nothing][109] and where "[s]euls les riches peuvent vraiment vivre" [only the rich could really live].[110] He condemns all the modalities of a state-/religion-induced repressive machinery acting in the name of so-called traditions, which are purposely commodified in order to deprive all the subaltern subjects of their intimate and sexual existences, and to maintain them in social misery.

Nonetheless, from *Un pays pour mourir* on, and this time targeting nowadays France and its militarized instances of police surveillance and brutal control—"la police, les militaires et les vigiles très armés (. . .) [dont] [o] n ne peut se retenir (. . .) d'avoir peur (. . .). Surtout les gens comme moi. Les Arabes" [the police, the military, and the heavily armed security guards (. . .) of whom you cannot stop yourself (. . .) from being scared (. . .) Above all people like me. Arabs]—[111]and more broadly the West,[112] the writer has made clear that he has no intention anymore to play the game of the Arab immigrant intellectual gratefully complacent with the France's coloniality[113] (which he self-disentangles through the character of Mounir in *La vie lente:*

> (. . .) à l'approche de la quarantaine, je voulais soudain (. . .) être dérangé, être bousculé, être dans l'échange vrai, même futile, et pas dans l'échange où tous les mots sont en permanence soupesés avant d'être dits, prononcés si sérieusement, proclamés avec tant de certitude et tant d'arrogance.
>
> Je devenais comme eux [= the Franco-French intellectuals], moi aussi. Je parlais précis. Je parlais en très bon français, parfait, faussement doux et incroyablement froid. Je parlais chic avec le sentiment d'être guindé. Et au fond, je ne disais rien. Rien ne se disait. Les jours passaient, les mois passaient, ma vie passait, et l'essentiel n'était pas là.
>
> [(. . .) approaching my forties, I wanted suddenly (. . .) to be bothered, to be moved, to be in the real exchange, even futile, and not in the exchange where are all the words are permanently weighty before they are said, pronounced, so seriously, proclaimed with such certainty and such arrogance.
>
> I was becoming like them [=the Franco-French intellectuals], me too. I spoke with precision. I spoke in such good French, perfect, falsely sweet and incredibly cold. I spoke chic with the feeling of being uptight. And deep down, I would say nothing. Nothing was said. Days passed, months passed, my life passed, and the essential part was not there.][114]

In a 2018 conversation with Edouard Louis, Taïa asserts that "resistance evolves" and he refers to Jean Genet and James Baldwin as models. I will get back to Genet further on. In an emotional (of course fictional) letter addressed in June 2020 to Baldwin[115] and which somehow confirms the argument developed in this essay, he writes in what is probably one of his firmest recent political statements, inserting the latter into his own existential imaginary, as he always does:

> Ta voix, tes mots et ton regard nous sont plus que jamais nécessaires, absolument indispensables pour oser continuer la révolte, la révolution, *sortir du regard blanc colonial et postcolonial.* (. . .) C'est ce que je ressens pour toi, depuis si longtemps déjà. (. . .) Je lis tes mots, (. . .) *j'entre avec toi dans ta radicalité,* au passé comme au présent, et je veux propager moi aussi ton message autour de moi, avec mes neveux, mes nièces, mes amis, ceux que je ne connais pas, *ceux que je croise dans les rues de Paris et que je reconnais immédiatement comme des frères, comme des sœurs.* (. . .) La littérature pour dire le désenchantement et le dégoût. *La littérature pour dire aux Blancs la Vérité sur ce qu'ils ont fait puisqu'ils persistent à nier l'évidence. Dire aux Blancs ce qu'ils font semblant d'ignorer sur eux-mêmes* (. . .) *Malgré la violence du pouvoir et de sa police, la peur a changé de camp. Elle est en train de changer de camp.* Les minorités n'ont pas peur ces jours-ci. Elles sont remplies de défi et de courage. Elles sortent pour manifester un peu partout. Elles imposent au monde entier leurs combats. On n'osera plus minimiser les thèmes qu'elles veulent lancer. *Le colonialisme. Le racisme systémique envers les Noirs et les "Indigènes." Les injustices sociales et économiques. L'intersectionnalité des combats des minorités, de toutes les minorités.*
>
> [Your voice, your words and your look are more than ever necessary for us, absolutely indispensable to dare to continue the revolt, the revolution, *to come out of the white, colonial and postcolonial gaze.* (. . .) That's what I feel for you, for so long already (. . .) I read your words, (. . .) I enter with you into your radicalness, in the past like in the present, and I too want to spread your message around me, with my nephews, my nieces, my friends, those whom I don't know, those I cross in the streets of Paris and whom I recognize immediately as brothers, as sisters. (. . .) Literature to recount the disenchantment and the disgust. Literature to tell the Whites the Truth about what they did since they persist in denying the evidence. To tell the Whites what they pretend to ignore about themselves. (. . .) Despite the violence of the power and the police, fear has changed camps. It's changing camps. The minorities are not afraid these days. They are full of defiance and courage. They come out to protest a bit everywhere. They impose their battles on the entire world. No one dares to continue to minimize the causes they launch. Colonialism. Systemic racism against Blacks and the "Indigenous." The social and economic injustices. The intersectionality of the battles of minorities, of all minorities.][116] (my emphasis)

He has actually started to develop even further a poetical-political literary strategy of what Ahmed, in *Celui qui est digne d'être aimé* defines as "une vengeance historique, post-coloniale" [a historic and postcolonial vengeance].[117] The latter is already expressed in a kind of immediate and almost instinctual rage by Aziz in *Un pays pour mourir* when he alludes to his Franco-French clients—"[Ils] ont les poches remplies d'argent. On est là pour le leur prendre" [They have pockets full of money. We're here to take it from them].[118] In *La vie lente*, a character named Sinan, whom Mounir says he "understands" because he was aware of the societal realities of contemporary France, "suivait tout ce qui se passait" [followed all that was happening] and "écoutait très attentivement les informations" [listened very attentively to the news]—something we know is part of Taïa's daily routine—evokes the "humiliation" (. . .) imposed on Muslim people and why they are led to "se venger" [avenge themselves].[119] In the aforementioned dialogue with Edouard Louis, the writer, who defines himself as "Moroccan, African, Muslim, and gay"—the words "French" or "residing in France" are conspicuously absent—explicitly rejects "the rigid imaginary of the France that only accepts 'good immigrants'." In a 2017 interview with Mabrouck Rachedi, he avows that he had to go through an existential experience and a political awakening which he describes, in a highly significative choice of words, as a *passage through France* (once again not using terms such as "residing in," or "living in" that country):

> [Il] *a fallu* que *je passe par la France pour comprendre de manière politique comment les Français blancs continuent de nous voir comme des corps totalement inférieurs aux autres.*
>
> [I had to pass through France to understand the political manner by which the white French continue to see us as totally inferior bodies to the others.][120] (my emphasis)

Such *passage through* the internal coloniality of the French nation-state has produced in Taïa a realization of his closeness to the "white French" people who continue to see "us" as "inferior bodies," along with an acute cognizance of his own objectively subaltern status—as part of a "we" ("*nous voir*"). It has also developed into an increased solidarity with *the decolonial resistance*.[121] But while being *solidaire*, as a writer and artist, he also remains *solitaire* [solitary], a conception of engagement similar to Jean Genet's.[122] Nacira Guénif-Souilamas has well perceived such dialectics between the existential, the political, and the poetic:

> Il s'est mis à l'abri des assauts d'amabilité et de condescendance mêlés qui font la marque de fabrique de la toxicité réorientalisante (. . .) Il a tout balancé et la bienséance avec, *rejoignant la foule des résistants et des rétifs, depuis sa place solitaire.*

[He puts himself/itself under the shelter of amiable attacks and tinged condescensions that are the trademark of re-orientalizing toxicity (. . .) He through all away and the rules of polite society with it, *rejoining the crowd of resistors and rebels, from its solitary place.*][123] (my emphasis)

In *Celui qui est digne d'être aimé*, Ahmed declares that he is "un indigène de la République française" [an indigenous of the French Republic].[124] Referring to the political organization of "Les Indigènes de la République" in his 2017 exchange with Mabrouck Rachedi,[125] Taïa intends to clarify that this statement must be understood as emanating from a fictional character he nevertheless qualifies as "mon double" [my double] but which is not to be seen as an abstract/conceptual delegate or a spokesperson of him as he pertains to "la réalité brute de la vie" [the raw brutality of life], adding: "Je n'écris [pas] pour faire plaisir à qui que ce soit ni en France, ni au Maroc" [I don't write to please anyone, be it in France or in Morocco]. But he is very straightforward in explaining *off literature* what his posture vis-à-vis the political movement of the "Indigènes de la République" is, along with its decolonial meaning: "[j]e *trouve que leur parole est plus que nécessaire, surtout aujourd'hui. Ils sont le produit du rapport de la France avec tous ces gens qu'elle a non seulement utilisés pendant le colonialisme, mais qu'elle a continué d'utiliser après la colonisation.* [I find their words are more than necessary, especially today. They are the product of the relationship between France and all of these people that it has not only used during colonialism, but that it continues to use after colonization] (my emphasis).

In another interview, this time with Ibtissam Ouazzani[126] published under the title "Qu'on le veuille ou non, l'homosexualité est une question politique" [Whether you like it or not, homosexuality is a political question], the writer describes *Celui qui est digne d'être aimé* as a novel treating non only queer desire and sex, but also "la justice" [justice], "les minorités" [minorities], and "la colonisation française" [French colonization]; and he associates "son corps" [his body] with the "*corps encore colonisés (. . .) des gens des banlieues parisiennes*" [bodies still colonized (. . .) of the people from the Parisian suburbs] (my emphasis). Pointing at what Pierre Tevanian and Saïd Bouamama have analyzed as "Un racisme post-colonial: un passé qui ne passe pas" [A postcolonial racism: a past that has not passed],[127] and refusing to participate in a nation-state conceived as "un tout préconstruit où (les immigrés) n'auraient qu'à s'assimiler en adoptant des normes pré-existantes (et qui) exerce une souveraineté exclusive sur leurs horizons identitaires ou artistiques" [a total preconstruct where (the immigrants) would only have to assimilate by adopting pre-existing norms (and who) exercise an exclusive sovereignty on their horizons of identity or artistry].[128] In his interview with Ouazzani, Taïa identifies the core of *Celui qui est digne d'être aimé*, from which everything commences and toward which everything returns, as *la question de la colonisation française qui perdure dans le corps d'un Marocain homosexuel de 40 ans qui vit à Paris* [the question of French colonization that endures in the body of a forty-year-old Moroccan homosexual living in Paris] (my emphasis). Having been disillusioned by France (or, I should say: by its colonial construction as it was and still is predominantly imposed in *both* the Hexagone and its neo-colony called Morocco), the writer (who nowadays is about Ahmed's age) grasped early on that he was actually *not in his place* in the middle of the average majority of the Franco-French people—"Je voyais ce que j'étais pour eux: un Marocain au milieu des Français! *Pas à ma place!*" [I saw what I was for them: a Moroccan surrounded by French people! Not at home!][129] (my emphasis). Through what he calls, in a conversation with Georgia Philipps-Amos published in *bombmagazine.org* (2016), his "postcolonial fight,"[130] he ended up sharing the destiny of all *ordinary* Maghrebi immigrants and their descendants who have tried to integrate/assimilate in the French nation-state, which, while proclaiming to be *universalist* and *hospitable/accommodating* toward diversity and alterity, is actually based on a restrictive and exclusive notion of its white Western "identity"[131] and totally controlled by its francocentric *owners* who are the only ones pretending to know "what it means to be at home."[132] For them, as the author states in an interview:

> (. . .) il n'y a plus sur terre aucun lieu pour les accueillir, les considérer, les reconnaître. Ils ont parfaitement conscience de la situation politique et sociale où ils survivent, les identités étroites qu'on leur propose, *aussi bien en France que dans leur pays d'origine. Ils n'ont plus de territoire.*
>
> [(. . .) there is nowhere left on Earth to welcome them, consider them, recognize them. They are perfectly aware of the political and social situation where they survive, the narrow identities proposed to them, as much in France as in their country of origin. They no longer have a land/territory.][133] (my emphasis)

Taïa is actually embarked in such statement as, while he assuredly speaks of "them," it is also in a way that concerns himself more and more, not only out of solidarity with "them" but because France's coloniality is a *system* that would (although marginally) accept him only if acting as a "francophone writer"[134] full of gratitude for having been illuminated by the nation-state's "enlightened values" and also only if becoming an objective ally of its alienating perversity, a condition that would demolish his own *existence.* This leads us once again to the question of this essay's title: "is there for Abdellah Taïa a *there* where to go and to *exist*?" While one cannot compress without mediation the writer and his fictional projections, one should nevertheless consider that such self-investigation is an intrinsic part of his *literary recasting* not only since having arrived in France but from the very beginning of his youth in Salé, as it is retro-projected and self-reflected in the beautiful short text entitled *Un jardin, en attendant* [*A garden, while waiting*][135] that could be read as a *primal scene* and in which he asks himself "Où aller quand on n'a rien? Où se promener, errer, quand on est rien?" [Where to go when you have nothing? Where to walk, to wander when you are nothing?]. In *Celui qui est digne d'être aimé*, Ahmed proclaims his desire to flee, this time not Morocco but Paris, and relocate in what Gilles Kespel (2012) has coined "la banlieue de la République," [the suburb of the Republic],[136] the "cités" [ghettoes] where the "intrangers" ["strange insiders"][137] are objectively determined to live, socio-culturally excluded but actually *encaged* under the permanent surveillance of a "disciplinary power."[138] These enclaves are situated by Ahmed "*ailleurs dans ce territoire français*" (my emphasis) [elsewhere in this French territory] as they—as were the *quartiers indigènes* [indigenous quarters] of the French colonial empire—are *de jure* [by law] in France and under its political and police control, but *de facto* in "[u]ne autre planète" [another planet][139] whose inhabitants are ejected outside the boundaries of the ideologically defined French "identity" and not recognized as truly and fully "French," while they do not have any other national belonging.

Ahmed/Taïa does not want to be anymore the type of "intellectuel" he dreamt to become under Emmanuel's/France's mentorship.[140] He has also lost all attempts at explaining to the latter the systemic reality of his colonized *suffering* condition.[141] But while being revolted against and even repulsed by *white France*, he is not sad at all to depart from a nation-state which has, at the end of the day, never truly accepted him, actually denying him the very right to fully be *who he is*, even more: has actually partly *teared down* who he is (culturally, linguistically, and even bodily and sexually), and has endeavored to transform him into a *failure*, somebody he could never be, always in the process of changing him—and even his first name[142]—into something that was structurally posited as unreachable.[143] He actually feels *liberated* as a finally decolonized human being having acquired his true independence. In what can be read as both a diegetic verisimilitude and an allegorical fable, he summarizes *French coloniality through Emmanuel* in these terms, with no regret, even with exhilaration, and a deep desire for avengement (just replace "tu"/"toi" = Emmanuel by "tu"/"toi" = la France):

> J'en ai marre. De toi et de tout ce que tu m'as *inculqué*. De tout ce que tu m'as *imposé* et que je n'ai jamais osé remettre en question. Et là, là, j'ai envie de tout foutre en l'air, de tout piétiner, de tout brûler et d'aller ensuite me jeter à la mer. J'ai envie de tout, absolument tout, quitter. *Te laisser seul pourrir dans ton monde propre et bien rangé. Aller ailleurs sans toi et sans ton regard sur*

> *moi. Sans ta bienveillance, qui n'en a jamais été une. J'ai la ferme envie de me venger*, de te faire du mal, non seulement te tuer en moi, mais encore faire en sorte de *ne plus marcher là où tu m'as dit de marcher, là où tu m'as fait croire que nous étions deux, égaux et partenaires, alors que tout avait été décidé par toi seul.*
>
> [I've had it. With you and with everything you've *taught me*. With everything you've *imposed* on me and that I've never dared to call into question. And now, now, I feel like fucking up everything, trampling everything, burning everything and then going and throwing myself into the sea. I feel like leaving everything, absolutely everything. *To leave you alone to rot in your neat and tidy world. To go elsewhere without you and without your gaze upon me. Without your kindness which never really was the case. I really feel like getting revenge*, hurting you, not only killing you in me, but also to really *no longer walk where you told me to walk, where you made me believe that we were two, equal and partners, where in fact everything had been decided by you alone.*][144] (my emphasis)

Beyond Ahmed's self-phenomenological description of his situation as a subject[145]—what Sartre once called "la transcendence de l'ego" [the transcendence of the ego][146]—all the isotopies revealing of a *colonial exacting*[147] are present in this passage: to have been instilled by a false benevolence, to have been coerced to "walk"/behave in imposed ways, to have been tricked by and trapped in the pretenses of equality and partnership, to have been decided outside of one's own will. . . . They could be applied not only to all the immigrants and the people of "immigrant descent" but also, symptomatically, to the author himself. His other narrator-vector, Mounir, after a long period of unconscious denial, sees "enfin (. . .) le lien entre eux et [lui]" [finally (. . .) the bond between them and (him)][148] and has decided to *encounter*[149] those who are compelled to be *assimilated* in the intangible manner of "une assignation intériorisée" [an internalized summons][150] by France's coloniality on behalf of a constraining and nevertheless always elusive supposed to be "French identity."

At the very same time Paris has become a militarized city in which state racism is obvious and visible—as it will be perceived by Mounir in *La vie lente.*[151] Ahmed aims at leaving the bourgeois Franco-French neighborhood (Paris 5th "arrondissement")[152] where he cohabitates with Emmanuel. He asserts that he will skedaddle, "[f]uir (. . .) dans un autre lieu," [flee (. . .) into another setting] and go "[e]n banlieue" [into the outskirts]. By proclaiming such intention, he precisely means to *withdraw from France as he did from Morocco* in order to *recover* in the immigrant populated areas that are *somewhere over there* where there is precisely no instance of "French welcome," consideration, and recognition, and where he could perhaps reconcile himself with the very reality, even if problematic, of being in some potential self-selected *homeland*. The latter is actually described for Mounir, in almost utopian terms, by Simone Marty in *La vie lente* as the place that will permit him to advent to *ce qu'* [*il est*] *vraiment (. . .) dans la résistance au monde d'ici* [what he really is (. . .) in the resistance of the world from here][153] (my emphasis):

> Je suis déjà de l'autre côté et je le vois. Je te vois. En classe devant tes élèves. (. . .) Tu es au milieu. Les élèves te regardent. Ils ont fini par t'accepter, par admettre que, malgré ton apparence juvénile, tu n'es pas un gamin arabe. Tu es un professeur.
>
> Ils t'aiment. Vraiment. (. . .)
>
> [I'm already on the other side and I see him. I see you. In class in front of your students. (. . .) You are in the middle. Your students look at you. They've ended up accepting you, by admitting that, despite your youthful appearance, you're not an Arab kid. You're a professor.
>
> They love you. Really. (. . .)][154]

Now, even if responding affirmatively to the following question could be seen as a hermeneutical *coup de force* [*forceful blow*], I will still ask it: *and if Mounir, in this specific instance, was Abdellah Taïa*? Let's imagine. He would have renounced his efforts at shining in order to subsist or even somehow survive within the Franco-French literati establishment where he is, like Mounir, "si réfléchi, si cultivé, si indépendant." [so reflective, so cultivated, so independent].[155] He would be prepared to leave the scene in which he performs excellently as both the actor and the director of his own theater play or film. After all, according to his (once upon a time) lover Vincent in *Celui qui est digne d'être aimé*—but it is of course the writer who deceptively speaks of and mirrors himself—he has acquired "si bien la maîtrise de l'art de la mise en scène, de la manipulation et de la tromperie" [such good mastery of the art of putting on the performance of manipulation and deception].[156] In the 2017 novel, Ahmed/Taïa mentions his own "distance entre moi vrai et moi dans un certain jeu" [distance between the real me and me in a certain game][157]—something which is by the way a topos of the author's works, as when he declares "Mon jeu t'amusait. Ma sincérité à être parfaitement arriviste te touchait" [My game was amusing you. My sincerity to be perfectly opportunist touched you].[158] In the order of (fictive?) possibilities, could he be, if not physically like Mounir, but definitely in literary and political terms, departing from Paris proper for its banlieue and rejoining its youth vilified by the domineering mass-media of "la France [qui est un] pays de race blanche," [France [which is a] country of the white race] to quote the ex-minister Nadine Moreno.[159] To pursue this hermeneutical fable, actually aroused by the writer's (often subtly) provocative narrative strategies, here is how Mounir/Taïa is addressing himself at the beginning of *La vie lente*:

> Regarde. Regarde bien dans le miroir. C'est qui? Toi? Non. Non, ce n'est plus toi. Tu n'es pas digne de ce beau prénom. Mounir. Tu devrais t'appeler Philippe ou Baptiste. Ou alors, tiens, pourquoi pas Fabien. Cela t'irait mieux. Ce n'est pas possible. Ce n'est pas possible. Tu n'es plus un Arabe, on dirait. Regarde-toi, c'est bien, regarde profond. Qu'est-ce que tu vois? Tu sais que j'ai raison. Tu as peur d'eux maintenant. Tu leur est soumis et tu te soucies trop de ce qu'ils pensent de toi. Bien élevé. Bien éduqué. Docile, quoi. (. . .) Tu ferais mieux de te jeter par la fenêtre puisque, depuis trois ans, tu as renoncé à cette flamme en toi, ce petit côté sauvage qui faisait que tu leur résistais un peu quand même. (. . .) Tu vas faire quelque chose pour changer, redevenir ce que tu as été?

> [Look. Take a good/hard look in the mirror. Who's that? You? No. It's no longer you. You are not worthy of this beautiful first name. Mounir. You should be called Philippe or Baptiste. Or, perhaps, then, why not Fabien. That would work better for you. It's not possible. It's not possible. You're no longer an Arab, it seems. Look at yourself, that good, look deep. What do you see? You know I'm right. You are afraid of them now. You're submissive with them and you worry too much what they think of you. Well raised. Well education. Docile, right. (. . .) You'd be better off throwing yourself out of the window since for three years now, you're renounced this flame in you, this little wild side which allowed you to resist a little all the same. (. . .) You are going to do something to change, to become again what you have been?][160]

Such an excerpt cannot be read literally and factually as an auto-critique in the sense that Abdellah Taïa has precisely begun, since the publishing of *Un pays pour mourir* in 2015 ("depuis trois ans" [for three years already]), what could be described as a turning point, a "rupture" [break],[161] a remarkable poetic and kaleidoscopic narrative strategy outside of and against the colonial social and mental borders of white France. According to Arnaud Genon, he has "trouvé sa voie qui est celle du politique" [found his path which is the one of the political].[162] Nevertheless, the above-quoted passage could still be read as one of the numerous *mises en abyme* of the writer in his work, and it is quite a damning one. Toward the end of *La vie lente* the author resorts once again to the mirror effect, but this time it is Madame Marty—who has "tous les éléments et toutes les clefs" [all the elements and all of the keys] of Mounir's life before he left the immigrant neighborhood of Belleville for the posh rue de Turenne located in *la France blanche* [white France]—who actually mediates that reflective echoing and sketches Taia's auto-portrayal:

> Ton âme aspire à tout maîtriser. Et si, pour cela, *il faut mentir, se mentir, faire de la fiction, se glisser dans la peau d'un autre personnage,* (. . .) tu n'hésites pas longtemps. (. . .) *Tu séduis. Tu fais la danse* (. . .) Tu inventes ce qu'il faut inventer et tu y crois, jusqu'au bout, jusqu'à l'effondrement.
>
> [Your soul aspires to master everything. And if, for that, *one must lie, lie to oneself, create fiction, slip into the skin of another character,* (. . .) you don't hesitate a longtime. (. . .) *You seduce. You do the dance* (. . .)[163] You invent what you need to invent and you believe in it all the way, until the collapse.][164] (my emphasis)

But having said that, she adds a little further:

> (. . .) *Veux-tu te rapprocher de quelque chose de musulman en toi et que tu ne peux trouver ni au Maroc ni ici en France?*
>
> *C'est vrai qu'on ne peut absolument pas s'éloigner trop longtemps de notre première origine.* Le sens du monde.
>
> [(. . .) *Do you want to blame me for something Muslim in you and that you cannot find neither in Morocco or here in France?*
>
> *It's true that it's not completely possible distance oneself too long from one's first place of origin. The meaning of the world.*][165] (my emphasis)

To pursue the "if question" even further, what *if* Mounir was Abdellah Taïa projecting himself in the novelistic imaginary of *La vie lente*, as someone braving the ideologically stereotype of *le garçon arabe* [the Arab boy] living in the *cités* [slums]?[166] Such stereotype has been dismantled and linked to its colonial genesis and meaning by Nacira Guénif-Souilamas and Eric Macé, but also, in a way or another, by Mehammed Mack and Todd Shepard, who have shown how young Arab males have been commodified, determined, and fabricated by a systemic racism into being hyper—misogynic and homophobe.[167] In Taïa's latest novel, Mounir is to become a queer Arab teacher of French in the prejudicially defined phallocentric and heterosexist abject periphery of Paris (or any other city of France) where the *indigènes de la République* [indigenous of the Republic] are socially ghettoized. Or will the writer pursue his wandering in *aporia*? Madame Marty/Taïa asks Mounir/Taïa precisely that, before her disappearance?[168]

Is there for Abdellah Taïa, who is in the process of accomplishing his decolonial destiny, a *there* where not only to go but also to *exist* within and through his very *queer body*,[169] as "un Je engagé dans le monde" [an I engaged in the world]?[170] I have attempted to address this question from a hermeneutical position located at the intersection of *both* the writer's three last novels and some of his extra literary interventions. These are actually often interconnected. For instance (and to take only one example among numerous ones), the writer asserts, in a statement that is directly echoed by Mounir's own words, that he is "si bien installé dans [son] égoïsme parisien, [sa] petite carrière" [so well situated in [his] Parisian egoism, [his] little career],[171] in effect alluding, in an auto-referential way, to the life Mounir has precisely decided to leave behind him. Indeed, and to reiterate one last time the "if": what if Taïa would have found his "point fixe qu'on appelle peut-être l'amour" [the set point that is perhaps called love].[172] The latter quote is from *Un captif amoureux* [Prisoner of Love] (1986) by Jean Genet, an author and political activist who actually became toward the end of his life somehow a "Maghrebi adopted writer,"[173] whom Taïa admires deeply, even if sometimes ambivalently, and who occupies a special place in his imaginary auto-genealogy, would it be *post-mortem* and in a fictionalized manner.[174] The enigmatic "point fixe" [set point] maybe named "love" could refer to one specific Palestinian feddayin Genet became found of, but beyond Hamza it also designates the Palestinian people and their resilient resistance, a cause the writer endorsed passionately. Genet was a *stateless wanderer* who used the French language to debunk France's coloniality and who found his *essential existence* only when joining the despised subalterns—including the Arab and African immigrants in France at a time almost *nobody* in the intellectual class was paying any attention to them (his friend Tahar Ben Jelloun being one of the few exceptions).[175] Moreover, while having definitely renounced any type of belonging to the French nation-state, he even *settled* three times: with the American Black Panthers (calling them, using a word he had *never* resorted to, his "compatriotes" [co- or fellow patriots][176]); with the Palestinian Feddayin; and with the humble people of the coastal city of Larache, in Northern Morocco, where he is buried (Taïa actually made a short movie in that town, entitled *Le tombeau de Jean Genet* [*Jean Genet's omb*]). These were for him the very *territories of solidarity where he enjoyed his rare moments of true existential happiness*.[177] It is in that regard worth quoting the author of *Les Nègres* [*The Blacks*] (1958), *Les Paravents* [*The Screen*] (1961), and *Un Captif amoureux* on his position (expressed in 1982) toward both the immigrants and the people of France's former colonies—which was already significantly present in his 1974 "Sur deux ou trois livres dont personne n'a jamais parlé" [About two or three books that no one ever spoke about]:

Tant que la France ne fera pas cette politique qu'on appelle Nord-Sud, tant qu'elle ne se préoccupera pas davantage des travailleurs immigrés ou des anciennes colonies, la politique française ne m'intéressera pas du tout.

[As long as France will not engage in this policy they call North-South, as long as it will no longer be worried anymore about the immigrant workers or the former colonies, French politics will not interest me at all.][178]

As he very precisely defines himself in a 2020 interview published in *L'Economiste* as "un Marocain qui vit en France" [a Moroccan who lives in France], could it be that Taïa's *nowadays there* where to go and to *exist* would be *anywhere in the nowhere* ("aucun lieu" [no setting/place]) alongside the resistance and fight of *both* the non-white so called *racaille* ["scum"][179] *and* the exploited, excluded and oppressed *subalterns* of his native country? On the two shores of the Mediterranean, these subjects, like the characters of *Un pays pour mourir*, are actually *internally exiled*, alienated in Morocco by the complicity of the local ruling class with the French neocolonial system; reduced to the category of racialized outcasts in France's coloniality of power:

(. . .) il n'y a plus sur terre aucun lieu pour les accueillir, les considérer, les reconnaître. Ils ont parfaitement conscience de la situation politique et sociale où ils survivent, les identités étroites qu'on leur propose, *aussi bien en France que dans leur pays d'origine. Ils n'ont plus de territoire.*

[(. . .) there's no longer on Earth anywhere to welcome them, consider them, recognize them. They completely understand the political and social situation where they survive, the narrow identities proposed for them, in France as much as in their country of origin. They no longer have a homeland.][180] (my emphasis)

Besides and beyond the writer's legal residency in France and his official Moroccan nationality, is he not himself, as are his fictional protagonists, "parfaitement conscient" [perfectly conscious] of his own refusal of the "identités étroites" [narrow identities] to which he is also so often reduced (including that of supposedly being *un écrivain "francophone"* [a "francophone" writer][181]) and of the *de-territoriality*[182] of his own existence—one could even say: his human condition? In the already mentioned *Tanger Urbain* interview, the writer declares the following, on which I want now to return in concluding this essay:

Je comprenais que mon salut en aucune façon n'était au Maroc, que j'allais être obligé de fuir, *que je ne voulais pas de ce pays pour mourir (. . .)*"

> [I understood that my salvation in no way was in Morocco, that I was going to be obliged to flee, *that I wouldn't want of this country for dying.*][183] (my emphasis)

But can France become for Taïa something more or something else than just "un pays pour mourir" [a country for dying] where he nevertheless has still to live: "tu dois vivre encore, Mounir" [you still have to live, Mounir].[184] *Tu dois vivre encore, Abdellah . . .* [*You still have to live, Abdellah*]. Has he anywhere else to go? Will he inhabit what the *Collectif Qui fait la France?* was naming, in 2007, "une société annoncée" [an announced society]? *La vie lente* was published in 2019. Time passes by and the French nation-state is by the day more and more a country—to quote the title of an essay by Luc Lamin—*en perdition sous l'image subliminale du racisme* [in trouble under the subliminal message of racism], overshadowed by "les mots-clefs [de] racisme, ostracisme, discrimination" [the key words (of) racism, ostracism, discrimination].[185] These are indeed the keywords which are *marking up* the coloniality of the national space *outside of which* Taïa seems to have decided, to borrow Mounir's words, to "réapprendre la vie" [relearn life] "à côté d'eux" [by their side]—"ces Français arabes, africains" [these French Arabs, Africans].[186] Would this be the author's ineluctable *situation*, in the meaning Sartre[187] gave to the term, that is: the ensemble of conditions in which his existence can acquire a signification, a subjectively asserted "essence" giving a sense to his *being in the world*?[188] Indeed, trying, if not to answer, at least to frame this essay's question on the sides of both the writer and the country where he seems to be compelled, for a series of reasons (including but not restricted to the access to publishing), to continue his literary and possibly cinematographic endeavors—in his *français arabe pauvre* [poor Arab French] radically outside of what is to be considered "l'écriture *chic*" [chic writing] and denying the French *beau langage* [beautiful language] he never considered as his, which *did not* "liberate" him and which he evenmore does not like at all[189]—is definitely also asking if France will be able to "refuser résolument l'injonction néocoloniale d'assimilation qui entend contraindre une partie de nos compatriotes (de culture musulmane, d'origine arabe, de peau noire, etc.) à s'effacer pour se dissoudre, à se blanchir en somme. Bref, qui ne les accepte que s'ils disparaissent" [to refuse resolutely the neocolonial injunction of assimilation that wants to force part of our compatriots (of Muslim culture, of Arab origin, of black skin, etc.) to efface themselves to dissolve themselves, to bleach themselves in sum. In short, who doesn't accept them unless they disappear].[190] Or, to phrase it otherwise and keep the question open, could there be, outside and even against a nation-state totally enveloped into its obedience to a permanently unsaid but systemic *white privilege*,[191] the *location of a poetic and political project for Taïa to inhabit*?—and, if so, which one and how?

At the very end of *Un pays pour mourir* the Moroccan Zined announces to her lover Gabriel, a French soldier, while they both are in Indochina (at the time part of the French colonial empire) that she wants to live in an imaginary India she knows only through movies:

> – *Moi, j'ai renoncé au Maroc.*
> – Et?
> – *Tu pourrais renoncer à la France.*
> (. . .)
> —Moi, c'est l' Inde. L'Inde ou rien du tout. *Je veux être dans ce rêve,* dans un pays où personne ne m'arrêtera, ne me rappellera mon passé de prostituée. *Ni les Marocains ni les Français.* Je veux passer directement à la lumière, sans intermédiaire.
>
> [– Me, I've renounced Morocco.
> – And?
> – *You could renounce France.*
> (. . .)
> – Me, it's India. India or nothing at all. *I want to be in this dream,* in a country where no one will stop me, will remind me of my past as a prostitute. Neither the Moroccans nor the French. I want to go directly into the light, without an intermediary.][192] (my emphasis)

Is the writer on his way departing *la vie lente* [the slow life] in order to *exist*? What and where will be Abdellah Taïa's "India"—the very place where he has direct access to his light?

NOTES

1. Abdellah Taïa, *La vie lente*, 71. For the title of my essay, I draw the expression "sortir de tous les territoires" [to come out of all territories] from Abdellah Taïa, *La vie lente*, 125. I would like to thank Denis Provencher for his help with the translations.
2. Taïa, *La vie lente*, 70.
3. Taïa, *La vie lente,* 204.
4. Abdellah Taïa, *Le rouge du tarbouche* (Paris: Séguier, 2004), 137–138.
5. Abdella Taïa, *L'armée du salut* (Paris: Seuil, 2006), 98. On this attraction toward the "mythical" Paris, see Ralph Heyndels, "'Je vis dans une nostalgie étrange. Dans le manque de cet autre que j'étais censé devenir (. . .).' La 'francophonie'

d'Abdellah Taïa," in *Langue française, écrivains francophones*, edited by Ridha Bourkhis (Paris: L'Harmattan, 2020), 113–124.

6. Abdellah Taïa, *Un pays pour mourir* (Paris: Seuil, 2015), 38, 125.
7. Taïa, *La vie lente*, 67.
8. Michel Lussault, "Ville," in *The City: Critical Essays in Human Geography*, edited by Jacques Lévy (New York: Routledge, 2008), 151–156.
9. Misra Tanvi, "The Othered Paris," *citylab.com,* November 16, 2017.
10. Taïa, *La vie lente*, 74.
11. Henri Lefebvre, *Le droit à la ville* (Paris: Anthropos, 1967).
12. Taïa, *La vie lente*, 92.
13. Taïa, *La vie lente*, 92.
14. Ralph Heyndels, "*Abdellah à jamais disparu*, ou les jeux de miroir du Je. Emergence et évanescence de soi dans la mise en scène de l'écriture chez Abdellah Taïa," in *L'écrivain et ses doubles*, edited by in Luc Fraisse (Paris: Classiques Garnier, 2014), 149–161.
15. Taïa, *Le rouge du tarbouche,* 144.
16. Olivier Le Cour Grandmaison, "Colonisés-immigrés et 'périls migratoires': origine et permanence du racisme et d'une xénophobie d'Etat," *Cultures et conflits* 69 (2008): 19–32.
17. Michel Foucault, *Il faut défendre la société* (Paris: Gallimard, 1976); and Pierre Bourdieu, *Sur l'Etat* (Paris: Editions du Seuil, 1984), 113–114; 359.
18. I consider that these novels constitute a trilogy.
19. Ralph Heyndels, "'Je suis un Indigène de la République'. L'atelier décolonial de l'écriture dans *Celui qui est digne d'être aimé* d'Abdellah Taïa," in *Around / Autour d' Abdellah Taïa. Poétique et politique de l'engagement et du désir / Poetics and Politics of Engaged Desire*, edited by Ralph Heyndels and Amine Zidouh (Caen: Passage(s), 2020), 117–145.
20. *Celui qui est digne d'être aimé* is actually a kind of rewriting of *L'armée du salut*, as I have tried to establish. See Ralph Heyndels, "'Je suis un Indigène de la République'. L'atelier décolonial de l'écriture dans *Celui qui est digne d'être aimé* d'Abdellah Taïa," 117–145.
21. Taïa, *La vie lente*, 70.
22. Taïa, *L'armée du salut*, 154.
23. On Taïa's complex relationship with his native country, see Ralph Heyndels, "'Qui suis-je si je ne suis plus Marocain?' Un espace imaginaire de l'autre côté de la Méditerranée dans l'auto-anthropologie viatique d'Abdellah Taïa," in *Voyages, représentations et conscientisations*, edited by Mohamed Lehdahda et Samira Elouli (Meknès: Editions de l'Université de Meknès, forthcoming).
24. Taïa, *La vie lente,* 67.
25. Taïa, *La vie lente*, 253.
26. Taïa, *La vie lente*, 253.
27. A fictional character named Samir expresses this *en abyme* in *La vie lente*, 52. Taïa has repeatedly asserted that he left Morocco to avoid being "destroyed" (see for instance Abdellah Taïa, Interview, *Urbain Tanger*, 2015.).
28. Abdellah Taïa, *Celui qui est digne d'être aimé* (Seuil: 2017), 101.

29. Abdellah Taïa, *La vie lente,* 41. On the problematic of language(s) in Taïa's work, see Ralph Heyndels, "'J'ai trouvé une autre langue': La France, le français et la 'francophonie' dans l'œuvre d'Abdellah Taïa," *Lasemaine.fr,* Universidade de Porto (2018), 57–72.

30. Taïa, *La vie lente,* 19.

31. Taïa, *La vie lente,* 14. See also p. 86.

32. Taïa, *La vie lente,* 23.

33. Taïa, *La vie lente,* 27.

34. Taïa, *La vie lente,* 38. See also p. 125.

35. Taïa, *La vie lente,* 29. Abdellah Taïa lived briefly on Rue de Turenne after having left the Rue de Belleville where he was occupying a small efficiency, and where he decided to return and resides again currently.

36. Taïa, *La vie lente,* 201–202.

37. Antonio Gramsci, *Cahiers de prison* (Paris: Gallimard, 1978 [1948–1951]).

38. Taïa, *La vie lente,* 152.

39. Taïa, *La vie lente,* 170–171.

40. Jasbir Puar, *Terrorist Assemblages: Homonationalism in Queer Times* (Durham: Duke University Press, 2007).

41. Taïa, *Celui qui est digne,* 40–41.

42. Florence Bernault, "Colonial Syndrome: French Modern and the Deceptions of History," in *Frenchness and the African Diaspora: Identity and Uprising in Contemporary France*, edited by Charles Thsimanga, Peter Bloom, and Didier Gondola (Bloomington: Indiana University Press, 2009), 168–206. On the intersectionality of racial and class consciousness, see Peter Hudis, "Racism and the Logic of Capitalism," *Monthly Review on Line*, August 2, 2018.

43. Abdellah Taïa, *Celui qui est digne*, 98, 82, 81. It is worth mentioning that the word "banlieue" appears here for the first time in Taïa's work.

44. Taïa, *Celui qui est digne*, 107, 109.

45. Taïa, *La vie lente,* 71.

46. Taïa, *La vie lente*, 260, and 256.

47. Taïa, *La vie lente,* 257.

48. Taïa, *Celui qui est digne*, 104, 97–98.

49. Abdellah Taïa, *Mon Maroc* (Paris: Séguier, 2000), 111.

50. Ralph Heyndels, "'Qui suis-je si je ne suis plus Marocain?' Un espace imaginaire de l'autre côté de la Méditerranée dans l'auto-anthropologie viatique d'Abdellah Taïa."

51. Taïa, *L'armée du salut*, 121.

52. Ralph Heyndels, "L'amour évidemment. Ecriture de la scène passionnelle et scène passionnelle de l'écriture: *L'armée du salut* d'Abdellah Taïa," in *Rhétorique de la passion dans la littérature francophone*, edited by Rhida Boukhris (Paris: L'Harmattan, 2010), 131–148.

53. Taïa, *L'armée du salut*, 78, 152.

54. Taïa, *L'armée du salut*, 98.

55. Abdellah Taïa, Interview with Georgia Philipps-Amos, *bombmagazine.org*, 2016.

56. Abdellah Taïa, and Frédéric Mitterrand, *Maroc 1900–1960. Un certain regard* (Arles: Actes Sud, 2007); Abdellah Taïa, "Postface," in *Grandes chaleurs* edited by François-Marie Banier (Gœttingen: Steidl, 2010), n.p.
57. Abdellah Taïa, "Regarder tout au fond du monde," *The Art Newspaper*, March 31, 2020.
58. Taïa, "Regarder tout au fond du monde," *The Art Newspaper*, March 31, 2020. See also Ralph Heyndels, "'Je suis un Indigène de la République'. L'atelier décolonial de l'écriture dans *Celui qui est digne d'être aimé* d'Abdellah Taïa," 117–145.
59. Louis Althusser, *Positions* (Paris: Editions Sociales, 1976).
60. Ralph Heyndels, "*Islam mon amour.* 'Nous réinventerons cette religion': la réinscription de l'Islam dans l'imaginaire fictionnel d'Abdellah Taïa," in *Les Francophonies de la Méditerranée*, edited by Ridha Boulaabi (Paris: Geuthner, forthcoming).
61. Ralph Heyndels, "Ecrire dans la loyauté infidèle: dialectique de la fidélité et de la trahison chez Abdellah Taïa," in *De l'ordre et de l'aventure: Langage, littérature, francophonie*, edited Alain Rey, Pierre Brunel, Philippe Desan, and Jean Pruvost (Paris: Hermann, 2014), 401–410.
62. Abdellah Taïa, *Infidèles* (Paris: Seuil, 2012), 83.
63. Taïa, *Un pays pour mourir*, 149, 156.
64. Taïa, *La vie lente*, 54.
65. Ralph Heyndels, "Configurations et transferts de la sexualité, du genre et du désir dans l'ouverture d'*Une mélancolie arabe* d'Abdellah Taïa, ou 'le dépassement des frontières," *Expressions maghrébines* 16 (2017): 85–105.
66. Taïa, *La vie lente,* 69.
67. On madness in Taïa's work, see Ralph Heyndels, "'*Je suis folle'*: folie de l'identité, du genre et du sexe chez Abdellah Taïa," in *Hermeneutics of Textual Madness / Herméneutique de la folie textuelle*, edited by M.J. Muratore et Etienne Barnett (Fasano: Biblioteca della Ricerca, 2017), 463–476.
68. Taïa, *La vie lente,* 69.
69. On the notion of *dislocation* in Taïa's work, see Amine Zidouh, *Phantom Arabic, Dislocated French: Auto-Anthropological Imaginaries (Jean Genet, Abdellah Taïa, Leila Sebbar, Nabil Ayouch).* https://scholarship.miami.edu/discovery/delivery?vid=01UOML_INST:ResearchRepository&repId=12355358260002976#13355481820002976.
70. See Marien Gouyon, "Abdellah Taïa et l'ethnologie de soi-même," *Tumultes* 41, no. 2 (2013): 185–204.
71. Taïa, *Mon Maroc*, 139–140.
72. Abdellah Taïa, ed., *Lettres à un jeune Marocain* (Paris: Editions du Seuil, 2009), Back cover.
73. Ralph Heyndels, "'Qui suis-je si je ne suis plus Marocain?' Un espace imaginaire de l'autre côté de la Méditerranée dans l'auto-anthropologie viatique d'Abdellah Taïa"; Ralph Heyndels, "'Je veux sortir de ta langue.' Comment (ne pas) devenir un écrivain francophone," in *Littérature marocaine d'expression française:*

ancrage culturel et défis scripturaux, *Oualili*, edited by Khalid Dahmani (Ecole Normale Supérieure de Meknès, forthcoming).

74. See Taïa, *Le rouge du tarbouche*; Taïa, *Infidèles*, 212, 83; Taïa, *Un pays pour mourir*, 156.

75. Taïa, *La vie lente,* 69.

76. Taïa, *Un pays pour mourir*, 39, 40, 61.

77. Taïa, *Celui qui est digne*, 104.

78. Taïa, *La vie lente,* 142.

79. Compare with Zahia Rahmani in the case of France vs. Algeria. See Ralph Heyndels, "'Je me voyais en dissidence avec le monde': Zahia Rahmani entre Algérie impossible et colonialité française," *Noria: Revue littéraire et artistique* (Paris: L'Harmattan, 2020).

80. Taïa, *La vie lente*, 13.

81. Taïa, *Un pays pour mourir*, 40.

82. Taïa, "Regarder tout au fond du monde," *The Art Newspaper*, March 31, 2020.

83. Abdellah Taïa, Interview, *Urbain Tanger*, 2015.

84. Taïa, *Un pays pour mourir*, 111, 117.

85. Robert Castel, *La discrimination négative. Citoyens ou indigènes?* (Paris: Editions du Seuil, 2007).

86. Taïa, *Un pays pour mourir,* 110.

87. Taïa, *Un pays pour mourir*, 36.

88. Taïa, *Un pays pour mourir,* 94.

89. Tahar Ben Jelloun, *Hospitalité française. Racisme et immigration en France* (Paris: Editions du Seuil, 1984); Mireille Rosello, *Postcolonial Hospitality: The Immigrant as a Guest* (Palo Alto: Stanford University Press, 2002).

90. Taïa, *Un pays pour mourir,* 49.

91. Taïa, *Un pays pour mourir,* 36.

92. Ralph Heyndels, "La prostitution sur la scène de l'écriture chez Abdellah Taïa," *@nalyses, Revue de critique et de théorie littéraire* 11, no. 3, (2016): 9–23.

93. Taïa, *Un pays pour mourir,* 13.

94. Taïa, *Un pays pour mourir,* 53.

95. Taïa, *Un pays pour mourir,* 53.

96. Taïa, *Un pays pour mourir,* 55.

97. Taïa, Un pays pour mourir, 68.

98. Taïa, ed., *Lettres à un jeune Marocain*, 10.

99. Arnaud Genon, "L'autofiction et comme je(u) politique dans l'oeuvre d'Abdellah Taïa," in *Lisières de l'autofiction*, edited by Arnaud Genon and Isabelle Grell (Lyon: Presses universitaires de Lyon, 2016), 235–257; Ralph Heyndels, "*Abdellah à jamais disparu*, ou les jeux de miroir du Je. Emergence et évanescence de soi dans la mise en scène de l'écriture chez Abdellah Taïa," in *L'écrivain et ses doubles: Le personnage autoréflexif dans la littérature européenne*, edited by Luc Fraisse and Eric Wessler (Paris: Classiques Garnier, 2014), 149–161.

100. Alberto Fernandez-Carbajal, *Queer Muslims in Contemporary Literature and Film* (Manchester: Manchester University Press, 2019).

101. Jean Zagarianis, *Queer Maroc: Sexualités, Genres et (Trans) Identités dans la littérature marocaine* (Morrisville: LuLu Publishing, 2014); Ralph Heyndels, "Trans-gendering, trans-sexualizing and decolonizing queer desire in todays' Morocco (Abdellah Taïa)," paper presented at the 2019 *Semana Arabe de Mexico City* = "Trans - genre, trans - sexualité, désir queer et destin décolonial au Maroc aujourd'hui (Abdellah Taïa)," to appear in *Queer Maghreb*, edited by Alfonso de Toro and Annegret Richter (forthcoming).

102. Denis M. Provencher, *Queer Maghrebi French: Language, Temporalities, Transfiliations* (Liverpool: Liverpool University Press, 2017).

103. Jean-Pierre Boulé, *Abdellah Taïa, la mélancolie et le cri* (Lyon: Presses universitaires de Lyon, 2020).

104. Ralph Heyndels, "L'amour évidemment. Ecriture de la scène passionnelle et scène passionnelle de l'écriture: *L'armée du salut* d'Abdellah Taïa," 131–148.

105. Ralph Heyndels, and Amine Zidouh, eds, *Autour d'/Around Abdellah Taia. Poétique et politique du désir engagé/Poetics and Politics of Engaged Desire* (Caen: Passage(s), 2020).

106. Ralph Heyndels, "'L'occasion, unique, de dégager nos sens': Modernité, primitivisme et homotexte chez Rimbaud," in *Rimbaud e la Modernità*, edited by Carolina Diglio and Giovanni Dotoli (Paris: Presses de l'Université de Paris-Sorbonne/Fasano: Schena Editore, *Transatlantique*, 2005), 103–135; Ralph Heyndels, "Ecrire pour dire que ce n'est rien, la vie: Arthur Rimbaud," *Revue Européenne de Recherches sur la Poésie* 2 (Paris: Classiques Garnier, 2016), 93–105; Ralph Heyndels, "Nuit politique du désir: l'engagement amoureux de Jean Genet," in *Pour Genet. Les Rencontres de Fontevraud*, edited by Hadrien Laroche (Saint-Nazaire: Maison des Ecrivains et Traducteurs Etrangers, 2011), 116–129.

107. Abdellah Taïa, "Genet, Abdellah et moi," in *Les passions de Jean Genet*, edited by Ralph Heyndels (Paris: Alain Baudry et Cie/Fasano: Schena Editore, 2010), 11–15; Ralph Heyndels, "Entremêlements narratifs sur la tombe de Jean Genet, Abdellah Taïa et Rachid O." *Travaux de littérature,* XXII (2009): 473–481.

108. Abdellah Taïa, *Le jour du Roi* (Paris: Seuil, 2010), 143.

109. Taïa, *La vie lente,* 61.

110. Taïa, *Le rouge du tarbouche*, 122.

111. Taïa, *La vie lente,* 135.

112. Taïa, *La vie lente,* 97.

113. Taïa, *La vie lente,* 86.

114. Taïa, *La vie lente,* 68; See also 177.

115. Abdellah Taïa, "Lettre à James Baldwin," in *Around/Autour d' Abdellah Taïa. Poétique et politique de l'engagement et du désir / Poetics and Politics of Engaged Desire*, edited by Ralph Heyndels and Amine Zidouh (Caen: Passage(s), 2020), 9–11.

116. Taïa, "Lettre à James Baldwin," 9–11.

117. Taïa, *Celui qui est digne*, 107–108; see also 82.

118. Taïa, *Un pays pour mourir*, 39.

119. Taïa, *La vie lente*, 235.

120. Abdellah Taïa, Interview with Mabrouck Rachedi, *Jeune Afrique*, 2017.

121. Ralph Heyndels, "'Je suis un Indigène de la République'. L'atelier décolonial de l'écriture dans *Celui qui est digne d'être aimé* d'Abdellah Taïa," 117–145.

122. Ralph Heyndels, "Nuit politique du désir: l'engagement amoureux de Jean Genet"; Ralph Heyndels, "'Cet Orient que je voyais à l'envers'. L'inversion de l'orientalisme chez Jean Genet," in *Voix d'Orient*, edited by Ridha Boulaabi (Paris: Geuthner, 2019), 177–198.

123. Nacira Guénif-Souilamas, "Par-delà frontière et division, rencontre avec Abdellah Taïa," in *Around/Autour d' Abdellah Taïa. Poétique et politique de l'engagement et du désir/Poetics and Politics of Engaged Desire*, edited by Ralph Heyndels and Amine Zidouh (Caen: Passage(s), 2020), 107–116.

124. Taïa, *Celui qui est digne*, 103.

125. Abdellah Taïa, Interview with Mabrouck Rachedi, *Jeune Afrique*, 2017.

126. Abdellah Taïa, "Qu'on le veuille ou non, l'homosexualité est une question politique," Interview with Ibtissam Ouazzani, *huffpostmaghreb.com*, 2017.

127. Pierre Tevanian and Saïd Bouamama, "Un racisme post-colonial. Réflexions sur un passé qui ne passe pas," *Le-blog-sam-la-touch.over-blog.com/ 2017.*

128. Tevanian and Bouamama, "Un racisme post-colonial. Réflexions sur un passé qui ne passe pas."

129. Abdellah Taïa, *Une mélancolie arabe* (Paris: Seuil, 2008), 56.

130. Abdellah Taïa, Interview with Georgia Philipps-Amos, *bombmagazine.org* , 2016.

131. Abdelmalek Sayad, *L'immigration ou les paradoxes de l'altérité* (Paris: Raisons d'agir, 2006).

132. Jacques Derrida, *Adieu to Emmanuel Levinas* (Palo Alto: Stanford University Press, 1999), 16.

133. Abdellah Taïa, Interview, *huffpostmaghreb.com*, 2015.

134. Ralph Heyndels, "'Je veux sortir de ta langue'. Comment (ne pas) devenir un écrivain francophone."

135. Ralph Heyndels, and Amine Zidouh, eds., *Autour d'/Around Abdellah Taia. Poétique et politique du désir engagé/Poetics and Politics of Engaged Desire.*

136. Gilles Kespel, *Banlieue de la République* (Paris: Gallimard, 2012).

137. Ilaria Vitali, *Intrangers: Post-migration et nouvelles frontières de la littérature* (Paris: L'Harmattan, 2012).

138. Michel Foucault, *Surveiller et punir* (Paris: Gallimard, 1975).

139. Taïa, *Celui qui est digne*, 107.

140. Taïa, *Celui qui est digne*, 109.

141. Taïa, *Celui qui est digne*, 102, 104.

142. Taïa, *Celui qui est digne*, 102.

143. Taïa, *Celui qui est digne*, 93, 99, 107.

144. Taïa, *Celui qui est digne*, 82.

145. José-Luis Bermudez, "Ownership and the Space of the Body," in *The Subject's Matter: Self-Consciousness and the Body*, edited by F. Vignemont, and A. Alshmith (Cambridge: M.I.T. Press, 2017), 117–144.

146. Jean-Paul Sartre, *La transcendence de l'ego* (Paris: Vrin, 1936).

147. Albert Memmi, *Portrait du colonisé précédé du portrait du colonisateur* (Paris: Gallimard, 1985 [1957]).

148. Taïa, *La vie lente,* 70.

149. Taïa, *La vie lente,* 70.

150. Nacira Guénif-Souilamas, and Eric Macé. *Les féministes et le garçon arabe* (La Tour d'Aigues: Editions de l'Aube, 2006).

151. Taïa, *La vie lente,* 135.

152. Taïa, *La vie lente,* 101.

153. Taïa, *La vie lente*, 254, 255.

154. Taïa, *La vie lente* 256.

155. Taïa, *La vie lente,* 67.

156. Taïa, *Celui qui est digne,* 52.

157. Taïa, *Celui qui est digne,* 109.

158. Taïa, *Celui qui est digne,* 108.

159. Jean Bernabé, *La France pays de race blanche: Réponse à Madame Nadine Moreno* (Paris: L'Harmattan, 2016).

160. Taïa, *La vie lente,* 14.

161. *Babelio*, Presentation of *La vie lente*, 2019.

162. Arnaud Genon, Review of *La vie lente*, in *La Cause littéraire,* April 2019.

163. Interestingly enough, Taïa has actually performed as a dancer in *Karantika*, a ballet produced for the Halles de Schaerbeek (Brussels), in October 2012.

164. Taïa, *La vie lente,* 247.

165. Taïa, *La vie lente,* 252.

166. Nacira Guénif-Souilamas, and Eric Macé. *Les féministes et le garçon arabe.*

167. Mehammed Amadeus Mack, *Sexagon: Muslims, France, and the Sexualization of National Culture* (New York: Fordham University Press, 2017); Todd Shephard, *France and the Arab Men* (Chicago: University of Chicago Press, 2018).

168. Taïa, *La vie lente,* 251, 253.

169. Sara Ahmed, *Queer Phenomenology: Orientations, Objects, Others* (Durham: Duke University Press, 2006), 66–68; Judith Butler, *Bodies That Matter: On the Discursive Limits of Sex* (New York: Routledge, 2011).

170. Maurice Merleau-Ponty, *Phénoménologie de la perception* (Paris: Gallimard, 2005 [1945]).

171. Abdellah Taïa, Interview, *huffpostmaghreb.com*, 2015.

172. See Ralph Heyndels, "'*Ce point fixe qu'on nomma peut-être l'amour*': les captivités amoureuses de Jean Genet," *Cahiers de l'Herne* (forthcoming).

173. Salim Ayoub, *Indigènes entre deux rives: Rimbaud, Genet, Goytisolo and Contemporary Maghrebi Diasporic Voices Questioning Coloniality in Literature and Film (Abdellah Taïa, Zahia Rahmani, Nabil Ayouch, Mehdi Ben Attia*). Dissertation, University of Miami, 2019.

174. On the genealogy of that relation of Taïa with French as it is fictionalized in his work, which is also part of many of the writer's media interventions, see Ralph Heyndels, "Écrire le tombeau de Jean Genet. Instants rêvés dans le cimetière espagnol

de Larache: Abdellah Taïa et Rachid O.," in *Toute les images du langage. Jean Genet*, edited by Frieda Ekotto, Aurélie Renaud, Agnès Vannouvong (Paris: Alain Baudry & Cie/Fasano: Schena Editore, 2008), 91–101.

175. See Subha Xavier, "Le désir militant: Genet, Ben Jelloun et la défense des immigrés," in *Les Passions de Jean Genet. Esthétique, poétique et politique du désir*, edited by Ralph Heyndels (Paris: Alain Baudry & Cie / Fasano: Schena Editore, 2008), 109–116.

176. See Ralph Heyndels, "Les Noirs sur la blancheur livide, ou le sens possible de l'Amérique selon Jean Genet," *Travaux de Littérature*, XXIV (2011), 319–331.

177. Ralph Heyndels, "Jean Genet's Mediterranean Cartography of Desire," in *Les Méditerranées de Jean Genet / Jean Genet's Mediterraneans,* edited by Ralph Heyndels and Salim Ayoub (Caen: Passage(s), forthcoming).

178. Jean Genet, "Entretien avec Bertand Poirot-Delpech" (1982), in Jean Genet, *L'ennemi déclaré. Textes et entretiens*, edited by Albert Dichy (Paris: Gallimard, 1991), 227–242.

179. Onana, 2006; Sadri Khiari, *Pour une politique de la racaille*: *Immigré-e-s et jeunes des banlieues* (Paris: Textuel, 2006).

180. Taïa, Interview, *huffpostmaghreb.com*, 2015.

181. See Heyndels, "'Je veux sortir de ta langue'. Comment (ne pas) devenir un écrivain francophone."

182. Such de-territoriality is also treated by Taïa in relation to the trans-gender/the trans-sexual. See Ralph Heyndels, "Trans-gendering, trans-sexualizing and decolonizing queer desire in today's Morocco: Abdellah Taïa," paper presented at the 2019 *Semana Arabe de Mexico*, to be expanded and translated in French for *Queer Maghreb*, edited by Alfonso de Toro and Annegret Richter (forthcoming).

183. Taïa, Interview, *Urbain Tanger*, 2015.

184. Taïa, *La vie lente,* 257.

185. Luc Lamin, *La France en perdition sous l'image subliminale du racisme* (BoD, 2019), 39.

186. Taïa, *La vie lente,* 71, 70.

187. Jean-Paul Sartre, *L'existentialisme est un humanisme* (Paris: Gallimard, 1946).

188. Martin Heidegger, *Being and Time* (New York: Harper, 2008 [1927]).

189. "Le français ne m'a pas libéré," declares Taïa in an interview with Antoine Idier. See Antoine Idier, "'Sortir de la peur'. Construire une identité homosexuelle arabe dans un monde post-colonial" (Entretien avec Abdellah Taïa), *Revue critique de fixxion française contemporaine* 12 (2016): 197–207.

190. Edwy Pinel, *Pour les musulmans* (Paris: La Découverte, 2014), 118.

191. Peggy McKintosh, "White Privilege: Unpacking the Invisible Knapsack," *Peace and Freedom,* July–August 1989.

192. Taïa, *Un pays pour mourir,* 157, 160.

BIBLIOGRAPHY

Ahmed, Sara. *Queer Phenomenology: Orientations, Objects, Others.* Durham: Duke University Press, 2006.

Althusser, Louis. *Positions*. Paris: Editions Sociales, 1976.

Ayoub, Salim. *Indigènes entre deux rives: Rimbaud, Genet, Goytisolo and Contemporary Maghrebi Diasporic Voices Questioning Coloniality in Literature and Film (Abdellah Taïa, Zahia Rahmani, Nabil Ayouch, Mehdi Ben Attia)*. Dissertation, University of Miami, 2019.

Babelio. Presentation of *La vie lente*, 2019.

Ben Jelloun, Tahar. *Hospitalité française. Racisme et immigration en France*. Paris: Editions du Seuil, 1984.

Bermudez, José-Luis. "Ownership and the Space of the Body." In *The Subject's Matter: Self -Consciousness and the Body*, edited by Frédéric de Vignemont and Adrian J. T. Alshmith, 117–144. Cambridge: MIT Press, 2017.

Bernabé, Jean. *La France pays de race blanche: Réponse à Madame Nadine Moreno*. Paris: L'Harmattan, 2016.

Bernault, Florence. "Colonial Syndrome: French Modern and the Deceptions of History," In *Frenchness and the African Diaspora: Identity and Uprising in Contemporary France*, edited by Charles Thsimanga, Peter Bloom, and Didier Gondola, 168–206. Bloomington: Indiana University Press, 2009.

Boulé, Jean-Pierre. *Abdellah Taïa: la mélancolie et le cri*. Lyon: Presses universitaires de Lyon, 2020.

Bourdieu, Pierre. *Sur l'Etat*. Paris: Editions du Seuil, 1984.

Butler, Judith. *Bodies That Matter: On the Discursive Limits of Sex*. New York: Routledge, 2011.

Castel, Robert. *La discrimination négative. Citoyens ou indigènes?* Paris: Editions du Seuil, 2007.

Collectif Qui fait la France? *Chroniques d'une société annoncée*. Paris: Stock, 2007.

Derrida, Jacques. *Adieu to Emmanuel Levinas*. Palo Alto: Stanford University Press, 1999.

Fernandez-Carbajal, Alberto. *Queer Muslims in Contemporary Literature and Film*. Manchester: Manchester University Press, 2019.

Foucault, Michel. *Surveiller et punir*. Paris: Gallimard, 1975.

———. *Il faut défendre la société*. Paris: Gallimard, 1976.

Genet, Jean. "Sur deux ou trois livres dont personne n'a jamais parlé" (1974). In *Jean Genet, L'ennemi déclaré. Textes et entretiens*, edited by Albert Dichy, 121–124. Paris: Gallimard, 1991.

———. "Entretien avec Bertand Poirot-Delpech" (1982). In *Jean Genet, L'ennemi déclaré. Textes et entretiens*, edited by Albert Dichy, 227–242. Paris: Gallimard, 1991.

Genon, Arnaud. "L'autofiction comme je(u) politique dans l'oeuvre d'Abdellah Taïa." In *Lisières de l'autofiction*, edited by Arnaud Genon and Isabelle Grell, 235–257. Lyon: Presses universitaires de Lyon, 2016.

———. Review of *La vie lente*, in *La Cause littéraire,* April 2019.

Gouyon, Marien. "Abdellah Taïa et l'ethnologie de soi-même." *Tumultes* 41, no. 2 (2013): 185–204.

Gramsci, Antonio. *Cahiers de prison*. Paris: Gallimard, 1978 (1948–1951).

Guénif-Souilamas, Nacira. "Par-delà frontière et division, rencontre avec Abdellah Taïa." In *Poétique et politique du désir engagé/Poetics and Politics of Engaged*

Desire. Around/Autour d'Abdellah Taïa, edited by Ralph Heyndels and Amine Zidouh, 107–116. Caen: Passage(s), 2020.

Guénif-Souilamas, Nacira, and Eric Macé. *Les féministes et le garçon arabe*. La Tour d'Aigues: Editions de l'Aube, 2006.

Heidegger, Martin. *Being and Time*. New York: Harper, 2008 (1927).

Heyndels, Ralph, and Amine Zidouh, eds. *Around/Autour d' Abdellah Taia. Poétique et politique du désir engagé/Poetics and Politics of Engaged Desire*. Caen: Passage(s), 2020.

Heyndels, Ralph. *La pensée fragmentée*: *Pascal, Diderot, Hœlderlin*. Bruxelles: Mardaga, 1989 (1985).

———. "'Qui suis-je si je ne suis plus Marocain?' Un espace imaginaire de l'autre côté de la Méditerranée dans l'auto-anthropologie viatique d'Abdellah Taïa." In *Voyages, représentations et conscientisations*, edited by Mohamed Lehdahda et Samira Elouli. Meknès: Editions de l'Université de Meknès, forthcoming.

———. "*Islam mon amour.* 'Nous réinventerons cette religion': la réinscription de l'Islam dans l'imaginaire fictionnel d'Abdellah Taïa." In *Les Francophonies de la Méditerranée*, edited by Ridha Boulaabi. Paris: Geuthner, forthcoming.

———. "'Je veux sortir de ta langue'. Comment (ne pas) devenir un écrivain francophone." In *Littérature marocaine d'expression française: ancrage culturel et défis scripturaux, Oualili*, edited by Khalid Dahmani. Ecole Normale Supérieure de Meknès, forthcoming.

———. "*Ce point fixe qu'on nomma peut-être l'amour*: les captivités amoureuses de Jean Genet." In *Jean Genet, Cahiers de l'Herne*, edited by Albert Dichy, forthcoming.

———. "Trans-gendering, trans-sexualizing and decolonizing queer desire in today's' Morocco (Abdellah Taïa)," paper presented at the 2019 *Semana Arabe de Mexico City* = "Trans - genre, trans - sexualité, désir queer et destin décolonial au Maroc aujourd'hui (Abdellah Taïa)." To appear in *Queer Maghreb*, edited by in Alfonso de Toro and Annegret Richter.

———. "Jean Genet's Mediterranean Cartography of Desire." In *Les Méditerranées de Jean Genet/Jean Genet's Mediterraneans*, edited by Ralph Heyndels and Salim Ayoub. Caen: Passage(s), forthcoming.

———. "'Je vis dans une nostalgie étrange. Dans le manque de cet autre que j'étais censé devenir (. . .).' La 'francophonie' d'Abdellah Taïa." In *Langue française, écrivains francophones*, edited by Ridha Bourkhis, 113–124. Paris: L'Harmattan, 2020.

———. "'Je me voyais en dissidence avec le monde': Zahia Rahmani entre Algérie impossible et colonialité française." *Noria. Revue littéraire et artistique*. Paris: L'Harmattan, 2020.

———. "'Je suis un Indigène de la République.' L'atelier décolonial de l'écriture dans *Celui qui est digne d'être aimé* d'Abdellah Taïa." In *Poétique et politique du désir engagé/Poetics and Politics of Engaged Desire. Around/Autour d'Abdellah Taïa*, edited by Ralph Heyndels and Amine Zidouh, 117–145. Caen: Passage(s), 2020.

———. "'Cet Orient que je voyais à l'envers.' L'inversion de l'orientalisme chez Jean Genet." In *Voix d'Orient*, edited by Ridha Boulaabi, 177–198. Paris: Geuthner, 2019.

———. "'J'ai trouvé une autre langue': La France, le français et la 'francophonie' dans l'œuvre d'Abdellah Taïa." *Lasemaine.fr, Universidade de Porto* (2018). https://ler.letras.up.pt/uploads/ficheiros/16135.pdf.
———. "Configurations et transferts de la sexualité, du genre et du désir dans l'ouverture d'*Une mélancolie arabe* d'Abdellah Taïa, ou 'le dépassement des frontiers." *Expressions maghrébines* 16 (2017): 85–105.
———. "'*Je suis folle*': folie de l'identité, du genre et du sexe chez Abdellah Taïa." In *Hermeneutics of Textual Madness/Herméneutique de la folie textuelle*, edited by M.J. Muratore and Etienne Barnett, 463–476. Fasano: Biblioteca della Ricerca, 2017.
———. "La prostitution sur la scène de l'écriture chez Abdellah Taïa." *@nalyses, Revue de critique et de théorie littéraire* 11, no. 3 (2016): 9–23.
———. "Ecrire pour dire que ce n'est rien, la vie: Arthur Rimbaud." *Revue Européenne de Recherches sur la Poésie* 2, 93–105. Paris: Classiques Garnier, 2016.
———. "*Abdellah à jamais disparu*, ou les jeux de miroir du Je. Emergence et évanescence de soi dans la mise en scène de l'écriture chez Abdellah Taïa." In *L'écrivain et ses doubles: Le personnage autoréflexif dans la littérature européenne*, edited by Luc Fraisse and Eric Wessler, 149–161. Paris: Classiques Garnier, 2014.
———. "Ecrire dans la loyauté infidèle: dialectique de la fidélité et de la trahison chez Abdellah Taïa." In *De l'ordre et de l'aventure: Langage, littérature, francophonie*, edited by Alain Rey, Pierre Brunel, Philippe Desan, and Jean Pruvost, 401–410. Paris: Hermann, 2014.
———. "Nuit politique du désir: l'engagement amoureux de Jean Genet." In *Jean Genet. Entretiens de Fontevraud*, edited by Hadrien Laroche, 116–129. Saint-Nazaire: Maison des Ecrivains et Traducteurs Etrangers, 2011.
———. "Les Noirs sur la blancheur livide, ou le sens possible de l'Amérique selon Jean Genet." *Travaux de Littérature*, XXIV (2011): 319–331.
———. "'L'amour évidemment', ou 'c'est par où le noir du monde?' Ecriture de la scène passionnelle et scène passionnelle de l'écriture: désir, trahison et mélancolie dans *L'armée du salut* d'Abdellah Taïa." In *La rhétorique de la passion dans le texte francophone*, edited by Ridha Bourkhis, 131–148. Paris: L'Harmattan, 2010.
———. "Entremêlements narratifs sur la tombe de Jean Genet, Abdellah Taïa et Rachid O." *Travaux de littérature,* XXII (2009): 473–481.
———. "Ecrire le tombeau de Jean Genet. Instants rêvés dans le cimetière espagnol de Larache: Abdellah Taïa et Rachid O." In *Toutes les images du langage: Jean Genet*, edited by Frieda Ekotto, Aurélie Renaud, and Agnès Vannouvong, 91–101. Paris: Alain Baudry & Cie., 2008.
———. "'L'occasion, unique, de dégager nos sens': Modernité, primitivisme et homotexte chez Rimbaud." In *Rimbaud e la Modernità*, edited by Carolina Diglio and Giovanni Dotoli, 103–105. Paris: Presses de l'Université de Paris-Sorbonne/ Fasano: Schena Editore (*Transatlantique*), 2005.
Idier, Antoine. "'Sortir de la peur'. Construire une identité homosexuelle arabe dans un mond post-colonial" (Entretien avec Abdellah Taïa). *Revue critique de fixxion française contemporaine* 12 (2016): 197–207.

Kespel, Gilles. *Banlieue de la République*. Paris: Gallimard, 2012.
Khiari, Sadri. *Pour une politique de la racaille: Immigré-e-s et jeunes des banlieues*. Paris: Textuel, 2006.
Lamin, Luc. *La France en perdition sous l'image subliminale du racisme*. BoD, 2019.
Le Cour Grandmaison. Olivier, "Colonisés - immigrés et 'périls migratoires': origine et permanence du racisme et d'une xénophobie d'Etat." *Cultures et conflits* 69 (2008): 19–32.
Lefebvre, Henri. *Le droit à la ville*. Paris: Anthropos, 1967.
Lussault, Michel. "Ville." In *The City: Critical Essays in Human Geography,* edited by Jacques Lévy, 151–156.New York: Routledge, 2008.
Mack, Mehammed Amadeus. *Sexagon: Muslims, France, and the Sexualization of National Culture*. New York: Fordham University Press, 2017
McKintosh, Peggy. "White Privilege: Unpacking the Invisible Knapsack." *Peace and Freedom* (July–August 1989): 10–12.
Memmi, Albert. *Portrait du colonisé précédé du portrait du colonisateur*. Paris: Gallimard, 1985 (1957).
———. *Portait du décolonisé musulman et de quelques autres*. Paris: Gallimard, 2004.
Merleau-Ponty, Maurice. *Phénoménologie de la perception*. Paris: Gallimard, 2005 (1945).
Pinel, Edwy. *Pour les musulmans*. Paris: La Découverte, 2014.
Provencher, Denis M. *Queer Maghrebi French: Language, Temporalities, Transfiliations*. Liverpool: Liverpool University Press, 2017.
Puar, Jasbir. *Terrorist Assemblages: Homonationalism in Queer Times*. Durham: Duke University Press, 2007.
Rosello, Mireille. *Postcolonial Hospitality: The Immigrant as a Guest*. Palo Alto: Stanford University Press, 2002.
Sartre, Jean-Paul. *La transcendence de l'ego*. Paris: Vrin, 1936.
———. *L'existentialisme est un humanism*. Paris: Gallimard, 1946.
Sayad, Abdelmalek. *L'immigration ou les paradoxes de l'altérité*. Paris: Raisons d'agir, 2006.
Shephard, Todd. *France and the Arab Men*. Chicago: University of Chicago Press, 2018.
Taïa, Abdellah. *Mon Maroc*. Paris: Séguier, 2000.
———. *Le rouge du tarbouche*. Paris: Séguier, 2004.
———. *L'armée du salut*. Paris: Editions du Seuil, 2006.
———. *Une mélancolie arabe*. Paris: Editions du Seuil, 2008.
———. *Le jour du Roi*. Paris: Editions du Seuil, 2010.
———, "Postface." In *Grandes chaleurs,* edited by François-Marie Banier, n.p. Gœttingen: Steidl, 2010.
———. "Genet, Abdellah et moi." In *Les passions de Jean Genet*, edited by Ralph Heyndels, 11–15. Paris: Alain Baudry et Cie / Fasano: Schena Editore, 2010.
———. *Infidèles*. Paris: Editions du Seuil, 2012.
———. Film director, *Salvation Army*, 2013.
———. *Un pays pour mourir*. Paris: Editions du Seuil, 2015.

———. *Celui qui est digne d'être aimé*. Paris: Editions du Seuil, 2017.

———. *La vie lente*. Paris: Editions du Seuil, 2019.

———. "Regarder tout au fond du monde." *The Art Newspaper*, March 31, 2020.

———. "Un jardin. En attendant." In *Poétique et politique du désir engagé / Poetics and Politics of Engaged Desire. Around / Autour d'Abdellah Taïa*, edited by Ralph Heyndels and Amine Zidouh, 351–354. Caen: Passage(s), 2020.

———. "Lettre à James Baldwin." In *Poétique et politique du désir engagé / Poetics and Politics of Engaged Desire. Around / Autour d'Abdellah Taïa*, edited by Ralph Heyndels and Amine Zidouh, 9–11. Caen: Passage(s), 2020.

———. Interview. *L'Economiste*, June 1, 2020.

———. Interview with Mabrouck Rachedi. *Jeune Afrique*, 2017.

———. "Qu'on le veuille ou non, l'homosexualité est une question politique." Interview with Ibtissam Ouazzani. *huffpostmaghreb.com*, 2017.

———. Interview with Georgia Philipps-Amos. *bombmagazine.org*, 2016.

———. Interview. *huffpostmaghreb.com*, 2015.

———. Interview. *Urbain Tanger*, 2015.

Taïa, Abdellah, and Frédéric Mitterrand. *Maroc 1900-1960. Un certain regard*. Arles: Actes Sud, 2007.

Taïa, Abdellah, ed. *Lettres à un jeune Marocain*. Paris: Editions du Seuil, 2009.

—, ed. *Jean Genet, un saint marocain*. Tanger: Librairie des Colonnes, 2010.

Taïa, Abdellah, and Edouard Louis. "We speak about violence." *The Paris Review*, July 2, 2018.

Tanvi, Misra. "The Othered Paris." *citylab.com,* November 16, 2017.

Tevanian, Pierre, and Saïd Bouamama. "Un racisme post-colonial. Réflexions sur un passé qui ne passe pas." *Le-blog-sam-la-touch.over-blog.com/ 2017.*

Vitali, Ilaria. *Intrangers: Post-migration et nouvelles frontières de la littérature*. Paris: L'Harmattan, 2012.

Zagarianis, Jean. *Queer Maroc: Sexualités, Genres et (Trans) Identités dans la littérature marocaine*. Morrisville: LuLu Publishing, 2014.

Zidouh, Amine. *Phantom Arabic, Dislocated French: Auto-Anthropological Imaginaries: Jean Genet, Abdellah Taïa, Leïla Sebbar, Nabil Ayouche*. Dissertation, University of Miami, 2018.

Chapter 2

Sexual Fluidity and Movements in Abdellah Taïa's *L'armée du salut*

The Birth of a Queer Moroccan Francophone Identity

Olivier Le Blond

L'armée du salut [*Salvation Army*], published in France in 2006, is Abdellah Taïa's third novel. It continues the distinctive autobiographical style the author has established since his first novel, *Mon Maroc* [*Another Morocco*], published in 2000 in France. *L'armée du salut* follows the relationship of young Abdellah and a Swiss academic: the blossoming of their relationship in Morocco, the constant round trips between the two protagonists' countries, and finally Abdellah's move to Geneva as a student finishing his *DESS*, a postgraduate diploma. Over the course of the novel, the concept of movement emerges as a persistent theme. It is evident in the geographical displacement of the characters, traveling around Morocco and from one country to another, but it can also be found in the structure of the novel. Motion helps develop Abdellah's identity in relation to other characters, and by doing so, allows him to define himself as an individual not only for himself but in the eyes of society as well. It is then essential to look at the importance of movement in order to understand its function in the novel and its function in creating a fluid queer Moroccan Francophone identity.

William Turner notes that "'queer' has the virtue of offering, in the context of academic inquiry into gender identity and sexual identity, a relatively novel term that connotes etymologically a crossing of boundaries."[1] Turner's definition, which focuses primarily on sexual and gender identity transgressions, could be extended to the crossing of boundaries from a diasporic point of view to help us define the fluidity of the queer Moroccan Francophone identity at play in *L'armée du salut*. Similarly, several recent studies address the intertwined implications of migrancy, sexuality, sexual identity, and gender.[2]

For example, Mack offers a vision of "interconnected perspectives into the sexualization of immigration" where each chapter is dedicated to these interconnections, looking at sexual diversity, psychoanalysis, the trope of the difficult Arab boy, and sexual undergrounds and pornography.[3] However, his study only looks at immigrants or their children already in France. Here, I propose to look at the different types of movements outlined above and offer a new perspective on how they shape self-definitions of masculinity. Within that intersectional framework, movement needs to be defined to grasp its integral part in the shaping of a queer Moroccan Francophone identity. Several types of movement stand out after reading the novel: geographical, narrative—alternating between pronouns—, and temporal, with the narration switching back and forth between the present and the past.

While defining masculinity in a few sentences can be a daunting task, one thing that many scholars do agree on is that masculinity is "no longer a monolithic category, but a competing set of definitions constructed by different groups."[4] In her groundbreaking work *Masculinities*, R.W. Connell offers two definitions of masculinity (essentialist and positivist) all the while noting that each of them exclude masculine women and feminine men.[5] Just like queer theory, masculinity seems elusive, since it will be different for everyone, yet is still defined in patriarchal societies as all the attributes belonging to the male sex. As we will see next, queer identity, masculinity, movement, and sexuality are all integral elements in Taïa's work, in which he lays the foundation of a specific queer Moroccan Francophone identity.

GEOGRAPHICAL, NARRATIVE, AND TEMPORAL MOVEMENTS

The most obvious kind of movement found in the novel, geographical mobility, is characterized by the physical displacement of the characters not only within Morocco but also between Morocco and other European countries. These journeys allow the narrator to create a sexual and gender identity that appears fluid, not fixed, and in line with his travels, which, by essence, are dynamic. Indeed, through his travels, Abdellah adapts to his surroundings, and as we will see later, not only does his identity change because of his travels, but his sexual identity is also influenced by his environment. In "Identity and Place: a Critical Comparison of Identity Theories," Hauge writes that: "Aspects of identity derived from places we belong to arise because places have symbols that have meaning and significance to us. Places represent personal memories, and [. . .] social memories (shared histories). Places do not have permanent meaning; their meaning is renegotiated continually and therefore their contribution to identity is never the same."[6] This is indeed what is at stake in *L'armée du salut*: Taïa puts great emphasis on the places where he finds himself, and this emphasis translates into a fondness for locale. Whether it be the family house in Hay Salam or the beach where he and Jean first walk together, there is a feeling of longing that transpires from the different places from his home country mentioned in the novel. This affective attachment changes between Morocco and Switzerland. Each country and cultural context also contributes its share of elements to the creation of the character's identity. For example, one element that defines Abdellah to greater or lesser degrees, at different points in the novel, is the eroticization of the male Arab body by the Western gaze. As Cervulle and Rees-Roberts note, the Arab boy is often objectified, and this conjures up a dominating/dominated schema, exacerbated by the dramatization of the precarity of the North African community in the projects, which becomes a locus of fantasy for many European men.[7] This objectification and schema of domination are remnants of the West's colonial past discussed at length by Joseph Boone in both his groundbreaking article and his book, in which he establishes what he calls the geographies of desire. In the second chapter of his book, aptly titled "Beautiful Boys, Sodomy, and *Hamams*: A Textual and Visual History of Tropes," he explores at length the discourses painting Arab boys as objects of desire as well as the age differences, and by extension the power, between the boys and the men who admire them.[8]

Because of this long history of viewing North African boys through the lens of visiting European men, it is novel that Taïa reverses the direction of migration—going from North Africa, both in geography and point of view, toward Europe. This shift in the travel narrative is discussed at length by Mack in the third chapter of his book, in which he notes that for authors like Taïa, their "literature of sexual dissidence embraces a transnational promise, relating a certain 'Arab' nomadism to, for example, stories of immigrant wanderlust in Europe."[9] Taïa's novel powerfully illustrates this reversal, since it exploits several types of flows connected with queer theory.

Another type of motion is found in the way the novel is divided into three parts. Although the novel ultimately concludes with Abdellah's experience, the first part of the novel focuses on his mother, M'Barka, and to a lesser degree her relationship with Abdellah's father, Mohammed. The second part is dedicated to his older brother, Abdelkébir. It is finally in the third and longest part of the novel where Abdellah becomes the focus through his experiences in Morocco and Switzerland. The transition—from *she* in the novel's first part, to *he* in the second, to finally *I*—represents the movement from the outside influence of one person in the narrator's life at one time and place to the influence of another person at another time and place. It is customary for the author of an autobiographical novel to put other characters at the center of their narration for several reasons: this process not only allows for the disclosure of information about characters important to the narrator, but it also allows the reader to understand the relationships that link these characters to the narrator.[10] Moreover, the use of the first person takes on a political dimension in the context of Moroccan authors: only important personalities could use this subject pronoun, not authors. Using this subject pronoun, talking about oneself, does not necessarily imply denying others as exemplified by this shift in pronouns.[11] By putting other characters at the center of the first two parts of the novel, Taïa explores the experiences and perceptions that young Abdellah lived and felt with his mother, father, and brother.

The use of the pronouns *he* and *she* in conjunction with the pronoun *I* creates a certain subjectivity. Indeed, it is the main character who uses the pronoun *I*, in this case the narrator who recounts to the reader what he has lived through contact with the other characters represented by *he* and *she*, but it does not tell what these other characters have lived in a precise manner or in a meticulous or historical way.[12] In Taïa's case, it is his brother and mother, about whom he writes in the third person singular, through the eyes of the narrator who uses the first person singular.

This choice of pronouns confirms not only the notion of an autobiographical novel, but also addresses the notion of movement, linking them through this never-ending waltz of different pronouns between each part. Movement is created between the different parts of the novel but also within each part. There is a constant shift between the *I*, representing Abdellah's thoughts and perspective, and the *she* and *he* representing the assumed perspectives of his mother and older brother. This alternation can be found in several places in the novel.

One example of the shift in pronoun usage is in the first chapter. Abdellah describes how his mother would slip out of the room where her children were all sleeping to go to her husband, and Abdellah would try to stay awake to witness this getaway: "Elle nous abandonnait alors, rassurée, pour aller assumer son devoir conjugal et rendre son homme heureux. J'ai essayé plusieurs fois de rester éveillé pour assister à ce moment magique [. . .]. En vain." [She'd leave us then, her mind at ease, to carry out her conjugal duties and make her man happy. Several times, I tried to stay awake to witness this magic moment [. . .]. In vain.].[13] This quote accentuates how *L'armée du salut* is first and foremost about Abdellah's experiences, his coming face-to-face with the active sexuality of his parents and his curiosity toward it. It is also about how the contact with these characters shaped and transformed him into the character he is at the end of the novel. By telling his mother's story in the first part and his brother's in the second, Taïa creates a narrative and temporal flow, further reinforcing the identity politics of the novel.

Another structural element that creates a sense of movement in the novel is the alternation of past and present. This temporal movement is made evident not only by the division of the novel into several parts, but also by the division made within each part. These three parts, in addition to having an independent subject, also have an independent temporal dimension. Each part covers a different period in the lives of M'Barka, Abdelkébir, and Abdellah, and allows the reader to understand what brought Abdellah to change, evolve, and become the person he is at the end of the novel. The first part reverts the furthest in time; it opens on their family life in the small house in Hay Salam, but Abdellah eventually reverts even further back to when his mother and father met and their wedding to explain the root of a recurring fight they have. This trip in the past creates a temporal displacement that informs the specific nature of the relationship between parents and children, to serve as a justification of a recent occurrence.

The second part of the novel, unlike the first, follows a chronological order: recounting the childhood and teenage years of Abdelkébir, ending with a vacation to Tangiers with his younger brothers, Abdellah and Mohamed, when he is already thirty years old. This portion of the novel opens with "Il était là avant moi. [. . .] Leur premier enfant! Un garçon!" [He was there before me. [. . .] Their first child! A boy!].[14] Out of these few sentences, the reader understands the importance of Abdelkébir in the Taïa family. Not only is he the older brother, so important for Abdellah, but he is also the first male child born of their parents' union. The use of exclamation points not only reinforces Abdelkébir's importance in the family, but also the importance he holds for Abdellah, for more personal, emotional reasons.

Most of Abdelkébir's chapter is dedicated to the vacation in Tangiers. This vacation represents the biggest geographical displacement in the novel until this point. This displacement and change in everyday life seemed exceptional for Abdellah: "Je ne sais pas pourquoi il avait soudain décidé de nous emmener en vacances. [. . .] Nous partions pour la première fois de notre vie en vacances, et ensemble. Il n'y eut jamais de deuxième fois." [I don't know why he suddenly decided to take us on vacation. [. . .] For the first time in our lives we were going on vacation, together. There would never be a second time].[15] This quote highlights how Abdelkébir's decision to take his younger brothers with him on vacation is unusual. The fact that this is the only time they all went on vacation together accentuates the uniqueness of this vacation, and the notion of departure prepares the reader for a new journey, a geographical one that will never happen again.

The last part of the novel is the most relevant when it comes to temporal shift. Abdellah, the narrator/character, moves back and forth between present and past in alternating chapters. Each chapter concerning the beginning of Abdellah's graduate studies in Geneva, Switzerland corresponds to the present of the novel, from Abdellah's arrival at the Geneva airport to his first days spent in the city. The chapters devoted to Morocco represent the past and correspond to the years when Abdellah was an undergraduate student and met Jean, who gradually became his lover. This budding relationship in the past is an important touchstone in Abdellah's identity formation and a connection with the present: his romance with Jean eventually pushes him to leave Morocco for Switzerland and therefore forces him, voluntarily or not, to change.

FLUID MASCULINITIES AS MOVEMENT

These different movements (geographical, narrative, and temporal) allow Abdellah, the main character, to build his own identity, characterized by both gender—whether it be masculinity or femininity—and sexuality. Taïa renders this identity building with a homodiegetic narration: these evolutions lived by Abdellah the character are told by Abdellah the narrator. In *L'armée du salut*, the concepts of traditional heteronormative masculinity and sexuality are transcended by motion, the major theme of the novel. Two very distinct types of masculinities exist in the novel. The first one can be perceived as conventional and is personified by Abdellah's father and, in some aspects, by his brother Abdelkébir. This heterocentric masculinity, very much in line with heterosexual traditions, is compliant with the expected role of men in Muslim societies. The second type of masculinity, queerer, is personified by Jean, Abdellah's lover. This masculinity, without a doubt, represents, the more fluid of the two, the type of masculinity to which Abdellah aspires. However, masculinity is now understood as a fluid concept, constantly changing.[16]

Since masculinity is dependent on the cultural traditions of specific milieux, it may seem difficult to define. However, as Morocco is a patriarchal society, the essentialist conception of masculinity (the masculine is active, the feminine is passive) seems to be the most commonly understood type of masculinity in Moroccan society, so much so that questions of gender are erased and masculinity becomes a negative concept. This is Nadia Tazi's main argument in her research (2004): "[C]ette culture ne se borne pas à servir l'homme-adulte-musulman au détriment des autres [. . .] minorisés. Elle sature, et elle polarise le *gender*. L'homme doit se postuler comme souverainement masculin, comme Un, et il ne cesse de se définir négativement en rapport à l'autre. Son éminence est visible au point d'en devenir aveuglante: la virilité est la tache aveugle de ce monde." [[T]his culture does not limit itself to serve the man-adult-Muslim to the detriment of the other [. . .] minoritized. It saturates and polarizes gender. Man needs to put himself as supremely masculine, as One, and he never stops to define himself negatively vis-à-vis other men. His eminence/superiority is visible to the point of being blinding: virility is the blind spot of this world].[17] According to Tazi, North

African culture is responsible for this hypervisibility and supremacy of an exacerbated masculinity that does not leave any space for minorities, whether it be women or alternative gender/sexual constructions. Virility, defined by strength and energy, thus becomes all-powerful and posits itself as the only way of structuring a society that is diminished by this power represented by traditional masculinity. For Tazi, North African society, very much like Western society, needs to question the concept of masculinity.

This tension is discussed by Abdessamad Dialmy when he conducted a survey asking Moroccan men about their own vision of masculinity from a legal, psychological, and sexual standpoint.[18] Results showed that men themselves were unsure of what masculinity meant for them, and that they are now becoming aware of a non-patriarchal conception of what it means to be a man. For them, this deterioration of the patriarchal vision of masculinity jeopardizes the identity of Moroccan men. They no longer know how to define themselves, all the while understanding that it is now necessary to create a new masculine identity. This paradox, which can be understood as a "crisis" in masculinity, is in accordance with the questioning developed by Western scholars. This is echoed by Osire Glacier who gives great attention to the sociopolitical emphasis placed on the feminine and the masculine, "presented as unchangeable biological truths"[19] that men and women are expected to be and act a certain way even before their births. Because of sociopolitical expectations, men and women do not know what their roles in society should be and start to question these roles. This paradox also shows that masculinity is not a fixed concept; it is constantly changing. This fluid concept reveals that there is not just one but several masculinities; thus, Moroccan men must redefine their conception of masculinity in order to embrace its fluidity. This lack of a fixed point in the notion of masculinity highlights a concept in constant flux.

So, what is masculinity in the novel? *L'armée du salut* offers a fluid vision of masculinity that not only criticizes the traditional concept, but also seeks to offer an alternate conception of patriarchy, if not several. Abdelkébir embodies an example of what fluid masculinity is. He personifies the questions raised and proposed by Dialmy's study about the paradox of a Moroccan masculinity that is searching for itself without being able to find it.

Abdelkébir is the most important male model for the narrator, and, indeed, the protagonistAbdellah idolizes his brother. This stems from the importance of the male first-born in Maghrebi culture and the importance placed on the role of the older brother who takes on a patriarchal responsibility when the father figure is absent. This idolatry slowly turns into love without Abdellah realizing it. This is highlighted when he explains how much he loved to wash his brother's hair: "Mettre mes doigts dans ses cheveux, jouer, tirer, dessiner. gratter, rêver . . . J'avais envie de tellement de choses quand j'étais avec

Abdelkébir. Je ne me contrôlais pas. Et je ne résistais pas." [I wanted to run my fingers through his hair, play with it, pull it, draw, scratch, dream . . . I wanted to do so many things when I was with Abdelkébir. I had no control. And I didn't resist].[20] This desire does not seem unnatural for Abdellah, as he loses himself in his feelings when he writes "and I didn't resist." The description of a mundane everyday scene, an exchange between two brothers, is transcended and therefore resembles a love scene, in which the desire for the other is dominant. However, this scene also lays the foundation for the complex nature of this admiration for the older brother, of the difficulty to resist temptation. This desire that Abdellah cannot yet name is present and will finally be given a name during their trip to Tangiers

In Tangiers, Abdellah comes to terms with his feelings: the love he feels for his brother is not a whim but something stronger, which he cannot understand. This realization happens in a city imbued with the movement of transience: geographical, fluid, and cosmopolitan. There is a diversity in Tangiers, or rather a fluidity that is exposed by Abdellah's commentary on the city's inhabitants: "Les Tangérois ont l'air perdu. J'ai l'impression qu'ils ne sont pas marocains. D'ailleurs ils parlent presque tous assez bien l'espagnol" [People in Tangiers seem lost to me, don't even seem Moroccan. Besides, most of them speak Spanish pretty well].[21] This quote shows how Tangiers is cosmopolitan, a Moroccan city that does not appear to be Moroccan, due not only to its proximity to Spain but also to the fact that it was colonized by Spain. Furthermore, this city is a locus of realization and of first times for Abdellah: it is in this city that he realizes what his feelings are for his brother, but it is also here that he has his first sexual experience. Finally, Tangiers is the place where Abdellah realizes the love his brother has for a woman, and thus his brother slowly slips from his grasp without him being able to do anything about it.

Although Tangiers is a city of transition, Abdelkébir and his personification of traditional and non-traditional Moroccan masculinities was Abdellah's rock. Yet this rock slowly crumbles as the vacation continues, and the most important example of masculinity Abdellah knew until then, the one he admired so much until this vacation, slowly changes. Up until the trip to Tangiers, and before his wedding, Abdelkébir alternately embraced and rejected the traditional notion of masculinity. He filled the role of the purveyor for his family, going as far as helping to build the house where the family lives. In some ways he is very similar to his father, all the while being his opposite; he does not speak much: "Abdelkébir ne parlait pas. Et quand il le faisait, c'était comme un prophète (un poète) qui annonçait un nouveau verset sacré" [Abdelkébir didn't speak. And when he did, he was like some prophet (a poet) who announces a new holy verse].[22] This vision of Abdelkébir does conjure up the patriarchal and essentialist conception of masculinity. Nevertheless, Abdelkébir is different from his father in the sense that while the latter collects books in Arabic, the former collects them in French. Taïa also mentions that his brother "n'écoute d'habitude que les Doors, Jimi Hendrix, les Rolling Stones, David Bowie" [usually listens to nothing but the Doors, Jimi Hendrix, the Rolling Stones, David Bowie].[23] With his choice of French literature and his musical tastes, Abdelkébir then represents for both the reader and his brother a Westernized vision of masculinity that does not align with the idea of a traditional Moroccan masculinity. Indeed, having learned French and listening to music made by famous, sometimes androgynous artists, pushes Abdelkébir into a less masculine realm, one that clashes with conceptions of Moroccan masculinities.

However, this trip to Tangiers jeopardizes these notions of a more fluid masculinity for both Abdelkébir and Abdellah. Abdelkébir changes right before his brother and goes from a modern man—a vision of masculinity that Abdellah reveres, due to the feelings he experiences for a brother who grew up bathed in Western culture—to a man who *Arabizes* himself. Abdelkébir is changed by this trip, crying while listening to Arabic music and committing to his traditional role by marrying a woman. Abdellah, who has just realized the nature of his feelings for his brother, dislikes this change. He had just come to terms with the feelings of love for this Moroccan man he saw as modern, different from what he was used to with his more traditional father. This changing vision of what Abdelkébir represents for Abdellah also highlights the fluid nature of the masculinity that attracts him.

Abdellah also comes out of this trip changed. Not only does he fully realize the nature of his feelings for his brother, but he also experiences for the first time a sexuality that is different from the heterosexuality he has been used to so far. During this trip, Abdellah meets Salim, a Frenchman of North African descent, and a short dialogue leads them to a sexual encounter in a movie theater. Salim introduces himself as a Moroccan man to Abdellah even though he does not speak Arabic. Abdellah is surprised, however that Salim can only speak French and knows very few words of Arabic. This exchange underlines the implications of migration: once a family moves to France, the mother tongue—and by extension the Arabic culture—can be forgotten by the children, replaced by French language and culture.[24] As a result, Salim does not seem to fully realize himself, as he is not Moroccan, but also not perceived as French by Abdellah.

His sexual experience with the French-Maghrebi man is, in and of itself, a movement in several ways. First, Abdellah lives an important progression, since he goes from childhood and innocence to a sexually active being, reflected by his quasi-sick reaction: "Je me sens mal, mal, mal. [. . .] Et le pire, c'est que j'ai aimé ça, être entouré par les bras forts de cet homme de 40 ans qui sentait bon et qui me parlait dans l'oreille en français tout en essayant de trouver un chemin vers mon sexe, mes fesses. Je me suis donné à lui. Il ne m'a pas fait souffrir. Oui, j'ai aimé ça. Mon Dieu!" [I feel sick, sick, sick [. . .]. And the worst is that, I loved it, loved having this forty-year-old man who smelled good wrap me in his strong arms and talk French in my ear while he tried to get at my penis, my ass. And I let him. And it didn't hurt. Oh, I loved it. Yes. Oh God!].[25]

Second, there is a motion related to gender and sexuality. Indeed, the only examples of sexuality and gender (masculinity) that Abdellah had previously experienced were those demonstrated by his parents and his older brother. This relation with Salim creates a displacement of gender and sexuality, with Abdellah moving from a heterocentric world to one where gender limitations happen to be blurred. However, despite a lack of displacement in Abdelkébir's gender or sexuality, the psychological progression undergone by Abdellah is the reverse of Abdelkébir's—Abdelkébir goes from a westernized young man to a much more traditional Moroccan one because of his love for a woman, whereas Abdellah just now begins his journey toward a more fluid westernized masculinity as a result of his interaction with Salim.

In the third part of the novel, Taïa brings the reader on new geographical movements to more far-flung locales that often intersect with movements of gender and sexuality. The most significant gender maneuvers occur during the trips between Morocco and Switzerland, taken by Jean first, and then by Abdellah. Jean personifies a masculinity that is very different from Abdelkébir's, being a gay European man, as well as demonstrating a sexuality that Abdellah only experienced once with Salim. Jean is a gay Swiss scholar in Morocco for a seminar. When Abdellah meets Jean, he is studying French literature at the University of Rabat, and meets "Jean au Maroc, à Rabat. À l'université Mohamed-V où il était venu participer à un colloque autour du thème 'le beau mensonge'" [Jean in Morocco, in Rabat, at Mohamed-V University where he had come to participate in a seminar on "The Beautiful Lie"].[26] The theme of the colloquium is forewarning of Abdellah and Jean's relationship, one that Abdellah thinks is exclusive but will turn out not to be. This meeting between the two characters introduces the theme of the Western man traveling to North Africa. As mentioned earlier in this chapter, these migrations are often linked to sexual tourism, to the attraction to the Arab male body that appears as exotic.[27]

EXOTICIZATION OF THE ARAB MAN AND REVERSE EXOTICISM

Jean and Abdellah's first meeting occurs outside of the university where Abdellah studies. The relationship that ensues represents yet another displacement that fits the overarching theme of movement, since its main characteristic involves the travels between Switzerland and Morocco. During this relationship, Abdellah learns a lot from Jean. For the latter, he has the satisfaction of having a young lover that personifies a certain exoticism steeped in Western clichés about the Orient. Jean tries to adapt to a culture he appreciates. This attraction and willingness to adapt are shown during one of his visits, when the two men end up on one of Salé's beaches. As both lovers are basking in the moment, "Puis [Jean] me surprit en passant sa main gauche dans mes cheveux. Enfin, il murmura lentement et avec beaucoup d'effort: "Mabrouke!" [. . .] Il était heureux pour moi (pour nous?) [. . .]" [Then [Jean] surprised me by running his left hand through my hair. Finally, and with great effort, he murmured: "*Mabrouke.*" [. . .]. He was happy for me (for us?) [. . .]].[28] This mark of affection from Jean as well as his attempt at speaking Arabic highlight Jean's interest in this culture, his willingness to possess Abdellah, and to do anything possible to make him happy. However, some doubts linger regarding the couple's happiness, as emphasized by Abdellah's question: "for us?"

Jean's attraction for Abdellah is mirrored in Abdellah's attraction for the scholar. Jean represents a form of counter-exoticism for Abdellah since he is attracted to European culture. The reader is faced with two different visions of exoticism. In Jean's case, it is colonial exoticism, the travel of the Western man to exotic countries for the purpose of sexual tourism. For Abdellah, the exoticism is in his attraction to European culture, his need to learn from and assimilate to this culture. However, even though on the surface these two views seem to differ, these exoticisms are brought face to face and joined.

In order to better understand what the notion of exoticism entails in the novel, Todorov (1989) comes to mind. He explains that the current understanding of exoticism developed in the nineteenth century with travel narratives of Europeans living or visiting the colonies.[29] Value was placed on countries and cultures that were exclusively defined in relation to the observer. The only characteristics were that the country and culture were not those of the observer. This perception of exoticism saw a reemergence in postcolonial studies in the 1980s. For example, Per Buvik (2006) notes that "l'exotisme est à la fois une recherche de ce qui est différent, ou autre, et une auto-critique, parfois implacable" [exoticism is both a search for what is different, or other, and a sometimes implacable self-criticism].[30] Indeed, by looking for what is different, those who advocate for exoticism soon recognize voids that exist in their own country. A lack of something is expressed, and it then creates a need to fill that lack by finding it in the Other. Exoticism therefore functions as complementary moves in opposing directions: the observer, looking for what they do not possess, and the observed who also finds in the observer something that they do not possess. Those who differ reinforce the nationalist views of the observer who, with an exacerbated nationalism, expresses a value judgement vis-à-vis those who are observed.

It is indeed the case with Jean. He is a scholar and therefore represents a constant source of knowledge for Abdellah, as well as a financial provider since Jean will later offer to take care of Abdellah's visa to go to visit him in Switzerland.[31] Furthermore, Jean is attracted to Morocco because it is a country that is not his home country, one where he goes to forget about Switzerland and to find something he cannot back home, which his money allows him to pay for. This monetary aspect of Jean's travels is felt by Abdellah after they both meet Mohamed, a young prostitute: "Mohamed acceptait d'être acheté. Cela ne lui posait aucun problème. Visiblement. Et moi? Jean était-il en train de m'acheter aussi? [. . .] Grâce à ses francs suisses, Jean pouvait tout avoir dans mon pays" [Mohamed allowed himself to be bought. He didn't have a problem with that, obviously. What about me? Was Jean trying to buy me too? [. . .] Thanks to his Swiss francs, Jean could have whatever he wanted in my country].[32] Jean desires everything in Morocco that is foreign to him. Todorov also highlights that all the notions desired by the other (in this case, the Westerner) are not fixed, which then creates a fluidity in exoticism, a displacement. The lack of stability that Todorov discusses, a cultural displacement, allows the observer to create their own identity vis-à-vis the *exote,* by which I mean "the person who is exoticized." The feeling of otherness felt by the physical or mental displacement generates a complex identity based on a lacuna.[33]

Silke Segler-Messner encourages a re-reading of exoticism by Francophone writers that displaces and subverts it, therefore creating a duality.[34] Jean and Abdellah's relationship illustrates this duality: Jean embodies the European viewpoint of exoticism, whereas Abdellah personifies this new subverted vision of it. This is very apparent when Taïa writes the following: "[. . .] j'étais ravi d'avoir un homme pour moi, qui s'intéressait à moi, qui me sortait de mon milieu populaire, un homme occidental, cultivé, quelque part un homme-rêve" [[. . .] I was delighted to have a man of my own, someone who was interested in me, someone who got me out of my working-class world, at least for a little while, a cultured man, a Western man, in some ways the man of my dreams].[35] This quote is a clear indication of this counter-exoticism. Abdellah finds in Jean what he cannot find in Morocco. Jean is European, cultured, and representative of a male ideal that does not exist in Morocco, an ideal that closely mirrors Abdelkébir. This man embodies an ideal that was shaped by the Western music, movies, and books Abdellah cherished so much growing up, though this ideal seems problematic; the narrator points it out himself: Jean is the "man of his dreams," a man that can only exist through the idea Abdellah has of him. There is a displacement of colonial exoticism, since Abdellah imposes on Jean his own European fantasy.

Segler-Messner further notes that "les observés deviennent les observateurs, se libérant de la position d'objet passif et devenant instance active de perception" [the observed become the observers, freeing themselves from the passive object position they were in to become an active authority of perception].[36] It is quickly established that for Jean, his relationship with Abdellah is based on the physical—having a lover and experiencing physical love—when for Abdellah, their relationship is perceived as an intellectual and economic exchange, an emulsion that combines his love for men and his love for Europe and its culture, personified by Jean, a scholar. Abdellah's view of Jean posits Abdellah as Segler-Messner's active observer—he is the narrator of this piece of Europe, personified by Jean, a Europe that he desires so much that the choices he makes do not seem fortuitous, whether it be for his college career or his decision to pursue his graduate degree in Switzerland.

With all the choices he makes, Abdellah learns what Europe is, familiarizing himself with what is different from him by studying and observing it, but also by "practicing" it. Abdellah experiments with everything Europe is, and this experimentation goes hand in hand with sexuality. There is a displacement of this sexuality: his first experience is with Salim who, despite being of Moroccan descent, is first and foremost a European man of "North African descent." Abdellah then transfers his sexual desire to another European man, Jean. Even though intercourse is not what Abdellah seeks, it is still a part of this observation, a means that will allow him to reach his European ideals personified by Jean.

This vision of the Western world happens through Abdellah's observation and his need to find an ideal man who is a Westerner, like Jean. This idealized vision of the scholar is therefore a biased one, since readers can only rely on what Abdellah tells them. Jean appears as nondescript—either that is all he is willing to show Abdellah, or that is all Abdellah sees in him, dazzled by his "Europeanizing blinders" (my own expression). These blinders fall for the first time when Jean and Abdellah initially meet Mohamed.

Mohamed, a young prostitute who identifies as heterosexual, occasionally takes men as customers, in hopes of leaving Morocco to go to Europe. Therefore, Mohamed is also seeking movement—a migration that will allow him to escape Morocco, a country where selling his own body is his only way of leaving it. Nevertheless, by doing so, he embodies what Europeans seek in Morocco: a country where they can satisfy the need for sexual intercourse with the Other. However, to be able to leave Morocco, a woman—not a man—will have to either fall in love with him or sponsor him. As such, Mohamed's genitalia are his best bet to leave for Europe, or better yet, for the United States with a woman who will be "dingue de lui, et de son zob surtout" [worthy of him, deserving of his cock].[37]

While he waits for this to happen, he offers his skills to men, and what the narrator then explains highlights the fluidity of masculinity in Morocco depicted in the novel:

> En attendant de trouver la bonne, celle qui serait douce, obéissante, respectueuse, généreuse et bandante, il s'était tourné depuis quelque temps, à peine un mois, vers les hommes. Ils étaient plus simples à satisfaire [. . .]. [I]l envisageait même de se laisser prendre lui aussi à son tour, une bite dans le cul, cela ne lui faisait pas peur, à partir du moment où ce don de ce qu'il avait de plus intime lui permettrait de foutre le camp de ce pays de merde.
>
> [For quite some time, maybe about a month, while he was still waiting to meet a good woman, someone who knew how to be sweet, obedient, respectful, generous and sexy, he gave men a try. They were easier to satisfy, simpler to please [. . .]. He even imagined letting them have a shot at him. He wasn't afraid, he'd give them his private gift if taking a cock up his ass was a way to get out of this shithole country].[38]

At first, Mohamed appears to be a cliché of a Moroccan heterosexual man: looking for a woman who, if one relies on the adjectives used, would be submissive while also being sexy. This description of Mohamed's female ideal parallels Jean's description as a "dream-man": Mohamed created this idea of an unattainable "dream-woman." While waiting for this elusive woman, he has sex with men, and even contemplates the passive position if it lets him leave Morocco.

Even though he claims not to be attracted to men, he explains his changing behavior when, a few lines later, he specifies that "Les hommes [. . .] ne l'intéressaient pas sexuellement auparavant, mais chaque chose arrivait en son temps, n'est-ce pas?" [Men [. . .] never interested him sexually before, but everything happens in its own good time, doesn't it?].[39] Mohamed refuses to identify as a gay man, since "[. . .] passer pour un *zamel* à Tanger lui inspirait une grande horreur. D'ailleurs, il n'était pas *zamel*, non, non, pas du tout [. . .]" [[. . .]the idea of being mistaken for a *zamel* in Tangiers filled him with horror. Besides, he was no *zamel*, no way].[40] Potentially being perceived as a homosexual (a *zamel*) is dreadful for Mohamed, and as such, he makes it a point to say that he is only interested in women and that it is "la vérité vraie. Il ne mentait pas. Il était prêt à le jurer sur le Coran, si on voulait" [the truth, the absolute truth. He wasn't lying. He was ready to swear to it on the Holy Koran].[41] However, he personifies a sexuality, albeit a chargeable one, that is nonetheless in motion and constantly changing. He embodies the Orient that is so liked by Europeans, an Orient where morals are supposedly more fluid than in Europe. Shortly after this exchange, Jean comes into the picture and fulfills the part of the Westerner who comes to Morocco to slum it, taking advantage of a fluid Moroccan male sexuality represented by Mohamed and slowly shedding his image of the ideal "dream-man" that Abdellah idolized up until that point: "Jean l'avait dragué dans la galerie Delacroix, à l'entrée de la vieille ville de Tanger. Mohamed l'avait suivi immédiatement. Je ne savais pas quoi penser de la situation. Jean, Mohamed et moi. Jean était au Maroc pour cela aussi: se faire de jolis petits marocains? Ne venait-il pas uniquement au Maroc pour moi?" [Jean cruised him in the Delacroix Arcade, the one at the entrance to the old part of Tangiers. And Mohamed followed him right away. I didn't know what to make of this scenario: Jean, Mohamed, and me. Was this another reason Jean had come to Morocco, to get laid by cute, young Moroccans? Hadn't he come to Morocco to spend time with me?].[42] It is in this instant that Abdellah realizes that Jean is not exclusive with him, but that he also comes to Morocco to quench his sexual needs. However, it must be remembered that this is only Abdellah's view, his own perception of Jean's intentions. In this quote, Jean is not an active character and does not have a line of dialogue. The reader can only rely on and trust Abdellah.

The negative aspects of Jean's personality, described by Abdellah, seem to intensify when Abdellah is in Switzerland. These different aspects of his personality put Abdellah face to face with a changing masculinity. Jean goes from this masculine ideal, caring and sweet when he is in Morocco, to a much sterner and more authoritarian version of himself when he is in Switzerland. Because of these changes, Abdellah understands that Jean is impersonal and different from the person he met in Morocco. Morocco, a country Abdellah has tried so hard to leave, begins to appear as a neutral place that lets the couple live their relationship in bliss, but as soon as Abdellah moves to Switzerland, everything changes. Ironically, this neutrality only exists in Morocco, not in Switzerland. Movement informs and modifies Jean's personality, and as such changes the couple's relationship. This mobility highlights the ephemeral aspect of Jean's masculinity: the masculinity first dreamed up by Abdellah, so close to his brother's with the commonality of the French language, literature, and education, now appears to be fleeting.

SAME-SEX MALE SEXUALITY AS MOVEMENT

Within the part of the novel entirely dedicated to Abdellah, chapters alternate between Morocco and Switzerland, and by extension between the past and present of the novel. However, in several instances, in the chapters of the past, travels to Switzerland are mentioned, in order to foster the long-distance relationship between Abdellah and Jean. These travels to Switzerland, always tainted by a certain negativity, paint a dystopian view of the country by the narrator. This migration sets in motion the creation of a new identity for Abdellah, one that asserts itself as a new example of masculinity as well as queer individuality. During one of his trips to Switzerland, Abdellah experiments with another type of relationship that allows him to blossom, and this relationship presages the foundations of a new identity.

On the ferryboat between Tangiers and Spain, Abdellah meets Matthias and Rafaël, two young men who tried to get into Morocco but were turned away because one of them did not have the visa required to enter the country. This meeting takes place on an actively moving means of transportation, linking Morocco and Spain—a neutral space that is not linked to either of the two countries. Out of the neutrality of this means of transportation, Abdellah's own neutrality emerges: he is neither in Morocco nor in Switzerland, is in between two continents, and is not influenced by outside elements or people that usually surround him. Abdellah is a blank slate, free to create new configurations for himself and a new identity.

This passage tackles the question of male sexuality in relation to movement. To this end, Mireille Rosello's "national-sexual" serves as a basis to define these two notions. According to Rosello, the national-sexual is "a code, a set of linguistic and cultural reflexes, a collection of myths, images, metaphors, and clichés by which each national entity defines the realm of the sexual, including the opposition between dominant and marginalized sexual preferences and practices."[43] Each national entity defines the sexual field in its own way, including the tension between dominant sexual practices/preferences and marginalized ones. Thanks to Rosello, masculinity can be understood as contingent upon a person's environment. The national-sexual is at the intersection of what a nation wants to impose as a norm and what the individual tends to define in terms of their own sexuality. As sexuality is not a fixed point, being constantly in movement, the individual's motions and the mobility of their own sexuality eclipses the limits prescribed by society.

In Abdellah's case, meeting these two young Europeans, and all of them taking a train through Spain, culminates in a sexual encounter that surpasses the norms imposed by society. The train transcends the nation because it is moving and represents neither Spain nor Morocco but a neutral space in which the characters can implement their own definition of sexuality and in which private and public spheres intertwine. It is in this train that a connection happens, symbolized by their nudity and lovemaking. It is important to note that this meeting, this connection, is only defined through movement:

> La nuit, dans le train qui nous emmenait à Madrid, nous avons fait connaissance [. . .]. Vers minuit, au moment où il fallait dormir, comme ça, sans avoir rien décidé, il faut croire que nous n'attendions que ça, nous nous sommes déshabillés et, nus, nous avons commencé à faire l'amour, tous les trois.

> Nous n'avons pas dormi. La nuit chaude nous maintenait éveillés pour l'amour et ses joies.
>
> Nous étions heureux. Jeunes et heureux. La terre d'Espagne comme cadre de nos élans et de notre partage.
>
> [That night, on the train to Madrid, we got to know one another. [. . .] Around midnight, just when we were supposed to sleep, the moment arrived, the single moment I think we all were waiting for, happened just like that, unplanned, no warning, and we took off our clothes and started to make love, all three of us naked together.
>
> We didn't sleep. The hot night kept us awake, ready for love and its pleasures.
>
> We were happy. Young and happy. The Spanish landscape hung like a frame around what surged within us and what we shared.][44]

This quote stresses a joy felt by the narrator with the help of the adjective "happy," which is highlighted through repetition. This encounter, this experience, is one of very few passages in the novel that does not have a sour aftertaste for the narrator. Moreover, the number three is of importance here; it reinforces a refusal of the binary, associated with a normative point of view—a point of view opposed to what appears to be a polyamorous encounter here. There is a multiplicity in sexuality that opens new horizons. The intersection mentioned by Rosello can be found here: "nous avons fait connaissance" [we got to know one another],[45] which underlines the fact that different cultures intertwine and fuse to form one entity, linked by sexuality.

Spain, despite being a country through which the characters only pass, represents a moment when Abdellah is the happiest and feels sexually fulfilled. This fusion achieved in a moving train shows again how movement is important in the novel. This specific journey is what lets Abdellah live the most fulfilling experience told in the novel. This encounter, told in one of the chapters related to Abdellah's past, can be compared to another one that he lives in the present of the novel, during his second day in Geneva.

As mentioned previously, Switzerland has a negative connotation in Abdellah's mind. Indeed, Jean's friend, who was supposed to pick up Abdellah from the airport, did not show up and did not answer his phone: "Personne ne m'attendait à l'aéroport de Genève. Au bout de deux longues heures il m'a fallu me rendre à l'évidence: Charles, l'ami de Jean, ne viendrait pas me chercher comme il l'avait promis [. . .]" [nobody was waiting to meet me at the Geneva airport. After two long hours, I had to face the facts: Jean's friend, Charles, wasn't coming to pick me up like he promised].[46] Morocco, his homeland, appears to be a lot more merciful now that he has left it. Abdellah's arrival in Switzerland forces him to move around, not knowing where he will be able to sleep, since the university dorms are not yet open. It is thanks to a conversation with a taxi driver that the novel's title takes on its full meaning: Abdellah will go to the Salvation Army to sleep until he can move into the dorm.

Geneva's Salvation Army emerges as a haven of peace for Abdellah. It is there that he will meet one of the most important people for him during his first days in Switzerland, an employee that he nicknames Michel Foucault. The character of Michel Foucault is of particular interest for several reasons: the fact that the narrator chooses this nickname explicitly links the character to the theoretician, and by extension, to his prolific work. As such, Foucault's work on power and sexuality comes to mind, two of the main themes in the novel itself. Another point of note is that when the character of Michel Foucault is first introduced, he is reading "[. . .] un roman que je connaissais très bien: *Adolphe* de Benjamin Constant" [[. . .] a novel I knew very well: *Adolphe* by Benjamin Constant].[47] The choice of this particular novel does not seem trivial: *Adolphe* is written in the form of a confession, a bildungsroman telling the story of a taboo relationship. The narrator of the novel, a twenty-two-year-old man, falls in love with a Polish woman, Ellénore, ten years older than him. These are but a few parallels that can be drawn between *L'armée du salut* and *Adolphe*, to the point that their outlines could be overlaid.

Geneva's Salvation Army is but one of the elements Abdellah needs to create his own army, in order to redefine himself. This army is possible through Abdellah's displacement: "[. . .] avancer seul. Être heureux seul. [. . .] Me perdre complètement pour mieux me retrouver. Constituer enfin, le matin d'un jour gris et de grand froid, une armée pour mon salut" [get ahead on my own. Be happy on my own. [. . .] Lose myself entirely, the better to find myself. To summon, one gray and very cold morning, an army for my own salvation].[48] Here lies the purpose of all of Abdellah's displacements: building his own army to save himself, to reinvent himself. All these movements, whether they be geographical, sexual, or in narrative form, are emphasized by the expressions "get ahead" and "lose myself" and highlight this notion of personal quest. All the experiences lived in Geneva bring a new element to the creation of this new identity and set the basis for the creation of this army for his own salvation. The salvation here can be understood in several ways. It may lie in his liberation from the confines of the patriarchal Moroccan society, by being in France, but can also be a way to escape the crumbling relationship that brought him to Geneva.

However, Abdellah's vision of Switzerland is still tainted with regret until he comes across an older man who cruises him. As he is wandering aimlessly in the city, going through places that are reminiscent of Jean, this anonymous man takes him to public restrooms in which other men are already engaging in different sexual activities. Motion is once again evident in this interaction. The anonymous man commands the move but there is a tacit understanding since despite being led by this man, Abdellah agrees to follow him. The place where he is led also alludes to transit. Urinals are a place where people just pass through, where no one stays longer than to relieve themselves. During this encounter in the urinals, a form of relief is experienced by Abdellah, but not the type of relief the reader may expect: a fellatio.

The urinals are described as a place of overflowing sexuality, and this overflow is reminiscent of the movement as defined by Rosello in the national-sexual. It is the intersection of two cultures, European and Moroccan, that meet and interweave. This meeting also triggers a reversal of Abdellah's perception of Geneva. Thus, for Abdellah, the urinal scene reveals a humanity he did not experience until then, "[. . .] l'humanité des êtres en Suisse" [the human side of the Swiss].[49] Through their sexuality, these men, whom Abdellah associates right away with Geneva, make visible a humanity that is present in this city and that he had not seen beforehand. It is then that his perception of Geneva slowly changes and evolves, and Abdellah realizes that things can change for the better, that these men may possibly be soldiers in his salvation army.

There is a symbiosis between these men, coming to the urinals to satisfy their sexual needs. By finding themselves in this place, they are all linked to one another through their desire. The idea of fusion created by these men is mirrored by the man performing fellatio on Abdellah. This sexual act strengthens this feeling of humanity that Abdellah notices when he arrives at the urinals. This notion of humanity is transcended at the end of the scene by the notion of exchange: whereas Abdellah is convinced the man mistook him for a prostitute, he received an orange as payment. As the man leaves him, telling him that they can meet again, Abdellah takes the orange up to his nose to smell it. He is already reminiscing about an experience that will not happen again, one that he tries to better understand. At that moment he notes: "J'étais heureux, de ce plaisir, soulagé. Il ne m'avait pas pris finalement pour un prostitué. Je lui avais plu, il voulait goûter à moi, et c'était aussi simple que ça. Rien de plus. Un échange équitable de jouissance" [I was happy, thanks to a moment's pleasure, relieved. When you come right down to it, he didn't take me for a prostitute. He liked me, wanted to get a taste of me, that's all, that's all this was about. Nothing but a mutual exchange of pleasure].[50] The orange is a symbol of equality. This equality, exemplified by the hookup between the two men ends with "a mutual exchange of pleasure." Even though there is a domineering/dominated relationship reflected in the spatial placement of the characters, it turns out that the pleasure shared by the two men is not defined by a ratio of power, of dominance, but is on the same level, an equality in the shared pleasure.

CONCLUSION

L'armée du salut offers an insight into what the newer generation of Moroccan authors, most of them living in France, seek to promulgate: a new definition of the individual that pays heed to the heteronormative norms imposed by Moroccan society. Throughout the novel, it appears that movement is the cornerstone of the definition of this new identity. This chapter has shown how movement exists in several forms in Taïa's *L'armée du salut*. Its most obvious representation is geographic; the characters move across Morocco and Switzerland, and within the confines of these countries or specific cities. This geographical displacement allows the different characters, and more specifically Abdellah, to define themselves as individuals before a society that does not understand or accept them. This geographical displacement is the key to escape the cultural, political, and social restraints of the different countries, as it cannot be contained. This self-definition relies first and foremost on a fluid sexuality that is almost multiple. In several instances, the passages in which sexuality is depicted include more than two characters. This fusion of beings allows the characters to define themselves and gives Abdellah a chance to start his own army, potentially his chosen family. Finally, movement is also temporal, with the constant back and forth between the stories in Morocco, that constitute the past of the novel, and Geneva, the present of the novel. This back-and-forth sheds light on the evolution of the character of Abdellah, revealing a definite growth between his life in Morocco and the beginning of his European life. Motion is a permanent feature of the novel and appears as the only way for individuals to define themselves opposite a normative society. However, it seems that at the end of the novel, Abdellah still does not know how to define himself; and Taïa, the author, does not offer a definite conclusion to the reader. This approach allows for the establishment of a fluid queer Moroccan Francophone character by presenting clues that establish the basis of this emerging identity.

NOTES

1. William Turner, *A Genealogy of Queer Theory* (Philadelphia: Temple University Press, 2000), 35.

2. For example, see among others, Inger Boer, *After Orientalism: Critical Entanglements, Productive Looks* (Amsterdam: Rodopi, 2003); Sam Bourcier, *Queers Zones, La trilogie* (Amsterdam: Editions Amsterdam, 2018); Mehammed Amadeus Mack, *Sexagon: Muslims, France, and the Sexualization of National Culture* (New York: Fordham University Press, 2017); and Denis M. Provencher, *Queer Maghrebi*

French: Language, Temporalities, Transfiliations (Liverpool: Liverpool University Press, 2017).

3. Mack, *Sexagon*, 256.

4. Michael S. Kimmel and Amy Aronson, *Men and Masculinities: A Social, Cultural, and Historical Encyclopedia* (Santa Barbara: ABC-CLIO, 2004), xi.

5. R. W. Connell, *Masculinities* (Stanford: University of California, 2005), 69.

6. Åshild Lappegard Hauge, "Identity and Place: A Critical Comparison of Three Identity Theories," *Architectural Science Review* 50, no. 1 (2007): 47.

7. This fascination for the *cité* (project housing) and for young French men of North-African descent resulted in the creation of an adult website, citebeur.com. Most scenes are filmed in the cellars of the project buildings of the suburbs.

8. See Joseph A. Boone, "Vacation Cruises; Or, the Homoerotics of Orientalism," *PMLA* 110, no. 1 (1995): 89–107, and *The Homoerotics of Orientalism* (New York: Columbia University Press, 2015).

9. Mack, *Sexagon*, 134.

10. Philippe Gasparini, *Est-Il Je? Roman autobiographique et autofiction* (Paris: Seuil, 2004), 160.

11. See Ilham Mellouki, "La Génération du je," *TelQuel* n.d. (2007): 10.

12. Gérard Genette, *Nouveau discours du récit* (Paris: Seuil, 1983).

13. Abdellah Taïa, *L'armée du salut* (Paris: Seuil, 2006), 15. All English translations come from the 2009 Semiotext(e) translation of the novel [15].

14. Taïa, *L'armée du salut*, 27; [27].

15. Taïa, *L'armée du salut*, 40; [37–38].

16. For masculinity as a fluid concept see among others R.W. Connell, *Masculinities* (Stanford: University of California Press, 2008); Jack Halberstam, *In a Queer Time and Place* (New York: New York University Press, 2005); and Michael Kimmel *Misframing Men: The Politics of Contemporary Masculinities* (New Brunswick: Rutgers University Press, 2010). For Arab masculinities, see Abdessamad Dialmy, "La Masculinité au Maroc: entre traditions, modernité et intégrismes," in *Masculinities in Contemporary Africa* (Dakar: CODESRIA, 2008), and Gibson Ncube, "Arab-Muslim Masculinity on Trial: Gay Muslim Writers Broaching Homosexuality," *Gender Forum* 47 (2014): 50–63.

17. Nadia Tazi, "Le Désert Perpétuel: Visages de la Virilité au Maghreb," in *La Virilité en Islam*, edited by Fethi Benslama (La Tour-d'Aigues: L'Aube, 1998), 44. My translation.

18. Abdessamad Dialmy. "La Masculinité au Maroc: Entre traditions, modernité et intégrismes," in *Masculinities in Contemporary Africa,* edited by Egodi Uchendun (Dakar: CODESRIA, 2008), 73–87.

19. Osire Glacier, *Femininity, Masculinity, and Sexuality in Morocco and Hollywood: The Negated Sex* (New York: Palgrave Macmillan, 2017), 80.

20. Taïa, *L'armée du salut*, 36; [35].

21. Taïa, *L'armée du salut*, 51; [47].

22. Taïa, *L'armée du salut*, 34; [33].

23. Taïa, *L'armée du salut*, 66; [60].

24. See Chantal Tetreault, *Transcultural Teens: Performing Youth Identities in French Cités* (Hoboken: John Wiley and Sons, 2015) in which she discusses at length how North African youth do not speak Arabic but incorporate some Arabic terms into their French.

25. Taïa, *L'armée du salut*, 61; [56].

26. Taïa, *L'armée du salut*, 81; [75].

27. See Boone, "Vacation Cruises; Or, the Homoerotics of Orientalism"; and Jarrod Hayes, *Queer Nations: Marginal Sexualities in the Maghreb* (Chicago: University of Chicago Press, 2000).

28. Taïa, *L'armée du salut*, 84; [78].

29. Tzvetan Todorov analyzes at length the works of Pierre Loti and how his travel narratives shaped France's visions of exoticism in *Nous et les autres: La réflexion française sur la diversité humaine* (Paris: Seuil, 1989), 348–364. It is also to be noted that the original meaning of exotic, before it changed in the nineteenth century, just meant foreign. (Dictionnaire Littré+: http://littre.reverso.net/dictionnaire-francais/definition/exotique).

30. Per Buvik, *L'exotisme, L'exotique, L'étranger: Actes du colloque tenu à la Maison des sciences de l'homme à Paris à l'initiative du Centre de coopération franco-norvégienne en sciences sociales et humaines, le 3 juin 2004* (Paris : Kailash, 2006), 11. My translation.

31. Taïa, *L'armée du salut*, 108; [100].

32. Taïa, *L'armée du salut*, 107–108; [100].

33. Todorov, *Nous et les autres; La réflexion française sur la diversité humaine*, 391.

34. Silke Segler-Messner, *Voyages à l'envers: Formes et figures de l'exotisme dans les littératures post-coloniales francophones* (Strasbourg: Presses universitaires de Strasbourg, 2009), 5.

35. Taïa, *L'armée du salut*, 98; [98].

36. Segler-Messner, *Voyages à l'envers*, 6. My translation.

37. Taïa, *L'armée du salut*, 105; [97].

38. Taïa, *L'armée du salut*, 106; [98].

39. Taïa, *L'armée du salut*, 107; [98].

40. Taïa, *L'armée du salut*, 107; [99].

41. Taïa, *L'armée du salut*, 107; [99].

42. Taïa, *L'armée du salut*, 108; [99–100].

43. Rosello Mireille, "The National-Sexual: From the Fear of Ghettoes to the Banalization of Queer Practices," in *Articulations of Difference: Gender Studies and Writing in French*, edited by Dominique D. Fisher and Lawrence R. Schehr (Stanford, CA: Stanford University Press, 1997), 246.

44. Taïa, *L'armée du salut*, 148; [138].

45. Taïa, *L'armée du salut*, 148; [138].

46. Taïa, *L'armée du salut*, 76; [70].

47. Taïa, *L'armée du salut*, 95; [87].

48. Taïa, *L'armée du salut*, 154; [143].

49. Taïa, *L'armée du salut*, 131; [122].

50. Taïa, *L'armée du salut*, 132; [123].

BIBLIOGRAPHY

Boer, Inge E. *After Orientalism: Critical Entanglements, Productive Looks*. Amsterdam: Rodopi, 2003.

Boone, Joseph A. "Vacation Cruises; Or, the Homoerotics of Orientalism." *PMLA* 110, no. 1 (1995): 89–107.

——. *The Homoerotics of Orientalism*. New York: Columbia University Press, 2015.

Bourcier, Sam, and Paul B. Preciado. *Queer Zones: La Trilogie*. Paris: Éditions Amsterdam, 2018.

Buvik, Per. *L'exotisme, L'exotique, L'étranger: Actes du colloque tenu à la Maison des sciences de l'homme à Paris à ;'initiative du Centre de coopération franco-norvégienne en sciences sociales et humaines, le 3 juin 2004*. Paris: Kailash, 2006.

Cervulle, Maxime, and Nick Rees-Roberts. *Homo Exoticus: Race, classe et critique queer*. Paris: Colin, 2010.

Connell, R. W. *Masculinities*. 2nd edition. Berkeley: University of California Press, 2005.

Dialmy, Abdessamad. "La Masculinité au Maroc: Entre traditions, modernité et intégrismes." In *Masculinities in Contemporary Africa*, edited by Egodi Uchendu, 73–87. Dakar: Council for the Development of Economic and Social Research in Africa, 2008.

Gasparini, Philippe. *Est-Il Je?: Roman autobiographique et autofiction*. Paris: Seuil, 2005.

Genette Gérard. *Nouveau discours du récit*. Paris: Seuil, 1983.

Gibson, Ncube. "Arab-Muslim Masculinity on Trial: Gay Muslim Writers Broaching Homosexuality." *Gender Forum* 47 (2014): 50–63.

Glacier, Osire. *Femininity, Masculinity, and Sexuality in Morocco and Hollywood: The Negated Sex*. Basingstoke: Palgrave Macmillan, 2018.

Halberstam, Jack. *In a Queer Time and Place: Transgender Bodies, Subcultural Lives*. New York: New York University Press, 2005.

Hauge, Åshild Lappegard. "Identity and Place: A Critical Comparison of Three Identity Theories." *Architectural Science Review* 50, no. 1 (2007): 44–51.

Hayes, Jarrod. *Queer Nations: Marginal Sexualities in the Maghreb*. Chicago: University of Chicago Press, 2000.

Kimmel, Michael S. *Misframing Men:The Politics of Contemporary Masculinities*. New Brunswick: Rutgers University Press, 2010.

Mack, Mehammed Amadeus. *Sexagon: Muslims, France, and the Sexualization of National Culture*. New York: Fordham University Press, 2016.

Mellouki, Ilham. "La Génération du je." *TelQuel* n.d. (2007): 10.

Provencher, Denis M. *Queer Maghrebi French: Language, Temporalities, Transfiliations*. Liverpool: Liverpool University Press, 2017.

Rosello, Mireille. "The National-Sexual: From the Fear of Ghettoes to the Banalization of Queer Practices." In *Articulations of Difference: Gender Studies and Writing in French*, edited by Dominique D. Fisher and Lawrence R. Schehr, 246–271. Stanford: Stanford University Press, 1997.

Segler-Messner, Silke. *Voyages à l'envers: Formes et figures de l'exotisme dans les littératures post-coloniales francophones*. Strasbourg: Presses universitaires de Strasbourg, 2009.

Taïa, Abdellah. *L'armée du salut*. Paris: Éditions du Seuil, 2006.

———. *Salvation Army*. Translated by Frank Stock. Los Angeles: Semiotext(e), 2009.

Tazi, Nadia. "Le Désert perpétuel: Visages de la virilité au Maghreb." In *La virilité en Islam*, edited by Fethi Benslama and Nadia Tazi, 27–58. La Tour-d'Aigues: L'Aube, 2004.

Tetreault, Chantal. *Transcultural Teens: Performing Youth Identities in French Cités*. Hoboken: John Wiley & Sons, 2015.

Todorov, Tzvetan. *Nous et les autres: La réflexion française sur la diversité humaine*. Paris: Seuil, 1989.

Turner, William B. *A Genealogy of Queer Theory*. Philadelphia: Temple University Press, 2000.

Chapter 3

Marginal Masculinities

Disidentifying Sexual Performativity across Abdellah Taïa's Novels

Daniel N. Maroun

Interpreting the various representations of queer sexuality across the greater corpus of Abdellah Taïa's novels involves uncovering subtle expressions of gender performativity in Moroccan culture. In the aforementioned quote from *L'armée du salut* [*Salvation Army*] (2006), the narrator anchors his notion of masculinity in normative performances: a notion from which he will ultimately deviate in this novel. This chapter uncovers how the author constructs narratives of masculinities across his greater corpus of texts. It argues that the evolution of queer sexualities, that is to say nonnormative positions regarding sexuality, in his works is one that is embedded in the concept of "disidentification"—that masculinity *à la Taïa* is always depicted, constructed, and assumed via the collision between "cultural logics of heteronormativity"[1] and queer iterations of Moroccan masculinity. To expand upon this, I suggest a new approach by first, showcasing how Taïa's works negotiate with and dismantle discourses on Moroccan patriarchy; and second, how these new performativities of queer sexuality uniquely occur in liminal spaces within the novels. This subversive act affords "new social formations" of Moroccan masculinities since their liminality rejects heteronormativity and demarks a zone for "productive spaces of hybridization," i.e., Moroccan, queer, and now masculine.[2]

Taïa's first texts are narratively reflective; texts whose aim is to recount to the audience how the protagonist of the novel came to "today," the present reading of the novel. *L'armée du salut, Une mélancolie arabe* [*An Arab Melancholia*] (2008), *Lettres à un jeune marocain* [*Letters to a Young Moroccan*] (2009), and even *Le jour du Roi* [*The Day of the King*] (2010), are examples of texts where the protagonist navigates various sociocultural restraints in an effort to construct a space for queer (homo)sexualities. This structure is opposed to Taïa's more recent novels, which highlight a continual presence of queerness. In *Celui digne d'être aimé* [*The One Worthy of Being Loved*] (2017) and *La vie lente* [*The Slow Life*] (2019), protagonists offer retrospective accounts of their lives affording the reader an opportunity to examine the intersection of Moroccanness, masculinity, and homosexuality from a presence and a posteriority. The composition of this division is not simply chronological, but just so happens to follow how the author begins to nuance how his characters engage with social expectations of sexuality and the clandestine sexual underbelly of homosexuality in Moroccan society, space, and geography. I divide these works into two sections: one in which there is either a prominent autofictive *je* and/or a clear trajectory of the protagonist moving *towards* a nonnormative identification; and a second where the shared common trait is a presence of a homosexual identity from the start of the novel. These more recent texts nuance life as a homosexual Moroccan, now, as opposed to earlier texts that carry the reader alongside a journey of queer discovery. At the heart of this chapter is a thorough examination of performative nonnormative masculinities in liminal spaces within Taïa's oeuvre.

These performances of Moroccan masculinities will draw upon the Butlerian notion that gender is performative. Judith Butler specifies "that gender is produced as a ritualized repetition of conventions, and that this ritual is socially compelled in part by the force of a compulsory heterosexuality."[3] Butler makes a distinction between performance and performativity that is critical to our understanding of how Taïa's protagonists *act*: a performance assumes an actor who acts either along the ritualized conventions of gender or against them; performativity is an act that constitutes the subject through public, repetitious rituals. The distinction is significant because both concepts, performance and performativity, are phenomenological. I thus propose a more focused examination of masculine performativity solely in the liminal spaces. His rejection of a compulsory Moroccan heterosexuality becomes a specific performance of what gender is for the author—a true disidentification which, according to Muñoz, is a "performative mode" that the minoritarian subject employs "in an effort to resist the oppressive and normalizing discourse of dominant ideology."[4] This unique interpretation differs from others because it will not simply underline how the queer is a rejection of sociocultural norms; instead, it will interrogate how the queer assumes and reappropriates the norm to define what queer Maghrebi masculinity is, a subversive act against Moroccan heteronormativity that ultimately manifests itself in liminal/border spaces. This framework scaffolds a distinctive look at the continuum of masculinity and its expression across Taïa's novels, giving readers an opportunity to better understand the politics at play concerning Moroccan sexual citizenship. The notion of sexual citizenship is a distinct, interpretive strategy that aids in bridging the public and private spheres—two disparate entities in Moroccan culture.[5] The term has come to express the socio-political implications that expressions of sexuality can have as they collide, affording marginalized sexualities the ability to confront the public with the private; a strong concept to confer how Taïa constructs a homosexual iteration of Moroccan masculinity.

DISIDENTIFYING FROM THE MOROCCAN MAN

The structures of performativity inside Taïa's novels appear to be fixed owing to sociocultural restraints he seeks to combat. Yet in *Disidentification,* José Esteban Muñoz claims that cultural producers "must negotiate between a fixed identity disposition and the socially encoded roles that are available for such subjects."[6] If we consider this in the context of Taïa's work, such fixed identities are pinned to patriarchal producers and by dismantling these structures, authors like Taïa rewrite the foundation of masculinity. This chapter explores said notion through three figures: the father, the king, and the brother. The continual erasure of cultural patriarchy across *L'armée du salut*, *La mélancolie arabe*, and *Le jour du Roi* and even his later novels *Infidèles* [*Infidels*] (2012) and *Celui qui est digne d'être aimé* is an important factor when considering transgressive sexualities like homosexuality and homosexual acts in Morocco. The patriarchy is analogous to normativity; it is the proposed constant against which deviant behavior is being compared and evaluated. By disassembling the various structures or processes that keep the father in power, Taïa renders the virile subject impotent. These processes will be examined at various stages in this chapter: dismantling the father as a symbol of the patriarchy, dismantling the family as a structure of support to the patriarchy, and finally dismantling the patriarchy as a social structure that relegates homosexuality in Morocco to liminal, private spaces.

In a recent public reading of a self-addressed letter, the author Abdellah Taïa retrospectively examines his past and his family. He starts: "Cher petit Abdellah, Je m'adresse à toi, à moi il y a longtemps" [Dear little Abdellah, I am writing to you, to me, a long time ago].[7] The letter is an opportunity for readers to witness how, thematically, the family unit remains a transformative figure in Taïa's literary universe and moreover, that the father is still a figure of continual conflict: "Et puis: ce père présent absent [. . .] un homme autrement homme" [And this absent father . . . a man who was a man in other ways].[8] His use of "autrement" underlines how his father was non-conforming to Moroccan masculine standards. This recent letter resonates with Taïa's epistolary text in *Lettres à un jeune marocain* where the author writes to his nephew Adnane. The author discusses his father, Adnane's grandfather, and his progressive erasure from the family: "Je ne retrouve plus l'image de ce père, sa présence, sa trace" [I can no longer remember his face, his presence, or any memory of him].[9] For Taïa, the father has never been an anchor off of whom to project a performance of Moroccan masculinity. He laments his father's death, stating "Je voulais par mes paroles le ressusciter" [I wanted to bring him back with my words],[10] for his presence was another nonnormative performance.

Some argue this could be seen as a type of mourning. Jean-Pierre Boulé articulately argues in favor of such a mourning when analyzing Taïa's reaction to his own father's death in *Lettres à un jeune marocain*, claiming that his discussion of the father is "a powerful desire to mourn and to reinstate the father," as a patriarchal figure in the protagonist's life.[11] I'd add that this mourning can also be conceived as a longing for—an attempt to reestablish a lineage, *une parenté* where the French notion of *filiation* plays an important role. Denis Provencher maintains that this type of communication—longing/remembering the parental past, is an act of transfiliation, but in reverse; one in which the progeny transmits back to the previous generation, flipping the teleological goal of transgenerational knowledge transmission.[12] These actors in the novel would then be reconstructing the father or father figure. However, as I suggested above, we should extrapolate this argument further, contending that Taïa's act of (re)writing his father is indeed an act of transfiliation, but it is one that is also transmitted to the reader, and again, in tandem with Provencher's argument. The reader becomes a generational offspring receiving a rewritten history of the father sharing in a communal mourning, as Muñoz would contend, where the readers are collective fragments mourning the loss of their whole.[13]

Patriarchy is a vital social structure in the understanding of queer masculinity in Taïa's works because the author needs to render its social power impotent in order for queer iterations of Moroccan masculinity to be legitimized. It is important to recall that Taïa disassembles the power of the father through various phases: subverting his leadership, the patriarchal structure of the family, and of society. Queer narratives, like Taïa's, are aptly positioned to break down the "compulsory heterosexuality" that is "inseparable from national identity" because their testimony showcases the "heterogeneous Nation,"[14] refusing the King, patriarchy, and heterosexual power over a homogenous state. To further understand this claim, we should first look at *Le jour du Roi*, which opens with a reverie-turned-nightmare sequence of the protagonist meeting the king, Hassan II. The novel's plot centers on two best friends, Khalid and Omar who share a strong bond as friends and adolescent lovers.[15] The duality of these two protagonists mirrors the intertwined dualities of Moroccan culture: rich vs. poor; successful vs. unsuccessful; and ultimately, "good" Muslim (i.e., heterosexual) vs. "bad" Muslim since wealth affords one access to structures that make said person successful. The opening passage of this novel is an important exposition of the ultimate figure of the patriarchy (after God)—the king, the guide of all believers. By undermining his power and his legitimacy, Taïa is destabilizing a powerful patriarchal figure in Moroccan culture. The dream starts with Omar being honored with the privilege of kissing the king's hand as obliged of any good Moroccan, a custom extended to parents and grandparents as well as a sign of respect.[16] The dream quickly transforms, however, as it turns from a pleasant interaction into an interrogation. The king innocently asks, "Comment je m'appelle?" [What's my name?] to which Omar replies, "Hassan II . . . Le roi Hassan II du Maroc" [Hassan II . . . King Hassan II of Morocco].[17] By naming the king, Omar is recognizing his power, his divine right of father to all, and rightful heir to the previous king, Mohammed V. The answer is unfortunately unsatisfactory for the king who then replies: "Non. Mon nom de famille? Quel est mon nom de famille?" [No, my last name? What's my last name?].[18] Naming someone gives them subjectivity, and individuality, realness in the Symbolic Order, which Omar is denying by not knowing/saying the king's last name.[19]

The insistence on a family name echoes Provencher's previous claim on reverse transfiliation in that by naming him, Omar legitimizes his reign as king and his role as metaphorical father to all. But Omar is not able to think of his name remaining "muet" [speechless][20] under pressure, which continues to mount as the king persistently demands, "Mon nom de famille? Vite, vite . . . mon nom de famille?" [What's my last name? Come on, come on . . . my last name?].[21] The deafening silence from Omar creates panic in the king who turns violent as he tries to kill the proverbial existential threat whose ignorance is denying him, the king, his patriarchal power. His lack of knowledge can be interpreted as simple ignorance but additionally, it underlines the social disparities and class differences since Omar, being poor, would not likely have said knowledge nor any sort of filiation with the king that a lot of affluent families do. After this exchange, Omar faints but is awoken by whispers of a female voice suggesting that he approach the king, his father: "C'est comme ton père. C'est ton père" [He's like your father. He is your father].[22] The semi-repetitious phrasing has a stark semantic difference. The lack of simile and use of the linking verb *être* [to be] in the second iteration emphasizes just how much the king is meant to be the cultural and religious father of all of Morocco. Recognition of his power is the king's most valuable patriarchal item and as a consequence, negating it disrupts the entire hegemonic and heteronormative masculine rule. With his symbolic power neutered, Taïa has created a literary space permitting various forms of same-sex desire, for masculinity in Morocco is in part linked to the construction of the family unit through marriage.[23] The king is the father of a Moroccan family, refusing his name is in fact repudiating his paternal role over his subjects. Omar does just that, shouting back, "Non, non il n'est pas mon père. Le Roi n'est pas mon père" [No, no he is not my father. The King is not my father].[24] The king has fallen, and his kingdom is troubled. By erasing the socio-sexual and cultural dominance of the king, Taïa is attempting to strip the social structure of its power.

The king represents a macro-cultural issue of paternity; however, a tertiary look across Taïa's novels affords a microcosmic glance at the family unit and the fading importance of the father figure predominantly erased by a maternal presence. In *Lettres à un jeune marocain*, Abdellah recounts to his nephew how his father dies, alone, isolated from the family for fear of spreading an unspecified infectious disease, a possible metaphor for his failed masculinity. This isolation, in Abdellah's eyes, causes his death because it represents how the father is quite literally, spatially cut off from the rest of the family. This theme of separating the father from his family (see *Celui qui est digne*, as well as *L'armée du salut*) is analogous to the tree cutting scene in *Infidèles*[25] where the protagonist Jallal discusses watching a tree fall as it is cut down—a poignant metaphor but also a scene that, as Siham Bouamer notes, is rich in familial unbuilding and queer familial rebuilding.[26] In *Le jour du Roi*, Omar's mother abandons the family causing his father to search endlessly becoming a defunct paternal figure, "[la]déchéance d'un homme," [the decline of a man][27] supplanted by his son who asserts, "Aujourd'hui c'est moi l'homme" [Today I am the man].[28] The father figure continues to be attacked in *Celui qui est digne d'être aimé*, an epistolary novel where the protagonist Ahmed, posthumously writes to his mother. Ahmed explains to her how after the father's death, she erased his existence: "tout reprendre, tout réécrire" [Took it all back, rewrote it all],[29] imposing her own tyrannical rule over the family and even when he was alive, he "cesser d'être homme" [stopped being a man][30] making his presence meaningless to the family. Analogous to *Le jour du Roi*, Ahmed in *Celui qui est digne* resents his father for even loving the mother, "J'avais honte alors. Je ne pouvais plus le voir, le considérer comme mon père" [I was ashamed. I couldn't bear to see him anymore, to even consider him as my father].[31] Finally, in an additional non-autofictional text, *Un pays pour mourir* [*A Country for Dying*] (2015), the reader observes the same motif—a fallen father, lacking any exemplary masculine qualities: "Ce père déchu, sans virilité" [This fallen father, with no virility][32] and even later, "J'oublie mon père" [I have forgotten my father][33] signifying a final blow to the paternal figure. By undermining paternity, Taïa discursively lays out what queer masculinity looks like—one that dis-identifies with the father and makes no reference to him. His texts testify to the sterilization of the father in the family, the family as patriarchy's weapon to power, and patriarchy as a social structure, thus enabling a textual queer space for Moroccan homosexual masculinities to be performed.

In fact, the only referent against which Taïa posits his protagonists is an older brother—the next paternal figure—both figuratively and legally. In *Celui qui est digne d'être aimé*, it's his older brother Slimane whom their mother simply adores, writing: "Ton fils aîné, Slimane, nous dépassait tous dans ton cœur" [Your eldest son, Slimane, he was by far the favorite in your heart],[34] but his reign ultimately comes to an end as Ahmed continues in his letter, "Dès que tu es morte, la révolte contre lui a commencé" [As soon as you died, the rebellion against him started].[35] His use of rebellion marks the figurative battle he is launching against patriarchal power with the last remnant of heteronormative Moroccanness. The author even discusses his real brother in a recent letter on Radio Télévision Belge Francophone, writing, "une odeur qui t'attire, une moustache, celle de ton frère, qui te fait fantasmer et qui te pousse à dire: je veux être comme lui" [a smell that attracts you, a mustache, that of your brother's for whom you're wild and who pushes you to say: I want to be like him].[36] This letter from 2020 corresponds to the 2006 text *L'armée du salut*.[37] In this novel, just like in his letter, the narrator sings his brother's praises as the true male referent: "Abdelkébir a 30 ans. C'est un homme" [Abdelkébir is 30 years old. He is a man now];[38] it is almost impossible for him to describe, venerating his status of a man to a Lacanian symbolic order: "Homme: je ne sais pas comment le décrire autrement" [A man: I don't know how to describe it any other way].[39] There is nothing queer about his brother; he is symbolic of a heteronormative ideology that permeates Moroccan culture—something Abdellah appears to long for in some sort of false ceremonial attempt at discovering a masculinity by consuming it: "Même le sperme de mon frère je le connaissais. Je le touchais, je l'étudiais, je le reniflais. J'ai même failli une fois le bouffer" [I even knew my brother's sperm. I would touch it, study it, smell it. I almost even ate it once].[40] His brother's ejaculate is symbolic of fatherhood so to consume it can be viewed as an attempt at becoming a man. However, its consumption would be through an incestuously homoerotic act, far from heteronormative and thus queer. I argue thus that since the brother remains in this literary world, Taïa has to deny his performance of masculinity, one cemented in heterosexuality: "Je renonçais à devenir cette sorte d'homme" [I refused to become that type of man],[41] thereby illegitimating his power in the eyes of the protagonist. Abdelkébir remains a benchmark against which heteronormativity is posited and frames masculinity for Abdellah, one that he ultimately expunges from the novel as the former marries off and abandons the family.

This discussion of the Moroccan family unit in Taïa's narratives foregrounds the need for him to reject these norms, undermine said norms' authority, and thus give way to new performances of what Moroccan masculinity can look like. The dismissal of these socio-sexual constructs gives power to new performances of masculinity that we will discover in liminal spaces using Muñoz's concepts I underlined earlier. Therefore, where these performances occur is equally important as we discover how transgressive sexualities find a place in the textual world of Taïa's narrative.

SEX AND THE CITY: CONTACT ZONES AND PERFORMATIVE SEXUALITY

At the heart of Taïa's representation of sexuality is a complex and entangled use of space in so much that an investigation into the locus of sex acts reveals unique sexual performances. For much of Taïa's earlier novels, sex acts are relegated to concealed spaces. *L'armée du salut* opens with Abdellah narrating to the reader his parent's equally violent and passionate sex consigned to his father's bedroom.[42] In the same novel, Abdellah would sneak into his brother's bedroom and find the latter's stained underwear concluding he masturbated.[43] While on vacation in Tangiers, Abdellah is invited to watch a movie at the local cinema with a stranger, Salim, where Abdellah ends up losing his virginity, off screen.[44] Even at the conclusion of the novel, this time in Belgium, Abdellah is approached by a stranger who leads him into a public restroom (*les pissotières*) where men are engaging in reciprocal sexual exchanges. Abdellah remarks, "Ils vivaient dans ce lieu souterrain et sale une sexualité clandestine et publique à la fois" [They were living out a clandestine and public sexuality in this subterranean and dirty place];[45] here the use of the clandestine echoes the privacy of queer sexual acts in the novel and the private solicits the antithesis of what public bathrooms represent. However, the reader is positioned voyeuristically, in an inbetweenness that echoes how these sex acts are depicted—presumed "hidden" from others but meant to be "viewed" by the reader. A similar bathroom scene appears in *La vie lente* as Mounir follows Antoine into a secluded bathroom at the Louvre, away from any visitors. Isolated, the two briefly, but intensely, share a sexual exchange that only the reader witnesses, in private.

The reader is the sole witness to most of these acts, a telescopic voyeur, suggesting that Taïa positions the reader in a sort of inbetweenness so that he can introduce newer depictions of Moroccan masculinity and queerness. Take for example the rape scene in *Une mélancolie arabe*, where the gang of adolescents forces Abdellah back to his home, sequestering him on an empty second floor with nothing but a "grand lit tout neuf" [a large new bed].[46] In *Le jour du Roi* Omar and Khalid share the same bed, away from parental supervision, "J'ai éteint la lampe, et je l'ai rejoint dans le petit lit vert" [I joined him in his little green bed].[47] Even in his recent novel, *Celui qui est digne d'être aimé*, Ahmed leaves his verbally abusive lover, writing him from the bedroom as they sleep: "Ma décision est prise. Cette nuit, dans le lit à côté de toi, j'ai vu clair [. . .] Je sors de toi" [I made up my mind. Tonight, in bed next to you, I saw clearly [. . .] I am leaving you].[48] These aforementioned examples of same-sex performativity are relegated to a private space, something detached but viewable to the reader—much like the train car sex scene in *L'armée du salut*. He reinscribes same-sex desire into a symbolic familial space—the bedroom. Such a tendency is reminiscent of Foucault's analysis of Victorian sexuality where sex acts outside of the bedroom are coded as abnormal. Taïa juxtaposes his bedroom acts with public, but hidden displays (bathrooms and cinemas). A focus on the bedroom keeps queer performativity private throughout a majority of his novels following religious precepts of Moroccan society. He reappropriates a coded heteronormative space—the bedroom—to queer its use and to legitimize his sexuality all the while still giving space to transgressive acts in public, albeit hidden, spaces.

Taïa's most recent novel, *La vie lente,* stands out in this respect of productive space of queer sexualities. It is in this novel that he moves performances of masculinity and same-sex relations to the border—the "where" of the sex act, its performance is shifting. Sex acts on the border itself are rather interesting to note because one has to interrogate what the border between two objects represents and delineates. Furthermore, in Taïa's narratives, it is not simply what is happening on one side of the border versus the other side, rather it is actually what is happening as one crosses the border. Queer masculinity, its performativity, is consigned to the borderland in particular when one takes into account Michel de Certeau's concept of the border: "À qui appartient-elle? Le fleuve, le mur, l'arbre fait frontière. Il n'a pas le caractère de non-lieu que la trace cartographique suppose à la limite. *Il a le rôle médiateur*" [Who does it belong to ? The River, the wall, the tree are all boarders. It does not have the quality of a non-place that cartographic representation presupposes][49] (emphasis my own). This privileges the transit, that area between the two borders,[50] because that area will ultimately become a non-place, a neologism coined by Marc Augé who contends certain spaces are relational, ahistorical, concerned with anonymity void of hierarchy.[51] It becomes a fascinating take when looking at Taïa's more recent novel in which the protagonist memorializes two different sex acts on mobile borders. The narrator recounts an adolescent story of his trip on a bus from Rabat, Morocco's capital—the location of the King's residence, a symbol of economic and social success, of capitalism, normativity, and coloniality—back to his home village of Salé. Even the character, Mounir, represents this dichotomy as the narrator self-describes as "petit, maigre" [small and frail] while his big-city lover whom he names Soufiane, is "grand et en très bonne forme" [tall and in good shape],[52] even later describing him "Il a l'air d'un homme éduqué. Il travaille au ministère." [He seems well educated. He works for the ministry].[53] The contrast is key because it emphasizes the importance of the transient border space, the area between that allows the two worlds to collide but also for the transgressive act to occur with no social consequence, that is, Mounir is not *le pédé du quartier* [neighborhood fag] in this moment on this bus and Soufiane does not lose his heterosexual allure to a public audience either. In fact, it is important to note that the border is a space that cannot be permanently inhabited. One can pass through it, as Mounir and Soufiane do on the bus, but one does not remain on it.

Mounir recounts, "Tout au long du trajet, l'homme n'avait cessé de se rapprocher de moi, de se coller à moi" [All along the route, this man did not stop approaching me, rubbing up against me].[54] This *trajet* sticks out to the reader as we are no longer confined to either side of Moroccan culture: Rabat as the patriarchally tied heteronormative space; Salé as the pitiable village where Mounir lives; but rather in a sort of non-place that is neither public nor private, but simply in-between. This mobile borderland affords the protagonist an opportunity to further explore his masculine performativity. It calls to mind Muñoz's concept that a postcolonial space permits new social formations of hybridity because of its liminality.[55] In fact, the transgressive act truly starts at the last stop leaving Rabat for Salé: "Au dernier arrêt, à Rabat, avant de commencer la descente vers chez nous, la ville de Salé, d'autres passagers sont montés. On a tous été poussés au fond du bus [. . .] Il était derrière moi. Contre moi. Dans mon dos" [At the last stop in Rabat, before we started to head down towards my house, in Salé, more passengers boarded. We all squished bunched up towards the back [. . .] he was behind me. Against me. Up against my back].[56] The notion of marginality reappears even on the bus as Mounir is pushed all the way back, but this time with those individuals from Rabat, a reverse hierarchy takes root as we enter the liminal space of the border. As the reader leaves Rabat with the protagonist, we enter a neutral space, a non-place as Augé would attest, where everyone is anonymous on the bus.[57] This anonymity, this lack of cultural impetus from either side—Salé, Rabat—offers a space in the de Certeauian fashion of a "lieu pratiqué" [practiced place][58] but also a productive space of "hybridization where complex and ambivalent" Moroccan sexual identities are produced" to bring Muñoz's concept of disidentification back into the fold.[59]

The concept of anonymity that a non-place affords its inhabitants is crucial here because one could argue that this sex act is public due to it being on the bus, in front of individuals but even the narrator remarks how the other riders never notice a thing: "Les passagers apparemment ne remarquaient toujours rien" [The passengers apparently did not notice anything].[60] The reader's voyeurism bears witness to the socially transgressive sex act, but society (on the bus) does not. As stated earlier, the flirting only starts as they leave Rabat for Salé while in transit. The transgressive, sexual act starts as they officially cross over the delineation between Rabat and Salé—the Bou Regreg river: "Dès qu'on a eu traversé le fleuve Bouregreg et qu'on a été de côté de Salé, chez nous, l'homme est redevenu sexuel" [As soon as we crossed over the Bou Regreg River and were in Salé, my neighborhood, the guy became sexual again].[61] The river can be read as an additional symbol of fluidity, non-conformity that promotes queer performances of marginal masculinities especially after they travel across it.

Their foreplay continues until the older gentleman climaxes—here again the socially transgressive act occurs while the bus is moving from one stop to another, a true Augian nonplace. But this ends as the former descends off the bus, getting off at "La Victoire," a possible metaphoric indication of Mounir's successful performative act of queer sexuality in a transient productive space. As Soufiane descends from the bus, Mounir remains. This distance gives Mounir a new perspective, one that allows him to rediscover that this gentleman is not similar to his conceived image: "Il est plus grand que je pensais [. . .] Je l'avais imaginé physiquement proche des gens comme moi. Pas trop sophistiqué" [He was bigger than I thought [. . .] I had imagined him physically closer in size to people like me. Not that classy].[62] The cleavage between them grows more as he continues, "C'est un autre homme. Bourgeois visiblement. Distingué. Cultivé. Intellectuel. Un immense tunnel soudain s'installe entre nous. Un abîme même [. . .] nous voilà étrangers" [He's a different type of guy, obviously bourgeois, refined, well-cultured, intellectual. A giant tunnel suddenly comes between the two of us, an abyss even [. . .] here we were, strangers again].[63] Taïa's imagery of the tunnel is useful for us to understand the importance of the in-between even more as on either side of it, queer performativity does not occur; but inside it, through it, it does since the tunnel connects two disparate spaces, i.e., Mounir and Soufiane.

Within Taïa's literary universe, the communal sex act can only occur on the bus between these two. Performativity is therefore relegated to this non-place. As a consequence, the reader observes that if queer masculine expression in the Moroccan context is to exist outside of these non-places, it will have to fight against the heteronormative framework of the patriarchy. Viewed as a threat to the patriarchy's hegemony, homosexuality is often denoted as feminine.[64] Moreover, this appellation of homosexual as female becomes a common trope denoting that queer Moroccan masculinity is an act, a performance.[65] Readers have likely noticed Zahira in *Un pays pour mourir* who explains, "J'étais un petit garçon. Je suis à présent une petite fille" [I was a little boy. I am now a little girl][66] and even more poignant is Omar in *Le jour du Roi* who emphasizes "Je ne suis ni garçon, ni fille. Je suis dans le désir" [I am neither a boy or a girl. I am in desire].[67] *Désir* becomes performativity. Queer Moroccan masculinity is not tied to the gender, it's tied to acts according to Omar. This is also why the border is interesting to study in Taïa's corpus because it is not on any particular side, it touches both. Omar's quote affirms the same principle, "ni garçon, ni fille," something in the middle that defines them but also reinforces their distance. The quote breaks away from a heteronormative tradition, which seeks to label males as either heterosexual, that is, "garçon" or homosexual, that is, "fille." For Taïa's characters, what counts is desire, "le moment du désir" [the moment of desire], a transformative place from which Taïa rewrites all of queer Moroccan sexuality reinvesting it into an action. This becomes increasingly important when discussing the duality of public vs. private and how it engages with the recognition of sexual orientation, which I propose is linked to place and space. Ultimately, Taïa is engaging in a historically queer act of resistance, much like Genet through both *Notre-Dame-des-Fleurs* [*Our Lady of the Flowers*] (1943) and *Journal du voleur* [*The Thief's Journal*] (1949) where the dynamic of public versus private aids in nuancing queer performativity.

Elaborating more on this concept of traveling on the border, the reader witnesses a similar trajectory in *L'armée du salut*, where Abdellah (protagonist) travels with his Swiss lover, Jean, from the beach in Salé to Rabat on a felucca.[68] Their entire trip is routed on this fluvial pathway and much like the voyage from Rabat to Salé via bus in *La vie lente*, nothing is said ("nous étions silencieux" [we remained quiet]), the only exchange is physical, further expanding upon this concept that the public displays of same-sex desire are confined to the border space not because of shame on the part of Taïa as an author but rather because this space affords queer representations of gender and same-sex desire to take place. The scene represents the common motif of colonizer and colonial subject since access to the felucca is behind a socioeconomic barrier that Abdellah, the poor Moroccan, would not have be able to afford without the intervention of his white, European lover Jean. The felucca remains a non-place that affords queer performativity a space, but we should not ignore the socio-economic implications it imposes as opposed to the bus from *La vie lente*. To exit, one has to cross over, into Rabat, or into Salé and thus succumb to cultural imposition on performativity. Both scenes of non-place sexual performativity put paramount importance on the actual traveling portion, the nomadic zig-zag trajectory the characters take in order to perform.

Such an idea becomes more evident when one reconsiders the bus scene from *La vie lente*. Mounir himself notes how this type of act should have never occurred for a myriad of reasons of which socioeconomics is at the forefront, "Que faisait-il dans le bus des pauvres?" [What was he doing on the poor people's bus?].[69] Soufiane likely takes advantage of his status to prey on poorer youth reinforcing a social hierarchy. Their worlds should not have collided, but they did through the obscurity provided by the bus as it traversed the border between Rabat and Salé. This scene becomes all the more important to the construction of the narrator's sexual identity because it reproduces itself, but with a shift, in Paris. Mounir meets Antoine, his supposed lover in *La vie lente*, on the metro system. The Parisian metro system is a mode of transportation that both the rich and the poor utilize (unlikely the apparent situation in Rabat/Salé where Soufiane's presence is odd); the Metro is socially syncretic. The protagonist arrives at Châtelet, one of Paris' biggest, most interconnected stops on the entire RATP (Parisian rail) system. This stop, its connections, lends to Deleuze and Guattari's concept of the rhizome because of the pathways it provides riders.[70] It permits users to connect to various *places*, each with distinct abilities of performativity. This rhizomatic effect affords more productive places for queer performativity as it transports users from the center to the periphery, through liminal space to manifest opportunities.

This rhizomatic effect of the RATP system is important as Mounir and his lover Antoine take the RER A line from the city center out to Nanterre, a suburb of Paris to the Northwest. On this "RER A bondé à l'heure de pointe" [RER line A, jam-packed at rush hour],[71] they share a sexually intimate moment similar to Mounir's earlier experience on the bus, albeit the social class difference is mute in this interaction. The occupancy of the RER car echoes earlier descriptions of the city bus being so packed no one is aware of any sexually transgressive act. Furthermore, it is only during the transit to the *banlieue*, that they act out this fantasy, "Quand le RER s'arrête à une station, Antoine se retire. Les portes se referment. Le train roule, prend de la vitesse. On se retrouve" [When the RER would stop, Antoine would pull away. The doors would close. The train would trug along gathering speed].[72] The RER is a transit border, a vacuum neither in nor out of the city during the actual transit moment. Brian Hunt elaborates on this concept when he states, "A border doesn't have to be traversed; it can be a passage, a border-as-bridge, that leads from one place of demarcation to another."[73] His argument underlines why the metro, during its movement between two stations, is a perfect place of performativity—it is liminal, a transition from one to the other offering space to hybrid performance as Muñoz would assert.

However, while in the city at a stop, their once anonymous act becomes more public. They arrive at Place Charles de Gaulle (still within the boundaries of Paris limits), get off to allow passengers to descend and then get back on. But they are separated upon reentry into the car. This is where the private becomes public as Mounir tells the reader, "Les passagers, étonnés et pris au dépourvu, lui font un chemin et le laissent venir jusqu'à moi" [The riders, surprised and caught off guard, cleared a path for him and let him come stand next to me].[74] They flirt and publicly display affection for one another, which is no longer left unnoticed within the confines of Paris: "Le monde autour de nous est un peu scandalisé. C'est visible. C'est palpable" [The world around us seems a bit horrified. You can tell. It's palpable].[75] Analogous to the Rabat vs. Salé juxtaposition from earlier where the sex act occurs out of the city (Rabat) on the journey home (Salé), these two characters are still within the city, not in route to the next stop. Antoine and Mounir are traveling toward the outskirts of the Parisian agglomeration. They lose their anonymity, and their performativity becomes public as other metro riders shout out: "Ce n'est pas un sauna gay ici. Un peu de tenue, les pédés" [This isn't a gay sauna. Get a hold of yourself, you faggots].[76] The vessel they ride affords them the prospect of manifesting a queer masculinity, one devoid of gender roles, but anchored in queer notions of reciprocity.[77]

I would argue that Taïa, as an author, attempts to confront this notion of transit and stagnation/ city vs. suburb. When Mounir writes, "Le monde c'est nous. Nous en public" [We are the world. Us, in public],[78] he links existence with public recognition. Taïa attempts to carve out a public display of queer Moroccan masculinity as he approaches the periphery. Admirers of his work should realize that this is a formative moment since queer expressions of Moroccan masculinity rest profoundly confined to the intimacy of the bedroom whether it's in the native Maghreb or in Europe albeit with different consequences. When these metro riders take note of Mounir and Antoine's intimacy, they render the act truly public. If Soufiane's act had been acknowledged on the bus back in Salé/Rabat, thus rendered public, the consequence would have been much more severe, the least of which is jail time. The contrast is stark, but the act of performance still occurs in transit. In the Parisian example, however, it is now made public because the reader is no longer a voyeur, but an additional rider on the metro watching. Nonetheless, Taïa's novel has finally written a performative act of gay Moroccanness into its story. The term gay is purposefully chosen as queer nomenclature is a choppy sea in particular with non-Western cultures. Taïa's novels tend to treat same-sex desire in phases: his early novels use *zamel* [fag] a stigmatized cultural world that feminizes the aspect of the male who is penetrated in Morocco. He later uses terms like *homosexuel* [homosexual] and even, although sparingly, the pejorative *pédé* [faggot]. However, it is not until this 2019 novel *La vie lente* that we notice the usage of "gay" and even here it is only used to describe Antoine[79] and not Mounir; or at most, the relationship between Mounir and Antoine.[80]

Mounir and Antoine then get off at Nanterre-Préfecture, they are outside the city limits, off the mobile border space and now on the periphery. They walk through the public park André-Malraux and later through the small *cité* Pablo-Picasso, named after the father of cubism. Malraux is known for his proto-existentialist philosophy; by walking through this park, we are forced to question the legitimacy of queer performativity. However, cubism is known as being a radical approach at representing reality and Mounir is bringing his gay lover, Antoine, into this space—Nanterre, lending to the idea that different realities can be expressed in this place than are permitted back in Paris—an interesting juxtaposition between the two philosophies. Mounir takes Antoine to his favorite bakery, La Clé du Paradis, run uniquely by women all wearing a veil of some sort. The reader's implicit bias concludes that they must all be Muslim and likely immigrant. More interesting is that the bakery is void of the masculine, where the profession of baker is traditionally coded male.[81] Consequently, this uniquely female bakery stands out to the reader due to the emphasis the author places on the abundance of female workers. This echoes earlier claims about the female presence (i.e., the mother) destroying patriarchal structures. Moreover, the *banlieue* is an important space as it is the only place in the novel that their relationship is recognized as "gay." More importantly, the recognition of their coupling comes from none other than the owner of the bakery, the metaphorical leader of this space: "Il n'y avait plus de doute pour la patronne, nous étions des gays, officiellement" [There wasn't any doubt left for the owner, we were officially a gay couple].[82] The comma plays an important grammatical role because, like all punctuations, it clarifies how we should read the sentence. The placement of the comma before "officiellement" suggests that they were and always have been gay; but through the recognition of their coupling by another party (*la patronne* [the boss]) in the *banlieue*, makes it official, or at least performs it into existence and being recognized temporarily queering the space. Taïa plays with the common trope of the *banlieue* and the "ever-present mother"[83] through the figure of the bakery owner who approves of Mounir as a gay Moroccan man living in Paris ambulating through the *banlieue*. The recognition is even more imperative when we take into account the socio-cultural context of the *banlieue* that refuses to negotiate with the identity politics of sexuality: "L'homosexualité, ça n'existe pas en banlieue" [Homosexuality, that doesn't exist here in the banlieue] to quote Houria Bouteldja, spokeswoman for *Les Indigènes de la République*, an anti-racist organization aligned with the political Left;[84] a comment Abdellah Taïa himself was aware of and commented upon.[85] His act of same-sex love recognition extra-muros is a purposeful performance by his protagonist.

Women play conflicting roles throughout Taïa's novels. There are those who are complicit in reinforcing patriarchal domination in Moroccan society like the female voice that wakes Omar during his reverie in *Le jour du Roi*, or the cancerous mother who privileged her eldest son in *Celui qui est digne* and embodied masculine traits of dominance. But there are those that also contribute to dismantling masculine hegemony or contribute to productive spaces of queer performativity like the bakery owner in Nanterre. Indeed, women hold special powers when useful for Taïa narrative goals. Sorcery and spells are conveniently enlisted to render typical male figures impotent both literally and figuratively, but the aforementioned example is one of the few times the only power employed is recognition.

Taïa's use of the banlieue in this scene allows for a performance of queerness because of how it permits Mounir an exploration of his own performative masculinity especially with Antoine. It is important to bring public recognition to the fore of this study because it will ultimately highlight the dyad of Morocco and Paris and how each interacts with queer protagonists. In *La vie lente*, Mounir laments his life to neighbor Madame Marty. His epistolary diatribe underlines how Moroccan culture constructs his gender identity:

> Je ne suis pas pédé. Je ne suis pas pédé. Ce n'est pas vrai ce qu'ils disent. Je suis quelqu'un de bien, mieux qu'eux. Pédé, c'est une insulte. C'est sale. Pédé, ça ne mène à rien. Pédé, ce n'est pas musulman et ce n'est pas correct. Ma mère me l'a dit. Mon père a confirmé. Même les violeurs de mon quartier au Maroc, après avoir joui à plusieurs reprises dans mes fesses, sont de cet avis. Tu n'es pas pédé, Mounir. Et nous non plus.
>
> [I am not a fag. I am not a fag. It's not true what they're saying. I am a good person, better than they are. Fag, that's an insult. It's dirty. Fag, that gets you nowhere. Fag, that isn't what a Muslim is, that isn't right. My mom told me so. My dad too. Even the rapists in my neighborhood in Morocco, after coming between my cheeks, were of the same opinion. You aren't a fag, Mounir, and neither are we.][86]

Notice how Mounir navigates the conundrum that man having sex with other men is not always *pédé*.[87] He is not putting a name to his actions and his performativity, rather he is simply performing. That is one of the hallmark traits of Taïa's depiction of queer identities—their performance. Indeed, this chapter has highlighted how Taïa's novels inscribe a place for performances of queer sexuality both in Morocco and in France, but recognition of this identity only occurs in France: "Je suis libre. À Paris et libre" [I am free. In Paris and free][88] and not in Morocco.

It's farfetched to believe Taïa is privileging the Hexagon, rather his work highlights the importance of how queer Moroccan masculinities and sexualities are negotiated in each locus. When Ahmed, the protagonist in *Celui qui est digne d'être aimé*, learns of his mother's passing, he stays in Paris never attending the burial and writes her a letter. In it, he states, "Tu es morte, Malika. Je suis homosexuel. Plus homosexuel que jamais maintenant" [You are dead Malika. I am a homosexual. More homosexual than ever now].[89] His final tie to his homeland, his family—his mother—now gone, he feels comfortable assuming his identity, but again, in Paris not back home, which he clarifies pages earlier when he states: "Que faire de moi, de ma vie au Maroc maintenant que tout le monde savait officiellement que j'étais pédé" [What should I do with myself, my life in Morocco now that everyone knows one hundred percent that I am a fag].[90] It appears the journey for the queer, male protagonist in Taïa's greater corpus is now complete. A journey during which his protagonists combat heteronormativity by patently rendering themselves more public. Again, the use of "officiellement" in this citation underlines that his homosexuality is no longer a tacit subject but a public affair, known to all.

Ultimately, this chapter is not a simple chronological look at the evolution of how Taïa, the author, constructs queer masculinity. It would be reductive to say that Taïa gets more comfortable and talks more openly as he continues to write; rather this study is a comparative analysis that seeks to investigate and unpack the ways Taïa nuances the complicated, and varied, iterations of queer Moroccan sexuality. Sexuality is a complex topic across the entire corpus of novels simply because of the fluidity he proposes between each gender in their own performativity or the performativity imposed on them. Taïa, the author, has even stated: "Les concepts du masculin et du féminin sont très récents, comme le concept de l'homosexualité" [the concepts of masculin and of feminine are very recent just like the concept of homosexuality][91] indicating that gender as a constant might not apply to his autofictive protagonists, rather that they assume the role of a Moroccan queerness. This chapter ultimately agrees with the fluidity Taïa proposes at the end of his interview with Philippe Panizzon, that he is "un écrivain plus transgenre que gay" [a transgender author more than a gay one];[92] all one has to do is look at Omar and Khalid from *Le jour du Roi* or Zahira from *Un pays pour mourir*, Abdellah (Leïla) in *Une mélancolie arabe,* or Samir (Samira) in *La vie lente*. At the same time, this chapter also argues against the idea that these protagonists are operating in a vacuum of gender performativity. I argue that these performances of a queer Moroccan masculinity find their true expression on the border, in a place that isn't inhabited but instead, traversed. Indeed, the discussion of queer performativity "on the border" is unique and novel to Taïa's work, but it also allows readers different ways of examining Taïa's characters, possibly affording further studies on concepts of hybridity, métissage, or transgenderism in the novel. If the border isn't fixed, but fluid, how does that reinforce Taïa's own assertion of gender fluidity in the novel? What is important, however, is the epistemic shifts we witness in his novels and how each contributes to a better understanding of queer Moroccan masculinity. Indeed, it will be interesting to see how the role of the border and the family continue to play in the future for this author and how he will continue to nuance both masculine and feminine performativity, but also everything in between.

NOTES

1. José Esteban Muñoz, *Disidentifications: Queers of Color and the Performance of Politics* (Minneapolis: University of Minnesota Press, 1999), 5.

2. Muñoz, *Disidentifications*, 91–92.

3. Judith Butler, "Melancholy Gender/Refused Identification," *Constructing Masculinity* (London: Routledge University Press, 1995), 31.

4. Muñoz, *Disidentifications*, 31.

5. David T. Evans, *Sexual Citizenship: The Material Construction of Sexualities* (Philadelphia: Routledge Press, 1993).

6. Muñoz, *Disidentifications,* 6.

7. The letter from 15 February 2020, was published on Radio Télévision Belge Francophone in a series entitled "Dans quel monde vit-on?" His letter is entitled "Cher petit Abdellah petit homosexual dans ce Maroc beau et terrible, intense et asphyxiant." All translations are my own.

8. Abdellah Taïa, "Cher petit Abdellah petit homosexual dans ce Maroc beau et terrible, intense et asphyxiant." Radio Télévision Belge Francophone, 15 February 2020.

9. Abdellah Taïa, *Lettres à un jeune marocain* (Paris: Editions du Seuil, 2009), 199.

10. Taïa, *Lettres à un jeune marocain,* 202.

11. Jean-Pierre Boulé, "Writing Selves as mourning and Vita Nova: Abdellah Taïa's Un pays pour mourir," *Contemporary French Civilization* 41, no. 1 (2016): 25–47.

12. Denis M. Provencher, *Queer Maghrebi French: Language, Temporalities, Transfiliations* (Liverpool: Liverpool University Press, 2017), 75.

13. Muñoz, *Disidentifications,* 73; Provencher, *Queer Maghrebi French*, 38.

14. Jarrod Hayes, *Queer Nations* (Chicago: University of Chicago Press, 2000), 16.

15. Omar narrates, "J'ai éteint la lampe, et je l'ai rejoint dans le petit lit vert. Cela ne l'a pas réveillé. Il avait l'habitude. De moi. De mon corps. De nous. Deux. Un" [I shut the lights off and climbed in bed with him. He didn't wake up. He was used to it. To me. To my body. Both of us. United.] (44).

16. "Baiser la main de Hassan II: c'est le rêve de presque tous les Marocains. Je suis devant ce rêve qui se réalise" [To kiss the hand of Hassan II, that is what every Moroccan dreams about. I am witnessing this dream come to life.] (16).

17. Abdellah Taïa, *Le jour du Roi* (Paris: Seuil, 2010), 10.

18. Taïa, *Le jour du Roi,* 10.

19. See Gibson Ncube, *La Sexualité queer au Maghreb à travers la littérature* (Paris: L'Harmattan, 2018), 53.

20. Taïa, *Le jour du Roi*, 11.

21. Taïa, *Le jour du Roi*, 11. It also should be noted that "muet" not only means "speechless," "silent," or "quiet" but also "dumb," or "unable to speak."

22. Taïa, *Le jour du Roi*, 12.

23. Vulca Fidolini, "Idéaux de masculinité et sexualité interdite," *Agora Débats/ Jeunesses* 69, no. 1 (2015): 23–35.

24. Taïa, *Le jour du Roi*, 13.
25. Abdellah Taïa, *Infidèles* (Paris: Seuil, 2012), 47.
26. Siham Bouamer, "De « River of no Return » à « Trouble of the World »: Parcours initiatique musical dans Infidèles (2012) d'Abdellah Taïa," *Expressions maghrébines* 19, no. 1 (2020): 107–124.
27. Taïa, *Le jour du Roi*, 31.
28. Taïa, *Le jour du Roi*, 35.
29. Taïa, *Le jour du Roi*, 13.
30. Taïa, *Le jour du Roi*, 14.
31. Abdellah Taïa, *Celui qui est digne d'être aimé* (Paris: Point, 2017), 16.
32. Abdellah Taïa, *Un pays pour mourir* (Paris: Seuil, 2015), 13.
33. Taïa, *Un pays pour mourir*, 14.
34. Taïa, *Celui qui est digne*, 19.
35. Taïa, *Celui qui est digne*, 20.
36. Taïa, "Cher petit Abdellah petit homosexual dans ce Maroc beau et terrible, intense et asphyxiant."
37. In his earlier novel, *L'armée du salut*, the older brother loses his familial status in the eyes of the protagonist as well.
38. Abdellah Taïa, *L'armée du salut* (Paris: Seuil, 2006), 43.
39. Taïa, *L'armée du salut*, 43.
40. Taïa, *L'armée du salut*, 35.
41. Taïa, *L'armée du salut*, 40.
42. Taïa, *L'armée du salut*, 12.
43. Taïa, *L'armée du salut*, 35.
44. Taïa, *L'armée du salut*, 65.
45. Taïa, *L'armée du salut*, 130–131.
46. Abdellah Taïa, *Une mélancolie arabe* (Paris: Seuil, 2008), 17.
47. Taïa, *Le jour du Roi*, 44.
48. Taïa, *Celui qui est digne*, 71.
49. Michel de Certeau, *L'invention du quotidien. Arts de faire* (Paris: Gallimard, 1990), 186–187.
50. For more information regarding the theory of traveling on and along a border and the productive/creative energy that it permits travelers, see Brian Hunt, *Mobile Limits and the Limits of Mobility in French Representations of Urban Space*, University of Illinois at Urbana-Champaign, PhD Dissertation, 2015.
51. Marc Augé, *Non-lieux, introduction à une anthropologie de la surmodernité* (Paris: Le Seuil, 1992).
52. Abdellah Taïa, *La vie lente* (Paris: Seuil, 2019), 43.
53. Taïa, *La vie lente*, 53.
54. Taïa, *La vie lente*, 43.
55. Muñoz, *Disidentifications,* 77–78.
56. Taïa, *La vie lente*, 46.
57. The protagonist in *La vie lente* even says "Je ne savais pas si les autres passagers avaient remarqué quelque chose ou pas" [I wasn't sure if the other riders had

noticed something or not] (45) further reinforcing the idea that the bus is a non-place and that anonymity affords queer masculine performativity.

58. de Certeau, *L'invention du quotidien. Arts de faire*, 173.

59. Muñoz, *Disidentification*, 92.

60. Taïa, *La vie lente*, 56.

61. Taïa, *La vie lente*, 56. "Chez nous" remains an interesting quandary in terms of analysis. A quick reading would allude to "nous" referring to both him, the adolescent, and his interlocuter Soufiane; however, the protagonist goes out of his way to emphasizes at length how the minister truly belongs to Rabat. I'd argue therefore that "chez nous" and "Salé" can be read metonymously for "chez les homosexuels" or at the very least indicating that he doesn't belong in this transgressive boundary.

62. Taïa, *La vie lente*, 60.

63. Taïa, *La vie lente*, 60.

64. There are numerous examples of sexual aggressors feminizing the males they will rape in Taïa's novel. In *Une mélancolie arabe* there is the Chouaïb who calls Abdellah "Leïla" (21–20) and Samir, Mounir's childhood acquaintance in *La vie lente,* who is forced to assume the identity of Samira by his aggressors (52).

65. In an interview with Philippe Panizzon from 2019, Taïa explains: "Et c'est ce qui fait de moi un écrivain plus transgenre que gay. Le transgenre traverse tout ce que j'ai écrit, cette idée que nous sommes traversés par des mélanges, le féminin et le masculin, sans qu'on en soit conscient." [This is what makes me more of a transgender writer than a gay one. Transgenderism can be found in almost everything I write, this idea that the mix of feminine and masculine go through us without us even knowing it]. In this interview he echoes what readers have been seeing across his novels. See Panizzon, "La vraie liberté n'existe nulle part: Un entretien avec Abdellah Taïa," *Francosphère* 8, no. 2 (2019): 183–207.

66. Taïa, *Un pays pour mourir*, 45.

67. Taïa, *Le jour du Roi*, 179.

68. Taïa, *L'armée du salut*, 84.

69. Taïa, *La vie lente*, 61.

70. "N'importe quel point d'un rhizome peut être connecté avec n'importe quel autre, et doit l'être" [Any point in a rhizome can be connected to any other and must be]. Gilles Deleuze and Félix Guattari, *Rhizome: Introduction* (Paris: Editions de Minuit, 1976), 20.

71. Taïa, *La vie lente*, 80.

72. Taïa, *La vie lente*, 80.

73. Brian Hunt, "Cinematic Borderlands: Jean Vigo's L'Atalante and the Allure of entre-deux," *Contemporary French and Francophone Studies* 21, no. 3 (2017): 266–273.

74. Taïa, *La vie lente*, 84.

75. Taïa, *La vie lente*, 85.

76. Taïa, *La vie lente*, 86.

77. In *Une mélancolie arabe* (2009), the protagonist, Abdellah, explains needing to take the metro back to his apartment in Belleville, a traditionally Arab neighborhood in Paris at the time. He discusses the possibility of taking Line 2 from Place de

Clichy to Belleville (51) but elects instead to simply walk in the rain. He fears the metro is too public and does not wish for others to view his sorrow. Historically, Place de Clichy is a place of resistance. This scene in particular lacks the "other"; there is no transgression culturally, sexually, socially. In this case, the protagonist is simply dealing with his own melancholia instead of needing a space for his queerness.

78. Taïa, *La vie lente*, 86.
79. Taïa, *La vie lente*, 96.
80. Taïa, *La vie lente*, 91.
81. Deborah Harris and Patti Giuffre elaborate more on how professional cuisine, even baking in this case, is typically associated with masculinity so as not to be confused with home cooking which is categorized as feminine. See their *Taking the Heat: Women Chefs and Gender Inequality in the Professional Kitchen* (New Brunswick: Rutgers University Press), 2015.
82. Taïa, *La vie lente*, 91.
83. Provencher, *Queer Maghrebi French,* 13.
84. Itay Lotem, "'L'homosexualité? ça n'existe pas en banlieue': The indigènes de la république and Gay Marriage, between Intersectionality and Homophobia," *Modern & Contemporary France* 27, no. 2 (2019): 205–221.
85. Taïa, "Non, l'homosexualité n'est pas imposée aux arabes par l'Occident," *Nouvel Observateur,* 2013.
86. Taïa, *La vie lente*, 203.
87. This quote form *La vie lente* dialogues with the Moroccan term *nouiba*, an Arabic term describing an act in which participants are both penetrators and penetrated. The practice comes up twice in Taïa's novels: once in *Une mélancolie arabe* where the narrator reflects on the childhood act; and also, in *L'armée du salut* while the protagonist is in Geneva, an adult this time. *Nouiba* does not appear to carry pejorative connotations in these works.
88. Taïa, *Un pays pour mourir*, 13.
89. Taïa, *Celui qui est digne*, 27.
90. Taïa, *Celui qui est digne*, 44.
91. Panizzon, "La vraie liberté n'existe nulle part: Un entretien avec Abdellah Taïa."
92. Panizzon, "La vraie liberté n'existe nulle part: Un entretien avec Abdellah Taïa.

BIBLIOGRAPHY

Augé, Marc. *Non-lieux: Introduction à une anthropologie de la surmodernité*. Paris: Seuil, 1992.

Bouamer, Siham. "De « River of no Return » à « Trouble of the World » Parcours initiatique musical dans *Infidèles* (2012) d'Abdellah Taïa." *Expression maghrébines* 19, no. 1 (2020): 107–124.

Boulé, Jean-Pierre. "Deuil et résolution dans Infidèles d'Abdellah Taïa." *@nalyse: Revue de Critique et de Théorie Littéraire* 9, no. 2 (2014): 276–307.

———. "Writing selves as mourning and Vita Nova : Abdellah Taïa's Un pays pour mourir." *Contemporary French Civilization* 41, no. 1 (2016): 25–47.
de Certeau, Michel. *L'invention du quotidien. Arts de faire*. Paris: Gallimard, 1990.
Evans, David T. *Sexual Citizenship: The Material Construction of Sexualities.* Philadelphia: Routledge, 1993.
Fidolini, Vulca. "Idéaux de masculinité et sexualité interdite." *Agora Débats/ Jeunesse* 69, no. 1 (2015): 23–35.
Guattari, Félix, and Gilles Deleuze. *Rhizome: Introduction*. Paris: Editions de Minuit, 1976.
Harris, Deborah, and Patti Giuffre. *Taking the Heat: Women Chefs and Gender Inequality in the Professional Kitchen*. New Brunswick: Rutgers University Press, 2015.
Hayes, Jarrod. *Queer Nations*. Chicago: University of Chicago Press, 2000.
Hunt, Brian. "Cinematic Borderlands: Jean Vigo's L'Atalante and the Allure of entre-deux." *Contemporary French and Francophone Studies* 21, no. 3 (2017): 266–273.
——— *Mobile Limits and the Limits of Mobility in French Representations of Urban Space*. University of Illinois at Urbana-Champaign, PhD Dissertation, 2015.
Lotem, Itay. "'L'homosexualité? ça n'existe pas en banlieue": The *indigènes de la république* and Gay Marriage, between Intersectionality and Homophobia." *Modern and Contemporary France* 27, no. 2 (2019): 205–221.
Muñoz, José Esteban. *Disidentifications: Queers of Color and the Performance of Politics*. Minneapolis: University of Minnesota Press, 1999.
Maroun, Daniel. "Comment échapper à la honte du zamel: Vers la construction de la masculinité queer maghrébine." *@analyse: Revue de Critique et de Théorie Littéraire* (2016): 135–154.
Ncube, Gibson. *La Sexualité queer au Maghreb à travers la littérature*. Paris: L'Harmattan 2018.
Panizzon, Philippe. "La vraie liberté n'existe nulle part: Un entretien avec Abdellah Taïa." *Francosphère* 8, no. 2 (2019): 183–207.
Provencher, Denis M. *Queer Maghrebi French: Language, Temporalities, Transfiliations*. Liverpool: Liverpool University Press, 2017.
Taïa, Abdellah. *La vie lente*. Paris: Seuil, 2019.
———. "Cher petit Abdellah, petit homosexuel dans ce Maroc beau et terrible, intense et asphyxiant." Radio Télévision Belge Francophone. 15 February 2020.
———. *Celui qui est digne d'être aimé*. Paris: Points, 2017.
———. *Infidèles*. Paris: Points, 2012.
———. *L'armée du salut*. Paris: Seuil, 2006.
———. *Le jour du Roi*. Paris: Seuil, 2010.
———. "Non, l'homosexualité n'est pas imposée aux arabe par l'Occident." *Nouvel Observateur,* 2013.
———. *Un pays pour mourir*. Paris: Seuil, 2015.
———. *Une mélancolie arabe*. Paris: Seuil, 2008.
———, ed. *Lettres à un jeune marocain*. Paris: Seuil, 2009.

Part II

AFFECTIVE MIGRATION

Chapter 4

He Loves Me, He Loves Me Not

Cruel Optimism in Abdellah Taïa's L'armée du Salut

Siham Bouamer

In his study of the representation of the "Arab boy" in French and Francophone literature, Mehammed Amadeus Mack examines the work of Abdellah Taïa. He contests the analysis of Taïa's work "in a celebratory mode."[1] Specifically, he regrets the fact that current scholarship on the Moroccan writer has exclusively praised his novels and film as being narratives of queer sexual liberation. As such, those studies fail to recognize problematic aspects of his work, such as the subjective divide between, on the one hand, "Arab sexual intolerance" and, on the other hand, "Western sexual liberation."[2] By reducing Taïa's work to an outlet to set free Arab queer sexual identity, critics miss part of the Taïa's efforts to dismantle specific structures that complicate such a dichotomy.

For example, Mack calls attention to Taïa's important discussion on sexual tourism. He insists on considering the writer's voice as a counter-discourse to the existing literary landscape on the subject matter since Taïa speaks from a Moroccan perspective.[3] Mack focuses on "Terminus des Anges" in *Le rouge du tarbouche* [*The Red of the Fez*] (2004) and the relationship between René, a European tourist, and M'hamed, a young Moroccan man. When the latter implores his lover to help him obtain a visa for Europe, he presents such a request as a fair exchange for the sexual favors he granted him. Such a plea shifts the bond between them from a possible romantic relationship to a transaction framed around their respective socioeconomic reality and the power dynamics founded on the colonial past between France and Morocco. Mack concludes that while such a strategy aims at dismantling "the globalization of homonormative discourses" imposed within a structure where economic imbalance and cultural differences are at play, Taïa leaves the reader sur *sa faim/fin* with an unfinished resolution based on "erotic promises."[4]

This sort of incomplete resolution based on possibilities of affective reciprocity is one of the reasons why critics often see Taïa's work as being tinged with optimism: an optimism that the writer describes, in a recent interview, as being imposed on him and his work. In the same discussion, Taïa further explains that for him, "The dream [. . .] is to be the darkest possible." He regrets failing every time and attributes this tendency to the reading of the presence of romantic moments in his work, but that ultimately, he does not "know where that hope comes from."[5]

In this chapter, I will argue that the hope imposed on his work stems from what Lauren Berlant has coined as "cruel optimism" to describe "the relation of attachment to compromised conditions of possibility."[6] This notion provides a way to dismantle the affective structure imposed on Taïa's work. Focusing on the film adaptation of *L'armée du salut* [*Salvation Army*] (2013), I will explore how Taïa destroys possibilities of "forever love"[7] for the main character, Abdellah. Berlant argues that attachment to such a fantasy, to which she prefers the expression "durable intimacy," is representative of the nurturing of ideals of "the good life" in liberal-capitalist societies.[8] I will stress here debunking such imagined possibilities aims to challenge western heteronormative structures—of family, success, and love—in which such ideality is engrained.[9] In the film, Taïa maps Abdellah's coming-of-age *out* of such oppressive structure for the queer subject, a process that I will explore through Kathryn Stockton's notion of "growing sideways."[10]

The impossibility of "forever love" and the acceptance of such a condition is set early in the movie and leaves no possibility for further nurturing of such a fantasy. Sitting alone in the family house's courtyard, Abdellah is playing the game "He loves me, he loves me not." Following the rules, he picks the petals off of a flower in order to determine if the object of his affection shares similar feelings. He repeats "*Taibrini, Mataibrinish*," which translates in English to "he loves me, he loves me not." While the French syntactic structure contains several levels of affection, *Il m'aime un peu, beaucoup, à la folie, passionnément, pas du tout* [He loves me a little, a lot, to madness, passionately, not at all], in Moroccan Arabic, like in English, the phrase cuts the range of possibilities in the structure of love; it is *quitte ou double*, all or nothing. The binary options structure Abdellah's ability to reach his goal and anticipate the way he receives the results during the game and throughout the film. According to the rules of the game, the last petal of the flower reveals if the love interest reciprocates the same feelings for the player. Abdellah accepts the discouraging results: *Mataibrinish* [He loves me not].

The scene only lasts for a few minutes, but it does not conclude Abdellah's repetitive acceptance of rejection throughout the film. While he does not disclose the identity of his love interest during the game, the film soon reveals several male figures in Abdellah's life who could play this role. I will pay particular attention to the importance of his relationships with his father Mohammed, his brother Slimane, and a Swiss professor named Jean. I argue that the individual negotiations of intimacy with the three characters leads to Abdellah's gradual detachment from cruel optimism and expectations of "durable intimacy" and the "good life" at different stages of his life. I will show that the multiple repetitions of Abdel Halim Hafez's song "*Ana Laka 3ala Toul*" [I am yours forever] from the Egyptian film *Ayyam wa layali* [*Days and Nights*] (1955) serve as markers for those transitions. Such inclusion is rather ironic since the lyrics nurture the ideality of forever love and echoes the linguistic binary of all or nothing love.

The same musical framework will outline this chapter. In the first section, I will focus on the first reference to the song. It will provide an understanding of Abdellah's initial realization regarding the unproductivity of cruel optimism through his dad and specifically his parents' toxic relationship. This initial lesson prepares the young protagonist to deal with unstable moments throughout his life, which I will identify in the second section with the acceptance of the impossibility of brotherly love (Slimane) and European love (Jean). We shall see that the song, in its intermediality within the film, serves as an indicator of moments of crisis, but also as a catalyst for overcoming precarity and accepting its ordinariness in everyday life, hence helping the dismantling of cruel optimism.

TOXIC FAMILIAL CRUEL OPTIMISM

Immediately after the scene of "He loves me, he loves me not," the song "*Ana Laka 3ala Toul*" appears for the first time. Mohammed, the father, is the character who allows the transitions between the two sequences. He comes out in the courtyard to smoke a cigarette. When he sees and hears Abdellah playing the game, he pauses to let him finish before breaking his solitude. Noticing Abdellah's sadness, Mohammed attempts to negotiate the meaning and origin of his son's sorrow. For example, he attributes his feelings to boredom due to the long summer break. He also suggests that he might not be feeling well because he is hungry and encourages him to eat something. His suppositions are part of his strategy of avoidance. He never mentions the possibility that Abdellah suffers from a heartbreak although he witnessed Abdellah plucking the last petal. While this scene could be seen as a positive and constructive exchange between a father and a son, it instead emphasizes the unproductiveness of the reasons the father presents. He bases his speculations on the notion that unhappiness is temporary with concepts such as vacation and hunger. Most importantly, he does not acknowledge Abdellah's queerness despite the fact that he heard his son using the Arabic masculine form of "He loves me not."

At that moment, the father becomes the vehicle for cruel optimism, which he then takes into the house to pass on to the next scene and to the rest of the family. In the house, Abdellah, his mother, and sisters are watching the black and white Egyptian film and musical *Ayyam wa layali* starring the young Abdel Halim Hafez. The poor condition of the family room, which also serves as a bedroom for the children and the mother, contrasts with the scene of the film captured on the small TV screen. Floating on the Nile river, Hafez sings the infamous song "*Ana Laka 3ala Toul*" which allows him to profess his selfless love to the actress Emane. For example, following a common trope in Arabic love songs, the singer promises his eyes as a token of his affection. The family is mesmerized by the Dark-Skinned Nightingale's voice.[11] As for M'Barka, the mother, she shows less enthusiasm for the performance, and after a few minutes, she asks Abdellah to turn down the volume of the TV because she does not like the Egyptian singer.

When the mother declares her aversion for Hafez, Emane appears on the black and white screen at the same time. Even though the young actress's radiant smile contrasts drastically with the mother's stern and jaded expression, it becomes clear that the superposition aims at emphasizing the similarities between the two women. This comparison is a reflection of the function of actresses and mothers as allegories of resistance in Taïa's life and work. At the 2015 Oslo Freedom Forum, Taïa stresses the influence of Egyptian actresses in his life. For him, women such as Soad Hosny and Nadia Lofti "were making political statements" by acting.[12] He refers here to their roles as performers in the theatrical meaning of the word. In the same fashion as Abdellah (the character) who is captivated by the film *Ayyam wa layali*, Taïa explains, in the same interview, his fascination for Egyptian movies during his childhood. It is clear that those productions played a crucial role in the shaping of his identity. For example, he reveals in the same speech how the acting profession inspired him to adopt real-life strategies for survival as a queer man in Morocco. From a Butlerian standpoint, he explains that they taught him how to negotiate his identity through the art of performative impersonation of imposed social expectations, without completely conforming to them.

Taïa highlights that the accessibility of Egyptian films on television made him feel that these role models were with him at home, in his everyday life. Within that space, notes Tina Dransfeldt Christensen, the mother holds a similar subversive position in Taïa's work. For example, in her study on the voices of resistance in the novel *L'armée du salut*, she explains:

> The different depictions of his mother—as a representative of those who are marginalized by the patriarchal norms; as the dictator of the family house; and

> as the empowered mother in opposition to the defeated or absent father—all serve the same purpose as resistance narratives that defy the traditional patriarchal norms of society.[13]

Christensen emphasizes, here in the case of the novel, the essential role of M'Barka for the dismantling of heteronormative structures in the household. Taïa further nurtures this function in the film. For example, when the mother asks Abdellah to turn down the music, she acts as an authoritarian figure who disregards the majority's opinion. This characteristic does not function as a criticism, but as a source of admiration. Visually, she is at the center of her children who serve as a frame for the painting that Taïa draws of her. She is laying down on the *sedari*, a Moroccan couch, like *La Grande Odalisque*. Through the metaphorical evocation of an ambiguous subversive feminine figure, Taïa presents his mother as another model for the possibilities of revolutionary acts within an oppressive space.

While those domestic acts take many forms in the film, I would like to focus here on the role of Abdellah's mother as what Sara Ahmed calls the "feminist killjoy." First, I choose this specific notion in order to evoke Ahmed's statement that feminist work must be firmly grounded at home, in everyday life.[14] I am also interested in the active role of such a figure as someone who "kill[s] other people's joy [and] [. . .] get[s] in the way of other people's investments."[15] I suggest replacing the expression "investment" with "cruel optimism." When M'barka asks Abdellah to turn down the music despite the fact that her son and his siblings are enjoying the song, she serves as an essential agent for the dismantling—the killing of joy—of some of the affective structures grounded in cruel optimism that the Egyptian film entertains.

It is important to note that Abdellah's mother does not express an aversion for the film; she only dislikes the singer, Abdel Halim Hafez. Considering the analogy that I have established between M'Barka and Emane, I would like to suggest that the rejection of the singer is an indirect attack of the father. As such, the black and white movie functions as a flashback of their past as young lovers. Turning down the music is thus an attempt to suppress cruel optimism that she once entertained within their relationship. When the father enters the family room, he reintroduces cruel optimism. He asks Abdellah to turn up the music and explains the reason for such request: "It is Saturday, so everybody should be happy."[16] By attributing the state of happiness to a specific day, Mohammed brings about promises of "the good life" in the same fashion as his conversation with Abdellah in the courtyard. Happiness and sadness are attached to temporary factors such as the summer break, hunger, and the weekend. His effort to impose solutions to solve what Sara Ahmed describe as "crises of happiness" to describe "the belief that happiness [. . .] [is] the reward for a certain loyalty" is doomed to failure.[17] He soon serves as the instigator who will destroy the same structure of happiness he nurtures. Through this vicious circle, Taïa emphasizes the unproductiveness of cruel optimism that he develops within the framework of the relationship between Abdellah's parents.

We understand that the object that will lead to the father's happiness is the mother. As such, his request to turn up the sound of the TV is a way to serenade her, in the same way that Hafez courts Emane. Mohammed attempts to reintroduce the same memories of their past as young lovers that the mother wanted to suppress because of, as we will see, the reality of everyday life forced her to give up on past memories. Despite her initial "killing of joy," the mother ends up reciprocating the attention by complimenting his shirt. This exchange announces the next scene. In the middle of the night, Abdellah wakes up and hears his parents having sex. More than the depiction of a teenager catching an intimate moment between his parents, the scene shifts the parents' sexual dynamic from "a private affair of the two" to "an intimate part of family life [. . .] that shapes Abdellah's whole existence and sexuality."[18] First, it seems to have a positive effect on Abdellah. He goes to the kitchen where he devours bread and honey. Getting his appetite back, in contrast to the scene on the patio, can appear as a sign of hopefulness for the possibility of durable intimacy for himself. However, the cruelly optimistic moment he is savoring is as short as *une lune de miel* [a honeymoon] since it is interrupted by his mother's screams. We soon understand that the father is hitting her.

The scene of abuse on the mother is hard to watch but is essential to our understanding of Taïa's cinematic style. In an interview, Taïa explains: "Cinema needs to feel real to me: concrete, sincere, complex and also melodramatic—like family life, when your parents fight, or when you hear them having sex; this intensity in the house, how you deal with the drama: there is some structure in that."[19] In other words, moments of trauma, which are part of everyday life, have to be part of the visual storytelling. Watching the children knocking on the door and begging their father to stop hitting their mother in the middle of the night can be seen as chaotic. However, Taïa sees structure in moments of crisis. Cinema allows him to re-center such moments into the reality of recurrent precarious situations. As such, he frames the scene of abuse as a critical moment of transition for Abdellah's journey sideways of his family structure.

IMPASSIVITY AND CRUEL OPTIMISM

In order to understand Abdellah's experience with his parents' relationship, I would like to first consider what Lauren Berlant calls "crisis ordinariness."

Instead of focusing on the exceptional nature of trauma, she proposes to consider moments of crisis in the everyday nature of ordinary life. Such a shift allows individuals to find ways of coping with instability daily.[20] The moment of crisis in his family offers Abdellah a foundation that will help him deal with future adversities. I will show how, through the effective management of "crisis ordinariness," Abdellah can build himself outside the heteronormative linear progression that his family tried to impose on him. The realization of the dysfunctional nature of cruel optimism in his household allows him to slowly reject such a structure.

In order to deal with "crisis ordinariness," Lauren Berlant suggests considering the strategy of impassivity. She identifies three specific types of impasse:

> First, there is the impasse after the dramatic event of a forced loss, such as after a broken heart, a sudden death, or a social catastrophe, when one no longer knows what to do or how to live and yet, while knowing, must adjust. Second, there is what happens when one finds oneself adrift amid normative intimate or material terms of reciprocity without an event [. . .]—coasting through life, as it were, until one discovers a loss of traction. Third, there are situations where managing the presence of a problem/event that dissolves the old sureties and forces of improvisation and reflection on life-without-guarantees is a pleasure and a plus, not a loss.[21]

While those impasses can be examined as independent transitional moments, the passage from the first to the third type can also be considered as progress on how to deal with crisis. Immediately after the fight between his parents, Abdellah goes through the first two types of impasses (adjustment to trauma and loss of control), which I propose to examine by engaging with Kathryn Bond Stockton's notion of growing sideways. Berlant describes impassivity as "[t]he way the body slows down [. . .] to clarify the relation of living on to ongoing crisis and loss."[22] In other words, impasses are transitional moments which, similarly to what Stockton calls "moving suspension," entail a form of delay.[23]

Specifically, during those two phases, Abdellah nurtures "sideways relations," an expression used by Stockton to define "forms of growing sideways [. . .] for children who have often not found it safe to express their "same-sex" longings to their peers without the fear of being ostracized or bullied."[24] Despite not explicitly revealing his homosexuality, it is clear that he cannot do so because he is already bullied for not fitting "male standards." For example, when he tries to join his mother and sisters to eat lunch with them, they reject him from their female space. When he expresses his sadness, they shame him for acting "like a girl." Other people also try to humiliate him because of his "nonnormative" behavior. For instance, while he is walking on the street, people throw stones at him from rooftops. To defend himself, he attempts to stand up to them by asserting his readiness to confront them without any fear. This response mainly aims at performing manhood to protect himself. However, it is truly in the following scene that Abdellah finds shelter when he meets one of the men from his neighborhood with whom he entertains a relationship. This "man/boy love" becomes, in the words Stockton, "a substitute lateral relation" for Abdellah to respond to the "arrested development and ghostly gayness thrust upon" him.[25] Here, the concepts of laterality and ghostly presence can help us understand Taïa's visual framing of Abdellah's sideways relations with this man and another one from his neighborhood during his adolescence.

First, the two men drag him into isolated spaces and Abdellah follows them to spaces that embody the last two impasses Berlant defines. First, the houses where the sexual exchanges happen are under construction. Symbolically, the unfinished structures challenge "the vertical [. . .] metaphor of growing up" and dismantle the concept of the household.[26] More than being fleeting moments of intimacy, the encounters sidetrack Abdellah from his family structure and some of the functions that he must fulfill as part of the expectations to grow "up" and become a man in the family. For example, the first man accosts Abdellah while he is on his way to accomplish a task traditionally attributed to the son in the family: carrying bread that his mother has prepared to the communal oven to be baked. On another occasion, Abdellah initiates the interaction with the second man from his neighborhood by asking if he needs help. This offer symbolically deprive his own family from his contribution to the well-functioning, a lack for which he is often reprimanded.

Abdellah does not reveal the nature of the help he is offering to this man, but we understand that he implies sexual favors. Because Abdellah initiates this last encounter, I would like to examine here the weight of his agency within those relationships in which he appears to be a victim. Stockton's notion "sideways motions" is here apt to help us make sense of this dynamic. I suggest that his experiences with these older men prepare Abdellah to become the "author of [. . .] [his] motions and emotions."[27] They set him up to enter the third type of impasses which, as defined by Berlant, consists of manageable and constructive moments of crisis that allows the acceptance of "life-without-guarantees."[28] In the film, the song "*Ana Laka 3ala toul*" allows us to identify those moments for Abdellah. During each crisis, Abdellah is successful in taking one step further from his family structures, while at the same time understanding that overcoming one difficult situation does not exclude the possibilities of more to come.

The first step in Abdellah's detachment from the familial structures stems from his ambiguous relationship with his brother. Taïa openly depicts

Abdellah's obsession with Slimane when, for example, the young man sneaks into his brother's bedroom and smells his underwear. If the scene left any further doubts, Abdellah takes this odd prized possession to the courtyard and touches the same flowers that served as prop for the game "He loves me, he loves me not," which leads us to think that the object of his affection was his older brother. Disheartened, Abdellah accepted the results of the game on the patio, the same way he takes Slimane's rejection and unkindness during their daily interactions. However, a trip organized to the seashore by Slimane with his two little brothers shifts this dynamic.

The transitionary nature of the concept of "vacation" echoes the fleeting moments of intimacy during Abdellah's previous sexual relationships with older men. As such, it opens a possibility for an incestuous relationship between the two brothers, but, at their arrival at the hotel, this probability is soon dismantled. While they are checking in, the song "*Ana laka 3ala toul*" is playing. After getting the keys, the hotel receptionist and Abdellah make eye contact to express their attraction for one another. Their age proximity breaks from his experience with intimacy thus far and this short encounter distracts Abdellah from his fascination for his brother.

This moment foreshadows Abdellah's further disconnection from Slimane. For example, Abdellah, who holds Slimane in high esteem, explicitly contests his conception of "the good life" while the two brothers are relaxing on the beach at the beginning of their vacation. Slimane is reading a book in French and tries to convince Abdellah to try to learn the language. His main arguments are based on the idea that French can open up opportunities for upward social mobility. In particular, while symbolically leaning on a boat, he mentions the possibility of crossing the Mediterranean Sea to live in France. Despite his admiration for his brother, Abdellah challenges his brother's perspective and asserts his belonging in Morocco, its people, and its language. Such a position is surprising considering Abdellah's experience in the country. He lives in a society that does not accept his queerness, whether on the street or in his family, which can lead us to think that he would want to leave the place of his oppression. However, more than a defense of Morocco, his reaction aims at attacking the oppressive structures of normativity that his brother nurtures. Specifically, he rejects the idea that the Western world unquestionably bring about possibilities of "the good life."

This standpoint is Abdellah's first step toward the process of disidentification which, in Muñoz's words, "is about managing and negotiating [. . .] systemic violence" grounded in whiteness and heteronormativity.[29] While Abdellah first stands up against the first system of oppression on the beach, he later attacks heteronormativity. Abdellah realizes that Slimane left him and his younger brother to meet up with a woman. He feels a strong sense of betrayal. To take his revenge, he decides to inform his mother about his brother's whereabouts. Despite the fact that Slimane was probably with the waitress he met at a restaurant, Abdellah tells his mother that he has left with a prostitute. By framing Slimane's escapade as unlawful, Abdellah decenters the "nonnormativity" of his sexuality. In turn, Abdellah abandons his little brother on the beach so he can meet up with a man he had met on the beach for a sexual encounter. With this act, Abdellah seems to reproduce the same toxic patterns to which he fell victim. The process is similar to previous transitionary moments of intimacy since it is happening in a house under construction.

We are left to wonder if Abdellah's progression has failed since he seems to have returned to the first (adjustment to trauma) and second types of impasse (loss of control) by this act. However, at the difference of other men, Abdellah embraces the man for comfort. While this new lover stays anonymous in the film, his name is Slimane in the novel. Such transfer symbolizes Taïa's effort in the film—in opposition to the novel—to clearly displace Abdellah's affective structure from filial relationship in his *famille de sang* [blood-related family] to his chosen family, as a queer act of resilience. Besides, such movement is highly symbolic since, more than being related by blood, the two brothers, notes Denis Provencher, are linked as "frères de sexe" [sex brothers] because they went through circumcision at the same time.[30] The ceremony is an important rite of passage in Islam as it prepares the child to "grow straight" into manhood. When Abdellah realizes that Slimane left, he "grows sideways" and abandon ties defined by Moroccan and Muslim heteronormative societies.

From this point forward, the family disappears from the screen. Taïa transports us forward in time, with an older Abdellah. In the scene that follows, he is having breakfast with Jean, a Swiss professor. They then decide to take a stroll on the beach where a man on a *fluka*, a boat, approaches them to ask if they would be interested in a ride. At this moment, Taïa sets the scene in a way that leads the audience to expect a romantic boat ride, which would echo the scene of *Days and Nights* with Hafez serenading Emane. However, a further reading of the scene can help us understand how Taïa destroys such possibilities. By setting the two lovers on the bark, he creates an indirect reference to the song and the love scene on the Nile from *Days and Nights*. The visual evocation of the clip serves as a reminder to presage that the boat ride will not end in a "forever love," the same way it failed for his parents. Prepared for a possible crisis, he accepts the ride, but we feel that he is concerned, and rightly so. The driver will not serenade the couple. He becomes another type of singer, a *maître-chanteur*.

The driver questions Abdellah's relationship with Jean and threatens to kill them if he does not pay him a higher fare. This blackmailing is grounded in the same economic reality previously discussed in *Le rouge du tarbouche* and the power dynamics at play in relationships between Western and Moroccan men. The extortionist rejects the possibility of an actual relationship between Jean and Abdellah, and instead, frames it as a capitalist transaction from which he can himself benefit. While Jean, who does not understand Arabic, ignores the seriousness of the situation, Abdellah handles the issue with calm, due to his ability to deal with "crisis ordinariness." The river metaphorically symbolizes another transitional moment; he is floating away to the realization that the fantasy of forever love is impossible. The shipwreck, welcoming them on the beach at the end of their boat ride, metaphorically confirms this outcome. Their relationship is doomed to destruction. The structure echoes the previous setting of unfinished constructions where Abdellah meets older Moroccan men during his childhood. It however takes a step further, since the boat can be seen as a symbol not as a refusal of "growing up," but as his realization of the necessity to dismantle expectations of forever love, instead of suffering through its decay.

After this scene, Taïa forwards the narrative to Geneva when Abdellah arrives at the airport. The fact that he leaves his bag in a locker is not surprising, although Jean lives in the Swiss city. The previous scene on the *fluka* has already prepared us and Abdellah for this conclusion. After days of wandering in the city and sleeping on benches, Abdellah seeks help at the Salvation Army where they give him a room to share with another young Moroccan man. As a sign of friendship, Abdellah offers to share an orange with him. His new roommate accepts but insists on paying him back by singing a song for him. Abdellah requests "*Ana Laka Hala Toul*" and cries while listening to the song. Here, he does not fall apart because the song reminds him of the traumatic experience involving the mother and the father, the failure of his relationship with his brother or with Jean. The song serves as a catharsis to reframe adversities within "crisis ordinariness." As such, the emotional release helps him find strength in another moment of failure.

CONCLUSION

Taïa's film could be described as an adaptation of his novel. However, I would like to offer an alternative expression. The term "remake" helps me here step away from expectations of faithfulness from one medium to another since I did not intend to make a comparison between the novel and the film. Throughout my analysis, a few references to the novel allowed me to understand the film in Taïa's overall autobiographical narrative. The inclusion of the song "*Ana Laka 3ala Toul*" in the film, absent in the novel, as a thread guiding us through Abdellah's escape from "cruel optimism," indicates

Taïa's efforts in making his original coming-of-age story less hopeful, less cruelly optimistic.

This process allowed Taïa to reflect on the constant transitional state of queer subjects against heteronormative expectations of "happiness" nurtured by cruel optimism. As such, he questions the problematic pursuit of happiness to borrow the title of Sara Ahmed in which she explores the following question: "What does it mean to be worthy of happiness?" Abdellah accepts being unworthy of the happiness attached to durable intimacy: he accepts to end on a "he loves me not" in the game he plays at the beginning of the film and to be called "a whore" by Jean at the end. Such acceptance is not unproductive because, to quote Halberstam, "[u]nder certain circumstances, failing, losing, forgetting, unmaking, undoing, unbecoming, [. . .] not knowing may, in fact, offer more creative, more cooperative, more surprising ways of being in the world."[31] His film *L'armée du salut* marks a clear transition in Abdellah Taïa's work. In his attempt to erase any trace of cruel optimism from the original novel, he prepares us for his future narratives that will further dismantle such a fantasy. In fact, such effort reaches its climax in his latest work *La vie lente* [The Slow Life] (2019) in which some of the closing words of the novel, "La solitude et la mort," leave no room at all for optimism (266).

NOTES

1. Mehammed Amadeus Mack, *Sexagon: Muslims, France, and the Sexualization of National Culture* (New York: Fordham University Press, 2017), 135.
2. Mack, *Sexagon*, 136.
3. Mack, *Sexagon*, 140.
4. Mack, *Sexagon*, 143.
5. Adbellah Taïa, "Our Monsters Are Like Us: An Interview with Abdellah Taïa," Interview with Sam Metz, *Los Angeles Review of Books*, January 9, 2017, https://blog.lareviewofbooks.org/interviews/monsters-like-us-interview-abdellah-taia/, Accessed December 10, 2018.
6. Lauren Berlant, *Cruel Optimism* (Durham: Duke University Press, 2011), 24.
7. Berlant, *Cruel Optimism,* 3.
8. Berlant, *Cruel Optimism,* 3. For Berlant, "The fantasies that are fraying include, particularly, upward mobility, job security, political and social equality, and lively, durable intimacy" (3).
9. In *The Queen of America Goes to Washington City: Essays on Sex and Citizenship* (Duke University Press, 2012), Lauren Berlant focuses on the heteronormative nature of the concepts of nationhood and citizenships.
10. Kathryn Bond Stockton, *The Queer Child, or Growing Sideways in the Twentieth Century* (Durham: Duke University Press, 2009).

11. Abdel Halim Hafez was nicknamed the "dark-skinned nightingale" (in Arabic, el-Andaleeb el-Asmar) for his uniquely soft voice.

12. Taïa, "African, Muslim, and Gay," Talk at the Oslo Conference. May 25–27, 2015, Consulted on: https://www.youtube.com/watch?v=THnQ9JmR_tk.

13. Tina Dransfeldt Christensen, "Writing the Self as Narrative of Resistance: *L'Armée du salut* by Abdellah Taïa," *The Journal of North African Studies* 21, no. 5 (2016): 863.

14. Sara Ahmed, *Living a Feminist Life* (Duke University Press, 2017), 7.

15. Ahmed, *Living a Feminist Life*, 65.

16. I am using the official English subtitles for the movies.

17. Sara Ahmed, "Multiculturalism and the Promise of Happiness," *New Formations* 63. (2007/2008): 122.

18. Tina Dransfeldt Christensen, "Writing the Self," 864.

19. Fernández Carbajal, "The Wandering of a Gay Moroccan: An Interview with Abdellah Taïa," 499.

20. Berlant, *Cruel Optimism,* 10.

21. Berlant, *Cruel Optimism,* 201.

22. Berlant, *Cruel Optimism,* 5.

23. Stockton, *The Queer Child*, 53.

24. Stockton, *The Queer Child*, 52–53.

25. Stockton, *The Queer Child*, 62.

26. Stockton, *The Queer Child*, 11.

27. Stockton, *The Queer Child*, 54.

28. Berlant, *Cruel Optimism,* 201.

29. José Estaban Muñoz, *Disidentifications: Queers of Color and the Performance of Politics* (Minneapolis: University of Minnesota Press, 1999), 161.

30. Denis M. Provencher, *Queer Maghrebi French: Language, Temporalities, Transfiliations* (Liverpool: Liverpool University Press, 2017), 173.

31. Jack Halberstam, *The Queer Art of Failure* (Durham: Duke University Press, 2011), 2.

BIBLIOGRAPHY

Ahmed, Sara. "Multiculturalism and the Promise of Happiness." *New Formations* 63 (2007/2008): 121–137.

———. *Promise of Happiness*. Durham: Duke University Press, 2010.

———. *Living a Feminist Life*. Durham: Duke University Press, 2017.

Berlant, Lauren. *Cruel Optimism*. Durham: Duke University Press, 2011.

———. *The Queen of America Goes to Washington City: Essays on Sex and Citizenship*. Durham: Duke University Press, 2012.

Christensen, Tina Dransfeldt. "Writing the Self as Narrative of Resistance: *L'Armée du salut* by Abdellah Taïa." *The Journal of North African Studies* 21, no. 5 (2016): 857–876.

Fernández Carbajal, Alberto. "The Wandering of a Gay Moroccan: An Interview with Abdellah Taïa." *Journal of Postcolonial Writing* 53, no. 4 (2017): 495–506.

Halberstam, Jack. *The Queer Art of Failure*. Durham: Duke University Press, 2011.

Mack, Mehammed Amadeus. *Sexagon: Muslims, France, and the Sexualization of National Culture*. New York: Fordham University Press, 2017.

Muñoz, José Esteban. *Disidentifications: Queers of Color and the Performance of Politics*. Minneapolis: University of Minnesota Press, 1999.

Provencher, Denis M. *Queer Maghrebi French: Language, Temporalities, Transfiliations*. Liverpool: Liverpool University Press, 2017.

Kathryn Bond Stockton. *The Queer Child, or Growing Sideways in the Twentieth Century*. Durham: Duke University Press, 2009.

Taïa, Abdellah. *L'armée du salut*. Paris: Seuil, 2014.

———, director. *L'armée du salut*. Les Films de Pierre, Les Films Pelleas, Rita Production, Ali N'Films, 7 May 2014.

———. "Our Monsters Are Like Us: An Interview with Abdellah Taïa." Interview with Sam Metz. *Los Angeles Review of Books*. January 9, 2017, https://blog.lareviewofbooks.org/interviews/monsters-like-us-interview-abdellah-taia/. Accessed December 10, 2018.

———. *La vie lente*. Paris: Seuil, 2019.

———. Taïa, "African, Muslim, and Gay." Talk at the Oslo Conference. May 25-27, 2015. Consulted on: https://www.youtube.com/watch?v=THnQ9JmR_tk.

Chapter 5

Queerness, Shame, and the Family in Abdellah Taïa's Epistolary Writing

Ryan K. Schroth

The careful reader of Abdellah Taïa knows the importance the author gives to epistolarity; and, since this feature of his writing has gone largely unstudied, it is the central focus of this chapter. From his short stories to his semi-autobiographical writing, from his feature-length adaptation of *L'armée du salut* [*Salvation Army*] (2014) to his fully epistolary novel, *Celui qui est digne d'être aimé* [*The One Who is Worthy of Being Loved*] (2017), Taïa makes use of the letter form in novel ways. Within Taïa's œuvre, the letter serves first and foremost as a bridge between subjects, a method to unite individuals without diminishing their specific differences, issues, or interests. These letters connect writer and reader in several ways, two of which I will study here: the question of shared origins and the common experience of shame. While these two categories may seem unrelated and even divergent, at first glance, I will argue that they are not. As we shall see, Taïa uses the letter form to motivate a discussion of origins—familial, platonic, amorous—through a sustained analysis of queer Arab shame that I will elucidate here.

Before we begin to identify queer Arab shame in Taïa's work, I would like to briefly discuss its constitutive elements. Following Dina Georgis and others, my understanding of queer Arab shame accounts for the specificity of the local without negating the effects of the global. In this sense, queer Arab shame is much less the outcome of specific shaming dynamics, like those associated with religion or homophobia, and more the hybridized manifestation of these dynamics coupled with universalizing homonormative structures, decades of colonial shame, and the shame brought upon subjects because of other related corporeal markers such as migrant status, ethnicity, and even gender expression. This form of shame is thus cumulative and cyclical.

Within the Moroccan context, and the Arab world more generally, *hchouma* is a specific form of shame that ensures group cohesion and the swift punishment of those who bring shame upon their family. Indeed, Fatima Sadiqi, in *Women, Gender and Language in Morocco* (2002), demonstrates that *hchouma* "may be defined as the 'fear of losing face in front of others'" and that "[t]his loss of face may be occasioned behavior that contravenes social norms, breaks Islamic precepts, or abrogates personal obligations inside or outside the family."[1] Often directed at women, *hchouma* assures cohesion because an individual's reputation, honor, and dignity are associated with the reputation of their family. Abdelhak Serhane, in *L'amour circoncis* [*Circumcised Love*] (1995), demonstrates that "le non-conformisme met en danger la cohésion du groupe. Exposé à l'insulte et à l'ostracisme, le marginal est sacrifié pour la défense des règles, des croyances et des projets de la société" [non-conformity endangers group cohesion. Exposed to insult and ostracism, marginal subjects are sacrificed for the defense of rules, beliefs and social goals].[2] Thus, while *hchouma* is often used against women, it can also be used against anyone who partakes in behaviors outside what society deems "normal," such as queer subjects.

In Dina Georgis' insightful "Thinking Past Pride: Queer Arab Shame in *Bareed Mista3jil*" (2013), the author makes the bold suggestion that one of the specificities of queer Arab communities is indeed a willingness to discuss shame. This willingness outright counters shaming processes like *hchouma*. Given the global and postcolonial realities these queer subjects face, Georgis argues, they do not subscribe to the post-Stonewall pride/shame politics that are well rehearsed in the West. To elaborate her argument, Georgis studies a collection of short stories published by Meem, a Lebanese group of lesbian, bisexual, and queer women and transgender individuals. While not letters in the strict sense, the title of the book, *Bareed Mista3jil*, does interestingly correspond to "Express Mail" in Arabic. Through these stories, Georgis proclaims that "collective queer experience is being mapped from the conditions of Western imperialism and localization, from the shaming legacies of a colonial past, and from everyday life in postwar Lebanon."[3] While Georgis' study focuses specifically on the Lebanese context, similar dynamics are at work in Morocco where globalization, Western imperialism, and the effects of the colonial past continue to shape the present. A unique feature of the *Bareed* stories is how often shame comes up, so much so that Georgis remarks: "a significant aspect of the process of becoming a [queer] community is, as I see it, an openness to talk about shame."[4] Georgis traces the genesis of this shame to the confluence of specific forms of Arab shame, like *hchouma*, the strong Islamic interdiction to minority sexualities, the vestiges of colonial shame, and the effects of neocolonial influence. Despite these elements, Georgis locates a queer Arab shame narrative that is generative in nature. Unlike the dominant post-Stonewall pride politics that have shaped heteronormative and homonormative relationships to shame in the West, Georgis' shame narrative is predicated on the revelation of shame as well as its negotiation. It is this same type of narrative that we will find in Taïa's epistolary writing.

While I have written elsewhere on the political effects of shame in Taïa's epistolary novel, I want to focus here on the relational effects of shame.[5] Shame is, first and foremost, relational because it implies at least two actors, much like letter writing, which we will discuss in a moment. But shame is also individuating in that one is most often shamed *by* another or one tries to hide one's own shame, lest it reveal one's secrets. Within Taïa's writing, the relational effects of shame will be most present in his dealings with his family, unlike the queer Arab shame Georgis locates in the *Bareed* writings, which is founded on the open, communal negotiation of shame. In "Shame, Theatricality, and Queer Performativity: Henry James's *The Art of the Novel*" (2009), Eve Kosofsky Sedgwick, writes on this relational element of shame, arguing:

> One of the strangest features of shame, but perhaps also the one that offers the most conceptual leverage for political projects, is the way bad treatment of someone else, bad treatment *by* someone else, someone else's embarrassment, stigma, debility, bad smell, or strange behavior, seemingly having nothing to do with me, can so readily flood me—assuming I'm a shame-prone person—with this sensation whose very suffusiveness seems to delineate my precise, individual outlines in the most isolating way imaginable.[6]

In short, shame connects us to one another in its double movement "toward painful individuation, toward uncontrollable relationality."[7] Douglas Crimp, in his essay "Mario Montez, For Shame" (2009) offers the following interpretation of Sedgwick's analysis of shame: "In taking on the shame, I do not share in the other's identity. I simply adopt the other's vulnerability to being shamed. In this operation, most important, the other's difference is preserved; it is not claimed as my own. [. . .] I put myself in the place of the other only insofar as I recognize that I too am prone to shame."[8] This is how shame seems to function in Taïa's oeuvre: writing from his own viewpoint or the perspective of a fictional character, he interrogates different forms of shame, not so much to eliminate them or to absolve, but rather to recognize the commonality of shame.

In *Blush: Faces of Shame* (2005), Elspeth Probyn articulates a remedial theory of shame. She understands shame as "both universal and particular, universalizing and particularizing, [and it] should be a resource, not a point of division."[9] Probyn goes on to argue that "when we disregard our human similarities, we can become blind to all the ways we remain connected to one another."[10] In this way, shame demonstrates what matters most to subjects because "whatever it is that shames you will be something that is important to you, an essential part of yourself."[11] Probyn seems to echo Georgis' ideas on queer Arab shame when she writes "[s]hame is not subversive. Shame just *is*. How it is experienced and theorized varies, but nonetheless it is a fact of human life"[12] (emphasis in original); indeed, Georgis sees the Lebanese queer group as forging community life through—rather than against—shame. Taken together, these arguments demonstrate the potential of shame to bring together subjects with similar experiences as well as those with very different experiences.

In the preface to his 2009 curated collection of letters, *Lettres à un jeune marocain* [*Letters to a Young Moroccan*], Taïa writes that "une lettre peut être le début, là, tout de suite, d'une révolte personnelle et collective. Une lettre pour exister. Faire exister les autres. Une lettre pour essayer de ne pas avoir peur. Ne plus se soumettre. Casser le paternalisme et le machisme. Parler et agir" [a letter can be the beginning, right there, all of the sudden, of a personal and collective revolt. A letter to exist. To make others exist. A letter to try not to be afraid. To no longer submit. To break the paternalism and male chauvinism. To speak and act].[13] Taïa assigns significant power to the letter form in this citation. For him, not only do letters carry the potential to ignite a revolution, they also possess the generative power to create other revolutions. Undoubtedly referring, at least in part, to his own open letter to his family, "L'homosexualité expliquée à ma mère" ["Homosexuality Explained to My Mother"] (2009), he understands letter writing as an attempt to make change, indeed as a form of revolt. The dynamic and transformational qualities Taïa locates within the letter form account in part for its prominence in his literary project.

It is by now axiomatic that epistolary writing attests to at least four figures: the letter writer and addressee, as well as the exterior author and exterior reader. Linda S. Kauffman in *Special Delivery: Epistolary Modes in Modern Fiction* (1992) demonstrates this schema in her discussion of Bakhtin's theory of dialogism: "the dialogue within the letter novel between letter writer and addressee is doubled by the dialogue between writer and reader."[14] This paradigm shortens the distance between exterior author and exterior reader, something that is not always possible in pure fictional writing. In other words, the direct interpellation and the use of the second person work collapses the space between author and reader, resulting in a more intimate narrative experience. Kauffman continues by delineating certain characteristics that typify her subject of study: love letters. However, we will still find many of these same elements in Taïa's letters: "writing in the absence of the beloved, mourning the inadequacies of language, transgressing generic boundaries, subverting gender roles, staging revolt through the act of writing."[15] Finally,

Kauffman demonstrates that the collection of letters presented in an epistolary novel necessarily deconstructs hegemonic and monolithic discourses, exposing in the process "the strategies of silencing, the tensions in power relations, and the mechanics of constructing those oppressed as 'other'."[16] This "decentering effect" is for Kauffman—and Taïa, I would argue—a central tenet of epistolary writing.

To be sure, the dynamic and transformational qualities Taïa locates within the letter form account for its prominence within his oeuvre. The first letter we will examine is Taïa's open letter written to his family; the letter is part coming out letter and part political manifesto in which he lays out a platform of progressive politics for the youth of Morocco. Published in 2009 in *TelQuel*, the letter was addressed to his family and is, ostensibly, an attempt to "explain" his sexuality to them. The second letter is again autobiographical. It appeared in Taïa's 2009 edited book *Lettres à un jeune marocain*, a collection of letters written by older Moroccans and addressed to the youth of the country. In Taïa's letter, he writes to his nephew Adnane and reveals family secrets in the process. The third letter, from *Celui qui est digne d'être aimé*, is from a fictional character, Ahmed, to his mother after her death. The fourth and final letter is from the same novel but details an early friendship Ahmed had with another queer boy during his childhood. All in all, the letter serves in each case as a conduit through which the author can reach the addressee in ways not accessible to pure fictional writing, and in the process explore shame through various positionalities. Furthermore, the doubling between writer and addressee—or author and reader—has a profound effect on our engagement with these works. In the end, the queer Arab shame found throughout this selection of Taïa's letters is rendered productive, made useful, or at least mitigated through the question of origins.

HOMOSEXUALITY EXPLAINED: FAMILIAL DIFFERENCES AND FAMILY ORIGINS

Published in the progressive French-language Moroccan newsmagazine *TelQuel*, Taïa's first letter was an open letter to his family in which he set out to presumably explain his minority sexuality. Entitled "L'homosexualité expliquée à ma mère," the letter borrows its title and dialogical structure from Tahar Ben Jelloun's essay, "Le racisme expliqué à ma fille" ["Racism Explained to My Daughter"] (1998). Constituting one of the first widely publicized revelations of nonnormative sexuality in North Africa, the letter aligns Taïa's sexuality with his liberal politics—his desire to do away with what he sees as the confining and constraining precepts of contemporary Moroccan life—as well as his political commitment to support the youth of

Morocco as they seek to reshape their own ties to the country. As such, the letter is more about the myriad ways the younger generations are questioning Moroccan values and ideals—such as citizenship, liberty, and the right to employment—and less about sexuality. In fact, in the thirty-paragraph letter, the word "sexuality" appears only five times.

The first paragraph of the letter focuses on Taïa's personal politics, rather than his sexuality. He begins by stating the objective of his letter: "Expliquer ma démarche, ce que je suis, ce que j'écris et pourquoi je le fais" [Explain my approach, what I am, what I write and why I do it].[17] He proposes that taking the time to explain one's position is a tacit method of valuing the other, and that this simple method of interacting with one another has been missing from Morocco for a long time: "Expliquer parce que depuis longtemps c'est ce qui nous manque au Maroc: qu'on nous considère enfin comme des êtres dignes de recevoir des explications, qu'on nous implique vraiment dans ce qui concerne ce pays et qu'on cesse de nous humilier jour après jour" [Explain because for a long time that is what we've been missing in Morocco: that they finally consider us humans worthy of explanations, that they truly implicate us in what concerns our country and that they stop humiliating us day after day].[18] It must be noted that the use of *digne*—"worthy" or "deserving" in English—prefigures his epistolary novel, *Celui qui est digne d'être aimé*. It also, interestingly enough, anticipates the political calls of various youth organizations following the 2010 Arab Spring uprisings in which students called for human rights and dignity.[19] Under this light, Taïa's earliest work manifests the desire to be worthy enough to receive explanations. He thus demonstrates through his letter, in an attempt to explain himself to his family, that he in turn values them.

In the second paragraph, Taïa invokes *hchouma*, the shame his family must have felt in learning about his minority sexuality. He writes: "Je sais que je suis scandaleux. Pour vous. Et pour les autres autour de vous: les voisins, les collègues au travail, les amis, les belles-mères" [I know that I am scandalous. For you. And for those around you: neighbors, work colleagues, friends, mothers-in-law].[20] Taïa's comments are instructive: first, the social groups in which the family travels are the real issue; second, it is the family that is the victim of this shame, not Taïa himself. This, of course, demonstrates one of the central social functions of shame: to ensure and enforce social cohesion, as Serhane observed. While Taïa is aware that by signing his real name to his writing, he "cause involontairement du 'mal,' des soucis" [involuntarily causes 'pain,' 'worries'], he cannot and will not change this because he has gained so much from the endeavor: "exister enfin! Sortir de l'ombre! Relever la tête! Dire la vérité, ma vérité! Être: Abdellah. Être: Taïa. Être les deux. Seul. Et pas seul à la fois" [exist at last! Come out of the shadows! Raise my head! Tell the truth, my truth! To be: Abdellah. To be: Taïa. To be both.

Alone. And not alone at the same time].[21] Thus, Taïa acknowledges that his actions cause pain and shame for his family, but he does not offer to stop writing with his real name. Instead, he returns to his self-proclaimed commitments to the younger generation, for those "voix nouvelles qui émergent pour dire ce pays autrement" [new voices that are emerging to describe this country differently].[22] Taïa's use of his real name counters shame as he inserts authenticity and solidarity into his political affirmations. In the end, it is not only his expression of minority sexuality that provokes the family's shame, it is also that he writes about these culturally "taboo" topics like "politique, [et] liberté" [politics, [and] freedom];[23] in both instances, going against the status quo provokes *hchouma*. However, Taïa's letter itself acts as a counter to this shame. His open discussion of shame, mirroring what Georgis found in the *Bareed* stories, constitutes his earliest deployment of queer Arab shame.

Taïa moves to further counter this shame by first focusing on his personal connection to his mother. He memorializes his mother's commitments to the family, even if her actions "devenait certains jours de la dictature [et s] a façon de parler était le cri, encore et encore le cri" [became certain days a form of dictatorship [and her] way of speaking was screaming, over and over again screaming].[24] Despite these traits, Taïa calls his mother and her abrasive ways "une école de féminisme" [a school of feminism].[25] Not only did she raise her children, she also coordinated the building of the family house in Salé, all while being "un homme à la place des hommes" [a man in a man's shoes].[26] Taïa offers his writing as a way to preserve her commitments and accomplishments, but he also goes further by suggesting that M'Barka herself has played a role in his personal politics. His political engagement, he proffers, comes from her: "Ma mère, tu ne le sais sans doute pas, le désir de révolte, c'est toi qui me l'as donné" [Mother, you doubtlessly don't know this, but the desire to revolt, you gave it to me].[27] He then announces to her that it is her turn to listen to him: "C'est important pour moi que tu m'écoutes à ton tour. Que tu saches que je suis comme toi. Pas dans la même révolte que toi mais, quand même, comme toi" [It's important to me that you listen to me. That you know that I am like you. Not in the same revolt as you, but like you nonetheless].[28] Indeed, it is the assertiveness of mother and son that brings them together; while their common forcefulness does not stem from the same motivations, it is nonetheless political for them both. And, of course, the shamefulness associated with being bold and assertive redoubles their similarity. Thus, Taïa's *prise de parole* is far from an empty act, but rather one that is motivated by his enactment of queer Arab shame; by figuratively forcing her to listen to him, he clears the way to speak about his shame.

Further on, Taïa appeals to his mother's sense of connectedness to Morocco, while tacitly reminding her that he is also from Morocco. He rehashes her journey to their family, "de Tadla à Salé, en passant par El-Jadida et Rabat" [from Tadla to Salé, passing through El-Jadida and Rabat], calling it "[u] ne épopée sans larmes" [an epic without tears].[29] Her individual journey becomes a valued collective and familial memory. He goes on to celebrate her way of talking: "Ta langue, ma mère, est ma langue. [. . .] J'écris en me rappelant tes cris. Je crie aujourd'hui pour rendre hommage à tes cris. Les fixer. Les donner à voir. Les faire entrer dans les livres, dans la littérature. C'est cela, entre autres, mon ambition. Tes cris comme une image du Maroc. Ton prénom comme symbole de la femme marocaine" [Your language, mother, is my language. [. . .] I write while remembering your screams. I scream today to pay homage to your screams. To get them down. To show them. To put them in books, in literature. That's my ambition. Your screams as an image of Morocco. Your name as a symbol of the Moroccan woman].[30] In a movement similar to Assia Djebar's documenting of women's "cris," Taïa writes his mother into the annals of Moroccan history, first through her journey and then through her own screams that register her power, assertiveness, and her own forms of violence. Throughout the letter, Taïa attempts to show his mother that they are not that different, that they both come from the same *terre*, and that they are embroiled in similar fights. Given the patrilineal structure of Moroccan society, this connection between collective memory, origins, and land is indeed significant. To possess land implies a sense of belonging, a place upon which to build memories that are free of the dogma associated with mainstream normativizing regimes. However, while Taïa attempts to show his mother that they are similar, he does not seem to consider that she is unwilling or unable to make her fight public, to have it traced down for perpetuity in books, like her son.

Denis Provencher, in *Queer Maghrebi French* (2017), rightly points out that Taïa connects his mother to not only the land, but also to forms of culture like poetry, art, and cinema, arguing that "in this letter, and elsewhere, the author ties his ancestry and that of M'Barka to these other cultural praxes—both internal and external to Morocco—in order to build his new transfilial model."[31] Provencher's conceptualization of *transfiliation*, the network of connections and relationships that enact and enable queer (re)production, does indeed work to bring queer son and mother together. I would also argue that it engages and facilitates Taïa's return to his homeland, because as he makes clear throughout the letter, and despite his sexuality and time spent living in Europe, he remains a Moroccan committed to fighting against Moroccan ideals that do not include him or people like him. Indeed, he uses the space of "L'homosexualité expliquée à ma mère" to reiterate the origins and memories he shares with his mother, his siblings, and the youth of Morocco in an attempt to underscore his ongoing commitment to his family, nation, and home. In the end, unlike Taïa's short stories and semi-autobiographical writing, this letter stands out in its bold confrontation of the shame directed at minorities of all types in Moroccan society. He figuratively reaches across the lines of demarcation in an attempt to show his mother how the Moroccan patriarchy positions them both, but his outlook is more optimistic here than in his later writing. While aligning himself with political and cultural movements of progressivism (he even mentions Barack Obama's presidency), he continues to hope for lasting change that will make his beloved nation a more welcoming home for all.

FAMILY SECRETS: SHAME AND AMBIGUOUS ORIGINS

The second letter we will study is found in *Lettres à un jeune marocain*. Entitled "Le Chaouche" [civil servant], the letter is addressed to Taïa's real-life nephew, Adnane. It focuses on the same themes as "L'homosexualité expliquée à ma mère"—an exploration of family origins, a call to the youth, and a reconciliation of shame—but the letter is instead focused on Taïa's father, Mohamed. The missive begins with Taïa admitting to his nephew that he is having trouble remembering his father: "je suis un peu perdu ces jours-ci: je ne retrouve plus l'image de ce père, sa présence, sa trace" [I am a little lost these days: I can no longer find the image of this father, his presence, his trace].[32] It is thus through the communal act of remembering with Adnane that Taïa will be able to recall his father, but this plea also serves as a device to unite the three generations of men. This letter to his nephew, at least with regard to the story that it tells surrounding the father's and nephew's origins, works differently, however, than the mother's genealogy that Taïa shared in "L'homosexualité expliquée à ma mère." Here it is the ambiguity of origins that produces the family. It is not through a connection to the land that paternal belonging is fortified, but rather through a commonality of ambiguous family origins and a shared tacit understanding of those origins.

To be sure, remembering his dead father is not the only goal of the letter. Taïa also intends to publicly reveal two family secrets. But, before doing so, he asks Adnane a series of questions: "ton père, mon frère Abdelkébir, t'a raconté l'histoire du nom de notre famille, Taïa, et du doute qui l'entoure? Est-ce que tu connais le malheur originel de ton grand-père?" [your father, my brother Abdelkébir, told you the story of our family name, Taïa, and about the doubt that surrounds it? Do you know the original misfortune of your grandfather?].[33] Taïa continues on disclosing that his father's brother accused Mohamed of being born out of wedlock. The older brother told Mohamed, "Notre mère t'a eu avec un autre homme. Tu n'es pas un Taïa. Mon père n'est pas ton père" [Our mother had you with another man. You are not a Taïa. My father is not your father].[34] The older brother took the younger brother's inheritance, that, of course, consisted of land: "avait-il inventé ce mensonge pour garder toutes les terres pour lui seul?" [had he invented this lie to keep the land for himself?].[35] Thus, Taïa's father is stripped of his family's land, while his mother, in "L'homosexualité expliquée à ma mère," is figuratively endowed with her own, further inverting the conventions of *hchouma*.

The doubt surrounding the grand/father's origins becomes a source of familial shame that impacts Mohamed's entire life: "Un homme a été brisé dès le départ et jeté dans un vide abyssal. Un homme a été déraciné, déshérité, moqué toute sa vie. On l'appelait le 'fainéant.' On ne le regardait pas comme il fallait" [A man was broken from the start and thrown into an abysmal void. A man was uprooted, disinherited, made fun of for his entire life. They called him a 'slacker.' They never looked at him the way they should have].[36] The ambiguity and doubt surrounding Mohamed's origins affected, in the end, generations of an entire family. Taïa articulates this when he writes: "Le doute des origines, le doute sur l'amour et son sens. Le doute sur soi: Qui suis-je? Qui est mon père?" [The doubt of origins, the doubt of love and its meaning. The doubt of oneself: Who am I? Who is my father?].[37] These questions work on two levels: they can be either the father's or the son's, at any rate this slippage brings Taïa and his father closer together. At this point in the letter, Taïa reminds Adnane that the doubt and shame produced by the grand/father's ambiguous familial origins will be of importance for the second family secret he intends to reveal: "Je veux que tu connaisses cette honte que nous avons subie [I want you to know this shame that we have experienced].[38] Again, Taïa's remark is not to project shame onto Adnane, but rather to share with his nephew the origins of their common familial shame in order to counter it.

Taïa slowly demonstrates that Adnane's origins, like the grand/father, are completely unknown to the family. He reveals that Adnane's parents were not able to have children. However, when Adnane was four months old, he suddenly appeared: "Oui, tu n'existais pas. Maintenant tu existes. Un bébé de quatre mois" [Yes, you didn't exist. Now you exist. A four-month-old baby].[39] Taïa increasingly becomes more direct in revealing that Adnane's parents adopted him. While adoption is prohibited in Islam,[40] Taïa remarks that the entire family was so happy to welcome Adnane into their lives that they were willing to be accomplices to the "crime:" "Nous étions tous dans la même transgression. L'adoption est interdite en Islam. Nous écrivions autrement la mémoire" [We were all part of the same transgression. Adoption is prohibited in Islam. We wrote memory differently].[41] As they rewrite familial memory together, they are also (re)writing the family's origins. Taïa goes on to explain that the extended family demonstrates the same willingness to look the other way: "Je ne sais pas si les autres membres de la famille s'en rendaient vraiment compte. Par amour pour toi et pour ta peau foncée, ils ne respectaient pas les lois" [I don't know if the other members of the family realized. Out of love for you and for your dark skin, they did not respect the laws].[42] Taïa also connects the story of Adnane's arrival into the family to the ambiguous origins of his own father: "J'aime que tu viennes d'ailleurs renouveler notre sang, redéfinir notre famille, porter différemment notre nom. Taïa. J'aime que l'histoire, grâce à toi, ne se déroule pas comme c'était prévu" [I like that you came from elsewhere to renew our blood, redefine our family, carry our family name differently. Taïa. I like that history, thanks to you, will not play out as planned].[43] In much the same way that Taïa's mother becomes a symbol for all of Morocco in "L'homosexualité expliquée à ma mère," Adnane comes to symbolize the progress often associated with the youth; not only will he renew and redefine their family, but his origins—mysterious as they are—will rewrite the family's history.

Ultimately, Taïa's letter to his nephew foregrounds the shame that his father and his family felt due to the ambiguous paternal genealogy. Within the letter, Taïa even calls into question the uncle's accusations, suggesting that the man perhaps wanted the entire family inheritance for himself. In an important moment towards the end of the letter, Taïa writes "Je ne veux pas être Cham qui a été maudit par son père, le prophète Noé" [I don't want to be Ham who was cursed by his father, the prophet Noah].[44] The exact meaning of the biblical story of Ham's curse, found in Genesis, Chapter 9, is unknown. Noah, drunken, falls asleep naked in his tent; his son Ham enters the tent without averting his eyes, nor does he cover his father. After Ham tells his brothers of their father's state of undress, the brothers return to Noah's tent and respectfully cover up their father. When Noah eventually awakens, he curses his son for his shameful actions. Given this background, Taïa's remarks can be understood as a reminder to respect the father, even when it might be easy to shame him. He goes on to say to Adnane, "Je ne veux pas que tu sois Cham non plus, Adnane" [I don't want you to be Ham either, Adnane].[45] Thus, in the end, Taïa issues the same warning to his nephew: even though he is adopted, he must never shame his father for this.

Ultimately, Taïa uses the space of this letter to connect himself, his father, and his nephew, thereby writing a new family history. Unlike "L'homosexualité expliquée à ma mère," this letter is a more sustained effort to rebuke *hchouma* or familial shame. While in the former letter, Taïa meticulously traced his own origins through his mother, he is unable to do so in the current letter because the patrilineal lines have been figuratively severed. Instead, Taïa uses the fragments of his memories with his father, as well as those of his nephew, to construct the man's portrait. The recuperative effects of this action call into question the bonds of the patriarchy. Provencher argues that Taïa "writes these two letters ["L'homosexualité expliquée à ma mère" and "Le Chaouche"] as a means of presenting a new Abdellah to his family, rediscovering and re-imagining his family and country, and inviting his family to imagine with him a queer future where they can all belong."[46] While this question of futurity is important, as we will see in the next section, it must also be said that the Abdellah presented in these two letters is not so much a new or (re)imagined Abdellah, but rather the Abdellah he has always been. To return to Provencher's concept, these letters lay bare the transfiliation that connects Taïa to his home, family, and country.

WHO IS WORTHY OF LOVE? A MOTHER'S SHAME

This section examines two letters from Taïa's 2017 epistolary novel, *Celui qui est digne d'être aimé*. As a fictional novel, *Celui* does not have the same markers of autobiography (for example, the protagonist is named Ahmed) featured in the first two letters examined. However, as we will see, the novel's letters still contain the same themes, namely the question of familial origins and expressions of shame. The first letter in the collection, written by Ahmed, is addressed to his mother. In this letter, Ahmed at first criticizes his mother for her shamelessness and neglect but resolves his ill will toward her by the end of the letter.

Ahmed's letter to his mother, Malika, combines elements from both of Taïa's letter to his family and his letter to his nephew analyzed above. Ahmed begins by describing his mother in ways that are very similar to the words of "L'homosexualité expliquée à ma mère": she is "effrontée, jusqu'au bout, les yeux durs, indifférente à tous, à moi surtout, dictatrice assumée" [shameless, until the end, with hard eyes, indifferent to everyone, to me above all, a proud dictator].[47] From the outset, the reader understands that this is not a letter to mourn his mother's passing, but rather one to settle scores. We learn that not only was Malika shameless in her dealings with her family and friends, but that she was also shameless in sharing her sex life with her children, which inevitably infuriated Ahmed because she remained unable to accept his own minority sexuality throughout her lifetime.

Ahmed writes that, as children, he and his siblings were forced to witness their parents' sex life. He judges his parents for allowing them to hear everything: "vos soupirs, vos râles, vos orgasmes bruyants, impudiques" [your moans, your gasps, your loud, shameless orgasms]. He wonders why his parents did not hide their love making, "pourquoi tu tenais tant à tout étaler devant nous [. . .] Pourquoi tu ne nous as pas protégés?" [why did you have to show us everything [. . .] Why didn't you protect us?].[48] This instance of shaming again reverses the dynamics of *hchouma*, in which the parents would typically shame the children for their transgressions. Thus, by directly shaming his parents, Ahmed ultimately suggests that Malika did not shield her children from what he considers to be their distasteful imposition of parental (hetero)sexuality.

Interestingly, Ahmed's description of shame in his letter to his mother remains focused on the shame his parents incite in him. Both Malika and Hamid push against gendered conceptions of "mother" and "father." While other children in the neighborhood have loving mothers, Ahmed describes Malika as having a "cœur dur, fermé, de plus en plus sec. Un cœur dictateur" [hard heart, closed, colder and colder. A dictator's heart].[49] He goes on to accuse his mother of publicly castrating his father; in fact, the neighborhood comes to think of Hamid as "moins qu'un homme" [less than a man].[50] Indeed, one day, the man finally proclaims, "Je suis une femme. Oui. Je suis Hamid, la femme de Malika" [I am a woman. Yes. I am Hamid, Malika's wife].[51] Because of his father's "failed masculinity," Ahmed writes, "J'avais honte alors [. . .] je le pleurais" [I was ashamed [. . .] I mourned him].[52] Thus, Ahmed's shame seems more motivated by the public nature of Hamid's gender shaming, and the hand his mother plays in it, rather than his actual discomfiture at having a submissive father. Interestingly, Malika is never condemned publicly for her "masculine" traits.

Like the other letters we have studied, origins remain an integral part of Ahmed's letter to his mother. However, here, the letter tells the origin story of Ahmed himself. At first angry that his mother "made" him in her image, Ahmed goes on to wonder what her ulterior motives might have been. To his dismay, he is like his mother: "Je suis froid et tranchant comme toi. Malin, calculateur, terrifiant parfois. Dans le cri, dans le pouvoir, dans la domination. Exactement comme toi" [I am cold and decisive like you. Sly, calculating, terrifying sometimes. In screaming, in power, in domination. Exactly like you].[53] He begins to wonder if his mother passed her personality on to him because of his nonnormative sexuality: "Pourquoi tu m'as choisi, moi? [. . .] Pourquoi? Parce que je suis homosexuel? C'est cela?" [Why did you choose me? [. . .] Why? Because I am homosexual? Is that it?].[54] On the one hand, this intentioned act would presuppose that she knew about her son's sexuality, without ever having acknowledged it, while, on the other hand, it presumes that she did not think Ahmed would be "strong" enough to face the abuse and isolation he would undoubtedly endure as a queer Moroccan.

Whereas with "L'homosexualité expliquée à ma mère," Taïa was able to produce a vision of the future in which the family might once again come together, this fictional letter is much less optimistic. Still, while the tone is biting and vicious, the letter still serves to mourn and memorialize the mother. In fact, towards the end, we learn that Ahmed is waiting for the phone call that will announce his mother's death. He accuses his mother of having never been fully honest with him: "Tu n'as rien dit de salutaire, Malika. Tu m'as juste tout entier imprégné de tes mises en scène et de ta dictature" [You never said anything salutary, Malika. You just filled me with your little dramas and your dictatorship].[55] Even so, it is as if life without his mother would be too unbearable, because he ends his letter with: "Je n'ai plus la force. Je n'ai plus envie ni de vivre ni de prendre l'avion. J'arrête ici, moi aussi" [I no longer have the strength. I have neither the desire to live nor to take the plane. I'm stopping here, me too].[56] In the end, Ahmed's letter demonstrates the unresolved anger at his mother and how it intersects with the man's ongoing love for her. Ironically, Ahmed is angered by his mother's shamelessness, perhaps because it was the one thing that she could not pass on to him.

SOME ORIGINS OF SHAME: RAPE AND SUICIDE

The last letter of *Celui qui est digne d'être aimé* is from Ahmed's queer childhood friend, Lahbib who writes for two reasons: first to memorialize his friendship with Ahmed; and, second, to warn the younger Ahmed about relationships with predatory men. Lahbib describes his shame-filled relationship with his European lover, Gérard. After he is rejected by Gérard for being "too old," Lahbib's letter turns into a suicide note. "Liés par le même secret" [Connected by the same secret],[57] Lahbib and Ahmed were regularly raped by men in their neighborhood of Salé.[58] They come together because of their similarities but do not discuss them: "se retrouver une fois par semaine devant les trains qui passent, parler de nous, toi et moi sans eux" [meet each other once per week in front of where the trains go by, to talk about us, you and me without them].[59] In the text, this "without them" is without antecedent and, thus, stands in for all the men who take advantage of the young boys, as well as all the adolescents who do not share Lahbib and Ahmed's secret.

Lahbib goes on to explain to Ahmed how Gérard broke up with him. Lahbib already knows that Gérard is planning to let him go because he has begun to inquire about Lahbib's younger friend, Ahmed, who is fifteen years old. Sadly, Lahbib writes that "[à] 17 ans, [il] ne faisai[t] plus l'affaire pour Gérard" [[at] 17 years old, [he] no longer do[es] it for Gérard], he knows that he has "expiré" [expired].[60] During one of their regular afternoon rendezvous, Gérard orders Lahbib to take a shower, like normal, but after the shower the French man refuses to get into bed with his younger lover. Whether it is Lahbib's "bad smell" that causes Gérard to order him to shower or the French man's controlling behaviors, this moment works, as Sedgwick explained in her comments on the relationality of shame, to transmit Lahbib's sense of shame to the reader. Gérard continues shaming him, announcing that he knows Lahbib took more money than their agreed-upon sum during their last tryst. His incommensurate reaction is to tell Lahbib: "Tu m'as trahi . . . Je ne peux plus te faire confiance . . . Je ne peux plus faire du sexe avec toi . . . Tu me dégoûtes . . ." [You betrayed me . . . I can no longer trust you . . . I can no longer have sex with you . . . You disgust me].[61] His remarks are clearly a pretense to end their relationship, but they nonetheless cause Lahbib immense shame. It is at this moment that he first considers taking his life.

After forcing Lahbib to take a second shower, Gérard still refuses to get into bed with him. Lahbib writes that this experience of shame "m'a rendu à moi-même, à ma pauvreté, à mon corps sale" [returned me to myself, to my poverty, to my dirty body].[62] A textbook definition of shame, the burden of Gérard's gaze refocuses Lahbib on his own body, uncovering the young man's oldest fears: his poverty and his "dirty" body. Here, Lahbib's experience is curiously similar to what Frantz Fanon describes in *Peau noire, masques blancs* [*Black Skin, White Masks*] (1952), when after having been interpellated by a young child, Fanon states, "Mon corps revenait étalé, disjoint, rétamé, tout endeuillé" [My body came back to me sprawled out, distorted, recolored, clad in mourning].[63] Thus, the humiliating gaze of his (white) European lover rips away his body, only to return it undone.

Having sacrificed his young body, Lahbib hoped for more than money in return. He sought protection and mutual respect. However, it is made clear in the letter that this is currently impossible in Morocco for subjects of minority sexualities. Lahbib asserts that Morocco "t'opprime et t'asphyxie" [oppresses you and suffocates you];[64] he assures Ahmed that there are no happy endings in queer life in North Africa, no possibility of finding (and keeping) one's "prince à tout jamais" [prince forever and ever].[65] This bleak realization motivates Lahbib to announce his suicide. Despite this, he urges Ahmed to "Garde[r] le monde et l'espoir vivants en [. . .] [lui]. Même difficile, tu dois porter jusqu'au bout cette mission" [Keep the world and hope alive in [. . .] [him]. Even when difficult, you have to carry out this mission].[66]

In the end, it is not a broken heart that kills Lahbib, but rather shame. His gradual realization that Gérard will never treat him as an equal partner is too much to bear. He writes: "Je croyais que Gérard allait me sauver, me garder avec lui pour toujours. Me trouver du travail, me guider dans l'enfer de mon existence marocaine. Je croyais que j'allais vieillir à ses côtés. Je croyais qu'il était mon prince à tout jamais" [I thought that Gérard was going to save me, keep me with him forever. Find me work, guide me through the hell that is my Moroccan existence. I thought that I was going to grow old next to him. I thought that he was my happily ever after prince].[67] While Lahbib does not find salvation with Gérard, he may find a divine form of it, for his name has special significance: "*Al-habib*. [. . .] L'amour. L'objet d'amour. Celui qui est proche de l'amour. Proche d'Allah. [. . .] un des 99 noms pour dire, s'adresser à Dieu en Islam. L'aimer. Le vénérer. Le chanter. Le caresser" [*Al-habib*. [. . .] Love. The object of love. He who is close to love. Close to Allah. [. . .] one of the 99 names to call, to address God in Islam. To love him. To venerate him. To glorify him. To caress him].[68] Because divine love is assured for Lahbib, he is not ashamed to take his own life. He is indeed the one worthy of love.

CONCLUSION: WRITING ORIGINS AND QUEER ARAB SHAME

In conclusion, the four letters studied here demonstrate the ways in which the letter form, throughout Taïa's writing, works to bring subjects together, to question social precepts, and challenge normative conceptualizations of shame. Taïa's first letter, "L'homosexualité expliquée à ma mère," uses tropes of migration and revolution to demonstrate to his mother that they are the same: they are both Moroccan, they come from the lower-class, and her story of emigration mirrors his own, from Morocco to France. In the second letter, Taïa writes to his nephew under the pretense of remembering his father, but he actually wants to reveal to his nephew that—like his father—he has unknown family origins. His nephew's adoption ultimately demonstrates the ambiguous nature of family while challenging the religious precepts of Islam.

The third letter, written by Ahmed to his mother after she has died, begins by shaming the mother and the father. Ahmed focuses on the role his mother's shame has played in his life, suggesting that she perhaps knew of his minority sexuality but could never accept it. This shame, as we saw, has both positive and negative effects in Ahmed's life; however, he is ultimately able to come to terms with his mother's role in making him who he is. The fourth and final letter, from Lahbib to Ahmed, traces the shame of an inter-generational, inter-ethnic relationship. Unfortunately for Lahbib, Gérard was never going to be the partner he was looking for. The shame of this realization proves to be too much, and Lahbib takes his life.

Each letter, of course, communicates with the other letters studied here. While all of the letters function as attempts to discuss and disclose shame, each one goes about doing so in a different way. In "L'homosexualité expliquée à ma mère," shame is charged with the hope of bringing mother and son closer together, it functions as the linchpin around which their possible (re)connection could turn. In the letter, shame is left smoldering with possibility. In "Le Chaouche," Taïa's experiment with shame goes further than in the former letter. Shame functions as a veritable tool, and its revelation serves to strengthen familial ties and reshape collective memory. It is not a coincidence that this letter is addressed to Taïa's nephew, as a member of the younger generation to whom he issued a call to action in "L'homosexualité expliquée à ma mère." As if Taïa's family was unable or unwilling to hear his pleas to accept his "shameful" secret—his minority sexuality—his most recent letters, in *Celui*, deploy shame in a more ruthless, even brutal way. In Ahmed's letter to his dead mother, he initially shames his mother for her role in manipulating him and his father, but eventually—somewhat fatalistically—demonstrates how lost he is without her guidance. Perhaps this is his shame. Finally, in Lahbib's letter to Ahmed, he revisits what is perhaps one of the first instances of shame experienced by the queer youth: their rape and sexual abuse at the hands of Moroccan and European men. By revealing this initial shame, culpability and shame can finally be directed at those men responsible for victimizing the youth. While the expression and revelation of shame does not, unfortunately, save Lahbib, it might very well liberate Ahmed.

In each of the letters, shame thus functions slightly differently. But it is never meant to serve as a threat to queerness itself. Instead, it works to make visible, unveil, build bridges, buttress newly formed connections; shame sets out to strengthen origins and work against the (hetero)norms of belonging. If shame is a constant experience of life, and it certainly seems to be so for queer Arabs, then it must be negotiated, rather than left to explode. Shame, as Sedgwick and Probyn have argued, is indeed relational; it "holds the promise of cultural production; in shame, what's possible is near because the gaze of the other evokes an intense vulnerability that cannot be easily disavowed."[69] This promise seems amplified by the epistolary mode in Taïa's œuvre, given its multiplication of the author-reader and writer-addressee relationships. Thus, to map these notions of relationality onto the epistolary genre is not difficult. Not only do letters circulate in much the same way as affect does, but a nexus of unending positionalities is opened, one that is not hierarchical in structure but rather reciprocal. Indeed, as Janet G. Altman argues: "The epistolary form is unique in making the reader (narratee) almost as important an agent in the narrative as the writer (narrator)."[70] Letter writing in Taïa's work does just that; the writer speaks directly to the reader, bringing himself closer to both *destinataires* [addressees]. Taïa's letters ultimately serve to connect people and places through experiences of shame, and to produce new possibilities for queers, Arabs, and queer Arabs alike; or, as Georgis reminds us "If we turn our attention to affects and their vicissitudes, we may learn how queer Arabs are negotiating in unexpected ways the interconnectivity of cultures and places."[71] The interconnectivity that is promised by both affect and epistolarity are indeed what constitutes the queer revolutionary power of letter writing.

NOTES

1. Fatima Sadiqi, *Women, Gender and Language in Morocco* (Leiden, Boston: Brill, 2002), 67.

2. Abdelhak Serhane, *L'amour circoncis* (Casablanca: EDDIF, 1995), 16; all translations are my own.

3. Dina Georgis, "Thinking Past Pride: Queer Arab Shame in *Bareed Mista3jil*," *International Journal of Middle East Studies* 45, no. 2 (2013): 234.

4. Dina Georgis, "Thinking Past Pride," 234.

5. Ryan K. Schroth, "Queer Shame: Affect, Resistance, and Colonial Critique in Abdellah Taïa's *Celui qui est digne d'être aimé*." *The Journal of North African Studies* 26, no. 1 (2021): 138–162. Published online October 22, 2019: DOI: 10.1080/13629387.2019.1683449.

6. Eve Kosofsky Sedgwick, "Shame, Theatricality, and Queer Performativity: Henry James's *The Art of the Novel*," in *Gay Shame*, edited by David M. Halperin and Valerie Traub (Chicago: University of Chicago Press, 2009), 50.

7. Eve Kosofsky Sedgwick, "Shame, Theatricality, and Queer Performativity," 51.

8. Douglas Crimp, "Mario Montez, For Shame," in *Gay Shame*, edited by David M. Halperin and Valerie Traub (Chicago: University of Chicago Press, 2009), 71.

9. Elspeth Probyn, *Blush: Faces of Shame* (Minneapolis: University of Minnesota, 2005), xvii.

10. Probyn, *Blush*, xiii.

11. Probyn, *Blush*, x.

12. Probyn, *Blush*, xviii.

13. Abdellah Taïa, *Lettres à un jeune marocain* (Paris: Seuil, 2009), 12.

14. Linda S. Kauffman, *Special Delivery: Epistolary Modes in Modern Fiction* (Chicago: University of Chicago, 1992), xix.

15. Kauffman, *Special Delivery*, xiii.

16. Kauffman, *Special Delivery*, xxi.

17. Taïa, "L'homosexualité expliquée à ma mère," *TelQuel*, April 10, 2009, Paragraph 1.

18. Taïa, "L'homosexualité expliquée à ma mère," Paragraph 1.

19. Moha Ennaji, "The Agency of Youth in North Africa: New Forms of Citizenship." February 11, 2020, Wake Forest University.

20. Taïa, "L'homosexualité expliquée à ma mère," Paragraph 2.

21. Taïa, "L'homosexualité expliquée à ma mère," Paragraph 2.

22. Taïa, "L'homosexualité expliquée à ma mère," Paragraph 25.

23. Taïa, "L'homosexualité expliquée à ma mère," Paragraph 4.

24. Taïa, "L'homosexualité expliquée à ma mère," Paragraph 10.

25. Taïa, "L'homosexualité expliquée à ma mère," Paragraph 9.

26. Taïa, "L'homosexualité expliquée à ma mère," Paragraph 9.

27. Taïa, "L'homosexualité expliquée à ma mère," Paragraph 9.

28. Taïa, "L'homosexualité expliquée à ma mère," Paragraph 16.

29. Taïa, "L'homosexualité expliquée à ma mère," Paragraph 11.

30. Taïa, "L'homosexualité expliquée à ma mère," Paragraph 12.

31. Denis M. Provencher, *Queer Maghrebi French: Language, Temporalities, Transfiliations* (Liverpool: Liverpool University Press, 2017), 157.

32. Abdellah Taïa, *Lettres à un jeune marocain* (Paris: Seuil, 2009), 199.

33. Taïa, *Lettres à un jeune marocain*, 201.
34. Taïa, *Lettres à un jeune marocain*, 208–209.
35. Taïa, *Lettres à un jeune marocain*, 209.
36. Taïa, *Lettres à un jeune marocain*, 209.
37. Taïa, *Lettres à un jeune marocain*, 209.
38. Taïa, *Lettres à un jeune marocain*, 210.
39. Taïa, *Lettres à un jeune marocain*, 207.
40. Adoption, in the Western sense, in which a child takes on the name of their adoptive family, is illegal in Arab countries; the Qur'anic verse "Proclaim their real parentage" (Qur'an 33.5) is understood to prohibit it. *Kafala* or guardianship, however, is not prohibited. For more on adoption in Morocco, see J.C.C.M. Fioole, "Give Me Your Child: Adoption Practices in a Small Moroccan Town," *The Journal of North African Studies* 20, no. 2 (2014): 247–264.
41. Taïa, *Lettres à un jeune marocain*, 208.
42. Taïa, *Lettres à un jeune marocain*, 208.
43. Taïa, *Lettres à un jeune marocain*, 207.
44. Taïa, *Lettres à un jeune marocain*, 210.
45. Taïa, *Lettres à un jeune marocain*, 210.
46. Provencher, *Queer Maghrebi French*, 169.
47. Taïa, *Celui qui est digne d'être aimé* (Paris: Seuil, 2017), 11.
48. Taïa, *Celui qui est digne*, 16.
49. Taïa, *Celui qui est digne*, 30.
50. Taïa, *Celui qui est digne*, 17.
51. Taïa, *Celui qui est digne*, 17.
52. Taïa, *Celui qui est digne*, 18.
53. Taïa, *Celui qui est digne*, 19.
54. Taïa, *Celui qui est digne*, 20.
55. Taïa, *Celui qui est digne*, 42.
56. Taïa, *Celui qui est digne*, 43.
57. Taïa, *Celui qui est digne*, 99.
58. Taïa, *Celui qui est digne*, 128.
59. Taïa, *Celui qui est digne*, 128.
60. Taïa, *Celui qui est digne*, 132.
61. Taïa, *Celui qui est digne*, 130.
62. Taïa, *Celui qui est digne*, 135.
63. Frantz Fanon, *Peau noire, masques blancs* (Paris: Seuil, 1952), 91.
64. Taïa, *Celui qui est digne*, 127.
65. Taïa, *Celui qui est digne*, 133.
66. Taïa, *Celui qui est digne*, 135.
67. Taïa, *Celui qui est digne*, 133.
68. Taïa, *Celui qui est digne*, 123.
69. Georgis, "Thinking Past Pride," 242.
70. Janet G. Altman, *Epistolarity: Approaches to a Form* (Columbus: Ohio State University Press, 1982), 88.
71. Georgis, "Thinking Past Pride," 237.

BIBLIOGRAPHY

Altman, Janet G. *Epistolarity: Approaches to a Form.* Columbus: Ohio State University Press, 1982.

Ben Jelloun, Tahar. *Le racisme expliqué à ma fille.* Paris: Seuil, 1998.

Crimp, Douglas. "Mario Montez, For Shame." In *Gay Shame,* edited by David M. Halperin and Valerie Traub, 63–75. Chicago: University of Chicago Press.

Fioole, J.C.C.M. "Give Me Your Child: Adoption Practices in a Small Moroccan Town." *The Journal of North African Studies* 20, no. 2 (2014): 247–264.

Fanon, Frantz. *Peau noire, masques blancs.* Paris: Seuil, 1952.

Georgis, Dina. "Thinking Past Pride: Queer Arab Shame in *Bareed Mista3jil.*" *International Journal of Middle East Studies* 45, no. 2 (2013): 233–251.

Kauffman, Linda S. *Special Delivery: Epistolary Modes in Modern Fiction.* Chicago: University of Chicago Press, 1992.

Moha, Ennaji. "The Agency of Youth in North Africa: New Forms of Citizenship." February 11, 2020, Wake Forest University.

Probyn, Elspeth. *Blush: Faces of Shame.* Minneapolis: University of Minnesota Press, 2005.

Provencher, Denis M. *Queer Maghrebi French: Language, Temporalities, Transfiliations.* Liverpool: Liverpool University Press, 2017.

Schroth, Ryan K. "Queer Shame: Affect, Resistance, and Colonial Critique in Abdellah Taïa's *Celui qui est digne d'être aimé.*" *The Journal of North African Studies* 26, no. 1 (2021): 138–162. Published online October 22, 2019: DOI: 10.1080/13629387.2019.1683449.

Sedgwick, Eve Kosofsky. "Shame, Theatricality, and Queer Performativity: Henry James's *The Art of the Novel.*" In *Gay Shame,* edited David M. Halperin and Valerie Traub, 49–62. Chicago: University of Chicago Press, 2009.

Serhane, Abdelhak. *L'amour circoncis.* Casablanca: EDDIF, 1995.

Taïa, Abdellah. *Celui qui est digne d'être aimé.* Paris: Seuil, 2017.

—. "L'homosexualité expliqué à ma mère." *TelQuel,* April 10, 2009.

—, ed. *Lettres à un jeune marocain.* Paris: Seuil, 2009.

The Bible. New International Version, https://www.biblegateway.com. Accessed 2 May 2020.

Chapter 6

Mourning and Reconciliation

Anger, Politics, and Love

Jean-Pierre Boulé

Published in January 2017, *Celui qui est digne d'être aimé* [*The One Worthy of Being Loved*] is a novel with a first-person narrator, as in some of Taïa's previously published works, but the narrator is called "Ahmed" rather than Abdellah (the names of some family members have also been changed). Nevertheless, the novel exploits an autobiographical stance: "Avec ce dernier roman, je poursuis quelque chose que j'avais arrêté après *Une mélancolie arabe* [2008], c'est-à-dire des romans pleinement autobiographiques. Il y a beaucoup de choses autobiographiques dans ce livre." [With this novel, I am carrying on something which I had stopped doing after *Une mélancolie arabe*[1] [2008], [*An Arab Melancholia*], that is fully autobiographical novels. There are many autobiographical elements in this book].[2] In a radio interview, Taïa confirms: "Donc, en tout cas, Ahmed et moi, c'est la même chose." [So, in any case, Ahmed and I, it's the same].[3]

Celui qui est digne d'être aimé is an epistolary novel composed of four letters. The first letter, written in the first person by Ahmed, is destined for his mother Malika (meaning "queen" in Arabic) who has recently died. The second one is written by Vincent, a French national, for Ahmed, who left him. The third one is also written by Ahmed and destined for Emmanuel, his French lover; it is a letter announcing the break-up of their relationship. The fourth letter is written by Lahbib and addressed to Ahmed; they were childhood friends. Lahbib puts pen to paper as Gérard, Lahbib's lover, has just left him. These letters are in reverse order (August 2015/ July 2010/ July 2005/ May 1990).

Even though Taïa claims to be renewing with autobiographical writings dating back to 2008, there is a clear thread with his more recent novels as the theme of mourning is also present in *Celui qui est digne d'être aimé*. I am going to concentrate on the theme of mourning, using a psychoanalytical approach, based notably on Melanie Klein, and will come back later in the chapter to the political message of the book, a constant in all of Taïa's writings, culminating with the third letter. I will then be able to demonstrate that the writing of the novel creates a movement toward reconciliation and appeasement, powered by the narrative and, more specifically, the epistolary genre, which can have a cathartic effect and allows a dialogue to continue, even after death. Because mourning is an evolving process, I will study the letters in their chronology, apart from the third one, which deals with the political message of the book, and demonstrate that the first phase of mourning is anger, which, when expressed, leads to unmasking love, and this in turn allows for reparation. It is a dynamic process which will parse out the main three axes of my chapter, together with the political. I will intermingle Taïa's interviews (as in the paratext) and some biographical details in an approach I call "biotextuality." This is not to say that I am going back to Sainte-Beuve, explaining the works by the life of the author. Taïa himself constantly uses autobiographical material; life and writing are intertwined in a melody, transcended by the act of writing and, notably, of writing the body. Instead of simply listening to the melody, my biotextuality approach also allows me to read the score on the partition. And because Taïa uses his life story for all his novels, my readers will not be surprised if I open my analysis with a previously published novel, *Un pays pour mourir* [*A Country for Dying*], published in 2015, as it will provide a key to unlocking some of the significance of *Celui qui est digne d'être aimé*. The intertextuality will reveal how a family tragedy has been a source for a writing stream in two separate novels, with very different results.

ANGER: COLONIALISM ENTERS THE FAMILY HISTORY

My starting point is an interview the author gave to Marie Richeux when *Celui qui est digne d'être aimé* was published. Taïa explains that, during his mother's funeral, he learned that the man whom she had married when she was very young (not his father) and who had died in the war (this information is given in *L'armée du salut* [*Salvation Army*][4] published in 2006) had in fact been sent by *France* in the 1950s to fight the war in Indochina. From their union was born a little girl, Amina, his half-sister.[5] Based on this information, I recall that the last part of *Un pays pour mourir* is called "Indochine, Saïgon, Juin 1954" [Indochina, Saïgon, June 1954].[6] In this last section of the novel, the father's sister, Zineb, reappears as a Moroccan prostitute and works for the French army, servicing the soldiers who do not like Asian prostitutes. There is also a character called Gabriel, a French soldier fighting in Indochina, and they fall for each other. If Gabriel had seemed unimportant to me when I first read the novel, he gains in gravitas when considering the family history. At the end of that story, having refused to become a deserter, Gabriel promises Zineb he will accompany her to India; his only wish is not to die in Indochina.[7] "Indochine, Saïgon, Juin 1954" represents a first attempt to write the family tragedy affecting Taïa's mother as revealed in the interview. Gabriel will not die in Indochina in the novel, unlike the first husband of Taïa's mother. It is almost as if the author wanted this character to stay alive in the fictional world because he had not known his existence for many years, as a form of *reparation* for his mother. I use the word in the sense given by Rosello: "The reparative is an energy, a process, a specific set of narrative choices that propose to offer a conscious or unconscious strategy to a double process of recapturing and recovering."[8]

Further on in the interview, we learn that after he died in service, the husband's family received some modest financial compensation from the French government. The money was so inadequately tiny that they decided to keep their granddaughter but threw Taïa's mother (M'Barka) in the street, penniless. The writer confesses to being upset because he did not ask his mother for the whole story while she was alive. He now has the opportunity to "repair" this state of affairs: "Donc, je me suis dit: 'Il faut écrire une lettre à cette femme, à ma mère, pour lui dire: voilà ce que j'ai appris sur toi et lui dire que cet événement excuse beaucoup de choses.'" [So, I told myself: "I have to write a letter to this woman, my mother, to tell her: this is what I learned about you, and this event excuses many things"].[9]

Listening to Taïa's intentions, I am struck by how dissonant they are from the ruthless letter addressed to his mother published in *Celui qui est digne d'être aimé*. In the same interview, Taïa shows his awareness of this discrepancy, blaming "les mystères de la littérature" ["the mysteries of literature"]. Rather than pointing the finger at the mysteries of literature, I want to focus my reading on the hazards of mourning as I believe they are the key to unlocking the discrepancy between intention and execution and, in turn, the act of mourning will allow for reconciliation.

Anger against the Mother

The starting point of the author's grief, which is the cornerstone of my reading, can be pinpointed to the mother's passing: Taïa was very much traumatized by her death. It brought to the surface unhappy episodes from his childhood and, in turn, made his day-to-day living very difficult to manage.[10] According to Melanie Klein, in the "normal" process of mourning, the loss of a loved one brings with it the need to reinstate the lost love-object[11]: "As we know, the mourner obtains great relief from recalling the lost person's kindness and good qualities, and this is partly due to the reassurance he experiences from keeping his loved object for the time being as an idealized one."[12] In this first letter, the opposite is true; the mother is described as a dictator, heartless. The author concedes that his character Ahmed "dresse un tombeau extrêmement cruel [. . .] de sa propre mère" [erects an extremely cruel gravestone [. . .] of his own mother][13]; he does not idolize her. If we follow Klein's reasoning, this action brings the following result: "[. . .] when hatred against the loved person wells up in the mourner, his belief in him breaks down and the process of idealization is disturbed."[14] Let us unpack the psychic phenomena at stake in this self *(auto)fiction*.

With Malika having only a few days left to live, one reads: "C'est le grand désespoir. Je suis abandonné. De nouveau abandonné" [It is the great despair. I am abandoned. Again, abandoned].[15] This feeling only intensifies: "Je commence à t'en vouloir. Tu n'as pas le droit de partir, de mourir comme ça, sans moi. Je t'en veux de plus en plus." [I am starting to bear a grudge against you. You do not have the right to go, to die like this, without me. I resent you more and more].[16] It appears that the narcissistic wound that opened up when the mother died caused the following reaction for the author: "His hatred of the loved person is increased by the fear that, by dying, the loved one was seeking to inflict punishment and deprivation upon him [. . .]."[17] Deprivation and the weight of carrying the deceased family member is a trope common in writing on the colonial past.

The aforementioned sentences express Ahmed's anger faced with his mother's death and, also, his anger against the whole world.[18] According to Taïa, "Pour arriver à la vérité, il faut passer par ce stade de la colère. Si on passe tout de suite à la compréhension et à l'apaisement, je pense [. . .] qu'on n'aura pas tout vécu ou compris]" [In order to arrive at the truth, first of all, one must go through this stage of anger. If one becomes straight away understanding and conciliatory, I think [. . .] that person will not have lived through nor understood everything].[19] We can now start to understand the difference between the intention of Abdellah Taïa to be compassionate, as expressed in his interview with Richeux, and the letter that the writer pens, thanks to an understanding of these psychic processes.

On the very first page, Ahmed switches from using "I" to using "we" when he speaks on behalf of his siblings, a first step toward collective mourning: "Chaque jour nous sommes un peu plus en colère" [Every day we are a little angrier].[20] The children try to reconstruct their lives without their mother . . . in vain. By speaking *for* his brothers and sisters, Ahmed gives more weight to his words. He addresses Malika directly and reproaches her for her hardness and indifference, especially toward him. His summary speech as in a prosecution evokes how speedily she got rid of his father's belongings after he passed away[21] and how she darkened his image. If we are to believe his mother, his father was only good for two things: smoking and "faire la chose" [doing it].[22] For Ahmed, she was castrating toward her husband and a dictator in life. She is also unfair to her children, giving everything to the eldest son, Slimane, raising him like a king, and treating the other children differently.[23] In the midst of this discourse, we find an autobiographical element that refers to the paratext (see Richeux): "Tu avais espéré trouver ton salut comme femme grâce à lui" [You had hoped to find salvation as a woman thanks to him].[24] Indeed, according to Taïa, the tragic event of his mother's life, and especially the fact that her first-born daughter had been taken away from her, explains why his mother had waged everything on a boy, her eldest son.[25]

Slimane does not escape the narrator's fury and he certainly does not escape his sisters' fury. As soon as their mother died, the day of the funeral, they demanded that he repair the injustice of the situation regarding the inheritance given to him by Malika.[26] Seeing his sisters change so much, Ahmed cannot help but think they are finally becoming like their mother who has probably planned this all along as she has raised and programmed Ahmed to be hard, with a closed heart.[27]

Evoking his novel, Taïa describes a painting by Poussin ("The Massacre of the Innocents") where the mother in the frame is shouting before stating: "Il fallait que le livre sorte comme ça" [The book needed to come out like this].[28] In another interview, he stresses that the four letters forming the novel are not waiting for a reply; they are a desperate act, a last resort, "un cri" [a shout][29]; they allow for a cathartic release. The painting by Poussin shows a mother who intercedes and places herself between her baby, *who is a boy*, and the centurion's sword coming down on him; she wants to spare his life. It is the exact opposite of the story narrated in the first letter where the mother wanted to abort her son (Ahmed), thinking she was going to have another daughter. Thanks to the dream of her eldest son who knew her true intentions (he dreamed she was in fact aborting a little baby boy), the narrator's life was spared as Slimane related his dream to his mother. This episode had already been narrated with the title "L'enfant endormi" [The Child Asleep] in the first short story published by Taïa in 1999.[30] Given this autobiographical information, the important focus in the painting is not so much the mother's shout as the young baby boy, unable to shout or cry because his throat is constricted by the centurion's foot.

Compassion for the Father

I have shown how this first letter criticizes both the mother and the eldest son. What about the father? To use Klein's terminology, the only "good internal object" is Ahmed's father, Hamid (in Arabic "the one who is praised"). He is idealized, not only by the narrator but also by his brothers and sisters:

"Entre nous, on se disait que dès les premiers jours de votre mariage tu l'avais fait mourir [. . .]" [Between us, we told each other that from the very first days of your marriage, you started to kill him].[31] Ahmed even finds sweetness in his father's use of violence against his mother while reproaching her for not protecting the children from the couple's sexual life, as if she wanted to bewitch them with her overbearing sexuality.[32] However, he concedes that, aged forty, he is still jealous of his parents' relationship and, above all, of his father.[33]

How can he be envious of an "emasculated" man he was ashamed of—to use his own description?[34] Ahmed is jealous of the fact that his father knew happiness in love; he was not afraid to love. At the time of penning his letter, he now perceives him as courageous. I believe he admires Hamid because of how different he was from his wife; he assumed his subservience and his dependency toward her. By contrast, Ahmed acknowledges his own cruel streak, just like his mother's: "Malgré moi, en tout, je te ressemble" [Despite myself, I resemble you in everything].[35] Ahmed then becomes self-critical, even though he feels manipulated by his mother as she still has the upper hand over him and has programmed him: "Tu as fait de moi la machine que je suis à présent"[You have made me the machine I am now].[36] Whereas, before, he saw these character traits of Malika as a blessing, he now sees them as a curse, wondering why it is him who is like his mother, rather than his brothers and sisters, and, above all, his eldest brother.

Self-destruction

Imperceptibly, Ahmed turns the anger displayed in the letter against himself. Psychologically, Ahmed is identifying with the lost object (his mother) before becoming self-critical. He accuses his mother of having turned him into a dictator, a heartless human being.[37] Klein explains this phenomenon as follows: "When hatred of the lost loved object in its various manifestations gets the upper hand in the mourner, this not only turns the loved lost person into a persecutor but shakes the mourner's belief in his good inner objects as well."[38]

This is a timely reminder that the time of writing, five years after the mother has passed, is still a painful mourning phase:

> Tu es morte, Malika.
> Je suis homosexuel. Plus homosexuel que jamais maintenant.
> [You are dead, Malika. I am a homosexual. Now, more homosexual than ever].[39]

Ahmed understands that when his mother was alive, she protected him from a certain truth: "La vérité ultime. L'enfer au sens propre" [The ultimate truth.

Hell, literally].[40] She acted like a barrier. From now on, he is alone in the world, without any protection.[41] And what can he foresee? "Je vois mon destin. Et je vois que plus rien n'arrêtera l'inéluctable. La mort dans la solitude absolue. Avec un cœur dur, fermé, de plus en plus sec. Un cœur dictateur" [I see my destiny. And I see that nothing will stop the inevitable. Death in absolute solitude. With a closed heart, shut in, more and more arid. A dictator's heart].[42] Which psychic processes are now at stake? Wanting so much to humiliate his object of hatred, his mother—a "hatred" derived from her death perceived as a punishment, an abandonment of her son—his intention has the opposite effect. In a vicious circle, Ahmed's own self becomes in turn a persecutor. He carries on with his *mea culpa*; he has destroyed those who loved him.

One could speculate that he inflicts on his lovers the suffering he has known at the hands of his mother. Ahmed acknowledges that he makes them taste paradise and then forgets them. After a while, they are no longer good enough, no longer worthy of him: "Je ne vous aime plus. Je ne suis plus à vous et mon cœur n'a jamais été complètement à vous" [I no longer love you (Note*: in French, he is addressing his lovers, not just one*). I am no longer yours and my heart never completely belonged to you].[43] Ahmed provokes in his lovers his biggest fear, what he experienced with his mother: rejection and abandonment. His behavior brings him a sense of relief as his anxiety lessens and he is more able to keep in control. He even talks, in relation to his attitude, of a "jouissance rare" [rare pleasure].[44]

I am wondering why he does not think about his father's example in these moments . . . His father who found happiness in being a "free slave" and who can proclaim: "Malika est digne de mon amour" [Malika is worthy of my love].[45] In some ways, he has not forgotten his father's lesson but he uses it negatively, for instance, when he writes that there is no longer anyone to enslave him with their feelings for him, with their affection, and with their sex—all the apparent "traps" in which Hamid fell willingly. By contrast, he describes himself as alone and hard.[46] If, beforehand, he was jealous of his father, he is now retaliating on his behalf by acting out with his own lover(s), as if he is now—in the realm of phantasy—Hamid's protector. He seems to project onto his lovers the fear and anxiety derived from his relationship with his parents. He is replaying the family drama and ends up with the same feeling he carried as a teenager, being alone, which brings on his biggest fear. Simultaneously, as he emulates his mother, it makes him feel closer to her: "J'avais l'impression que j'existais enfin [. . .] dans le rapprochement avec toi, maman [. . .] " [I felt that I finally existed [. . .] in my drawing closer to you, mommy].[47] Because of the planned abortion of his fetus, he compares her to a criminal before writing: "Comme toi, je suis un criminel. Pédé et criminel. Pédé, seul et criminel" [Like you, I am a criminal. Queer and criminal. Queer, alone and criminal][48]; the identification is complete. It is to be noted that Ahmed inserts queer in the equation, perhaps as a way of showing that Malika is also "transgressive."

In many ways, while he is talking to Malika and, at the beginning of the letter, directing his anger toward her, Ahmed is keeping her alive. This presents a paradox because, while she is "alive," he cannot move on to mourning. If, for him, his mother is still living ("Les morts sont vivants" [the dead are alive])[49], for his sisters, their mother is dead[50] and this allows them to go into mourning and subsequently to heal. Let us listen to one of his sisters, Samira: "Je lui pardonne. Nous lui pardonnons, toutes. Absolument toutes" [I forgive her. We all forgive her. Absolutely all of us].[51] As for Ahmed, he cannot forgive anything.[52]

As his mother is drawing her last breaths in Morocco, Ahmed is still in Paris. On learning that she has become unconscious, he goes to the public swimming pool twice a day and shouts under the water: "Je crie. Je recommence. Encore et encore" [I shout. I start again. And again and again].[53] Symbolically, his ritual makes him plunge in the amniotic fluid: "Je suis dans l'eau de la piscine et je veux y rester" [I am in the swimming pool water and I want to stay there].[54] As Siham Bouamer explains, this is a return to the womb, or to what Pascal Quignard called "le dernier royaume" [the last kingdom], which is often associated with loss/death.[55] He identifies with his mother again to the point where he finishes the letter by saying he wants to depart with her. Immersed in the swimming pool, he opens his mouth to let the water in: "Je n'ai plus envie ni de vivre ni de prendre l'avion" [I no longer want to live nor to catch the plane].[56] Yet again, Klein's analysis of mourning brings some light on his behavior: "The poignancy of the actual loss of a loved person is, in my view, greatly increased by the mourner's unconscious phantasies of having lost his *internal* 'good' objects as well. He then feels that his internal 'bad' objects predominate, and his inner world is in danger of disruption"[57]; precisely, Ahmed wants his world to *explode*.[58]

LOVE

Toward Reconciliation?

The second letter offers a change of narrator; it is written by Vincent and addressed to Ahmed. Despite this change, the second letter continues the work of criticizing Ahmed's personality. He is described as a heartbreaker, a dictator, and, in a nutshell, a persecutor. This letter continues to illustrate the behavior described by Klein whereby some people in mourning question their own good interior objects, including themselves. Ahmed has done his *mea culpa*; now Vincent is doing it for him. After twenty-four hours spent together where Vincent said he tasted paradise (I reported earlier that Ahmed made his lovers taste paradise then forgot them) and the promise of meeting in a café the next day (La Veilleuse in Belleville), Ahmed disappears without a trace.[59] There is, however, a major difference with the first letter. Whereas the son was not prepared to forgive his mother, Vincent wants to find his companion to start again and realize their dreams. He does not hate him anymore; on the contrary, he wants to renew contact with him.[60] Reminiscent of the daughter's attitude toward their mother, Vincent is ready to forgive.

In the paratext, Taïa explains this character with a certain nostalgia: "Vincent est un mélange de plusieurs histoires d'amour. Il est cet homme qui m'a attiré, que j'ai fait souffrir et que, impitoyablement, j'ai quitté [. . .] Vincent est le fantôme qui me hante et me hantera longtemps" [Vincent is a mix of various love stories. He is that man I was attracted to; I made him suffer and, implacably, I left him [. . .] Vincent is the ghost who haunts me and who will haunt me for a long time].[61] The decision to have Vincent write this second letter is a way of providing the reader with an outsider's point of view, so that Ahmed is seen from the outside. Through the description of his conduct, we come to realize what he has done to others close to him.

At the end of the first letter, Ahmed identified so much with the mother that he wanted to die with her. Now that he can measure the impact of his own actions on Vincent, notably his cruelty, he starts again identifying with his mother *but not only as a hate object*. Klein is again helpful at this juncture: "This distress is related not only to the past but to the present as well [. . .] sadism is in full swing. It needs a fuller identification with the loved object [. . .] for the ego to become aware of the state of disintegration to which it has reduced and is continuing to reduce its loved objects."[62] This second letter is an important illustration of the mourning process, with the example of Vincent who is working toward reconciliation. He illustrates the qualities of the father that Ahmed was so jealous of. He too can say "Je t'aime [. . .]" [I love you].[63] According to Vincent, in their relationship, Ahmed was the one leading. He took control as he mastered "[. . .] l'art de la mise en scène, de la manipulation et de la tromperie" [the art of staging, of manipulating and of deceiving], even of bewitching.[64] These attributes are the ones Ahmed reproaches to his mother in the first letter. Vincent has understood that, through his behavior and his capacity to be cruel, Ahmed is taking revenge on a troubled past,[65] which echoes my own analysis that Ahmed is doing to his lovers what he has endured from his mother.

Vincent then narrates his origins, a story he had kept back to share with Ahmed when they were due to meet the next day, but the latter never showed up for the meeting *he* had set up. Vincent had a weak father and a strong mother who controlled everything. After her death, the same question that was asked in Ahmed's family surfaced: "Après elle, sans elle, comment survivre ?" [After her, without her, how to survive?].[66] It is when his mother died that Vincent learned about his father's childhood. He was a Moroccan Jew from Meknès whose parents suddenly vanished. Vincent's father told him how he regretted having let his wife fill all the space and manage everything[67] echoing Vincent who deplores the fact that he did not share his story with Ahmed, he did not assert himself and he let Ahmed orchestrate everything. The stories of the two letters intermingle and, through Vincent's words, resonate with the first letter: "J'aurais dû faire comme maman le dictateur" [I should have been a dictator, like my mother] and also: "Sans pays. Sans réelles racines [. . .] je meurs et, seul, je résiste" [Stateless. Without any real roots [. . .] I am dying, and, alone, I resist].[68]

Vincent's father died six months after he met Ahmed. Unlike the anger of the first letter, a feeling of love permeates the second one. Ahmed should have been the one uttering the words Vincent says, so as to mourn his mother and to integrate her within himself as a "good" object: "Ton amour. Je le reprends. Je le reprends en moi et, plus fort que jamais, je te le renvoie" [Your love. I reclaim it. I reclaim it back in me and, stronger than ever, I send it back to you].[69] Reminiscent of the first letter, when Ahmed asked his mother to hold his hand for her last journey,[70] Vincent invites Ahmed to die with him, pleading: "Prends ma main, Ahmed. Je t'en supplie" [Take my hand, Ahmed. I beg you].[71] There is, however, a final twist to this story: even for Vincent, reconciliation is impossible. The text ends with a confession. Vincent has not forgiven anything; he is not at peace and his anger is still palpable. While we hear these revelations, he is still calling for Ahmed, the letter leaving the door open as the last word is "Viens . . ." [Come . . .].[72]

The process of mourning reaches a new stage and comes full circle with the fourth letter, fitting together all the pieces of the puzzle of my analysis. It is written in Lahbib's head and dated May 1990. It is both a reminiscing letter and a testament addressed to "Ahmed. Mon petit frère . . ." [Ahmed. My little brother].[73] Lahbib is seventeen and Ahmed is two years younger. Lahbib is composing this letter so that Ahmed does not make the same mistakes he has made: "Il faut que cela serve de leçon à quelqu'un. Toi. Toi, Ahmed." [This needs to serve as a lesson for someone. You. You, Ahmed].[74] Lahbib has been having a sexual relationship with a Frenchman called Gérard who is now rejecting him. He has even asked Lahbib to bring Ahmed to replace him because, at seventeen, Lahbib is becoming too old for his taste. Lahbib thinks about dying but then he hopes to be given a second chance. This ends in an even more powerful rejection and the thought of ending it all comes back again.[75] According to Ahmed, Lahbib is Gérard's slave.[76]

The text provides a powerful contrast when it describes how Simone, Gérard's mother, treats Lahbib. In a way, she accomplishes what Ahmed's mother was unable to do with her own son. She listens to him and wants to get to know him: "[. . .] elle m'a demandé des choses sur moi, sur ce que je suis au fond [. . .]" [she asked things about me, about who I really am].[77] This attitude toward him has opened his heart, unlike Ahmed's heart which remains closed. Simone has protected Lahbib and shown him love. She has told him to leave Gérard, her own son, because of the way he treats him.

"The One Worthy of Being Loved"

The title of the novel is found in this fourth letter. The words are uttered by Simone while Lahbib tries to explain the meaning of his first name in Arabic. She tells him: "Tu es celui qui est digne d'être aimé." [You are the one worthy of being loved].[78] There is a certain ambiguity in the text as to the recipient of this declaration because it comes just after the first sentence of this letter: "Ahmed. My little brother . . .," and it could equally be addressed to Ahmed. It is only in the paratext that the ambiguity is lifted: "Lahbib a un très beau prénom. Il est le héros un peu caché de ce livre. Mais, dans le titre, il n'est question que de lui. Je l'aime de tout mon cœur." [Lahbib has a beautiful first name. He is the partly hidden hero of this book. But the title is all about him only. I love him with all my heart].[79] The title has already come up twice in the novel before the aforementioned passage. Hamid is the first to have voiced: "Malika is worthy of my love."[80] The second instance is when Ahmed writes, while he is alluding to his older brother who has the affection of his mother and who is the king of the family: "Le grand frère. Le plus beau. Le plus fort. Le plus instruit. Celui qui est digne d'être aimé, adoré, vénéré, déifié" [The big brother. The most beautiful. The strongest. The cleverest. The one worthy of being loved, adored, venerated, deified"].[81] This is not free from sarcasm and cynicism.

In the first letter, Ahmed wished to walk toward death holding his mother's hand. In the second letter, Vincent wanted to do the same, holding Ahmed's. Those wishes did not come true. In the fourth letter, Lahbib takes Ahmed by the hand and walks toward death by jumping in the Bou Regreg river, echoing the passages about the pool/amniotic fluid. He asks Ahmed to keep both the world and hope alive within himself and to avenge him one day by bringing him justice. As he is about to jump, Lahbib remembers that he *is* worthy of being loved in exhorting himself: "Saute. Saute, Lahbib! Tu es celui qui est digne d'être aimé, saute." [Jump. Jump, Lahbib! You are the one worthy of being loved, jump].[82] Committing suicide is his way of reclaiming his human dignity by extricating himself from the abusive relationship with Gérard, and of staying forever with the feeling that he is worthy of love. There is a lesson in this tale that presents a major drawback: an open heart cannot cope with the suffering of this world. I will come back to this point in my conclusion.

THE POLITICAL

In the introduction, I mentioned the political dimension of the novel upon which I will now elaborate. This dimension was in evidence, even before the novel was written. As we saw in the aforementioned interview with Richeux, Taïa was thinking about writing the story of his mother that he learned at her funeral (the fact that her first husband fought in the Indochina war on behalf of the French army and had fallen in the line of duty). From that moment on, his family history became directly impacted by colonization. According to the interview, it is because the pension given by France was so miserly that his family threw M'Barka in the street, keeping only the daughter born during their union. The paratext helped me to establish a link with the character of Gabriel in *Un pays pour mourir* and with the character of Zineb, the father's sister, who was a Moroccan prostitute for the French army. *Celui qui est digne d'être aimé* is dedicated to Taïa's aunt, Massaouda. When we know (as revealed in an interview) that she was in fact a prostitute,[83] the dedication is also a political statement.

In the first letter, Ahmed describes Maghrebi homosexuals belonging to his generation who live in Paris. He scorns the fact that they see France, the country of freedom, as their savior.[84] According to him, they are treated like any other immigrant. He rages against the fact that these men, under the cover of integration, start to use the theoretical language of the French and, in the process, forego their origins. In the third letter, he tarnishes himself with this same behavior: "Comme eux, j'ai été d'abord un excitant et exotique objet sexuel en France. Je ne le suis plus." [Like them, I have been at first an exciting and exotic sexual object in France. This is no longer the case].[85] The novel also criticizes or rather questions what a homosexual identity is and what it means to be an Arab homosexual and a Muslim living in Paris.[86]

In the second letter, Vincent narrates the story of the Moroccan singer, Zahra el-Fassiya, who immigrated to Israel. She symbolizes Ahmed's life in exile in France. Zahra has recreated a corner of Morocco in her apartment in Israel. She appears to doubt herself, wondering why she emigrated. Vincent explains to Ahmed that, like his own father, she is stateless, without any real roots, and driven by the world to end it all.[87] As he is finishing his letter, he confides to Ahmed that he is in the same state of mind as Zahra. Another political dimension lies in the reason why Ahmed did not turn up for their meeting in the café. Perhaps he thought he was an exotic consumer object for Vincent and, by turning up, he would fall into the trap of neo-colonialism.

In the fourth letter, the character of Gérard illustrates a strong political message. He is a forty-five-year-old Frenchman with an important job at the French embassy. He lives in a prosperous area of Rabat (Hassan) in a nice villa. Given his social class, Lahbib can only be attracted to these trappings; he is impressed by him.[88] As he confesses to Ahmed, and I need to report his exact words as they betray the power relationship between the two lovers: "Il était tout ce que nous ne serons jamais toi et moi. Un Français qui a tout, qui a la belle vie, qui a le Maroc à ses pieds. Gérard est ce que nous ne deviendrons jamais, Ahmed." [He was everything you and I will never be. A Frenchman who has everything, a good life, who has Morocco at his feet. Gérard is what we will never become, Ahmed].[89] Gérard has been using Lahbib as a sex object since he was fourteen, often shaming him: "Va prendre une douche, je t'attends au lit. Tu es sale, comme d'habitude. Va te laver!" [Go and take a shower; I will wait in bed. You are dirty, as usual. Go and have a wash!].[90] Echoing colonial discourses on "cleanliness and race," Gérard loves it when he smells of soap, especially the make DOP, which is the French brand used by poor people in Morocco. In his "generosity" Gérard has passed around Lahbib among his friends. Even though Lahbib remains very discreet on the subject, we learn: "J'ai accepté ce qu'ils me faisaient. Je me suis vendu" [I accepted what they did to me. I sold myself].[91] He has not told Ahmed everything, simply describing the situation as a "[. . .] un massacre interminable" [never ending massacre].[92]

The following anecdote is revealing. We find out that Lahbib steals a little pocket money from a willing Gérard, tacitly. As he writes: "Cela l'excitait d'avoir un petit voleur marocain pédé dans son lit" [He was excited to have a little gay Moroccan thief in his bed][93]; all stereotypes are united. But, as he is turning seventeen, he is becoming too old for his lover. Gérard desires younger flesh. He has his eyes on Ahmed who is fifteen; he wants the three of them in bed together. Lahbib knows the "rules"; he must find his own replacement before being booted out.[94] Using the excuse that, the previous week, he stole from him more than the sum implicitly agreed between them (even though an amount had never been discussed), Gérard tells him he no longer wants to have sex with him.[95] This means that their relationship is over as it was the sum of it. The narrative implies a different reason. Lahbib is too old and Gérard is also jealous of his relationship with his mother. Lahbib thinks that, given his social status, Gérard could have saved him, kept him, offered him work, and guided him through the hell of daily life in Morocco.[96] In Gérard's eyes, Lahbib was a consumer object with a perishable date. Tragically, Lahbib concedes on several occasions that he loved Gérard. As he is about to commit suicide, he claims that his love for him will always be alive. When the novel was published, Taïa said on the radio: "J'ai essayé de montrer la colonisation dans l'endroit le plus loin possible, le plus nu possible: l'amour et le sexe" [I tried to show colonization in the most far away part, the most naked part: love and sex][97]; this letter is an illustration of his intention.

The third letter sees the most powerful political message of the novel, hence my wish to study it last. It is written by Ahmed and addressed to his lover, Emmanuel; they live together in Paris. The existence of this letter is already mentioned in *L'armée du salut* in a chapter where the narrator "Abdellah" had left Morocco to go and study in Geneva and to be with Jean. "Abdellah" narrates how, one morning, having woken up early, he wrote Jean a letter, telling him he could no longer carry on with their relationship, and that he needed to leave, to breathe, and to think of his future.[98] This is the gist of the message Ahmed conveys to Emmanuel. They met when he was seventeen (the very age when Lahbib will commit suicide) at a time when he still lived in Morocco—thirteen years before the time of writing the letter. The story between Lahbib and Gérard prefigures that between Ahmed and Emmanuel (from the point of view of the chronology rather than the ordering of the letters). Discussing the novel's structure, Pierre Ahnne uses the expression "court-circuit temporal" [temporal short circuit] . According to him, the structure opens an abyss, that of causation (why do these stories of exploitation and injustices repeat themselves?): "Faut-il les chercher dans l'histoire personnelle et la structure familiale ou dans une histoire coloniale qui n'en finit pas de se répéter?" [Should we look [for answers] in the individuals' histories, their family structures or in a colonial history that keeps on repeating itself?].[99]

In comparison with their milieu and deprivation, Gérard and Emmanuel appear as saviors for the two young boys/men. Ahmed is ready to give thanks to Allah for Emmanuel being in his life. He will now be able to live, to exist, and to leave poverty behind.[100] One realizes the extent of his dream when he smells Emmanuel for the first time and thinks he is smelling France![101] Ahmed is the first one to admit he tried to charm and bewitch his companion. For example, at the beginning of their relationship, he forces himself to hold Emmanuel's hand in order to seduce him,[102] linking his behavior to that which he learned from his mother[103] and anticipating, thanks to this new relationship, power, revenge (toward society), and a certain comfort of living.[104] From their very first meeting, Emmanuel corrects his French. Ahmed is both honored and crushed by this[105]; it is a microcosm of their future problems. This personal story soon takes a political and a historical dimension.

The last two letters intermingle when Ahmed evokes Lahbib twice in the third letter to Emmanuel. The latter asks him to stop focusing on his memories when he was poor, now that he lives in Paris[106]; he listens to him. In Paris, Emmanuel purged Lahbib from their conversations. Ahmed realizes that he also killed Lahbib in himself.[107] He now understands that, through Lahbib, it is *his* stories "émouvantes, naïves [. . .] [qui] ont fini par tomber, par sombrer dans le noir, ne plus exister" [moving, naive [. . .] that have fallen by the wayside, that have sunk in a dark pit, and that no longer exist].[108] Because Emmanuel saw his past as *folkloric*, Ahmed dissociated himself from it. Instead of protecting him and reconciling him with his world, Emmanuel has made him turn his back on his past.[109] The two "brothers" have the same destiny. Just like Lahbib, Ahmed is going to be replaced by Kamal, younger than him; he is already waiting in the wings. Ahmed writes: "J'ai 40 ans. Je suis vieux, fini, asséché, déjà." [I am forty. I am old, finished, dried up, already].[110] History repeats itself, as Ahnne suspected; the same applies to colonial powers.

I have already established that Taïa's original intention for this novel—to show a certain empathy for his mother by pointing out the tragedy of the death of her first husband killed in Indochina—had not materialized. However, one finds this narrative about colonialism and its injustices, as the author himself acknowledges:

> Cette histoire, parce qu'elle n'est pas sortie, a emmené les autres lettres. L'impossibilité d'accepter la mort (de la mère), le courage de ne plus avoir peur devant la langue française, devant certains Français [. . .] Emmanuel a perpétué sur Ahmed la pénétration coloniale, l'éducation de ses indigènes, la colonisation de ses indigènes.
>
> [This story, because it did not come out, brought into existence the other letters. The impossibility of accepting the death (of the mother), the courage to no longer be afraid in front of the French language, in front of certain French people [. . .]. Emmanuel has perpetuated colonial penetration on Ahmed, the education of its indigenous people, the colonization of its indigenous people].[111]

Ahmed is particularly lucid about this historical context. He writes to Emmanuel that he let himself be *colonized*,[112] having learned from him how to be a "true" Parisian, not too Arab, not too Muslim, not too "[. . .] de là-bas" [from over there].[113] He even agreed to change his first name to "Midou" as, according to his French lover, his Parisian friends found "Ahmed" impossible to pronounce.

Because of him, Ahmed has become *another*.[114] He lives in a strange nostalgia, not even able to speak Arabic like before, concluding: "Ma langue n'est plus ma langue" [My language is no longer my language].[115] While at the beginning, when he still lived in Morocco, Ahmed felt himself to be even more Muslim in Emmanuel's arms,[116] he has become in Paris "[. . .] un petit pédé parisien bien comme il faut" [a little Parisian queer, well to do].[117] *Of his own volition*, he has wanted to abandon everything, to leave, to replace his sensibility by a different one, his words by those of Emmanuel and the

Arabic language by the French language.[118] It is the expression "of his own volition" that hurts. Ahmed gives a telling example. One day, he did a presentation at the University of Rabat on Oscar Wilde who "gave" André Gide his first boy. Influenced by Emmanuel, he decided to conceal the real hero of this story from his presentation, the little Arab boy given as a gift, in order to concentrate on "les deux écrivains faisant du tourisme orientalo-sexuel" [the two writers engaged in orientalist sexual tourism].[119] With hindsight, he now thinks that, at the time, he was still totally colonized in his head.[120] This little Arab boy he betrayed, was he in fact none other than Lahbib and himself? Does he have excuses? As he repeats,[121] at seventeen, he was naïve, he knew nothing.

With hindsight, Ahmed sees that Emmanuel is in control and has ruled their relationship. This has echoes of the mother, as if he has left one dictator for another, and he is submissive to them both. He even wonders if this break-up with his companion has not been programmed by his mother, just as he was wondering earlier if his sisters' rebellion at his mother's funeral was not in fact planned by her. He now realizes that his partner has reproduced with him, on his body and in his heart, everything that France refuses to see: neo-colonialism.[122] And this extends to the French language; having conquered it, he now wants to emancipate himself from it. From the start of the letter, Ahmed declares he wants to leave Emmanuel as he wants to renounce the French language. His partner had presented this language as a means to leave poverty behind and to be free and strong.[123] He now realizes that the French language has enslaved him. He must forsake it, for it reminds him of his lover, as he must leave Emmanuel.[124] He feels colonized by the French language: alienated from who he was at seventeen, losing his primary identity, his roots. I argued above that the fourth letter illustrated Taïa's declaration that he had tried to show colonization in the most far away part, the most naked part: love and sex.[125] We can now include the third letter and add the French language to love and sex.

Following this linguistic *tabula rasa*, Ahmed wants to find his origins again; the political reading of the novel carries on and meets my psychoanalytical interpretation. Having wondered why, at the beginning of his relationship with Emmanuel he no longer saw what was happening around him in Morocco, what his sisters were going through, he now wants to "[. . .] [s]e réconcilier avec [s]on premier monde" [reconcile himself with his first world].[126] In this third letter, Ahmed seems more at peace with Malika. He wants to reconcile himself with his mother and sisters, create a new bond, even if they refuse to talk about his homosexuality.[127] He wishes to think the world through their eyes.[128] I would argue that he wants to integrate them in himself as "loved objects," for Klein tells us that a successful mourning is one where "[. . .] the individual is reinstating his actually lost loved objects."[129] If

Ahmed is ready to hear their harsh words, it is because he knows that these words are key to connectedness with them.

LAHBIB: A KEY CHARACTER FOR RECONCILIATION

After penning his letter to Emmanuel, Ahmed's violent feelings are disappearing, and he feels again some tenderness for his lover.[130] Following his anger toward his mother in the first letter, he recovers some affection for her in the third letter, a reconciliation already foreseen in the second letter where he no longer perceived her exclusively as a "bad object." He can now feel and own his pain, caused by the alienation from his primary identity and from the Arabic language. If the book has erected a cruel gravestone for Malika, it also builds her a mausolea and therefore doubles up the process of mourning/reconciliation. The mother has center stage: "Son esprit est là, de la première à la dernière lettre. Dans chaque phrase, chaque mot, il y a son souffle" [Her spirit is here, from the first to the last letter. Her breath is in every sentence, in every word].[131] This breath is a breath of life. We learn in an interview: "Je suis seul dans ce monde, au sens propre. Alors, dans ma tête, je parle en permanence à ma mère, je lui écris des lettres" [I am alone in this world, literally. So, in my head, I am always speaking to my mother, I write her letters].[132] Even if these letters never reach the intended addressee, they serve a cathartic function by the scream they let out; they are a form of reparation. It seems that the whole of the novel has been building up toward this crescendo, and that if reconciliation is in evidence, it rests with the title as it also applies to the *author* since the front cover reads: "Abdellah Taïa: *The one worthy of being loved.*"

Taïa said on television that, in order to arrive at the truth, one must go through anger first, otherwise "[. . .] on n'aura pas tout vécu ou compris" [that person will not have lived through nor understood everything].[133] And what have the characters in the novel lived through or understood? The fourth letter talks about the origins of the two friends, Ahmed and Lahbib. In committing suicide, Lahbib has forced his own destiny because he could no longer carry on with the life he was living. He also predicted the future of the one he called "his little brother" because he wanted to protect him from what lay ahead. We saw that Lahbib's heart had been opened (unlike Ahmed's heartlessness—according to him, programmed by Malika) when Simone, Gérard's mother, accomplished what Ahmed's mother could never do with her own son: she listened to him, took time to get to know him and, above all, made him feel that he was worthy of being loved. The character of Lahbib speaks to me: he died at seventeen, the very age at which Ahmed met Emmanuel. In the third letter, Ahmed, who is by now thirty, wants to rediscover himself at age seventeen, as if he wants to make Lahbib alive again through himself or in order to start again, unless he is pointing out that Lahbib is his alter ego.

The character of Lahbib seems to represent a way of exploring what happens when one is open-hearted and lives through what he and Ahmed have lived through. And for someone open-hearted, the (literary) response is to commit suicide. The writing process—through the prism of the various characters and, above all, the modulation of the narrator—opens the way for reconciliation with the mother. Taïa analyzes: "Ce qui m'a sauvé, ce qui a sauvé le personnage d'Ahmed dans le livre, c'est que, dans un monde dur, je vais être dur avec le monde. La dureté, c'est ce qui m'a sauvé et c'est ce qui m'emprisonne aujourd'hui" [What saved me, what saved the character of Ahmed in this book is that, in a harsh world, I am going to be hard with the world. Being hard is what saved me but it is also what incarcerates me today].[134] This hardness can also be found in Malika. By the end of the novel, one understands that Malika, like Ahmed, could not have survived as an open heart. According to the paratext, being a closed heart is both a reason and an excuse whilst remaining a form of incarceration. If, in the first letter, Ahmed saw his mother as a jailer, he now feels compassionate toward her and sees her like him, as a prisoner; this is what he has understood. The tragedy is that what "saved" them is killing them softly. Isn't lucidity the tragedy of this novel? "Dans mon roman, il me semble que mes personnages sont bloqués justement parce qu'ils sont capables de voir clair en eux, dans ce qu'ils vivent d'amoureux. Mais cette clairvoyance ne les aide pas du tout" [In my novel, it seems to me that my characters have a mental block, for the very reason that they see clearly in themselves, in their love life. But this lucidity does not help them in the least].[135]

What mental block is the author referring to? Jean Zaganiaris encapsulates Ahmed's personality when he writes: "Plus que son identité et sa culture, Ahmed a perdu la capacité d'aimer autrui avec innocence [. . .] l'impossibilité de *ressentir l'abandon amoureux*" ["More [problematic] than his identity and his culture, Ahmed has lost the capacity to love the other with innocence [. . .] it is impossible for him to *feel loving surrender*"] (my emphasis).[136] This impossibility condemns him to a life of solitude; he thinks that happiness is simply another form of captivity.[137] Zaganiaris goes beyond colonialism and neo-colonialism to strike at the heart of the matter, echoing my analytical reading. Ahmed is narcissistically wounded; he was never the child basking in his mother's love (he describes Malika's "yeux durs" [cold eyes]),[138] *surrendering* because he is secure in love and worthy of being loved, growing into an adult capable of feeling loving surrender. Isn't he jealous of his father, *precisely* because he can experience loving surrender? His father had the strength to love, hence showing his courage—an attitude repeated by Vincent in the second letter.

Mourning and reconciliation have taken us through several stages: anger, politics and, finally, love. When narrating the story of the near abortion of his fetus in the first letter, the narrator writes: "Je suis perdu, depuis le départ, dans ton ventre déjà, en France encore plus que jamais." [I am lost, since the beginning, in your womb already, in France even more than ever].[139] Uprooted, separated from his mother tongue, battling with the French language, with a closed heart and prisoner of his own behavior but fighting, shouting, like his mother. And writing: "J'écris et je crie" [I write and I shout].[140]

NOTES

1. Abdellah Taïa, *Une mélancolie arabe* (Paris: Seuil, 2008).
2. Abdellah Taïa, "J'ai été choqué par la façon dont on a traité la mort de George Michael," interview by Christophe Martet, *Hornet*, January 16, 2017, https://hornetapp.com/stories/fr/abdellah-taia-george-michael. All translations are my own.
3. "Lettres françaises" dans "Les nouvelles vagues," interview by Marie Richeux, *France-Culture*, March 9, 2017, https://www.franceculture.fr/emissions/les-nouvelles-vagues/la-france-vue-de-letranger-45-lettres-francaises.
4. Abdellah Taïa, *L'armée du salut* (Paris: Seuil, 2006), 28. See also 17.
5. Taïa, *L'armée du salut*, 28.
6. Abdellah Taïa, *Un pays pour mourir* (Paris: Seuil, 2015), 141–164.
7. Taïa, *Un pays pour mourir*, 161.
8. Mireille Rosello, *The Reparative in Narratives: Works of Mourning in Progress* (Liverpool: Liverpool University Press, 2010), 22.
9. "Lettres françaises" dans "Les nouvelles vagues," interview by Marie Richeux.
10. The last interview to mention this is given to Antoine Idier: "[. . .] ma mère est morte à l'été 2010. Pour moi la vie n'est plus pareille. Je suis à la fois le pédé de cette famille et le pédé seul dans la vie. Désormais, dans la vie, je suis seul, au sens propre. Davantage encore que je ne le ressens depuis que je suis petit [. . .] Or cette révélation a eu lieu alors que je vivais en France depuis douze ans déjà. Malgré tout ce que j'avais fait, tous les liens que j'avais tissés, rien n'a pu combler le vide et la solitude immense que je ressentais. C'était comme une énorme explosion." [My mother died during the summer of 2010. For me, life is no longer the same. I am both the queer of that family and the queer, alone in the world. From now on, I am alone in life, literally. Even more so than I felt when I was small [. . .] Now, this realization came to me whilst I had been living in France for twelve years. Despite everything I had achieved, all the relationships I had formed, nothing was able to fill the lack and the immense solitude I felt. It was like an enormous explosion]. "Sortir de la peur. Construire une identité homosexuelle arabe dans un monde postcolonial," interview by Antoine Idier, *Fixxion*, no. 12 (2016), 202.
11. Juliet Mitchell, *The Selected Melanie Klein* (London: The Free Press, 1986), 174.

12. Mitchell, *Melanie Klein*, 158.
13. "Les nouvelles vagues," interview by Marie Richeux.
14. Mitchell, *Melanie Klein*, 158.
15. Abdellah Taïa, *Celui qui est digne d'être aimé* (Paris: Seuil, 2017), 28.
16. Taïa, *Celui qui est digne*, 29.
17. Mitchell, *Melanie Klein*, 158.
18. Taïa, *Celui qui est digne*, 39.
19. "Abdellah Taïa dans La grande librairie," *France 5*, January 29, 2017.
20. Taïa, *Celui qui est digne*, 11.
21. Taïa, *Celui qui est digne*, 11.
22. Taïa, *Celui qui est digne*, 14–15.
23. Taïa, *Celui qui est digne*, 21.
24. Taïa, *Celui qui est digne*, 21.
25. "Les nouvelles vagues," interview by Marie Richeux.
26. Taïa, *Celui qui est digne*, 22.
27. Taïa, *Celui qui est digne*, 25.
28. "Les nouvelles vagues," interview by Marie Richeux.
29. "Abdellah Taïa: 'L'amour n'est pas une chose pure,'" interview by Olivier Rachet, *Le Site info*, February 9, 2017.
30. Texts presented by Loïc Barrière, ed. *Des Nouvelles du Maroc* (Paris: Paris-Méditerranée, 1999).
31. Taïa, *Celui qui est digne*, 15.
32. Taïa, *Celui qui est digne*, 16.
33. Taïa, *Celui qui est digne*, 17.
34. Taïa, *Celui qui est digne*, 18.
35. Taïa, *Celui qui est digne*, 19.
36. Taïa, *Celui qui est digne*, 19.
37. Taïa, *Celui qui est digne*, 13.
38. Mitchell, *Melanie Klein*, 156.
39. Taïa, *Celui qui est digne*, 30.
40. Taïa, *Celui qui est digne*, 30.
41. Taïa, *Celui qui est digne*, 30.
42. Taïa, *Celui qui est digne*, 30.
43. Taïa, *Celui qui est digne*, 30–31.
44. Taïa, *Celui qui est digne*, 31.
45. Taïa, *Celui qui est digne*, 17.
46. Taïa, *Celui qui est digne*, 31.
47. Taïa, *Celui qui est digne*, 31.
48. Taïa, *Celui qui est digne*, 39.
49. Taïa, *Celui qui est digne*, 12.
50. Taïa, *Celui qui est digne*, 26.
51. Taïa, *Celui qui est digne*, 26.
52. Taïa, *Celui qui est digne*, 40.
53. Taïa, *Celui qui est digne*, 42.
54. Taïa, *Celui qui est digne*, 28.

55. Siham Bouamer, "De 'River of no Return' à 'Trouble of the World': Parcours initiatique musical dans *Infidèles* (2012) d'Abdellah Taïa," *Expressions maghrébines* 19, no. 1 (Summer 2020): 120.

56. Taïa, *Celui qui est digne,* 43.

57. Mitchell, *Melanie Klein*, 156.

58. This has echoes of the interview discussed in note 10 where Taïa talks about an "enormous explosion" regarding his mother's death.

59. Taïa reveals in an interview that this story did happen in 2006. He met a Jewish man. They spent the weekend together, but he is the one who waited in vain for his lover at the café La Veilleuse. Abdellah Taïa: "J'ai été choqué par la façon dont on a traité la mort de George Michael," interview by Christophe Martet, *Hornet.*

60. Taïa, *Celui qui est digne,* 47.

61. "Abdellah Taïa: 'L'amour n'est pas une chose pure,'" interview by Olivier Rachet.

62. Mitchell, *Melanie Klein*, 124.

63. Taïa, *Celui qui est digne,* 48.

64. Taïa, *Celui qui est digne,* 52, and 67.

65. Taïa, *Celui qui est digne,* 51.

66. Taïa, *Celui qui est digne,* 70.

67. Taïa, *Celui qui est digne,* 72.

68. Taïa, *Celui qui est digne,* 74 and 77.

69. Taïa, *Celui qui est digne,* 77.

70. Taïa, *Celui qui est digne,* 43.

71. Taïa, *Celui qui est digne,* 77.

72. Taïa, *Celui qui est digne,* 78.

73. Taïa, *Celui qui est digne,* 123.

74. Taïa, *Celui qui est digne,* 126.

75. Taïa, *Celui qui est digne,* 132.

76. Taïa, *Celui qui est digne,* 126.

77. Taïa, *Celui qui est digne,* 124.

78. Taïa, *Celui qui est digne,* 123.

79. Abdellah Taïa, "Je ne pardonne absolument pas au Maroc ce qu'il m'a fait," interview by Fadwa Islah, *Tel Quel*, no. 746, January 6, 2017.

80. Taïa, *Celui qui est digne,* 17.

81. Taïa, *Celui qui est digne,* 39.

82. Taïa, *Celui qui est digne,* 135.

83. "J'ai aussi appris l'art de la séduction qui frise la manipulation grâce à ma tante, Massaouda, prostituée" [I also learned the art of seduction bordering on manipulation thanks to my aunt, Massaouda, a prostitute], "Portrait: 'Abdellah Taïa: Paria gagné,'" interview by Dounia Hadni, *Libération*, January 5, 2017.

84. Taïa, *Celui qui est digne,* 40.

85. Taïa, *Celui qui est digne,* 41.

86. It is the sub-title of the interview with Idier: "Construire une identité homosexuelle arabe dans un monde postcolonial" [How to construct an homosexual Arab identity in a postcolonial world].

87. Taïa, *Celui qui est digne,* 77.
88. Taïa, *Celui qui est digne,* 126.
89. Taïa, *Celui qui est digne,* 129–130.
90. Taïa, *Celui qui est digne,* 129.
91. Taïa, *Celui qui est digne,* 134.
92. Taïa, *Celui qui est digne,* 134.
93. Taïa, *Celui qui est digne,* 128.
94. Taïa, *Celui qui est digne,* 130.
95. Taïa, *Celui qui est digne,* 130.
96. Taïa, *Celui qui est digne,* 133.
97. "Tire ta langue: Abdellah Taïa," interview by Rachida El Azzouzi and Antoine Perraud, *Mediapart,* January 25, 2017, https://www.youtube.com/watch?v=HiIlNpqmisk.
98. Taïa, *L'armée du salut,* 152.
99. "Celui qui est digne d'être aimé, Abdellah Taïa (Seuil)," interview by Pierre Ahnne, January 28, 2017, [blog], http://pierreahnne.eklablog.fr/celui-qui-est-digne-d-etre-aime-abdellah-taia-seuil-a128207950.
100. Taïa, *Celui qui est digne,* 87.
101. Taïa, *Celui qui est digne,* 88.
102. Taïa, *Celui qui est digne,* 94.
103. Taïa, *Celui qui est digne,* 91.
104. Taïa, *Celui qui est digne,* 92.
105. Taïa, *Celui qui est digne,* 84.
106. Taïa, *Celui qui est digne,* 99.
107. Taïa, *Celui qui est digne,* 100.
108. Taïa, *Celui qui est digne,* 100.
109. Taïa, *Celui qui est digne,* 83.
110. Taïa, *Celui qui est digne,* 41.
111. "Les nouvelles vagues," interview by Marie Richeux.
112. Taïa, *Celui qui est digne,* 99.
113. Taïa, *Celui qui est digne,* 81.
114. Taïa, *Celui qui est digne,* 93.
115. Taïa, *Celui qui est digne,* 93.
116. Taïa, *Celui qui est digne,* 89.
117. Taïa, *Celui qui est digne,* 89.
118. Taïa, *Celui qui est digne,* 96.
119. Taïa, *Celui qui est digne,* 118.
120. Taïa, *Celui qui est digne,* 118.
121. Taïa, *Celui qui est digne,* 83.
122. Taïa, *Celui qui est digne,* 104.
123. Taïa, *Celui qui est digne,* 94.
124. Taïa, *Celui qui est digne,* 98.
125. "Tire ta langue: Abdellah Taïa," interview by Rachida El Azzouzi and Antoine Perraud.
126. Taïa, *Celui qui est digne,*109.

127. Taïa, *Celui qui est digne,* 109.
128. Taïa, *Celui qui est digne,* 110.
129. Mitchell, *Melanie Klein*, 174.
130. Taïa, *Celui qui est digne,* 111.
131. Abdellah Taïa, "L'amour n'est pas une chose pure," interview by Olivier Rachet.
132. Abdellah Taïa, "Je ne pardonne absolument pas au Maroc ce qu'il m'a fait," interview by Fadwa Islah.
133. "Abdellah Taïa dans *La grande librairie*," *France 5.*
134. Abdellah Taïa, "J'ai été choqué par la façon dont on a traité la mort de George Michael," interview by Christophe Martet.
135. "Abdellah Taïa: 'L'amour n'est pas une chose pure'," interview by Olivier Rachet.
136. Jean Zaganiaris, "Dans le fond de la piscine," *Libération*, January 5, 2017.
137. Taïa, *Celui qui est digne,* 97.
138. Taïa, *Celui qui est digne,* 11.
139. Taïa, *Celui qui est digne,* 29.
140. "L'homosexualité expliquée à ma mère," *Tel Quel*, no. 367, April 4–10, 2009, https://www.asymptotejournal.com/nonfiction/abdellah-taia-homosexuality-explained-to-my-mother/french/. I would like to thank the editors, Siham Bouamer and Denis Provencher, for their judicious comments on my work; any remaining inadequacies are solely mine. This chapter has already been published in French: "Deuil et réconciliation" [Mourning and Reconciliation] as part of my monograph, *Abdellah Taïa, la mélancolie et le cri* (Lyon: P.U.L., series: Autofictions, etc., 2020). My thanks go to P.U.L. for granting me permission to publish this chapter in English.

BIBLIOGRAPHY

Barrière, Loïc, ed. *Des Nouvelles du Maroc*. Paris: Paris-Méditerranée, 1999.

Bouamer, Siham. "De 'River of no Return' à 'Trouble of the World': Parcours initiatique musical dans *Infidèles* (2012) d'Abdellah Taïa." *Expressions maghrébines* 19, no. 1 (Summer 2020): 107–124.

Boulé, Jean-Pierre. *Abdellah Taïa, la mélancolie et le cri*. Lyon: Presses universitaires de Lyon, 2020.

Mitchell, Juliett. *The Selected Melanie Klein*. London: The Free Press, 1986.

Rosello, Mireille. *The Reparative in Narratives: Works of Mourning in Progress*. Liverpool: Liverpool University Press, 2010.

Taïa, Abdellah. *L'armée du salut*. Paris: Seuil, 2006.

———. *Une mélancolie arabe*. Paris: Seuil, 2008.

———. "L'homosexualité expliquée à ma mère." *Tel Quel*, no. 367, April 4–10 2009. https://www.asymptotejournal.com/nonfiction/abdellah-taia-homosexuality-explained-to-my-mother/french/.

———. *Un pays pour mourir*. Paris: Seuil, 2015.

———. "Sortir de la peur. Construire une identité homosexuelle arabe dans un monde postcolonial." Interview by Antoine Idier. *Fixxion* 12 (2016): 198–207.
———. *Celui qui est digne d'être aimé*. Paris: Seuil, 2017.
———. "Portrait: 'Abdellah Taïa: Paria gagné'." Interview by Dounia Hadni. *Libération*, January 5, 2017.
———. "Je ne pardonne absolument pas au Maroc ce qu'il m'a fait." Interview by Fadwa Islah. *Tel Quel* 746, January 6, 2017.
———. "J'ai été choqué par la façon dont on a traité la mort de George Michael." Interview by Christophe Martet. *Hornet*, January 16, 2017. https://hornetapp.com/stories/fr/abdellah-taia-george-michael.
———. "Tire ta langue: Abdellah Taïa." Interview by Rachida El Azzouzi and Antoine Perraud. *Mediapart* January 25, 2017. https://www.youtube.com/watch?v=HiIlNpqmisk.
———. "Celui qui est digne d'être aimé, Abdellah Taïa (Seuil)." Blog by Pierre Ahnne. January 28, 2017. http://pierreahnne.eklablog.fr/celui-qui-est-digne-d-etre-aime-abdellah-taia-seuil-a128207950.
———. "Abdellah Taïa dans La grande librairie." *France 5* January 29, 2017, https://www.youtube.com/watch?v=8syaSvRz320.
———. "Abdellah Taïa: 'L'amour n'est pas une chose pure.'" Interview by Olivier Rachet. *Le Site info*, February 9, 2017. https://www.lesiteinfo.com/cultures/abdellah-taia-lamour-nest-pas-une-chose-pure/.
———. "Lettres françaises" dans "Les nouvelles vagues." Interview by Marie Richeux. *France-Culture* March 9, 2017. https://www.franceculture.fr/emissions/les-nouvelles-vagues/la-france-vue-de-letranger-45-lettres-francaises.
Zaganiaris, Jean. "Dans le fond de la piscine." *Libération*, January 5 2017.

Part III

POSTCOLONIAL TEMPORALITIES

Chapter 7

Abdellah Taïa's Melancholic Migration

Oscillation between Solitude and Multitude

Thomas Muzart

In an op-ed published in March 2012, Abdellah Taïa abruptly introduces himself to the readers of the *New York Times* as "A Boy to Be Sacrificed." Under this disturbing title, a portrait of the Moroccan author looking straight at the camera with a soft yet determined gaze, shows however that, despite his persistent youthful appearance, Taïa overcame such a sacrificial destiny and became instead an important voice for protest against prejudices and violence toward sexual minorities. Initiating this political intervention from his own personal experience, the author associates the social alienation that he suffered in Morocco with his homosexuality. As he explains, the taboo surrounding such a nonnormative sexuality not only condemned him to hide who he was, but also exposed him to the lust of men who considered him nothing more than a sexual object, an effeminate boy to be sacrificed. Taïa specifically recalls how one night, when he was twelve, a group of drunken men gathered by his house and cried out that they wanted him to come down to have sex with them. What particularly shocked him was the absence of reaction from his family members who witnessed the scene. Perceiving their silence as their own way to turn their back on him, the young boy realized that night that no one was there to save his skin but himself, which he did, as he writes in the article, by "killing himself." Albeit on a symbolical level, the image of suicide adequately captures the violence on the self that constitutes breaking all the social ties that one once had. Far from succumbing to the tragic, the young boy understood this radical gesture as a necessary step that led to the creation of a new Abdellah, who would eventually immigrate to Europe in 1998 in order to seek what Michel Foucault would define in "The Ethic of Care for the Self" (1984) as a freedom to practice his own aesthetic of existence.

Retrospectively, Taïa confesses in his article that he feels nostalgic about the effeminate boy he used to be and evokes the interior struggle that such a longing generates in him: "He was innocence. Now I am only intellect. He was naïve. I am clever. He was spontaneous. I am locked in a constant struggle with myself."[1] By refusing to mourn the young Abdellah he had left in his home country, Taïa presents the main symptom that affects what Sara Ahmed calls, in *The Promise of Happiness* (2010), the melancholic migrant. Taïa's departure to France may indeed have more to do with migration than immigration because it derives from a political history, which is unfinished.[2] In *Le rouge du tarbouche* [*The Red of the Fez*] (2004), Taïa equates leaving his family to chosen exile,[3] which confirms Hamid Naficy's observation on the redefinition of such a term "from a strictly political expulsion and banishment to a more nuanced, culturally driven displacement."[4] Whether big or small, external or internal, forced or voluntary, exile always presupposes a relation to homeland and the possibility of return.[5] Taïa's unfinished history and openness toward the possibility of return are manifest in his tendency for melancholia, which, as Ahmed observes, serves as a pathologizing diagnosis against migrants who do not mourn their past lives completely: "the distinction between mourning and melancholia can easily be translated into ethical imperative: 'to let go' becomes a healthy relation to loss, and to 'hold on' becomes a form of pathology."[6] Far from being a disinterested gesture, Ahmed perceives the encouragement to mourn as an injunction to be happy—a feeling intended to subsequently bind migrants to the national ideal of the country hosting them. On the contrary, by holding on to something that has been lost, the melancholic subject cultivates negative feelings that complicates if not prevents integration and the formation of new attachments.

Rather than a condition from which Taïa has to recover, I argue that the resistance to happiness that characterizes the melancholic migrant allows him to critically reconsider his primary attachments with Morocco, which ultimately opens him to new political potentialities. While Ahmed mainly focuses on attachments based on objects, whose quality and property may be unclear to the melancholic subject, I will show that attachments in Taïa's work are directed toward well-defined subjects such as his younger self and his family members. I read this choice of reclaiming specific intimate attachments as a political effort to reconcile with his Moroccan origins and his people. This gesture does not mean, however, that Taïa decides to conform himself to the social imperatives that had led to his initial alienation. As he specifies in his *New York Times* article, the refusal to let go of the past is also an attempt to "do justice to the little Abdellah, to never forget the trauma he and every Arab homosexual like him suffered." It is important to highlight the fact that Taïa's act of reconnection takes place in the context of the 2011 Arab Spring, a popular movement, which emerged in many Arab-speaking countries such as Egypt, Libya, Syria, and Tunisia, in order to overthrow the authoritarian regimes in place. The author considers this political and historical event as a turning point for Arabs who came to understand the necessity to fight for individual freedom. It is because such a political struggle revolutionizes one's relation to subjectivity and collectivity that Taïa sees an opportunity to make visible and further include homosexuals among the agents of this ongoing liberation movement.

Beyond expressing a desire to return to his origins, the figure of the child mobilized by Taïa further allows him to reevaluate how he intends to participate in this revolution. Instead of taking pride in becoming "only intellect," the author equates such a condition with self-doubt and yearns for the spontaneity he used to enjoy as an innocent and naïve child. In doing so, I believe Taïa follows the recommendation of Frantz Fanon who, in *The Wretched of the Earth* (1963), invites native intellectuals to give up on their way of thinking focused on details in order to reconnect with their people and their material demand.[7] They must not speak on behalf of the people and fall into the trap of populism, but instead, immerse themselves into the collective. As Bourdieu underlines in his essay "The Social Space and the Genesis of Groups" (1985), intellectuals nonetheless play a key role as cultural producers. They can help people question the scripted aspect of reality and shape new representations that better defend minorities' interests.[8] They are what Bourdieu calls dominated agents among the dominant given that even though they occupy an undervalued position in the social space, they benefit from a cultural capital providing them with an influence if not an authority on politics.

As a queer subject who became a writer, Taïa embodies such an ambivalent position, which I propose to investigate in this chapter through the concept of multitude developed by Michael Hardt and Antonio Negri. As an alternative to the notion of community, which tends to develop commonality through the dilution of singularities, multitude considers coalition-building as a process deriving from the communication among singularities.[9] Hardt and Negri explain that thanks to the globalization of the world, especially with the rise of immaterial labor, which increased the production of communication, affective relationships, and knowledge, the commonality experienced by people have allowed them to develop collective forms of resistance against western capitalism and assimilation to nation-states. From this perspective, migrants, who undermine geographical barriers, represent significant contributors to the development of multitude. Migration, Hardt and Negri further assert, is "a training of the desire for freedom," which corresponds well to Taïa's initial motive to leave Morocco's repressive measures against homosexuality.[10] In the first part of this chapter, I will show how the author's desire for freedom expressed in his autofictional novels, *Le rouge du tarbouche, L'armée du salut*

[*Salvation Army*] (2006), and *Une mélancolie arabe* [*An Arab Melancholia*] (2008), corresponds to what Michel Foucault characterizes as an aesthetic of existence, which I discuss further below. Even though such a gesture appears individualistic and leads Taïa to experience isolation because of his inability to adapt to France's way of life, I demonstrate in the second part of this chapter that his immigration constituted the necessary step for him to reconcile with the Moroccan people. If public letters such as "L'homosexualité expliquée à ma mère" [Homosexuality Explained to My Mother] (2009) and *Lettres à un jeune marocain* [*Letters to a Young Moroccan*] (2009) demonstrate the author's intention to initiate a dialogue from a position of critical observer, his subsequent texts "Lettre à Mohamed Bouazizi" [Letter to Mohamed Bouazizi] (2011) and *Infidèles* [*Infidels*] (2013) reflect on the potential as well as the limits for queer subjects to become active agents in a collective resistance. In parallel with the condition of melancholic migrants oscillating between the West and the Arab world, Taïa and the characters he imagines oscillate between moments of solitude and multitude.

LEAVING TO FIND ONE'S PLACE: TAÏA AND THE AESTHETIC OF EXISTENCE

In "The Ethic of Care for the Self as a Practice of Freedom," Foucault promotes what he calls an aesthetic of existence, which consists of an exercise of the self on the self through which an individual elaborates, transforms himself, and accesses a certain mode of being.[11] Taking the example of Ancient Greece, Foucault argues that this form of self-care is ethical in the sense that it allows the individual to occupy, in the city, in the community, and intersubjective relations, a specific and proper place.[12] In *Saint Foucault* (1995), David Halperin specifies that Foucault refers to ancient Greek morality because unlike the modern sexual ethics, its aim is not to implement interdictions and normalize subjects but rather to operate distinctions through stylization, in other words, to marginalize or "queer" subjects.[13] Therefore, what is at stake in the self-care promoted by Foucault is not to find a place in the social sphere already existing but to create one for oneself. Because, despite its emphasis on singularity, self-care also implies relations to others; it cannot escape dealing with issues of power and freedom. The choice of a term such as "freedom" over "liberation" comes from Foucault's skepticism toward the possibility for self-care to get rid of all forms of repression. Using the example of sexuality, he explains that what is at stake is not liberating sexuality but rather trying to discover practices of freedom through which individuals can experiment with pleasure and erotic relations.[14] Power relations are, according to Foucault, inherent to any form of sociality in which practices of freedom take direct part. Mobile and present at different levels (among a family, in pedagogical relations, in the political body), power is the object of constant negotiation between individuals. Explaining that individuals' degrees of power vary according to various circumstances, Foucault warns about the risk of situations of domination in which an individual or a social group succeeds in fixing relations of power, thus preventing any possibility of reversibility.[15] Consequently, there needs to be a certain degree of liberation for practices of freedom to develop.

Following this line of thought, it is possible to consider Taïa's discovery of his homosexuality and the socio-political stigmatization of such a marginal sexuality in Morocco as the main factors that led him to leave his country and find in Europe, and particularly in France, a place more open for the practice of freedom.[16] Prior to his sexual awakening, Taïa recounts in his novel, *L'armée du salut*, that as a child, he had no desire to leave a country that had everything he needed, especially a loving older brother, Abdelkébir, whom he admired and desired. The coast of Spain that he sees during a stroll with his brother through the streets of Tangier does not represent an invitation for future travel experiences. He perceives this "maudite Europe" [damned Europe] right across the Mediterranean Sea as a cynical and unbearable scene, in which he has no intention to participate, finding all that he considers essential in his own country.[17] In the film adaptation that he directed himself, Taïa added a scene at the beach that reinforces the skepticism he had as a child toward the Western world. While Abdellah's older brother reads a book in French and advocates for the learning of such a language for succeeding in life, the young boy does not seem to subscribe to this point of view and has a hard time imagining the utility of French for his future life. However, the moment of rupture appears sooner than expected when Abdellah realizes that his brother's ultimate motive for their trip to Tangier was to meet a woman whom he was considering marrying. This compliance with social norms is, according to Daniel Maroun, what constitutes for the narrator his first experience of a betrayal.[18] Claiming that "[c]'était une trahison, non de sa part, mais de la part de la société" [It was a betrayal, not on his part, but on the part of society],[19] Abdellah absolves his brother from any responsibility and denounces instead the social injunction to normality that caused the separation from his brother, to the extent that the latter ceases to represent the masculine ideal he aspired to attain one day.

The beginning of *Une mélancolie arabe* depicts a more radical scene of rupture that better reveals how Taïa will eventually leave his hometown and become a writer. Recalling a sexual encounter he had as a child with young boys from his neighborhood, the narrator underlines his unease toward the behaviors of his partners who feminize him by calling him "Leïla" and a *zamel*, a derogatory Arabic term used to shame homosexuals.[20] Resisting such deprivation of his social identity by stating his real name and hoping to show that, through this gesture, an equal homosexual relation based on tenderness and respect toward gender identity is possible, Abdellah realizes that on the contrary, his assailant increases his violence and threatens him with rape.[21] Managing to escape, he nonetheless foresees through this event the life of shame that awaits him if he remains in his town: "Je savais au fond le destin de petite vie programmée par les autres qui m'attendait. Je savais la honte intime, publique, qui allait me poursuivre partout. Je refusais et l'une et l'autre" [I knew too well the kind of life people would expect me to live, off in the margins somewhere. I already knew the level of private and public shame that would follow me everywhere. And I said, no way].[22] The narrator refuses a fate in which others decide for him and condemn his sexual orientation to public, and consequently, personal shame. That is why he decides to start a new life, in which he will be the agent of his own choices: "Mon histoire, désormais, j'allais l'écrire seul, en silence, loin du groupe, loin du mauvais oeil" [From now on, I'd tell my story alone, write about it in silence, away from other people, away from the evil eye].[23] In this passage, Abdellah assumes that seizing control of his own life necessarily implies exclusion from the group. The expression "en silence" [in silence] furthermore emphasizes that despite gaining agency, he still needs to conceal his difference. The refuge he will eventually find in music, literature, and cinema, provides him nonetheless with role models that will help him live and write his own story: "La littérature et la vie réelle sont à jamais unies pour moi, l'une ne peut exister sans l'autre. La vie sans les mots des livres me semble impossible à vivre" [Literature and real life are forever united within me—one cannot exist without the other. To me, a life without words from books seems impossible to live].[24] The desire for escape through art glimpsed by Abdellah further awakens his desire for an elsewhere that implies both discovery and self-discovery.

This state of mind partly explains why he falls in love with Jean, an older French scholar whom he met at a conference in Rabat. Described as "un homme occidental, cultivé, quelque part un homme-rêve" [a cultured man, a Western man, in some ways the man of my dreams],[25] Jean initially embodies the role of the prince charming fulfilling Abdellah's desire to see the world as an intellectual and escape his working-class milieu. Even though Jean gives him the opportunity to study in Switzerland, the narrator understands after his arrival in Europe that he needs to take his independence from his Western partner to fully experience freedom. Jean's behavior does indeed display entitlement and prevents Abdellah from transcending his condition as an exotic sexual object. Far from being the end of his social and sexual construction, the arrival in Europe constitutes not only a new start but an opportunity to deconstruct all certainties about himself in order to reflect better on his relationship with his culture of origin: "[s]e perdre complètement pour mieux

[s]e retrouver" [Lose myself entirely, the better to find myself].[26] The necessary break-up with Jean eventually leads the narrator to find shelter at Geneva's Salvation Army whose manager looks exactly like Michel Foucault. While this resemblance may appear coincidental, it seems actually quite logical that the narrator would identify the person providing him support to experience his freedom with the philosopher who theorized it.

While at the end of *L'armée du salut*, the narrator seems rather hopeful about his new beginning in Europe, his account in *Une mélancolie arabe*, as the title itself suggests, appears less idealized. Remembering the young Abdellah he once was, the narrator underlines in this passage the necessity he felt to escape his country and to be uprooted as a sort of initiation ritual toward adulthood: "Il pleurait. De joie. De déchirement. De Paris. [. . .] D'être parti de là-bas, du Maroc. D'avoir quitté le monde et la foule. L'enfance" [He would cry. Cry because he was happy. Because he was afraid. Because he was heartbroken. Cry over Paris itself. [. . .]. Cry because he had left Morocco, left its crowds, left its childhood].[27] Describing his conflicted feelings, Taïa does not romanticize his immigration to France but rather insists on the difficulty of leaving behind the world and the people he always knew. Despite the necessity of his departure, he experiences the melancholic aspect of migration identified by Ahmed, which manifests in his case through the equally freeing and burdening power of loneliness: "Seul, pour son plus grand bonheur. Seul, pour son plus grand malheur." [He was alone and happier than ever to be that way. All alone and sadder than ever because of it.][28] Taïa considers nonetheless that his isolation and disappointment about Paris are the factors that led him to become a writer: "Les promesses de la France n'avaient pas été tenues. La déception était le quotidien. La déception nécessaire. [. . .] Et une surprise. Il ne s'était jamais rêvé écrivain. Paris lui avait donné l'écriture comme cadeau" [France wasn't all it was supposed to be. Every day, he was in for another letdown. Disappointment had to happen. [. . .] And then came a surprise: He never dreamed he'd become a writer. Paris gave him writing as a gift].[29] Emerging through the dissatisfaction that Taïa finds in both Morocco and France, writing offers him an opportunity to reflect as a writer without borders on his social self through a constant back and forth between the two countries.

The refusal to "let go" and the cultivation of negative feelings observed by Sara Ahmed in the melancholic migrant are also prevalent in the last chapter of Taïa's *Le rouge du tarbouche*. The narrator realizes the loss of desire that he has been experiencing in his Parisian life and the solitude resulting from such a state of mind: "j'éprouvais un immense sentiment de solitude, d'abandon [. . .] je ne comptais vraiment pour personne. J'étais vraiment seul dans cette ville. La liberté ne voulait tout d'un coup plus rien dire, n'avait ni sens ni goût. Livré à moi-même, je pouvais commettre toutes sortes de folies. Paris est une ville dangereuse pour les solitaires" [I experienced an immense feeling of loneliness, of abandonment [. . .] I did not really matter for anyone. I was really lonely in this city. All of a sudden, freedom no longer made any sense, it had neither meaning nor taste. All by my lonesome, I could have wrought all kinds of havoc. Paris is a dangerous city for loners].[30] This passage challenges the Foucauldian idea according to which the practice of freedom through an aesthetic of existence allows a subject to find their position in the social realm. If freedom brings isolation, is it still freedom or simply indifference? Is freedom still something worth pursuing? In reaction to this loss of meaning, Abdellah decides to follow his intuition and return to Morocco for the holiday: "répondre à l'appel marocain" [respond to the Moroccan call].[31] Once arrived there, he discovers however the increased poverty of his home country where, according to him, the motto has become "every man for himself." His return among his compatriots provokes mockery given his failure to embody the successful emigrant who made fortune in Europe. Confronted with the alternative "becoming rich or not coming back," the narrator realizes that he no longer belongs to the Moroccan society either. What he was holding on to was already dead. Consequently, he decides to leave again for France.

DISTANCE AS AN OPPORTUNITY FOR DIALOGUE AND THE RISE OF MULTITUDE

If Taïa's estrangement from both Moroccan and French society is undeniable, it is however possible to envision his status as a migrant as an opportunity rather than as a problematic condition. According to Rosi Braidotti, the nomadic subjectivity resulting from the distanciation between oneself and one's homeland may be a painful process but also allows minorities to escape the scripted way of life that had until then inhibited them.[32] Braidotti's concept of nomadism directly takes inspiration from Deleuze and Guattari's *Mille Plateaux* [*A Thousand Plateaus*] (1980), which correlates the figure of the nomad with the state of "becoming." The nomad embodies a subjectivity in transit and therefore resists the identity process consisting of a fixation into a state of "being." By doing so, such a subject also breaks away with pre-established power relations and gives way to power dynamics, which emerge from unsuspected encounters and interactions with people, but also with knowledge and ideas. Rather than reproduction and imitation, nomadic becoming produces new interconnections. Therefore, even though the extraction from a hegemonic habit of thinking may imply a moment of alienation, the creative process generated by nomadism is not individualistic or exclusionary but relational and collective.

Mehammed Amadeus Mack's specific analysis of "Arab" nomadism in *Sexagon* (2017) identifies Taïa as one of the main authors contributing to the "transnational promise" that includes Arab subjects into the elaboration of sexual modernity.[33] While Mack mainly considers these Arab nomads' movements across cultures, races, and borders as a search for romantic and erotic fulfillment, I would argue that both their quest and the transnational promise that they carry within them and through their actions transcend the realm of sexuality while remaining embedded within it. Moreover, instead of connecting this "romantic transnationalism of sorts" to a transnationalism idealizing mobility and reinforcing the hegemonic position of Western cultures, what Françoise Lionnet and Shu-mei Shih call a "transnationalism from above," I will show how Taïa's nomadic tendencies contribute to political efforts that have more to do with a "transnationalism from below." Despite its intended desire for a unifying world order, transnationalism has produced multilayered spatio-temporalities that simultaneously provided minoritized cultures with opportunities to create networks within and across national boundaries.[34] According to Lionnet and Shih, the various forms of cooperation that constitute "transnationalism from below," or minor transnationalism, represent a welcome alternative for minority subjects who often identify themselves in opposition to a dominant discourse rather than vis-à-vis each other and other minority groups. No longer seeking recognition and citizenship through a vertical struggle, in other words, depending on the approval of the dominant norm, minorities horizontally reconfigure modes of living, belonging, and political practice.

In *Les prémices littéraires des révolutions arabes* [*The Literary Signs of Arab Revolutions*] (2014), Samir Patrice El Maarouf also acknowledges the fact that extracting oneself from the dominant group and being part of the margin offers a significant political advantage, particularly to observe collective movements. The role of observer supposes a critical distance that allows one to reflect on the dynamics of the crowd and its relations with the historical events and the power in place. As a homosexual and emigrant, Taïa embodies such a role and participates in the elaboration of what El Maarouf calls "une éthique de la marge" [an ethic of the margin].[35] "L'homosexualité expliquée à ma mère," published in the Moroccan magazine *TelQuel* in 2009, represents such an ethical gesture coming from an author not only socially marginalized due to his sexuality but also living at the margins of his country of origin. Thanks to such a geographical distance, Taïa benefits from less pressure to respond to attacks such as the one conducted in 2009 by Morocco's interior Minister who announced the intensification of repression toward writings seeking to attack the moral and religious values of Moroccan society. While the Minister did not name anyone specifically, Taïa felt that this attack targeted him and decided to respond publicly with

"L'homosexualité expliquée à ma mère," in which he explicitly ascribes a political meaning to homosexuality.

As the title suggests, the text takes the form of a letter to the author's mother. While his first intention was to address the Minister directly, Taïa explained that because his speech would not necessarily be heard, he preferred to write to someone related to him.[36] This decision appears nonetheless more as a literary strategy than a simple attempt to dialogue with his mother, given the fact she does not understand French and does not know how to read. Taïa mobilizes the power of the intimate to emotionally color a political text addressed to the Moroccan people. In his letter, the author returns to the reception of his coming out and the inability of his family members to understand a gesture that they interiorized as shameful for them. While regretting the wound he inflicted on his relatives, Taïa reclaims his right to affirm his sexual identity without renouncing inclusion in his family and by extension his community: "Je m'expose en signant de mon vrai prénom et de mon vrai nom. Je vous expose avec moi. Je vous entraîne dans cette aventure, qui ne fait que commencer pour moi et pour les gens comme moi: exister enfin! Sortir de l'ombre! Relever la tête! Dire la vérité, ma vérité! Être: Abdellah. Être: Taïa. Être les deux. Seul. Et pas seul à la fois" [I expose myself by signing my real first name and my real last name. And I expose you along with me. I drag you along on this adventure, which is just the beginning for me and for people like me: to exist finally! To come out of the shadows, head held high! To tell the truth, my truth! To be: Abdellah. To be: Taïa. To be both. Alone. Yet not alone at the same time].[37] In this passage, the author addresses the importance of "telling" along with the one of "naming." By connecting, Abdellah, the symbol of his individuality, and Taïa, the one of his family heritage, the author also expresses the possibility of articulating his singularity with collectivity. If, by signing with his actual name, Taïa might have contributed to the transgressive aspect of his coming out, Denis Provencher considers that with such a gesture, the author also "grounds himself in the normative familial system."[38] Both coming out and performative filiation of his Moroccan identity, the letter demonstrates that breaking the family circle and tradition and leaving for Europe not only helped Taïa to live his sexuality more freely, but also was the only possibility for him to reconnect with his family: "Je rêve du dialogue. Un dialogue impossible jusqu'à aujourd'hui" [I dream of dialogue. A dialogue that has been impossible until today].[39]

Far from limiting itself to the recognition of homosexuality and LGBTQI rights, Taïa reflects in "L'homosexualité expliquée à ma mère" on the inclusion of sexually marginalized subjects in the movement of resistance against the authoritarian Moroccan regime that imposes a moral order and values that no longer represent the actual society. As Provencher astutely notes, Taïa's letter is, beyond the central aspect of homosexuality, also a coming out as a writer and a thinker who must act.[40] By stating in his address to his family, "[j]e ne suis pas dans la minorité. *Je suis vous, avec vous, toujours avec vous*, même quand je brise les tabous" [I am not in a minority. *I am you, with you, always with you*, even when I break taboos][41] (emphasis mine), the author underlines his refusal to consider his sexual orientation as an obstacle. However, let us note that Taïa asserts that he is "not in a minority," which differs from saying "I am not a minority." Having that distinction in mind, I would argue that the author does not deny his sexual marginality but rather considers it the way through which he can belong not in a minority but in a group in which individuals as singularities can act on the basis of what they have in common, that is, Hardt and Negri's multitude. Homosexuals are, according to him, part of a revolution that needs to happen and can only happen through "provocation and scandal."[42] That is why they have a significant role to play as agents of change, but they also *are the multitude, with the multitude, always with the multitude.*

Taïa particularly praises the youth that, according to him, has already embraced post-modernism and therefore challenges the unicity of Moroccan culture: "Je ne supporte plus qu'on ne voie pas la richesse réelle de ce pays: l'imaginaire, les histoires, le mystère. LA JEUNESSE. Je ne supporte plus qu'on n'aide pas assez le Maroc à se relever et à grandir. Je ne supporte plus ce système qui casse du matin au soir le Marocain et qui fait taire les voix nouvelles qui émergent pour dire ce pays autrement" [I can no longer stand the fact that people cannot see the real wealth of this country: the imaginary, the stories, and the mystery. THE YOUTH. I hate the fact that we don't do enough to help Morocco stand up and grow. I can no longer stand the system, which breaks Moroccan people day and night and silences new voices that are struggling to talk about this country differently].[43] Taïa's stress on "the imaginary, the stories, and the mystery," to open the people to Morocco's diversity, reveals his faith in the literary power of representation. Beyond recognizing the importance of his country's and family's traditions on his literary performance, it is also necessary to acknowledge its mixing with Western references. Taïa explains in his text the influence of the Portuguese poet Fernando Pessoa, the Anglo-Irish painter Francis Bacon, and the French-Algerian actor and singer Isabelle Adjani on his identity construction. Their respective artistry inspired Taïa to "surpass" and "transform" himself, "revelation" leading to "revolution."[44] That is why, according to Provencher, the text appears as a microcosm of his family "where [Taïa] can test out his performance of identification, disidentification, queer temporalities, and *transfiliations*" that can extend to the Moroccan society.[45] By mixing the intimate with the political as well as cultural references from the Arab world with some from the West, Taïa invents a new imaginary that overcomes alienation and challenges the status-quo defended by the regime.

Published the same year as "L'homosexualité expliquée à ma mère," *Lettres à un jeune marocain* further confirms the author's desire for multitude, for "une révolte personnelle et collective" [a personal and collective revolt].[46] This articulation from personal to collective derives directly from the project of this text that Taïa had initially planned to write based on his own experience before deciding to include other Moroccans' voices:

> Au départ, je voulais faire ce livre tout seul, j'avais suffisamment d'éléments, d'histoires et de colère en moi pour écrire un livre qui s'adresse à toute la jeunesse marocaine. Puis je me suis rendu compte ensuite qu'il y avait d'autres voix très intéressantes au Maroc à qui on ne donne pas la possibilité de s'exprimer. Au lieu de le faire tout seul, j'ai réuni autour de moi toutes ces voix qui, à leur manière, sont aussi dans un combat et dans une résistance.
>
> [At the beginning, I wanted to write this book by myself. I had enough elements, stories and anger within me to write a book that speaks to the whole Moroccan youth. Then I realized that there were other very interesting voices in Morocco that had no possibility to express themselves. Instead of doing this book by myself, I gathered around me all these voices which, in their own way, are also in conflict and resistance.][47]

Lettres à un jeune marocain gathers eighteen contributors from Moroccan origins whose diverse profiles reflect the complexity and plurality of contemporary Morocco. While four of them still live in their country, the others, like Taïa, emigrated to European countries such as Belgium, France, the Netherlands, or Spain. Authors like Fadwa Islah and Mounir Fatmi, respectively living between Paris and Rabat and between Paris and Tangier, have the particularity of evolving in an intermediary space. More than just revealing that Taïa's fluctuating geographical position is far from being unique, *Lettres à un jeune marocain* takes advantage of such a position to reflect on the social and political challenges faced by Moroccan society. Examining the intergenerational aspect of *Lettres à un jeune marocain,* Khalid Lyamlahy notes that eleven of the authors were born in the 1970s, including Taïa. Besides this majoritarian generational group, two contributors (Tahar Ben Jelloun and Abdelhak Serhane) were born before the 1960s, two during the 1960s, and finally three in the 1980s. While acknowledging the benefit of giving a voice to young authors, Lyamlahy finds regrettable that the text becomes a pretext "pour dialoguer avec soi-même ou, du moins, avec sa propre génération" [to dialogue with oneself or, at least, with one's own generation].[48] The concession introduced by "at least" is however crucial. In my view, the dialogue established through the text is not a dialogue of youth with itself but a dialogue between a youth with transnational experience and cultural capital and the Moroccan youth that remained in the home country. *Lettres à un jeune marocain* represents an attempt for intellectuals to reconnect with the people. The wide distribution of the text itself is proof of such a desire to reach as many young Moroccans as possible. Based on the information provided by Taïa to Jalila Sbaï, author of the article "Réformes politiques et enjeux sociaux au Maroc," the magazine *Tel Quel* distributed for free 50,000 copies of the text in August 2009 before its release in France in September.[49] More than what Lyamlahy calls a linguistic transposition,[50] the translation of the book into Arabic in December 2009 attests to a will of initiating a transnational dialogue, which the distribution of 40,000 copies, thanks to the Arabic-speaking magazine *Nichane,* further supported.

Addressed to his nephew Adnane, Taïa's letter consists first of all of a tribute to his recently deceased father, Mohamed. The author wishes through writing to revive his father and return justice to the man he was, a *chaouche,* a minor civil servant in the *Bibliothèque générale* in Rabat. Unlike the life of servitude of Taïa's father, Adnane must question the social values of his country and rebel if necessary. Taïa chose Adnane as a symbol of revolt because like his father, his biological origins are uncertain. Even though, as we have seen with "L'homosexualité expliquée à ma mère," Taïa's letters convey political messages that extend beyond his family circle, Lyamlahy questions the author's tendency to favor his personal story to the detriment of the actual preoccupations of Moroccan youth. Identifying this bias in other contributions, he concludes that *Lettres à un jeune marocain* might have actually missed the mark that it intended to hit: "À trop vouloir se raconter, on finit par oublier, ou du moins négliger, la visée initiale de l'ouvrage et par transformer l'écriture *pour l'autre* à une écriture *de soi.* À trop vouloir raisonner à partir de son expérience personnelle, l'autre risque inévitable est de se poser en moralisateur et d'omettre les attentes et les inquiétudes de la jeunesse marocaine" [By wanting to describe oneself too much, one ends up forgetting, or at least neglecting, the initial aim of the work and by turning the writing *for the other* into a writing *of oneself.* By wanting to reason too much from one's own personal experience, the other inevitable risk is to position oneself as a moralizer and to forget the expectations and the worry of the Moroccan youth].[51] As mentioned in the introduction, in "The Social Space and the Genesis of Groups," Pierre Bourdieu characterizes such an ambivalent position, typical of intellectuals, as the one of the "dominated among the dominant."[52] In this model, while intellectuals are dominated in the field of power and therefore aware of the effects of domination preventing social change, they occupy at the same time a dominant position as cultural producers compared to the rest of the people. As an author, Taïa can offer the dominated people the tools to initiate a rebellion and consider a new path for the Moroccan youth. But as Bourdieu explains, the homology of positions between intellectuals and lower classes is often the basis of ambiguous alliances because of the reproduction of the dynamics of domination. In the context of the decolonization of Algeria, Frantz Fanon's *The Wretched of the Earth* identifies in the figure of the intellectual the same potential and limits to implement resistance as Bourdieu. Even though a native intellectual who sided with the West played the role of "a vigilant sentinel ready to defend the Greco-Latin pedestal," Fanon recognizes during the struggle for liberation the possibility for such a subject to reject his individualistic mindset after realizing the colonialist regime would not keep its promises for upward mobility and equality.[53] However, despite being a great asset, the native intellectual also tends to position himself as the holder of a truth that he imposes on the people by using populist methods.[54] According to Fanon, the truth does not emerge from the individual but from a people willing to liberate itself from the colonial yoke. That is why he invites the native intellectual to an exercise of self-criticism in order to reconnect with the masses: "the more the intellectual imbibes the atmosphere of the people, the more completely he abandons the habits of calculation, of unwonted silence, of mental reservations, and shakes off the spirit of concealment."[55] If Taïa's emigration may have been perceived through his autofictions as a collusion with the West, "L'homosexualité expliquée à ma mère" and *Lettres à un jeune marocain* prove on the contrary his desire to implement the dialogue and reconnection with the people that Fanon advises. However, by focusing on his individual experience, Taïa positions himself as one of the holders of truth instead of seeking inclusion in already existing grassroots movements and rediscovering what Fanon calls "the substance of village assemblies, the cohesion of people's committees, and the fruitfulness of local meetings and groupments."[56] Mack also observes that, as an author who writes from France about North Africa, Taïa may sometimes fall into the role of a "transnational informant" for his tendency to corroborate a reductive divide between an intolerant Arab world and a Western world more accepting of sexual minorities.[57] Taïa's ambiguous position therefore calls into question the ways he can actively participate in the resistance struggle taking place in his home country, especially during the Arab Spring of 2011.

THE ARAB SPRING OR HOW TO BECOME AN ACTIVE AGENT WITHIN A RESISTANCE COLLECTIVE

In the preface of *Égypte, les martyrs de la révolution* (2014), Taïa acknowledges that before the Arab Spring, he did not think that a collective movement of contestation was possible: "Je ne voyais pas d'où pouvait venir le vent fort d'une émancipation, à la fois collective et individuelle" [I could not see where the strong wind of an emancipation could come from, at once collective and individual].[58] He explains his misjudgment by the fact that he was blinded by ideas of others, whether the one of the Moroccan regime or the West. Admitting his own internalization of divisions, Taïa now prefers to see beyond the differences, the commonality between him and the Arab people, and consequently shift from the role of simple observer to the role of agent within the crowd. In a tribute addressed to Mohamed Bouazizi, the fruit seller who started the Revolution in Tunisia by setting himself on fire in an act of despair after being deprived of his work tools, Taïa lays out the specific role he intends to play in this revolution, the one of a writer:

> Je suis écrivain, cher Mohamed. Je sais que mon devoir est d'être avec ces révolutionnaires. D'être fort avec eux. Alors j'écris. À toi. Et ailleurs. Écrire pour marquer ce mouvement. Le voir et le revoir. Le porter haut. Le porter grand. Je me libère grâce à toi, grâce à eux, à ces frères et sœurs dans la révolte. Nous n'écrirons plus comme avant dans le monde arabe. Nous ne penserons plus comme avant. Tout change. Tout bouge.

> [I am a writer, dear Mohamed. I know that my duty is to be with these revolutionaries. To be strong alongside them. So I write. To you. And elsewhere. I write to mark this movement. To see it again and again. To carry it high. To carry it expansively. I am liberating myself thanks to you, thanks to them, to those brothers and sisters in revolt. In the Arab world, we will never write in the same way again. We will never think the same way. Everything is changing. Everything is shifting.][59]

It is worth noticing in this quote the shift from the "I" to the "We" and its association to the liberation of the self *alongside* the revolutionaries. Indeed, Taïa reveals that more than observing others' actions, he found brothers and sisters who inspired him to join the fight. Unlike "L'homosexualité expliquée à ma mère" and *Lettres à un jeune marocain,* the letter to Bouazizi does not position Taïa as a guide but rather as a follower of a movement initiated by the people. The intellectual's reconnection with the people promoted by Fanon is also crucial for Alain Badiou, who in *Le réveil de l'Histoire* [*The Awakening of History*] (2011) examines contemporary resistance movements and claims: "le seul réveil possible est celui de l'initiative populaire où s'enracinera la puissance d'une Idée" [the only awakening possible is the one from the popular initiative, where the power of an Idea will take root].[60] In the case of the Arab Spring, the awakening comes from the immolation of Bouazizi that generated what Badiou calls an instantaneous riot.[61] An instantaneous riot takes place in the area of those who participate in it and only disseminates by imitation, meaning that similar groups of people follow the example of the ones who initiated the rebellion. One of the determining factors that turn an instantaneous riot into a historical one is when it extends to parts of the population who are diverse in terms of status, social class, sex or age.[62] While Badiou mentions the involvement of women as a sign of generalized extension, I would claim that the involvement of sexually marginalized subjects manifests as well the shift toward a historical riot. The extension of the historical riot no longer results from similar groups imitating each other but instead from the gathering of almost every component of the society, which thus creates "une foule multiforme valant pour le peuple entier" [a multiform crowd equating to the entire people].[63] Taïa's writing, especially his letter to Bouazizi promising to "carry high" the movement, places sexually marginalized subjects among the people and for the first time on the stage of history. The tribute to Bouazizi, in the passage quoted previously, further suggests that after the riots, it is no longer possible to write and think the same way. By turning now to Taïa's post-Arab Spring novel, *Infidèles*, I will examine to what extent such an event influenced his writing and his approach to collective movements.

At first, *Infidèles* emphasizes the opposition between marginal singularities and the rest of the people. The young protagonist, Jallal, for example, feels he has to defend his mother, a prostitute, from the people of his hometown who reject her: "Je crache sur cette ville, Salé, et sur tous ceux qui ne te reconnaissent pas" [I spit on this city, Salé, and everyone who pretends they don't know you].[64] Jallal's mother represents, for Taïa and his protagonist, a character that is a central figure of the society. She is the one who guarantees the respect of traditions while knowing the hypocrisy sustaining them. Indeed, Slima is in charge of teaching sex to men the day of their marriage and of making sure blood appears on the white sheet to prove the bride's virginity. In taking part in the most intimate moment and knowing what everybody else ignores, Slima is "un être à part" [a being apart].[65] Later in the novel, Jallal's mother is tortured in the south of Morocco by the police for refusing to provide information about a former client of hers considered as a dissident soldier. When finally liberated, Slima concludes that there are no longer true Muslims in Morocco but only obedient slaves thirsty for blood.[66] That is why she decides to renounce her citizenship: "Brûler mon passeport marocain. Brûler ma carte d'identité marocaine. Renaître pour toi, Jallal. Pour nous" [Burn my Moroccan passport. Burn my Moroccan identity card. Be born again for you, Jallal. For us].[67] By claiming about her son "je suis son origine, son pays, son avenir" [I'm his origins, his country, his future][68] and subsequently electing Cairo as a place for them to be resurrected, Slima undermines the importance of homeland and promotes instead through displacement, a regaining of agency for the identity construction of Jallal, who comes to embody the future of Arab youth. Escaping the burden of national identity that she qualifies as "une peau qui n'est plus la nôtre" [a skin that's not ours], she and Jallal find in Cairo a place that belongs "à tous les Arabes sans racines" [to all rootless Arabs].[69] Slima and Jallal's position is reminiscent of Taïa's immigration to France, which allowed him to redefine his attachment to his cultural heritage and create a system of symbolic references in which he could freely exist and invite others, especially the youth, to liberate themselves. However, Taïa's *Infidèles* elects Cairo as a place for reinvention and practices of freedom, which differs from his autofictional works where Europe played such a role. I consider this to be a significant change: this return to the Arab world is directly influenced by the 2011 uprisings that took place in the Tahrir Square or "Liberation Square" in Cairo. As stated in his letter to Bouazizi, Taïa writes and thinks differently by imagining characters other than himself willing to rebel against the status quo imposed by authoritarian regimes within the Arab world.

This regained faith in his Arab revolutionary fellows is of crucial importance for a movement that the Western media, according to Badiou, often interpreted as a desire for Western democratic society.[70] Denouncing what he calls the modern version of imperial interventionism, Badiou advocates for a complete de-westernization of the uprising in order to implement true change.[71] Even though *Infidèles* participates in the representation of a rebellion from and for Arab subjects, the novel does not reject Western cultural influence as Slima's fascination for Marilyn Monroe can testify. Unlike Badiou, who bases his argument on a dichotomy between the West and the Arab world, Taïa uses the reference to Marilyn Monroe to illustrate their commonality and create an imaginary that differs from the one imposed by the Moroccan authoritarian regime and the imperialistic West. The similarity between the West and the Arab world is first acknowledged by Jallal who establishes a parallel between Marilyn and his mother. One as a sex symbol and the other as a prostitute, they are both at the same time idolized and deprecated by society. It is their common condition rather than their geographical and cultural difference that reunites them: "les âmes se rencontrent, se reconnaissent et se parlent même quand les mers, les océans les séparent" [Souls meet, recognize each other and speak, even when gulfs, oceans lie between them].[72] Even the language is no longer a barrier: "Elle [Marilyn] parle anglais et, dans mes oreilles, mon cœur, c'est comme si c'était de l'arabe" [She speaks English and to my ears, my heart, it's Arabic].[73] It is also important to note that the novel specifically associates Marilyn Monroe with her role in Otto Preminger's film, *River of No Return* (1954). Obsessed with this film, Jallal shows a particular interest in the portraying of a crowd of cowboys and marginalized people in search of gold:

> C'est une foule sauvage, en rupture, à la recherche d'un moment fugitif de tendresse. On boit. Et on boit. Et on boit. Au milieu de ces hommes, un petit garçon, un petit homme. 10 ans. 11 ans peut-être. Il est chez lui ici, dans cette foule

dangereuse, à la limite du désespoir. [. . .] Il a tout vu ici dans ce camp. Les assoiffés. Les désaxés. Les fous. Les saints. Les prostituées. Les prêtres. Les chanteuses. Les guerriers. Les morts. Les survivants. Les chefs. Une mère. Marilyn Monroe.

[A wild crowd at breaking point in search of a fleeting moment of tenderness. They drink. And they drink. And they drink. In the middle of these men, a little boy, a little man. Ten years old. Maybe eleven. He's at home in this dangerous crowd on the brink of despair. [. . .] He's seen everything, here in this camp. The thirsty. The deranged. The mad. The saints. The prostitutes. The priests. The songstresses. The warriors. The dead. The survivors. The leaders. A mother. Marilyn Monroe.][74]

This heterogeneous list of marginals, part of the Klondike Gold Rush, is reminiscent of the diverse Egyptian population united to demand social justice, the sought-after golden rule. This parallel further allows Taïa to represent how his protagonist finds a way to imagine collective actions despite everyone's singularities. Similar to Marilyn who represents Slima's alter ego, Jallal identifies with the young kid in the film, who, as described, feels at home in this crowd. This interpretation is further reinforced by the final section of the novel where *River of No Return* becomes the inspiration for Jallal and Mahmoud, a young Belgian recently converted to Islam with whom the young boy fell in love, to organize a bombing in Morocco. The purpose of such an attack is brought by Jallal and displays, I would argue, the tension that Taïa feels between his opposition to an obedient crowd and his faith in a collective rebellion:

Donner à méditer un geste. Être contre cette plaie qui se répandait partout au Maroc. La banalité. L'étroitesse. L'enlisement. La soumission. L'enlisement dans le faux et l'ignorance. La destruction programmée des individus, de ceux et celles qui, comme ma mère Slima, osent un jour tenter la liberté, la résistance, une autre voie. S'élever contre tout un pays. Contre tout un peuple. Poser enfin les vraies questions. Qui nous a amenés jusque-là, à cette déchéance, à ce malheur, à cette négation de nous-mêmes, à cet aveuglement contagieux ? Qui empêche nos âmes de voler et d'écrire une autre histoire avec un nouveau messager ? Qui nous bloque, nous pétrifie et nous dénie le droit d'être ce que nous sommes à l'origine: des hommes debout?

[Perform an action to make people think. To stand firm against the plague spreading through Morocco. Banality. Narrow-mindedness. Confinement. Submission. Mired in falsity and ignorance. The programmed destruction of individuals, of people like my mother Slima who dare one day to try for freedom, resistance, a different road. To rise up against an entire country. An entire people. Finally, to try to ask the real questions. Who brought us to this point, this state of collapse, this misfortune, this self-negation, this infectious blindness? Who is preventing our souls from taking flight and writing another History with a new messenger? Who is blocking us, turning us to stone and denying us the right to be what we are: men, standing?][75]

First of all, the bombing is intended to convey a message of resistance addressed to the people. Even though at first glance the act of resistance phrased as to fight against a people and a country might appear antisocial if not nihilistic, the "We" emerging in the questions Jallal wishes to ask, does not only include the two friends preparing the bombing but those who were originally "standing," in other words, the people. The dramatic effect of these questions further leads me to consider them as a way for Taïa to cross the fictional realm in order to include the readers into the collective. His expansion toward cinema with his reference to *River of No Return* further extends the set of spectators who could participate in the uprising. Therefore, the attack organized by the protagonists seems against a national discourse provoking "Banality," "Narrow-mindedness," "Confinement," and "Submission," and those supporting it, rather than against society itself. Badiou explains that riots include people who, in a world structured by exploitation and oppression, have no voice and therefore no existence outside of the one determined by the oligarchy in power. The historical significance of a riot, in other words, its possibility of changing the world, emerges when those who had no existence begin to exist with the highest intensity: "C'est exactement ce que disaient et disent encore les gens dans les rassemblements populaires en Égypte: on n'existait pas, et maintenant on existe, on peut décider de l'histoire du pays. Ce fait subjectif est doté d'une puissance extraordinaire. L'*inexistant est relevé.* C'est pourquoi on parle de *soulèvement*: on était couché, plié, on se lève, on se relève, on se soulève" [It is exactly what people used to say and still say in the popular gatherings of Egypt: we were not existing, and now we exist, we can decide on the history of the country. This subjective fact has an extraordinary power. The non-existent has been raised up. That is why we talk about an uprising: we were lying, bended, we stand up, we arise, we rise up].[76] Jallal's desire to remind people that they were originally "standing" coincides with Badiou's "relève de l'inexistant" [arising of the non-existent] taking place during the Arab Spring. That is why under the influence of such an event, Taïa elaborates through the queer character of Jallal, a way to connect the individual struggle he recounted in his autofictions to socially exist with the others' struggle for existence.

Badiou explains that during historical riots, the various categories that used to separate people fade in front of the demand for justice: "la norme, au lieu d'être identitaire, est devenue générique: quiconque prouve, par ses actions, qu'il se soucie du genre humain, doit être traité, égalitairement, comme un des nôtres" [The norm, instead of being determined by identity, has become generic: whoever proves by their actions, that they care about mankind, must be treated, in equal way, like one of ours].[77] Andrea Khalil's *Crowds and Politics* (2014) confirms the Arab people's will to undermine the dichotomies established by the state, which serve as a shield against solidarity movements of resistance: "The crowd performed a refusal of the atomized, the so-called 'free,' modern individuals organized according to the dichotomies of the state. The collective self was replicated through contagion, which threw off the divisions of the dictatorship."[78] In his letter to Bouazizi, Taïa describes this moment of contagion at the same time sudden and inevitable: "Elle arrive par surprise. Elle arrive comme ça, d'un coup. Elle explose. Elle nous entraîne avec elle. En elle. Impossible de résister. Impossible d'ignorer ce révolutionnaire qui sommeillait en nous. En moi" [It comes as a surprise, just like that, all of a sudden. It explodes. It carries us along with it. In it. Impossible to resist, impossible to ignore the revolutionary who was sleeping inside us. Inside myself].[79] With the expression "sleeping inside," Taïa suggests that a revolutionary self already existed within the Arab people, thus connecting them beyond their individuality and illustrating Khalil's analysis of "person-as-crowd." Influenced by the post-structuralist approach of Gilles Deleuze and Félix Guattari, Khalil advances that "the individual is not the opposite of crowds, or a structural model for a crowd, but rather already exists as a crowd, in a constitutive coexistence within a crowded field."[80] Since the individuals are already together in the crowd, their joining in a collective is supposed to be a "becoming human" or a "becoming oneself." Because such a concept concerns any individual, it represents a significant threat for the authoritarian regimes, which develop their power through divisions. Aware that it is Mohamed Bouazizi's gesture that lit this collective "becoming human" in the Arab people, Taïa commits to maintaining the intensity of the revolutionary flame: "Tu n'es pas mort pour rien. Nous continuerons le combat. Nous relèverons chaque jour un peu plus la tête. Et nous t'écrirons dans nos poèmes, nos romans, nos légendes" [You did not die for nothing. We will continue the fight. We will lift our heads up a bit more every day. And we will write you in our poems, in our novels, in our legends].[81]

In "The Counter-Revolution is Just a Passing Storm Cloud" (2013), Taïa refuses to consider the electoral victory of Islamist nationalism after the Arab Spring as the end of the revolutionary movement: "I still believe in it, in this Revolution that came as such a shock, to so many people and to myself, when it occurred. I still refuse to fall into political realism that considers this political moment (in all senses of the term) to be dead to Arab lives."[82] Far from being a blinded form of optimism, resisting political realism implies permanent criticism and self-criticism in order to keep the spirit of the Arab Revolution alive through the formation of collective forces always in the becoming. In his two latest novels, *Celui qui est digne d'être aimé* [*The One Who Is Worthy of Love*] (2017) and *La vie lente* [*The Slow Life*] (2019), Taïa takes the reader back to the West by focusing on the anger of postcolonial subjects tired of being simultaneously validated as exotic objects and excluded as proper members of French society. Written in the aftermath of the terrorist attacks of January 2015 and November 2016, these texts demonstrate Taïa's will to connect with the political urgency of the time no matter on what side of the Mediterranean Sea it takes place. Unlike doctors without borders, his status of writer without borders might not provide the certainty of a cure but reveals instead "an acute awareness of the nonfixity of boundaries."[83] His words have transcended his state of solitude and become necessary gestures that challenge the traditional approach of citizenship by weaving the voices of minorities into a social fabric, and advocate, like Hardt and Negri's multitude, for a state of becoming that would accommodate subjects' singular practices of freedom with their needs for collective belonging.

NOTES

1. Abdellah Taïa, "A Boy to Be Sacrificed," *New York Times,* May 24, 2012. https://www.nytimes.com/2012/03/25/opinion/sunday/a-boy-to-be-sacrificed.html.
2. Sara Ahmed, *The Promise of Happiness* (Durham: Duke University Press, 2010), 17.
3. Abdellah Taïa, *Le rouge du tarbouche* (Paris: Seuil, 2004), 73.
4. Hamid Naficy, *Home, Exile, Homeland: Film, Media, and the Politics of Place* (New York: Routledge, 1999), 9.
5. Naficy, *Home, Exile, Homeland,* 3.
6. Ahmed, *The Promise of Happiness*, 139.
7. Frantz Fanon, *The Wretched of the Earth* (New York: Grove Press, 1963), 49.
8. Pierre Bourdieu, "The Social Space and the Genesis of Groups," *Theory and Society* 14, no. 6 (1985): 737.
9. Michael Hardt and Antonio Negri, *Multitude, War and Democracy in the Age of Empire* (New York: The Penguin Press, 2004), 204.
10. According to article 489 of the Moroccan penal code, "indecent act" or "act against nature" with someone of the same sex is a criminal offense punishable by six months to three years of imprisonment and a fine of 200 to 1000 dirhams.
11. Michel Foucault, "The Ethic of Care for the Self as a Practice of Freedom," interview by Raúl Fornet-Betancourt, Helmut Becker, Alfredo Gomez-Müller, translated by J. D. Gauthier, *Philosophy & Social Criticism* 12, no. 2–3 (1987): 113.
12. Foucault, "The Ethic of Care," 118.
13. David Halperin, *Saint Foucault: Toward a Gay Hagiography* (Oxford: Oxford University Press, 1995), 111.
14. Michel Foucault, "The Ethic of Care," 114.
15. Foucault, "The Ethic of Care," 114.

16. In France, homosexuality has been decriminalized since 1982. See Antoine Idier's *Les alinéas au placard: l'abrogation du délit d'homosexualité (1977-1982)* (Paris: Cartouche, 2013). Homosexual couples have had access to civil union (Pacte Civil de Solidarité - PACS) since 1999 and to marriage since 2013. This progress on social issues generated nonetheless significant oppositions from conservative groups, which nuances the image of France as a tolerant country toward homosexuals and LGBTQI rights. For more details on the reception of the PACS, see Éric Fassin's *L'inversion de la question homosexuelle* (Paris: Éditions Amsterdam, 2008), and on the reception of gay marriage, see Bruno Perreau's *Queer Theory: The French Response* (Palo Alto: Stanford University Press, 2016).

17. Abdellah Taïa, *L'armée du salut* (Paris: Seuil, 2006), 52; Abdellah Taïa, *Salvation Army,* trans. Frank Stock (Los Angeles: Semiotext(e), 2009), 48.

18. Daniel Maroun, "Comment échapper à la honte du *zamel.* Vers la construction de la masculinité maghrébine queer," *@nalyses* 11, no. 3 (2016): 151.

19. Taïa, *L'armée du salut*, 69; Taïa, *Salvation Army*, 36.

20. Specifically attributed to the passive partner, this word shows the importance of sexual roles in the modes of identification in Muslim cultures. The active partner is indeed usually not considered a homosexual.

21. Abdellah Taïa, *Une mélancolie arabe* (Paris: Seuil, 2008), 25.

22. Taïa, *Une mélancolie arabe*, 30; Abdellah Taïa, *An Arab Melancholia,* trans. Frank Stock (Los Angeles: Semiotext(e), 2012), 30.

23. Taïa, *Une mélancolie arabe*, 33; Taïa, *An Arab Melancholia,* 33.

24. Taïa, *Le rouge du tarbouche*, 57. All translations are my own.

25. Taïa, *L'armée du salut*, 98; Taïa, *Salvation Army*, 90.

26. Taïa, *L'armée du salut*, 152; Taïa, *Salvation Army*, 143.

27. Taïa, *Une mélancolie arabe*, 71; Taïa, *An Arab Melancholia,* 69.

28. Taïa, *Une mélancolie arabe,* 71; Taïa, *An Arab Melancholia,* 69.

29. Taïa, *Une mélancolie arabe*, 70; Taïa, *An Arab Melancholia,* 68.

30. Taïa, *Le rouge du tarbouche*, 141.

31. Taïa, *Le rouge du tarbouche*, 143.

32. Rosi Braidotti, *Nomadic Subjects: Embodiment and Sexual Difference in Contemporary Feminist Theory* (New York: Columbia University Press, 2006), 16.

33. Mehammed Amadeus Mack, *Sexagon: Muslims, France, and the Sexualization of National Culture* (New York: Fordham University Press, 2017), 134.

34. Françoise Lionnet and Shu-mei Shih, *Minor Transnationalism* (Durham: Duke University Press, 2005), 7.

35. Samir Patrice El Maarouf, *Les prémices littéraires des révolutions arabes. Yasmina Khadra, Assia Djebar, Abdellah Taïa* (Paris: L'Harmattan, 2014), 177. All translations are my own.

36. He provided such an explanation during a conversation on "Writing and Resistance Today" organized by the Center for the Humanities of the Graduate Center, CUNY, on April 9, 2018.

37. Abdellah Taïa, "L'homosexualité expliquée à ma mère," *TelQuel*, April 10, 2009; Abdellah Taïa, "Homosexuality Explained to My Mother," trans. Riccardo Moratto (Semiotext(e), 2014), 8.

38. Denis M. Provencher, *Queer Maghrebi French: Language, Temporalities, Transfiliations* (Liverpool: Liverpool University Press, 2017), 152.
39. Taïa, "L'homosexualité expliquée"; Taïa, "Homosexuality Explained," 14.
40. Provencher, *Queer Maghrebi French: Language*, 158.
41. Taïa, "L'homosexualité expliquée"; Taïa, "Homosexuality Explained," 14.
42. Taïa, "L'homosexualité expliquée"; Taïa, "Homosexuality Explained," 15.
43. Taïa, "L'homosexualité expliquée"; Taïa, "Homosexuality Explained," 14.
44. Taïa, "L'homosexualité expliquée"; Taïa, "Homosexuality Explained," 12.
45. Provencher, *Queer Maghrebi French*, 158.
46. Abdellah Taïa, *Lettres à un jeune marocain* (Paris: Seuil, 2009), 12. All translations are my own.
47. Marc Endeweld, "Abdellah Taïa, une colère marocaine," *Minorités,* 2009. All translations are my own.
48. Khalid Lyamlahy, "Une mélancolie marocaine: portrait de l'intellectuel et pouvoir de l'écriture dans *Lettres à un jeune marocain,*" *@nalyses* 11, no. 3 (2016): 84. All translations are my own.
49. Khalid Lyamlahy, "Une mélancolie marocaine," 86.
50. Khalid Lyamlahy, "Une mélancolie marocaine," 87.
51. Khalid Lyamlahy, "Une mélancolie marocaine," 86.
52. Pierre Bourdieu, "The Social Space and the Genesis of Groups," 737.
53. Fanon, *The Wretched of the Earth*, 48–49.
54. Fanon, *The Wretched of the Earth*, 50.
55. Fanon, *The Wretched of the Earth*, 48.
56. Fanon, *The Wretched of the Earth*, 47.
57. Mack, *Sexagon,* 136.
58. Denis Dailleux, *Égypte, les martyrs de la révolution* (Marseille: Le bec en l'air éditions, 2014), 11. All translations are my own.
59. Abdellah Taïa, "Lettre à Mohamed Bouazizi," *Polka Magazine*, no. 12 (2011); Abdellah Taïa, "Letter to Mohamed Bouazizi," trans. Noura Wedell (Los Angeles: Semiotext(e), 2014), 30.
60. Alain Badiou, *Le réveil de l'Histoire* (Paris: Nouvelles éditions Lignes, 2011), 27. All translations are my own.
61. Badiou, *Le réveil de l'Histoire*, 38.
62. Badiou, *Le réveil de l'Histoire*, 41.
63. Badiou, *Le réveil de l'Histoire*, 56.
64. Abdellah Taïa, *Infidèles* (Paris: Seuil, 2012), 13; Abdellah Taïa, *Infidels,* trans. Alison L. Strayer (New York: Seven Stories Press, 2016), 9.
65. Taïa, *Infidèles*, 47; Taïa, *Infidels,* 35.
66. Taïa, *Infidèles*, 111; Taïa, *Infidels,* 83.
67. Taïa, *Infidèles*, 111; Taïa, *Infidels,* 84.
68. Taïa, *Infidèles*, 83 ; Taïa, *Infidels,* 62.
69. Taïa, *Infidèles*, 83; Taïa, *Infidels,* 62.
70. Badiou, *Le réveil de l'Histoire*, 76.
71. Badiou, *Le réveil de l'Histoire*, 81.
72. Taïa, *Infidèles*, 69; Taïa, *Infidels,* 51.

73. Taïa, *Infidèles*, 69; Taïa, *Infidels,* 51.
74. Taïa, *Infidèles*, 72; Taïa, *Infidels,* 54.
75. Taïa, *Infidèles*, 158; Taïa, *Infidels,* 120–121.
76. Badiou, *Le réveil de l'Histoire*, 87.
77. Badiou, *Le réveil de l'Histoire*, 116.
78. Andrea Khalil, *Crowds and Politics in North Africa* (New York: Routledge, 2014), 27.
79. Taïa, "Lettre à Mohamed"; Taïa, "Letter to Mohamed," 30.
80. Khalil, *Crowds and Politics in North Africa*, 26.
81. Taïa, "Lettre à Mohamed"; Taïa, "Letter to Mohamed," 32.
82. Taïa, "The Counter-Revolution is Just a Passing Storm Cloud," trans. Noura Wedell (Los Angeles: Semiotext(e), 2014), 62.
83. Braidotti, *Nomadic Subjects,* 66.

BIBLIOGRAPHY

Ahmed, Sara. *The Promise of Happiness.* Durham: Duke University Press, 2010.

Badiou, Alain. *Le réveil de l'Histoire.* Paris: Nouvelles éditions Lignes, 2011.

Bourdieu, Pierre. "The Social Space and the Genesis of Groups." Translated by Richard Nice. *Theory and Society* 14, no. 6 (1985): 723–744.

Braidotti, Rosi. *Nomadic Subjects: Embodiment and Sexual Difference in Contemporary Feminist Theory.* New York: Columbia University Press, 2006.

Dailleux, Denis. *Égypte, les martyrs de la révolution.* Marseille: Le bec en l'air éditions, 2014.

Deleuze, Gilles, and Félix Guattari. *Mille Plateaux.* Paris: Les Éditions de Minuit, 1980.

El Maarouf, Samir Patrice. *Les prémices littéraires des révolutions arabes. Yasmina Khadra, Assia Djebar, Abdellah Taïa.* Paris: L'Harmattan, 2014.

Endeweld, Marc. "Abdellah Taïa, une colère marocaine." *Minorités,* no. 11 (2009).

Fanon, Frantz. *The Wretched of the Earth.* Translated by Richard Philcox. New York: Grove Press, 1963.

Fassin, Éric. *L'inversion de la question homosexuelle.* Paris: Éditions Amsterdam, 2008.

Foucault, Michel. "The Ethic of Care for the Self as a Practice of Freedom." Interview by Fornet-Betancourt Raúl, Becker Helmut, Gomez-Müller Alfredo. Translated by J.D. Gauthier. *Philosophy & Social Criticism* 12, no. 2–3 (1987): 112–131.

Halperin M., David. *Saint Foucault: Toward a Gay Hagiography.* Oxford: Oxford University Press, 1995.

Hardt Michael, and Antonio Negri. *Multitude, War and Democracy in the Age of Empire.* New York: The Penguin Press, 2004.

Idier, Antoine. *Les alinéas au placard: l'abrogation du délit d'homosexualité (1977-1982).* Paris: Cartouche, 2013.

Khalil, Andrea. *Crowds and Politics in North Africa.* New York: Routledge, 2014.

Lionnet, Françoise, and Shu-mei Shih. *Minor Transnationalism.* Durham: Duke University Press, 2005.

Lyamlahy, Khalid. "Une mélancolie marocaine: portrait de l'intellectuel et pouvoir de l'écriture dans *Lettres à un jeune marocain.*" *@nalyses* 11, no. 3 (2016): 80–104.

Mack, Mehammed Amadeus. *Sexagon: Muslims, France, and the Sexualization of National Culture.* New York: Fordham University Press, 2017.

Maroun Daniel. "Comment échapper à la honte du *zamel.* Vers la construction de la masculinité maghrébine queer." *@nalyses* 11, no. 3 (2016): 135–154.

Naficy, Hamid. *Home, Exile, Homeland: Film, Media, and the Politics of Space.* New York: Routledge, 1999.

Perreau, Bruno. *Queer Theory: The French Response.* Palo Alto: Stanford University Press, 2016.

Provencher, Denis M. *Queer Maghrebi French: Language, Temporalities, Transfiliations.* Liverpool: Liverpool University Press, 2017.

Sbaï, Jalila. "Réformes politiques et enjeux sociaux au Maroc: quand le migrant se fait expert et s'invite au débat." *Hicham Halaoui Foundation* (2012): 1–11. http://www.hichamalaouifoundation.org/wp-content/uploads/2017/08/R%C3%A9formes-politiques-et-enjeux-sociaux-au-Maroc.pdf.

Taïa, Abdellah. "A Boy to Be Sacrificed." *New York Times,* May 24, 2012. https://www.nytimes.com/2012/03/25/opinion/sunday/a-boy-to-be-sacrificed.html.

———. *L'armée du salut.* Paris: Éditions du Seuil, 2006.

———. *Salvation Army.* Translated by Frank Stock. Los Angeles: Semiotext(e), 2009.

———. *Celui qui est digne d'être aimé.* Paris: Édition du Seuil, 2017.

———. "L'homosexualité expliquée à ma mère." *TelQuel,* April 10, 2009.

———. "Homosexuality Explained to My Mother." In *Arabs are No Longer Afraid - Texts on a Revolution Underway,* translated by Riccardo Moratto, 7–15. Los Angeles: Semiotext(e), 2014.

———. *Infidèles.* Paris: Éditions du Seuil, 2012.

———. *Infidels.* Translated by Alison L. Strayer. New York: Seven Stories Press, 2016.

———. *Lettres à un jeune marocain.* Paris: Éditions du Seuil, 2009.

———. "Lettre à Mohamed Bouazizi." *Polka Magazine,* no. 12 (2011).

———. "Letter to Mohamed Bouazizi." In *Arabs are No Longer Afraid - Texts on a Revolution Underway,* translated by Noura Wedell, 24–32. Los Angeles: Semiotext(e), 2014.

———. *Une mélancolie arabe.* Paris: Éditions du Seuil, 2008.

———. *An Arab Melancholia.* Translated by Frank Stock. Los Angeles: Semiotext(e), 2012.

———. *Le rouge du tarbouche.* Paris: Éditions du Seuil, 2004.

———. *La vie lente.* Paris: Éditions du Seuil, 2019.

Chapter 8

From the "Garçon du bled" to "Tintin's Dog"

The Interplay between Race and Sex in Abdellah Taïa's Un pays pour mourir *and* Celui qui est digne d'être aimé

Philippe Panizzon

In his more recent work, especially in *Un pays pour mourir* [*A Country for Dying*] (2015) and *Celui qui est digne d'être aimé* [*The One Worthy of Love*] (my translation of the title) (2017), Abdellah Taïa critically examines the place of the ethnic homosexual Other within the primarily white French gay community and the French Republic. Asked to speak about his relationship to gay identity, in a recent interview Taïa stated:

> Je suis homosexuel. Mais je suis un homosexuel qui n'exclut pas les autres. Je ne veux pas être gay, faire partie de la communauté gay [. . .] La réalité [de l'identité gay] est étroite. Peut-être le vœu, le désir du départ ne l'est pas, mais la réalité est étroite. Tout groupement est dans la limitation et dans la reproduction de ce qui l'a fait souffrir au départ. Il suffit d'aller voir sur une application gay.
>
> [I am homosexual. But I am a homosexual who does not exclude others. I don't want to be gay, be part of the gay community. The reality of the gay identity is too narrow. Perhaps this isn't what gay people want, but its reality is narrow. Each group limits itself and reproduces the mechanisms from which it has suffered at the beginning. Just open a gay app.][1]

Taïa reveals here the mechanism of exclusion and ostracization to which homosexuals who do not identify with the rather contingent western gay identity are exposed. His words address a thematic that will be central to this chapter, namely the fraught relationship between the homosexual ethnic Other and primarily white French gay men in France today.

Cultural Studies scholars and sociologists have recently revealed the tensions between homosexuals with an Arab/Muslim cultural background and white gay French men due to a relatively new creed, which has seen white gay men assimilating Republican values. In his work on sexual democracy, Eric Fassin shows, for example, how according to the French Republican model today, in which the law on same-sex marriage and the equality of homosexuals with their heterosexual counterparts were finally codified, the ethnic Other is often earmarked as patriarchal or homophobic.[2] In the article "Homosexuels des villes, homophobes des banlieues" (2010), Fassin discusses, for example, the debates in the French media in 2009 triggered by two books, namely Franck Chaumont's *Homo-ghetto: gays et lesbiennes dans les cités: les clandestins de la République* (2009) and Brahim Naït-Balk's *Un homo dans la cité: La descente aux enfers puis la libération d'un homosexuel de culture maghrébine* (2009), both depicting exposure to homophobia while growing up as homosexual in the Parisian outskirts.[3] While French journalists utilized the authors' denunciation of homophobia and the importance of hypervirility in the French banlieue in order to mark a clear line between the enlightened, progressive French citizen in the city center and the "banlieusards" of different ethnic origin, mainly Arabs and Blacks, their branding of Muslims/Arabs as homophobic was enhanced the same year by the football club Créteil Bébel's refusal to compete against the club Paris Foot Gay.[4] As Fassin observes, as a consequence of Créteil Bébel's refusal there was a tendency in the media to criticize Muslims/Arabs as backward and patriarchal. The French media accused their values to be opposed to France's stated creed of equality between the sexes and sexualities.[5] In a later article, "Same-sex marriage, nation, and race: French political logics and rhetorics," Fassin observes that during the debates on same-sex marriage in France in 2014, LGBTIQ rights were characterized through the lens of white French citizenship. Non-white people, according to certain media, supposedly joined the right-wing party in their opposition to same-sex marriage.[6]

In a similar vein, in *Queer Maghrebi French: Language, Temporalities, Transfiliations* (2017), Denis M. Provencher recognizes that Franck Chaumont's *Homo-ghetto* and Brahim Naït-Balk's *Un homo dans la cité* play into the common French narrative of the liberation of the protagonist from traditional, immigrant Muslim families and their discovery of a city and a society that is associated with modernity, secularism, and progress.[7] For Provencher, this narrative is that of the "good sexual citizen," namely that concerning the citizen who left "conservative Islam" and his Muslim family behind in order to adopt a visible gay identity, a consumerist lifestyle, and neoliberal values associated with wealth and affluence.[8] The good homosexual citizen adapts to French Republican values and builds this homonormative community, distinguishing him or herself from those with different ethnic backgrounds and subversive lifestyles.

These anxieties around integration into the French Republic that occur at the expense of the ethnic Other are also discussed in *Homo exoticus, race, classe et critique queer* (2010) by Maxime Cervulle and Nick Rees-Roberts. Both cultural historians recognize in France's contemporary gay culture a tendency to exoticize Arab/Muslim men along with their sensuality in order to respect the gay culture's own respectability. Studying gay film production and pornography, these scholars observe how the gay erotic imaginary connotes stereotypes informed by past white supremacist colonial discourses, such as unbridled sexuality, aggression, "the uncivilized," and so on.[9] If they rightly observe that this erotic imaginary informed by colonial discourse far from pertains only to the gay community, perhaps it reveals a specific tendency within the French gay community to distinguish themselves as respectable citizens of the French Republic from the ethnic Other with its different sexual and bodily practices. Cervulle and Rees-Roberts observe: "L'exotisme gay et ses avatars nous renseignent ainsi sur la définition en creux d'une politique de l'identité gay en quête de respectabilité, fermement ancrée dans la classe moyenne blanche [Gay exoticism and its various expressions tell us indirectly about gay politics which is in search of respectability, firmly anchored in the white middle class]."[10] The eroticization and sexualization of the Other is purposefully deployed in order to stress the French gay male's own respectability and modernity. Cervulle and Rees-Roberts astutely show how gay cultural production, be it film or pornography, coat what would normally be colonial discourses in politically correct terms in order to conceal the resonance of French colonial history and imperialist ideologies. If the porn industry sells "ethnic" porn, racial stereotyping as epitomized in "Y'a bon banania" —a slogan used by a French cocoa brand *Banania* in 1914 depicting a smiling *tirailleur sénégalais* who was supposed to pronounce this incorrect French sentence and which has for decades, until banned in 2015, exemplified France's racialization of the inhabitants of its former colonies[11]— is nevertheless barely hidden. The display, in contrast to white actors, of sexual attributes and the emphasis on the nudity of Arab/Muslim actors recalls photographs of nude Algerian and Moroccan men and women on postcards that circulated in France and North Africa during colonial times.[12]

This chapter examines the interplay of racialization and sexualization of the ethnic Other in *Un pays pour mourir* before turning to the more recent work *Celui qui est digne d'être aimé*. Taïa's *Un pays pour mourir* and *Celui qui est digne d'être aimé* depict white French gay anxieties regarding the ethnic Other evinced, for example, in casting the Arab/Muslim man into the role of the libidinous, oversexualized Other or by denying his cultural background. Both novels expose these mechanisms of exclusion to which North African homosexuals and North Africans generally are exposed in the French Republic with its ongoing political tensions around sexual and ethnic minorities.

Denis M. Provencher, in his *Queer Maghrebi French* and Jean-Pierre Boulé in his recent *Abdellah Taïa, La Mélancolie et le cri* (2020), point out that Taïa regularly associates the literary with the political in his writings and public activities.[13] It is this "'local' political and poetic voice," as Provencher calls it, which interests me, this voice which, through the literary medium of *Un pays pour mourir* and *Celui qui est digne d'être aimé,* indicts the racialization and sexualization North Africans are subjected to in the French gay community and in France generally.[14] I am interested how Taïa, through complex narrative structures, particularly by juxtaposing stories and voices, all interrelated, reveals the complex temporalities and position of the ethnic and sexual Other in the French Republic today.

Un pays pour mourir and *Celui qui est digne d'être aimé* also show how Taïa re-appropriates French literary heritage in order to denounce French racialization and ethnicization. By adopting and subverting narrative forms and symbols referring to the French cultural legacy, Taïa succeeds in subtly denouncing France's neo-imperialist and neo-colonialist attitudes toward the ethnic Other. As Joanne Brueton demonstrates in her analysis of Taïa's preface to the Tangiers journal *Nejma* special issue *Jean Genet, un Saint Marocain* (2010), Taïa recalls Genet's narrative: "and in the rewriting, ascribes a French literary heritage to his own Moroccan culture" (2020).[15] Deploying narrative forms, symbols and figures from a French cultural legacy in *Un pays pour mourir* and in *Celui qui est digne d'être aimé,* the current chapter illustrates that Taïa not only ascribes a French literary heritage to his own culture but, by means of this heritage, also sheds light on the injustice and specific societal and political issues that North Africans have to contend with in France today.

Finally, the protagonists in both novels reveal new forms of queer sexuality, which are at tension with gay sexuality. In his book *Sexagon: Muslims, France and the Sexualization of National Culture* (2017), Mehammed Mack analyses sexual sub-cultures in the French banlieue and describes how France's Arab/Muslim and banlieue sexual subcultures exist in opposition to homosexual emancipation and values such as visibility and alignment with the French Republic.[16] These sexualities queer dominant gay culture in that they remain in what Mack calls the: "unregulated space of sexual diversity."[17] Consonant with Mack, I argue that Taïa's protagonists, especially in *Un pays pour mourir*, queer homonormativity and gay white sexuality and reveal a more diverse, "unregulated" sexuality. Hereafter, when using the term "gay" or "good" homosexual citizen, I refer to the homosexual citizen who has assimilated neoliberal, consumerist values and whose life-style is associated with modernity, integration, and progress. As opposed to the term "queer" where that individual betrays a more invisible, unregulated sexual space.

UN PAYS POUR MOURIR

In *Un pays pour mourir*, Taïa has created a polyphonic novel in which he gives voice to the social outcasts and migrants who lived at the time of the demise of the French empire and in Paris today. The term *pays* in the title alludes perhaps to France and more precisely to its capital, to this ambiguous place where subjects from France's former empire come to live united in solidarity and die. *Pays*, however, also refers to a fantasized space without geographical and national borders in which the novel's protagonists are no longer subjected to ostracization, rejection, and racial stereotyping. The novel is divided into three parts, each composed of first-person narratives that take the reader to different spatio-temporal contexts throughout the twentieth century. In the first two parts, entitled "Paris, juin 2010" [Paris, June 2010] and "Paris, août 2010" [Paris, August 2010], we follow three characters through their downtrodden daily lives in Paris: Aziz, an Algerian hustler who is about to embark on a sex change; Zahira, a Moroccan prostitute who works in Paris; and Motjaba, a young homosexual political activist who has fled Iran. In "Indochine, Saigon, juin 1954" [Indochina, Saigon, June 1954], the third and last part of the novel, we are taken back to the colonial era and witness the life of Zineb, a Moroccan prostitute and Zahira's aunt, who works in seedy brothels for the French army. Within this web of first-person narratives, while subtly juxtaposing and linking the characters' queer migratory lives today with those of their parents and life under colonial rule, the reader comes to realize that, despite France's politics of color-blindness, not much has changed since colonization for North African subjects. Under the cover of a liberal economy and free-trade agreements between Europe and Morocco, North African subjects are still exploited by France, and are still the victims of insidious forms of racism and white supremacy.

However, in the figure of Aziz, Taïa also reveals different and new forms of queer sexuality that exist in the French Republic today alongside the homonormative gay model. Aziz's gender fluidity and Arab/Muslim cultural background gestures towards a queer migrant identity that stands in contrast to the homonormative model often embodied by French gay men. Furthermore, by identifying to a certain extent with the historical French icon Jeanne d'Arc, Aziz re-appropriates French cultural heritage and iconic figures to make a point about contemporary French sexual politics. Just as Jeanne d'Arc—an outcast—denounced a patriarchal society, Aziz fights against homonormativity and, concomitantly, the racialization and sexualization of the Other.

The juxtaposition of past colonial violence with present forms of violence is revealed in Zahira's and Aziz's life narratives. By working as a prostitute and providing sexual services mainly to illegal immigrants or construction workers from North Africa and the Middle East, Zahira barely makes a living in Paris. Zahira ponders: "C'est devenu ma spécialité. Les hommes arabes ou musulmans de Paris. La plupart sans papiers. La plupart usés par cette ville qui les maltraite sans remords et par des patrons français blancs qui les exploitent au noir sans éprouver aucune culpabilité" [They've become my specialty, Arabs or Muslim men in Paris. Most of them undocumented. Most of them worn out by that city which mistreats them without guilt and abused by white French patrons who exploit them on the black market without remorse].[18] Zahira is part of a system that exploits cheap labor: in the same way as illegal workers offer their services on construction sites or on farms, she sells her body to the lowest in the French Republican hierarchy. She provides men some sort of satisfaction, however fleeting, thus keeping this exploitative system going. Frequenting the poorest in society, she can herself barely make a living and hopes to marry Iqbal, a man of Sri Lankan origin. She reflects: "Sinon, à quoi bon trimer du matin jusque tard dans la nuit, accueillir entre mes jambes tous les émigrés troisième classe de Paris" [Otherwise, why toil day and night, opening my legs to all third-class immigrants from Paris]?[19] The money and the benefits of these toiling bodies, however, belong to the owners and bosses, the "patrons blancs."[20]

That Zahira's exploitation resonates strikingly with that of colonial subjects during France's colonial past is revealed through the juxtaposition of her life narrative and that of her father and that of his sister Zineb, her aunt. We read that her father fought for the French army during the war in Indochina and when the war ended he never received his indemnities ("La France m'a jeté elle aussi [. . .]. Elle m'a renvoyé au Maroc et elle m'a oublié" [France dumped me [. . .]. She sent me back to Morocco and forgot me]).[21] In the final part of the novel the secret veil around Zahira's aunt, Zineb, is finally lifted. In "Indochine, Saigon, juin 1954" we learn that her virginity was taken from her by the French police in Marrakesh, and that she was then passed on from one Frenchman to another until she ended up in the brothels of the French army.[22] From then on, she drifted from place to place, following the French army, in order to provide the soldiers of the newly founded Republic with sexual services. By interweaving the lives of Zahira, her father, and Zineb, Taïa shows how Zahira's life perpetuates Zineb's experience. Just as her aunt was ostracized during the colonial era, Zahira also belongs to the marginals of the French Republic.

Zahira's activity as a prostitute in France has wide-reaching consequences for her community in Morocco and is illustrated in the figure of Allal, her suitor. When he hears that Zahira works on a land bought by Zahira's "dirty" money and that he is paid with the same money, he comes to France in order to kill her and redeem his honor. He feels degraded by being dependent upon a countrywoman who "belongs" to the French and earns her money by offering her sexual services in France. Allal's feelings of degradation and hurt pride echo anthropologist Jean-Jacques Courtine's observation about North African men being humiliated by the French who built brothels in North Africa in which Muslim girls would work.[23] Melding Zineb's with Zahira's and her father's lives, Taïa reveals that sexual and bodily exploitation of North Africans in France today distressingly recalls colonial exploitation.

If Zahira is exploited in France in the sense that she services illegal migrants and construction workers, Aziz in a similar vein is utilized by the French white gay community. For French gay men, he embodies an exoticized object onto which they can channel their desire for unbridled sex while living in all appearances a respectable life. The racialized and sexualized role of the exotic Other Aziz embodies in French gay society is especially striking in episodes featuring the gay couple Jean-Jacques and Pierre, two Parisian intellectuals from the Vosges, who teach at the Ecole Normale Supérieure. During one of Aziz' meetings with Zahira, Aziz, almost in a comic vein, tells his friend Zahira about how he entertains Jean-Jacques and Pierre. Apart from invigorating their sexual life by sharing the couple's bed and providing them with sexual services ("Il n'y a que comme ça qu'ils jouissent" [That's the only way they come]),[24] he cooks Maghrebi food for them ("Je leur ai cuisiné des tas de couscous et de tagines" [I cooked a lot of couscous and tagines for them]),[25] and takes them to the *hammam* where he gives them massages, embodying these orientalist-erotic fantasies on which the European imaginary has been fed for centuries. The young prostitute concludes that it is only thanks to him that the two men are still together ("Tu le sais, ce vieux couple français trop parisien, qui a totalement oublié le coin perdu dans les Vosges d'où il vient, ne tient plus que grâce à moi" [You know it. This old French couple too Parisian throughout, which has totally forgotten their place of origin in the Vosges where they are from, they are only together thanks to my efforts].).[26] Thanks to Aziz's queer, nonconforming sexuality, the old couple still stays together. In his role of the queer outsider providing sexual services, Aziz recalls Slima and her mother in *Infidèles* who in a similar vein "spice up" heterosexual couples' sexual lives.

As the queer sexual outsider within the French gay community, Aziz also features in another episode in the novel. He recalls, while talking to Zahira, how, on his arrival in France from Algeria, he would prostitute himself at the Porte Dauphine in Paris for French clients: "Je venais d'arriver à Paris. Je me prostituais habillé en garçon arabe un peu sauvage de là-bas, d'Algérie. C'est ce qu'ils aimaient, les clients, que je sente le bled, la sauvagerie du bled, comme ils aimaient dire" [I've just arrived in Paris. I sold myself clad as an Arab boy, a bit wild, from down there, from Algeria. That's what they fancied, the clients, that I smelt of the village, the "wildness of the village," as they liked to say].[27] Aware that his attractiveness lies, first and foremost, in orientalist clichés such as wildness, which in turn betrays his, to the European mind, untrammeled sexuality, he performs the undomesticated boy from Algeria. As he emphasizes, the term *bled,* stemming from the Arabic word *blad*, or country, and meaning in French "village in the countryside," evokes for his French client wildness and exoticism. In the French imaginary he is, together with the *bled*, linked to the remote, uncivilized countryside of Algeria.

At the same time, however, while serving clients, Aziz craves lipstick and wishes to change sex. During these moments at the Porte Dauphine, he remembers his childhood during which he performed, dragged in women's clothes, ceremonial dances with his sisters. Aziz's gender identity here is mobile and fluid, starkly opposing that of the cis-sexual French gay men who are his clients. In contrast to these men, Aziz embodies a queer migrant identity that does not ossify into rigid categories. By oscillating between the masculine and the feminine gender ("Je danse. En fille. Je danse. En garçon" [I dance. As a girl. I dance. As a boy])[28] and later, after his operation, between the male and female sex, he queers hetero- and homonormativity and introduces new ways of desiring and living one's sexuality. As a queer migrant from Algeria, he deviates from the normative French understanding of sexuality and introduces new, marginalized possibilities of living out one's sexuality in the French Republic.

Jean-Jacques and Pierre, and others ("Certains d'entre eux ont des maisons à la campagne ou au bord de la mer" [Some of them own houses in the countryside or on the seacoast])[29] then need the young Algerian prostitute to fulfill their erotic fantasy and to live out a licentious sexuality which is no longer possible if they want to live according to the homonormative model and belong to the French Republic. In their race for assimilation, to be a good homosexual citizen firmly anchored in the French Republic, Jean-Jacques, Pierre and other French gay men need the racialized, orientalized Other who offers them the possibility of outwardly being a couple despite the fact that their attraction for each other has seemingly vanished and that they can no longer enjoy a vibrant sexual relationship ("Tous les fantasmes qu'ils avaient dans leurs pauvres têtes de clients coincés, je les ai réalisés" [I realized all the phantasms these arrogant customers had in their poor heads]).[30] In public, they can be a homonormative couple, but behind closed doors we learn that their relationship can only be sustained due to Aziz's services. While these men pride themselves on France's progressiveness, on the importance of human rights, on the freedom they enjoy as citizens of the French Republic, they need Aziz at night for their fantasies to be fulfilled.

At the same time, Aziz is aware that he has no place and will never have a place as a citizen of the French Republic. Enumerating all the clients who enjoy his services, he states at the end:

> Ça leur sert à quoi toutes ces lois si elles ne les empêchent pas de reproduire le même monde, beau de l'extérieur et, au fond, tellement coincé. À la limite je veux bien croire que leur Jeanne d'Arc s'est réellement battue pour la liberté et que leurs ancêtres ont inventé les droits de l'homme. En 1789. Mais, au bout du compte, qu'est-ce qu'on trouve ici, à Paris, au cœur du cœur de la France? De la bourgeoisie bien étriquée, trop fière de sa culture et toujours bien contente d'elle-même.
>
> [What's the point of all the laws if they do not prevent them from reproducing the same world, beautiful from the outside but in the end so arrogant? Of course, I want to believe that Joan of Arc really fought for freedom and that their ancestors invented human rights. In 1789. But in the end, what do you find here in Paris, at the very heart of France? The smug bourgeoisie, too proud of its culture and always satisfied with itself.][31]

Frequenting the intellectual circles and well-established citizens of Paris, Aziz denounces their hypocrisy when they pride themselves on the belief in human rights and inclusiveness invented in France. Despite the existence of the French law according to which every French citizen is equal, be they from a different ethnic background, belonging to a sexual minority, and so on, the ethnic Other faces insurmountable hurdles if he wants to access French society at the heart of Paris. Alongside these official laws, there are these hidden lingering colonial and imperialistic attitudes in French society which racialize and ostracize the Other without openly admitting it.

It is not by chance that Aziz mentions Jeanne d'Arc here. Evolving in a patriarchal, military society, during her lifetime Jeanne was marginalized. Strategic decisions concerning the military and warfare were taken without her. However, by fighting and at times leading French soldiers, she betrayed gender norms, which required women not to interfere in the public military sphere. This mobile and unstable gender identity is also reified in the only existing painting of Jeanne d'Arc at the time. With her long flowing hair, sporting women's clothes yet carrying a sword, the painting's rendition of Jeanne emphasizes her unstable gender identity.[32] Aziz, it seems, is interested in this figure who liberated the French yet at the same time remained marginalized by patriarchy. Jeanne d'Arc bears some similarity to Aziz himself.

In his unstable gender performativity, oscillating between the feminine and the masculine, queering French homonormativity, Aziz's behaviour in *Un pays pour mourir* resonates with that of Jeanne. Like Jeanne d'Arc, Aziz is marginalized yet fights against powerful structures, here homonormativity, in the name of inclusion and fluidity.

In *Un pays pour mourir*, Abdellah Taïa creates a web of interrelated voices and lives that reveal past and present sexual exploitation of the ethnically different in France. Within this polyphony and through the figure of Aziz, Taïa illustrates how queer migrant sexuality disturbs the gender conformity and homonormativity of the French Republic. Finally, through the parallels drawn between Jeanne d'Arc and Aziz, I have illustrated how Aziz uses a French cultural symbol to proffer toward greater inclusivity and a different image of Frenchness, one in which unstable gender figures and the ethnically different become integrated. Taïa re-appropriates the ubiquitous and loaded cultural symbol of Jeanne, which has been used by Marine Le Pen's nativist National Party, in order to invent into it with a new queer potential. If Jeanne d'Arc, who was burnt alive by the English, symbolizes for Le Pen intrinsic Frenchness threatened by a larger, multicultural French Republic, Jeanne is used by Taïa and Aziz in the opposite sense, in that she symbolized integration, gender fluidity, and multiculturalism. These are values that oppose the homonormative and intrinsically "French" views of the mainstream. Through a French cultural symbol, then, Taïa denounces racism and at the same time points toward new ways of being "French" and being a citizen of France.

CELUI QUI EST DIGNE D'ÊTRE AIMÉ

If *Un pays pour mourir* illustrates the racial and sexual stereotyping to which North Africans in France were exposed during colonial times and still today, the epistolary novel *Celui qui est digne d'être aimé* centers around processes of cultural effacement that North Africans undergo if they wish to patronize French bourgeois society today. The novel is, first and foremost, an account of the life of Ahmed, a forty-year old queer Moroccan who lives in Paris. The novel is composed of four letters, "Août, 2015" [August, 2015], "Juillet, 2010" [July 2010], "Juillet, 2005" [July, 2005], and "Mai, 1990" [May, 1990]. In "Août, 2015," Ahmed comes out to his mother as a homosexual and also analyzes the relationship he had with her. The second letter, "Juillet, 2010," is Vincent's letter to Ahmed in which we learn about Vincent's unrequited love for him. Vincent had a brief love affair with Ahmed; however, Ahmed has not pursued this affair further and left Vincent without any news. In the third letter, "Juillet, 2005," we learn in Ahmed's farewell letter to Emmanuel that Ahmed left Morocco as an adolescent in order to follow

Emmanuel, a French intellectual and scholar with whom he was passionately in love at the time of their encounter, to Paris. At the time Ahmed wrote the letter, Ahmed had decided to leave Emmanuel who has begun dating a younger Moroccan boy. The last letter, "Mai, 1990," a coda and echo of the preceding letter, is written by Lahbib, Ahmed's childhood friend, in which Lahbib recounts his frustrated love affair with a French diplomat in Rabat. Here I am mainly interested in Ahmed's letter to Emmanuel in that it reflects the tension around homonormativity, or in other words, progressive sexuality, and non-western sexualities, thus it introduces a further aspect to my discussion of the place of the ethnic Other in Taïa's work in France's Fifth Republic.

In Ahmed's letter to Emmanuel we learn that their encounter on a beach in Salé was importantly sexual, and later developed into love. Back in Morocco, Emmanuel was keen to hear about Ahmed's budding sexuality, which he explored with his friend Lahbib. Once in Paris, when Ahmed attempts to talk to Emmanuel about his sexual experiences with his best friend Lahbib while roaming the streets and the beaches, Emmanuel loses interest: "Là-bas, tu voulais tout entendre de mes aventures enfantines, sexuelles, avec lui. Ici, à Paris, Lahbib a fini par ne plus représenter qu'un passé que tu m'incitais non pas à oublier mais à ne plus toujours prendre en considération. 'Encore tes histoires de pauvres! Tu devrais te concentrer sur autre chose. . .Tu es à Paris. . .Tu es arrivé. . .'" [There, you wanted to hear everything about my childish, sexual adventures with him. Here in Paris, Lahbib ended up representing only a past that you did not make me forget but rather not take into account. "Again, your stories of the poor! You should focus on something else . . . You are in Paris . . . You've made it . . ."].[33] In Emmanuel's eyes, uninhibited sexuality is linked to poverty and underdevelopment, in contrast to the civilized life they lead in Paris. Whereas Emmanuel was seemingly interested in Ahmed's stories about his first sexual experiences with Lahbib in Morocco, in that they belonged to orientalist stereotypes of adolescents having sex, he has lost interest in this in Paris. Ahmed's "childish" stories belong to a folkloric past seemingly out of place here ("Et plus jamais ce passé, désormais folklorique à tes yeux, n'est revenu entre nous" [And this past, now folklore in your eyes, has no longer interfered in our relationship].).[34]

Making it as a Moroccan boy in Paris means entering into the civilization and citizenship of the French Republic as exemplified by the good white homosexual, embodied by Jean-Jacques and Pierre in *Un pays pour mourir*, and leaving the queer past behind. Emmanuel's attitude toward Ahmed thus betrays his imperialist attitude toward the ethnic Other and resonates with the British art historian and black studies scholar Kobena Mercer's observation that:

> Imperialism justified itself by claiming that it had a civilizing mission—to lead the base and ignoble savages and "inferior races" into culture and godliness. The person of the savage was developed as the Other of civilization and one of the first "proofs" of this otherness was the nakedness of the savage, the visibility of sex. This led Europeans to assume that the savage possessed an open, frank, uninhibited "sexuality"—unlike the sexuality of the European which was considered to be fettered by the weight of civilization.[35]

The attitudes of Emmanuel, Jean-Jacques, and Pierre betray the new imperialism inherent in homonormativity and good homosexual citizenship. For the latter to exist, it needs to oppose their own seemingly "civilized" sexuality (in other words, "sexual democracy," with its concomitant gay rights, gender equality, same-sex marriage, and so on) to non-European sexuality, according to the European view of "uncivilized" sexuality. In Emmanuel's view, France and Paris, the place of progressive sexual politics, save Ahmed from homophobia and "backward" sexuality and give him the opportunity to live out his sexuality as a good homosexual citizen in the French Republic. Like Jean-Jacques and Pierre in *Un pays pour mourir*, Emmanuel seemingly has adapted to a homonormative lifestyle. Emmanuel is interested in the "uncivilized" side of Ahmed's sexuality only to the extent that it spiced up his own sexual life long ago during a sexual escapade in Morocco.

France's new imperialism inherent in its sexual politics, defended by Emmanuel and his family, is vividly described by Ahmed elsewhere. He becomes aware of Emmanuel's and his family's attitude towards the ethnic Other, their wish to erase every trace of a different ethnic background, when he meets Emmanuel's sister and her Tunisian husband Jamal. Ahmed is shocked when he learns that Emmanuel's sister and Jamal have named their two daughters Jeanne and Marguerite, two names that remind him of Jeanne Moreau and Marguerite Duras, and at the same time efface every trace of their father's Tunisian culture.[36] Unlike Aziz in *Un pays pour mourir* who re-appropriates French cultural symbols such as Jeanne d'Arc, Emmanuel's sister and her Tunisian husband Jamal mimic blindly French culture in order to erase Arab/Muslim culture. For Ahmed, this process is "une nouvelle étape dans l'effacement programmé" [a new step in the programmed erasure][37] and he remarks: "Non seulement il faut s'intégrer de force dans la société française, mais si, en plus, on réussissait à faire oublier notre peau, notre origine, ça serait parfait" [Not only do we have to integrate ourselves by force into French society, but if, in addition, we succeed in making people forget our skin and origins, that would be perfect].[38] Integration into Emmanuel's family and into French society in general happens only at the cost of giving up one's own ethnic difference.

This cultural compromise—linked to France's sexual politics—is also clearly alluded to at the moment when Ahmed attempts to establish a connection with Jamal so as to talk about their common past and Arab culture. However, Ahmed becomes aware that Jamal has completely denied his past and has become assimilated to France. Furthermore, Jamal remarks to Ahmed: "Heureusement que tu as rencontré Emmanuel. Il t'a sauvé, c'est sûr . . . Les homos, là-bas, on les . . . tu sais . . . On les tue . . .." [Luckily, you met Emmanuel. He saved you, that's for sure . . . homosexuals over there . . . you know . . . are being killed . . .],[39] whereupon Ahmed reflects: "Là-bas . . . Des gens de là-bas . . . Des sauvages, voilà ce que nous sommes, Jamal et moi. Sauvés par toi et ta famille. Je devrais être reconnaissant. Je devrais être gentil. Bien élevé" [Over there . . . People from over there . . . Savages, that's what we are, Jamal and me. Saved by you and your family. I should be grateful. I should be nice. Well-mannered . . .].[40] Jamal is a Tunisian himself and he has paradoxically turned into the mouthpiece of French sexual politics. France opens itself up to the sexually different and to sexual minorities, integrates them, and allows them to live out their sexuality at the costs of branding, as Fassin shows, the culture of the ethnic Other as patriarchal or homophobic. In other words, being a homosexual and at the same time standing up for one's North African identity is impossible in the eyes of Emmanuel's family. In order to belong to Emmanuel's family and to the French Republic in general, Ahmed has to deny his Arab past or at least dismiss it as barbaric and Other.

As Ahmed writes in his letter to Emmanuel, he was, at the time of their relationship, not aware of the systematic effacement of his Moroccan cultural background. Thus at the beginning, when Ahmed's name caused awkwardness among Emmanuel's Parisian friends and family, both Emmanuel and Ahmed decided to change Ahmed into "Hamidou." However, "Hamidou" still bore too much resemblance to Arab culture, and so they decided to name him "Midou," which was reminiscent, as both realized, to Tintin's dog "Milou." At the time, Ahmed used to laugh about this comparison; now, however, he has realized that he has turned into a docile, faithful servant over whom Emmanuel could have complete mastery and whom Emmanuel could mould according to his wishes. Not only was his new name an allusion to Belgian culture—another former colonizing nation, but also to the notion of a servile dog. Thus Emmanuel draws on a Belgian cultural heritage, which is itself problematic. *The Adventures of Tintin*, the famous comic strip by the Belgian cartoonist Hergé (Georges Remi), is not uncontested in the sense that, for example, *Tintin au Congo*, one of the installments in the series, reveals in its depiction of indigenous people all the racist and colonial stereotypes Europeans entertained at the time toward Africans. This imperialist view of non-Europeans is perpetuated a hundred years later, in Emmanuel and Ahmed's relationship.

In his letter to Emmanuel, Ahmed blames his French lover not only for the systematic effacement of his background but, concomitantly, for his personality and human qualities. According to Ahmed, Emmanuel had no interest in Ahmed, the Moroccan boy, but rather in a young, handsome, cultivated Arab man he could display to his friends and family. Ahmed becomes aware of his interchangeability, his objectification, when he realizes that Emmanuel is already courting another, younger Arab boy who, like himself at the time, is about to begin his studies at the university. Ahmed writes: "Je ne suis qu'un objet qui pourrait être remplacé facilement par un autre. Un jeune Arabe très cultivé grâce à toi qui pourrait du jour au lendemain être jeté et échangé contre un autre jeune Arabe" [I am just an object that could easily be replaced by another. Thanks to you I am a young and very cultured Arab who could overnight be dumped and traded for another young Arab].[41] In fact, Ahmed knows that Kamal, "[qui] sera là pour te satisfaire" [who will be there to satisfy you], is waiting in line.[42] The Arab, in the view of Emmanuel, becomes thus the mute, interchangeable object at the beck and call of the whites, in reminiscence of colonial times.

In interviews, Taïa remarks that the form and content of *Celui qui est digne d'être aimé* is inspired by *Les lettres portuguaises* (1669), an epistolary novel now commonly attributed to Gabriel de Guilleragues.[43] *Les lettres portuguaises*, published in France, consists of five letters written by a Portuguese nun to a French officer who deserted her.[44] The letters are emotional complaints in which the nun revives her feelings for her lover. The letters written by Ahmed to his mother and to Emmanuel, by Vincent to Emmanuel, and by Lahbib to Ahmed, draw upon *Les lettres portugaises* in that in each letter the writer depicts his love or past love. As critics of the epistolary novel have remarked, in no other genre is the consciousness of the character better revealed than in the epistolary genre in which the letter writers drafts unmediated thoughts on paper.[45] This, however, has been contested by Joe Bray, for example, who argues that, through their correspondents, the novelists illustrate how the letter-writers are conscious of their word choice and steer their writings in order to impart certain impressions to the reader.[46] What Taïa seemingly attempts to do in *Celui qui est digne d'être aimé* is chiefly to provide Ahmed's subjective point-of-view about this encounter and the ensuing love affair with Emmanuel. Through the epistolary form, Taïa gives voice to Ahmed and, by extension, to the generic Arab boy, who has been, for decades, muted by orientalist discourse and whose perspective the western reader never got to know. If French writers such as Gide or Barthes described their encounters with Arab men from their point of view, Taïa here offers the Arab boy's version. Furthermore, as Mack shows, French literary gay circles such as those that revolved around Roland Barthes, Frédéric Mitterrand, Renaud Camus, or Patrick Cardon have often despised the Arab masculine voice as "dim-witted," unreceptive to the French gay writers' "aesthetic appeals." Through the letter, Taïa offers a counter-example of a man who portrays himself in all his complexity.[47] Furthermore, Ahmed's complexity is enhanced through Vincent's and Lahbib's letters in which we are given their perspective on Ahmed. As the title, suggests, *Celui qui est digne d'être aimé* are these Moroccan men in all their fragility and complexity, displaying multifaceted personalities, while muted or loved perhaps for the wrong reasons by their French counterparts.

Retrospectively, while writing to Emmanuel, Ahmed recalls a presentation he gave at the University of Rabat about the significance of Gide's encounter with adolescents from the Maghreb. While approaching this topic from a Gidean perspective, he remarks now in his letter:

> L'émancipation sexuelle d'André Gide, je l'avais vécue à l'époque comme si elle avait été la mienne. Mon identification mystique, littéraire et sexuelle était la preuve de mon intelligence. [. . .] Plus tard je me suis rendu compte que j'avais fait un oubli impardonnable. Tragique. J'avais traité le garçon arabe offert à André Gide en ne parlant pratiquement pas de lui. [. . .] j'avais tué à Rabat une énième fois le garçon qui devrait être le véritable héros de cette histoire. J'aurais dû lui servir de voix, d'avocat, d'ami, de frère lointain.
>
> [André Gide's sexual emancipation, I had experienced it at the time as if it had been my own. My mystical, literary and sexual identification was proof of my intelligence. [. . .] Later I realized that I had made an unforgivable omission. Tragic. I had analyzed the Arab boy offered to André Gide by hardly mentioning him. [. . .] I had killed in Rabat for the umpteenth time the boy who should be the real hero of this story. I should have served as his voice, his advocate, his friend, his distant brother.][48]

While remembering his first encounter with Emmanuel on the beach, Taïa appropriates Gide's experience from Ahmed's point of view, recalling the Algerian boy given to him by Oscar Wilde on their trip to Algiers. Thus, in his description of his encounter of Emmanuel, Ahmed clearly draws upon Gide's *Si le grain ne meurt* (1926). The gesture Ahmed makes in order to draw Emmanuel to the floor is described in the following terms: "J'ai pris ta main et avec force je t'ai entraîné" [I took your hand and with force I dragged you down to the soil],[49] which resonates with Gide's text, "Mais, saisissant la main qu'il me tendait, je le fis rouler à terre" [But, grabbing the hand, he held onto me, I made him roll to the ground],[50] with the difference that Ahmed here has self-agency.

On the whole, the letter reveals Ahmed's regaining of self-identity and shedding French acculturation. "Je veux devenir Un sans toi, Emmanuel"

[I want to become One without you, Emmanuel], says Ahmed at one point in the letter.[51] He rejects this new identity epitomized by the name Midou, with all its concomitant characteristics. He wants to shed Emmanuel's influence, regain independence, and return to his own roots and culture ("Un sans toi"). He will abandon the center of Paris, the 5th arrondissement, and move to the banlieue ("dans un quartier que tu ne connais pas. En banlieue. A Gennevilliers. A Clichy." [In a neighborhood you don't know. In the suburbs. In Gennevilliers. In Clichy.]),[52] the places, as we have seen, of Aziz and Zahira. This return to his own identity can also be seen in the fact that he now tries to understand his own family's and Moroccan attitudes towards homosexuality. He distances himself from this western attitude, which conceives of sexuality as the primary characteristic of one's identity. He writes to Emmanuel:

> Je reviens à ma première solitude, où, je l'espère, je pourrai me réconcilier avec mon premier monde. Ma mère dure, sans Hamid, mon père. Mes sœurs trahies par la vie. Je vais aller vers elles et, même si elles s'obstinent à refuser de parler de mon homosexualité, je les forcerai à créer un lien nouveau. Je veux parler avec elles d'elles et de moi. Je ne veux pas que tout tourne autour de mon homosexualité.
>
> [I return to my first solitude, where I hope I can come to terms with my first world. My tough mother, without my father, Hamid. My sisters betrayed by life. I will go to them and, even if they persist in refusing to talk about my homosexuality, I will force them to create a new bond. I want to talk to them about them and about me. I don't want everything to revolve around my homosexuality][53]

In this letter Ahmed realizes that the imposition of this western idea of gay identity means deprivation of freedom and, as we have seen, objectification. With his acculturation in France, the European notion of sexuality that privileges sexuality as the essence of the self, the innermost core of one's personality, has been imposed on him. Thus, as Mercer comments, "it comes as no surprise to see the development of a particular stereotype of a gay man whose consciousness contains nothing else but sexuality, who is perpetually troubled by his sexual desires and who is always looking for the truth of his identity in his sex,"[54] a stereotype from which Ahmed now wishes to distance himself ("Je ne veux pas que tout tourne autour de mon homosexualité"). While he wished to turn into a Parisian white gay man, he despised his sister and his family and their silencing of homosexuality. Now he is keen to get to know his family, facing hardship he has ignored during the luxurious, alienated Parisian life he had led and re-developing his relationships with his mother and sisters. He is no longer afraid of solitude and of perhaps facing his family's troubled attitude towards his sexual orientation. He has understood that these are the challenges he must face and that these form his identity.

CONCLUSION

In these two novels, Taïa creates a web of narratives in which he links past colonial exploitation with (sexual) exploitation of North Africans in the present. Aziz, Zahira, Zineb, and Ahmed are all caught in a broader colonial and contemporary machinery, which capitalizes on cheap human labor. Furthermore, Taïa reveals these subtle dynamics in France's gay community whereby, in the desire to be a good citizen of the Republic, the ethnic Other must either be exoticized and racialized, as it were, or then assimilated to the extent that they have to deny their own ethnic background. Being first a writer, it is through narrative strategies that Taïa denounces and reveals the links to colonialism that still pervade French society, exploit the North African, and imprison them in stereotypes. Taïa's words on the back cover of *Un pays pour mourir* succinctly summarize this exploitation: "Ils sont nombreux ceux qui se trouvent dans le même cas. C'est notre destin: payer par notre corps l'avenir des autres" [There are many who find themselves in the same situation. It is our destiny: to pay with our body for the future of others]. If the author with this rather obscure *ceux* and *nous* leaves it open who exactly he has in mind, his statement certainly describes the lot of protagonists in *Un pays pour mourir* and *Celui qui est digne d'être aimé* who are caught in the nexus of colonialism, neo-colonialism, racism, and sexual exploitation.

NOTES

1. Philippe Panizzon, 'La vraie liberté n'existe nulle part': un entretien avec Abdellah Taïa," *Francosphères* 8, no. 2 (December 2019): 202. All translations are my own. I take here the opportunity to thank Siham Bouamer and Denis Provencher for their encouragement and insightful comments on this chapter.
2. Eric Fassin, "Homosexuels des villes, homophobes des banlieues," *Métropolitiques* (2010) <http://www.metropolitiques.eu/Homosexuels-des-villes-homophobes.html> [accessed September 2020].
3. Franck Chaumont, *Homo-ghetto: gays et lesbiennes dans les cités: les clandestins de la République* (Paris: Le cherche-midi, 2009), and Brahim Naït-Balk, *Un homo dans la cité: La descente aux enfers puis la libération d'un homosexuel de culture maghrébine* (Paris: Calmann-Lévy, 2009).
4. Fassin, "Homosexuels des villes, homophobes des banlieues." Bébel-Créteil's members are mainly of Arab/Muslim origin.

5. Fassin's analysis in the article "Homosexuels des villes, homophobes des banlieues" encompasses not only France. He also discusses the case of the Dutch politician Pim Fortuyn who openly claimed to have had affairs with Moroccan boys while rejecting Islam, and who was eventually murdered.

6. Eric Fassin, "Same-sex Marriage, Nation, and Race: French Political Logics and Rhetorics," *Contemporary French Civilization* 39, no. 3 (2014): 297–299.

7. Denis M. Provencher, *Queer Maghrebi French: Language, Temporalities, Transfiliation* (Liverpool: Liverpool University Press, 2017), 13.

8. Provencher, *Queer Maghrebi French,* 17–18.

9. Maxime Cervulle and Nick Rees-Roberts, *Homo exoticus, race, classe et critique queer* (Paris: Armand Colin, 2010), 17.

10. Cervulle and Rees-Roberts, *Homo exoticus*, 17.

11. Noémi Michel, "Accounts of Injury as Misappropriations of Race: Towards a Critical Black Politics of Vulnerability," *Critical Horizons: Journal of Social & Critical Theory* 17, no. 2 (May 2016): 240–259.

12. Cervulle and Rees-Roberts, *Homo exoticus*, 53.

13. Provencher, *Queer Maghrebi French*, 149. Jean-Pierre Boulé, *Abdellah Taïa, La mélancolie et le cri* (Lyon: Presses universitaires de Lyon, 2020), 209.

14. Provencher, *Queer Maghrebi French*, 149.

15. Joanne Brueton, "Abdellah Taïa's Literary Palimpsests," *RELIEF—Revue électronique de littérature française* 14, no.1 (2020): 56.

16. Mehammed Mack, *Sexagon: Muslims, France and the Sexualization of National Culture* (New York: Fordham University Press, 2017), 13.

17. Mack, *Sexagon*, 14.

18. Abdellah Taïa, *Un pays pour mourir* (Paris: Seuil, 2015), 61.

19. Taïa, *Un pays pour mourir*, 61.

20. Taïa, *Un pays pour mourir*, 61.

21. Taïa, *Un pays pour mourir*, 30.

22. Taïa, *Un pays pour mourir*, 143.

23. Jean-Jacques Courtine, "Virilités coloniales et post-coloniales," in *Histoire de la virilité*, edited by Alain Corbin, Jean-Jacques Courtine, Georges Vigarello (Paris: Seuil, 2011), 403.

24. Taïa, *Un pays pour mourir*, 36.

25. Taïa, *Un pays pour mourir*, 36.

26. Taïa, *Un pays pour mourir*, 36.

27. Taïa, *Un pays pour mourir*, 49.

28. Taïa, *Un pays pour mourir*, 46.

29. Taïa, *Un pays pour mourir*, 39.

30. Taïa, *Un pays pour mourir*, 39.

31. Taïa, *Un pays pour mourir*, 39–40.

32. François Neveux, "Les voix de Jeanne d'Arc, de l'histoire à la légende," *Annales de Normandie* 62, no. 2 (2012): 274.

33. Taïa, *Celui qui est digne d'être aimé* (Paris: Seuil, 2017), 99.

34. Taïa, *Celui qui est digne*, 100.

35. Kobena Mercer and Isaac Julien, "Race, Sexual Politics and Black Masculinity: A Dossier," in *Male Order: Unwrapping Masculinity*, edited by Rowena Chapman and Jonathan Rutherford (London: Lawrence & Wishart, 1988), 106.
36. Taïa, *Celui qui est digne*, 105.
37. Taïa, *Celui qui est digne*, 105.
38. Taïa, *Celui qui est digne*, 105.
39. Taïa, *Celui qui est digne*, 106.
40. Taïa, *Celui qui est digne*, 106.
41. Taïa, *Celui qui est digne*, 106–107.
42. Taïa, *Celui qui est digne*, 108.
43. See, for example, https://lebudelarue.com/rencontre-avec-abdellah-taia-1re-partie/ and https://www.franceinter.fr/emissions/chasse-croise/chasse-croise-15-juillet-2017, [accessed 14 July 2020].
44. Joe Bray, *The Epistolary Novel: Representations of Consciousness* (London: Routledge, 2003), 29.
45. Laurent Versini, *Le roman épistolaire* (Paris: Presses universitaires de France, 1979), 50.
46. Bray, *The Epistolary Novel*, 55.
47. Mack, *Sexagon*, 47.
48. Taïa, *Celui qui est digne*, 118.
49. Taïa, *Celui qui est digne*, 87.
50. André Gide, *Si le grain ne meurt* (Paris: Gallimard, 1995), 299.
51. Taïa, *Celui qui est digne*, 107.
52. Taïa, *Celui qui est digne*, 107.
53. Taïa, *Celui qui est digne*, 109.
54. Mercer and Julien, "Race, Sexual Politics and Black Masculinity," 106.

BIBLIOGRAPHY

Boulé, Jean-Pierre. *Abdellah Taïa, La mélancolie et le cri*. Lyon: Presses universitaires de Lyon, 2020.

Bray, Joe. *The Epistolary Novel: Representation of Consciousness*. London: Routledge, 2003.

Brueton, Joanne. "Abdellah Taïa's Literary Palimpsests." *RELIEF – Revue électronique de littérature française* 14, no. 1 (2020): 49–62.

Cervulle, Maxime, and Nick Rees-Roberts. *Homo exoticus, race, classe et critique queer*. Paris: Armand Colin, 2010.

Chaumont, Franck. *Homo-ghetto: gays et lesbiennes dans les cités: les clandestins de la République*. Paris: Le cherche-midi, 2009.

Courtine, Jean-Jacques. "Virilités coloniales et post-coloniales." In *Histoire de la virilité*, edited by Alain Corbin, Jean-Jacques Courtine, Georges Vigarello, 387–412. Paris: Seuil, 2011.

Fassin, Eric. "Homosexuels des villes, homophobes des banlieues." *Métropolitiques* (2010). <http://www.metropolitiques.eu/Homosexuels-des-villes-homophobes.html> [accessed 22 May 2018].

———. "Same-sex Marriage, Nation, and Race: French Political Logics and Rhetorics." *Contemporary French Civilization* 39, no. 3 (2014): 281–301.

Gide, André. *Si le grain ne meurt.* Paris: Gallimard, 1995.

Julien, Isaac, and Kobena Mercer. "Race, Sexual Politics and Black Masculinity: A Dossier." In *Male Order: Unwrapping Masculinity*, edited by Rowena Chapman; Jonathan Rutherford, 97–148. London: Lawrence & Wishart, 1988.

Mack, Mehammed Amadeus. *Sexagon: Muslims, France and the Sexualization of National Culture.* New York: Fordham University Press, 2017.

Michel, Noémi. "Accounts of Injury as Misappropriations of Race: Towards a Critical Black Politics of Vulnerability." *Critical Horizons: Journal of Social & Critical Theory* 17, no. 2 (May 2016): 240–259.

Naït-Balk, Brahim. *Un homo dans la cité: La descente aux enfers puis la libération d'un homosexuel de culture maghrébine.* Paris: Calmann-Lévy, 2009.

Neveux, François, "Les voix de Jeanne d'Arc, de l'histoire à la légende." *Annales de Normandie* 62, no. 2 (2012) : 253–276.

Panizzon, Philippe. "“La vraie liberté n'existe nulle part": un entretien avec Abdellah Taïa." *Francosphères* 8, no. 2 (2019): 183–207.

Provencher, Denis M. *Queer Maghrebi French: Language, Temporalities, Transfiliations.* Liverpool: Liverpool University Press, 2017.

Versini, Laurent. *Le roman épistolaire.* Paris: Presses universitaires de France, 1979.

Taïa, Abdellah. *Celui qui est digne d'être aimé.* Paris: Seuil, 2017.

———. *Un pays pour mourir.* Paris: Seuil, 2015.

Chapter 9

Abdellah Taïa's *Transfilial* Mythmaking and Unfaithful Realms of Memory

Denis M. Provencher

INTRODUCTION: GLOBAL CINEMA AS AN EXAMPLE OF TRANSGRESSIVE AND TRANSFILIAL MYTHMAKING AND MEMORY

From Abdellah Taïa's very first novel, *Mon Maroc* [*My Morocco*] (2000), the power and importance of global cinema for the author and his protagonist, Abdellah, come into clear focus. In the chapter "Du pain et du thé" [Bread and Tea], Taïa recounts his main character's pleasure and fascination when going to the Cinéma Opéra in the Tabriket district of Salé, where he discovered the double-featured matinee that becomes known in his social circle as "bread and tea."[1] This involves Chinese karate and kung-fu cinema ("bread") followed by Indian—early Bollywood—cinema ("tea") and indeed, for many filmgoers of the 1970s in Salé, these two cinematic genres went hand in hand. Abdellah admits he loves karate and kung-fu films yet often finds the never-ending Indian films too "syrupy" for his liking, which he does not bother staying to watch at first.[2]

On this visit to the cinema, Abdellah discovers the film *La Fureur du Dragon* [*The Way of the Dragon*] (1972) where he immediately falls in love with Bruce Lee. Abdellah proclaims his "fidelity"[3] to the bare-chested Lee and situates himself in the camp of children from Salé who prefer this "Chinese"[4] hero over the kids who prefer Jackie Chan—the other renowned male actor of Hong-Kong origin associated with karate and kung-fu cinema. After watching the double feature, Abdellah and the rest of the movie-goers return home later that day with a shared sense that all is right in the world because of good guys like Lee who triumph ultimately over evil, as exhibited in the first film in this double feature.[5] The village spectators will repeat this viewing practice by returning to the cinema every week for reassuring doses of visual "bread and tea." This ritualized act is indeed reminiscent of the type of simultaneity Benedict Anderson claims is necessary for cohesion in any "imagined community."[6] At the same time, however, "bread and tea" in this context could also be read as just another form of "bread and circus" that is fed to the masses in what Taïa often refers to as a "sterile"[7] Morocco of the 1970s—empty of real leadership in government or real opportunity for its citizens—in order to appease and calm the people through cheap and mindless diversion.[8]

In this same chapter, Abdellah also develops an appreciation for a variety of cinematic traditions that will admittedly also include Indian films starring Amithab Bachchan and Shabana Azmi. At the same time, in an act of cinematic transgression, the protagonist will abandon his "fidelity" to Bruce Lee when he discovers the American and French cinematic traditions. Taïa writes:

> En 1984, *E.T.* de Steven Spielberg sortit à Rabat. Abdelkébir nous emmena le voir, mon petit frère Mustapha et moi. Il ne savait pas qu'il m'ouvrait, par ce geste, une autre porte dans le cinéma, la porte du cinéma occidental qui me conduirait à d'autres rencontres: Truffaut, Hitchcock, Renoir, Scorsese, et bien d'autres. Je changeai de cinéphilie. Je devins infidèle.
>
> [In 1984, Steven Spielberg's *E.T.* opened in Rabat. Abdelkébir took us to see it, my little brother Mustapha and me. He didn't know he was opening, through this gesture, another door of the cinema, the door of western cinema that would lead me to other encounters: Truffaut, Hitchcock, Renoir, Scorsese, and many others. I changed my viewing habits and love for cinema. I became an infidel.][9]

Abdellah's eldest brother Abdelkébir plays an important role here introducing him and his younger brother to cinema, in the same way he will later introduce Abdellah to the French language and literature.[10] This is a form of filiation, a symbolic link between and symbolic transmission from elder to younger brother, allowing Abdellah to discover and familiarize himself with other "father figures" who inspire: Spielberg, Truffaut, Hitchcock, Renoir, Scorsese, and the like.

What is most striking about this passage on global cinema, infidelity, and transgressive figures is that it occurs in Taïa's very first novel and it points to what will become, as I have argued elsewhere,[11] one of the author's most salient trademarks: his transmission of "transgressive filiations" or *transfiliations*, which are sites of connection, mythmaking, and memory for himself and his world-wide readership of "infidels." I am defining *transfiliation* as a process that involves the creation of familial and filial (parent-child) ties across generations through subversive and transgressive artistic and cultural productions, the transmission of those models across genres and generations of producers and consumers, and across transnational networks of communication.[12] In this context, Taïa will leave a trail of "disloyal" or "unfaithful" signifiers and cultural mythologies for his readers to follow and, cinematic references and their transgressive bodies are just one such set of examples. These links are "disloyal" or "unfaithful" because they disrupt both his place of origin (Morocco) as well as the postcolonial metropole (France), the two spaces to which the postcolonial subject is often supposedly attached.[13] Indeed, cinema is a disruptive force that goes beyond just the transgressive and disruptive nature of language. Indeed, the cinematic images enter Taïa's home through the television screen and hold the potential to unsettle both his and his family's world view. It is also in part for this reason that I have chosen to open this chapter with a disruptive image from global cinema. At the same time however, this disruption occurs for the author both when watching movies and reading books about Europe and other sites in the world, and we will consider both types of cultural production in this chapter.

Taïa's ability to not only create but also redefine cultural myths and realms of memory for the postcolonial subject is also present in this chapter on bread and tea. It is noteworthy here that Bruce Lee is actually an American-born actor and film director of Hong Kong origin—born in San Francisco—who has been reappropriated in this tale by Abdellah and the other children of Salé, like other global viewers, as a "Chinese" figure. A community will generally reappropriate cultural icons and myths in a way that evacuates them of some of their original significance in order to bring meaning to the local group.[14] Similar to realms of memory, cultural myths also involve a certain level of forgetfulness in order to maintain their contemporary significance or coherence.[15] Indeed, and as we will see in this current chapter, Taïa's use of signifiers, cultural myths, and realms of memory from his writings generally transcends references to the Hexagon, the French empire, and the larger Francosphere (larger French-speaking world). The fact that Moroccan boys in his very first novel are watching Chinese and Indian movies from a young age in the 1970s suggests that the French realms of memory and cultural myths we would suspect to be central to a postcolonial Morocco are always and already disrupted. It is worth noting here that there is also a gender transgression at work here by staying on to watch the Indian movies with its singing and dancing that goes against the heterosexual macho culture of the action (karate/king-fu) films. Hence there is also already a sort of "trans" sorority with the author's sisters, regarding the singing and dancing.[16]

As Taïa experiences new cinematic traditions and chronicles them in his oeuvre—while sitting on the crowded floor either in the Cinéma Opéra or in front of the TV in his family's living room, or throughout time and space during his physical migrations over two decades, to Geneva, Brussels, Paris, Cairo, and beyond—he also flexibly accumulates language and semiotic codes beyond Morocco and the Hexagon. The flexible accumulation of language is defined here as "an accrual of scripts and other symbols' across time and space."[17] Although flexible accumulation also helps the subject to disidentify with—that is, both draw on and debunk—the claims to belonging that neoliberal self-sovereignty supposedly requires.[18] Flexible accumulation of language also includes "seemingly contradictory elements"[19] that work on and against dominant ideologies of the culture where this performance takes place. For example, and as I have argued elsewhere, Taïa's ability to use statements and images related to being simultaneously a "terroriste, pédé, et le fils de Marilyn Monroe" [terrorist, fag, and the son of Marilyn Monroe], allows him to escape his quotidian existence as a poor kid from Morocco by creating transgressive filiations as he moves across multiple borders. Speakers like Taïa are able to create new scripts of survival and resilience, and this resembles the process that Françoise Lionnet and Shu-mei Shih refer to as a "transnationalism from below."[20] In fact, and as we will see in this chapter, Taïa points in his work to a transnational and transgressive set of myths and sites of memory for the queer[21] diasporic author and the members of his imagined readership. This process of transnational and transgressive referencing, a form of *transfilial* myth and memory making, is, as I will argue, central to Taïa's grand project of *infidelity* to the nation and to the French empire.

My goal in this chapter is twofold. First, I will briefly present some of the recent scholarship on postcolonial mythmaking and postcolonial realms of memory. Next, I will draw from my own work on transfiliation and the flexible accumulation of language in order to illustrate how these tools can help us to better understand the identities of "postcolonial" and "queer" Maghrebi migratory writers such as Taïa.[22] My aim here is to argue that these additional concepts—transfiliation and flexible language—can serve as complementary analytical tools to those involved in the field of postcolonial Francophone studies and especially where mythmaking and sites of memory involve queer migratory bodies. While all of Taïa's writings include elements of "transfilial cultural myths and realms of memory," I will limit my discussion in this chapter to a relatively small but salient set of cinematic and literary examples that move us "unfaithfully" from the local (Moroccan), to the postcolonial French metropole and Francosphere, and finally to the transfilial on a global scale, largely informed by the United States. Like Taïa, my own work in this chapter can be read as a kind of disloyal act to some of the work currently being done in postcolonial Francophone studies because I argue that this important scholarship maintains its own limitations and falls short in any analysis that involves migratory queers of color[23] from the former French-speaking colonies.

POSTCOLONIAL AND TRANSFILIAL SITES OF MEMORY AND MYTHMAKING FOR THE EVERYDAY QUEER

> J'ai compris deux autres choses importantes durant ce premier voyage en Europe. D'abord, à quel point la fascination qu'exerçait sur moi la culture occidentale était réelle. Et ensuite, à quel point ce même Occident était une autre chose à vivre au quotidien, une autre réalité que celle que j'avais pendant des années imaginée à travers les films et les livres.
>
> [I understood two other important things during this first trip to Europe. First, to what point the fascination thrust upon me by Western culture was real. And then, to what point this same West was altogether something else to experience on a daily basis, another reality than what I had for years imagined from films and books.][24]

In *Mythologies postcoloniales: Pour une décolonisation du quotidien* (2018), postcolonial Francophone studies scholars Etienne Achille and Lydie Moudileno revive the work of Roland Barthes some sixty years later in order to "penser autrement la République postcoloniale" [think differently the postcolonial Republic] and "(re)lire le réel sous le double signe de l'héritage théorique barthésien et d'un héritage colonial qui est indissociable de l'Histoire française" [to reread the real under the double sign of the Barthesian theoretical heritage and a colonial heritage that is inseparable from French history].[25] Through an analysis of public space, popular culture, literature, media, the world of sports, and consumer products, among other realms, these scholars aim to expose the underlying racial stereotypes and blind spots that still undergird many institutions and cultural phenomena in contemporary France. By doing so, they further the conversation beyond the mythmaking texts of the 1950s that Barthes originally analyzed in order to expose the largely naturalized middle class and white ideologies, which still continue today to erase other forms of belonging and difference. These scholars draw on the work of Achille Mbembe, Pap Ndiaye, Léopold Senghor, Edward Saïd, Valentin-Yves Mudimbe, Frantz Fanon, and Didier Fassin, among others, to ensure that race in particular remains an important analytical category. Of course, this is particularly important in an era where the erasure of race or other forms of difference by French political figures—like Emmanuel Macron, Nicolas Sarkozy, François Hollande, and others—remains common practice. Achille and Moudileno argue that we must rethink mythmaking by questioning the way a multicultural citizenry reads the signs and myths around them: "Il est évident que le rapport au quotidien *se vit* différemment aujourd'hui selon que l'on est français, étranger, touriste, sans papiers, réfugié, et bien sûr, blanc ou non-blanc" [it is evident that the relationship to the everyday *is lived* differently today according to whether or not you are

French, a foreigner, a tourist, an undocumented person, a refugee, and of course, white or non-white].[26]

Inspired also by the work of Henri Lefebvre, Michel de Certeau, and Georges Perec, among others, they emphasize the fact that there is nothing "anondin" [harmless][27] about the cultural myths that comprise the everyday for people of color or other minorities in France and they call upon us to help to decolonize the everyday. Achille and Moudileno define the everyday as "un palimpseste où persistent les traces d'histoires plus ou moins lointaines et plus ou moins partagées. En cela, il est intimement lié à l'écriture et à la représentation de la nation" [is a palimpsest where more or less faraway and more or less shared historical traces persist. Hence, it is intimately linked to writing and to representation of the nation].[28] They also qualify the nation as a paradoxical space built on many tensions including but not limited to: liberty vs. surveillance; hospitality vs. rejection; visibility vs. invisibility; and forgetting vs. memory.[29] Indeed, many French cultural myths are imbued with these frictions and remain harmful for French citizens of Caribbean, North African, and sub-Saharan African descent as well as for immigrants from these former French colonies.

While Achille and Moudileno focus on the citizens of France who are descendants of immigrants from the former colonies, we could also easily apply their framework to immigrants such as Taïa from a postcolonial Francophone context. This is elucidated clearly in the quote above from Taïa where he describes his first trip to Europe. We see therein how his experience as a Moroccan *immigré* to France in the late 1990s shares many of the same aspects of the lived reality and everyday experiences of first- and second-generation French citizens of Caribbean, Maghrebi or Sub-Saharan African origin. The initial fascination with Europe, which is narrated largely through films and literature, is strong for his protagonist Abdellah. However, living the everyday in Europe will become something quite different and this pushes Taïa and his character ultimately to continue to imagine themselves elsewhere through transgressive myth and memory making in order to construct new forms of belonging for their migratory queer bodies of color.[30] For this reason, I answer, at least hypothetically, Ralph Heyndels' question in this volume, "is there a there where to go and exist?"

Another important volume that helps us to understand the "elsewhere" where people look to find new forms of belonging and memory includes the recent *Postcolonial Realms of Memory: Sites and Symbols in Modern France* (2020). In this book, Etienne Achille, Charles Forsdick, and Lydie Moudileno take up an important perspective on belonging for French citizens of color and immigrant origin by reexamining French historian Pierre Nora's multivolume set *Les lieux de mémoire* [*Realms of Memory*] (1984–1992). Building on scholarship in anthropology, history, memory studies, and postcolonial Francophone studies, among others, Achille, Forsdick, and Moudileno aim to "address systematically the flaws"[31] in Nora's volumes. Quoting from a manifesto against decolonial thinking published in *Le Point* in 2018, the authors underscore how a certain class of intellectuals in France who signed the document, including Pierre Nora himself, remain largely in denial about the need for a postcolonial understanding of the French Republic and accuse decolonial thinking as a form of "shameful hijacking of the values of liberty, equality and fraternity on which our democracy is built."[32] Achille, Forsdick and Moudileno aim to correct the omissions of a nationalistic historiography initiated by Nora and others during the latter part of the twentieth century, which was largely shaped by these thinkers' preoccupation with the "Greater France" of the Third Republic. This was part of a larger agenda of nation building in light of France's own bicentennial celebration (1989) alongside the nation's own growing anxiety surrounding its waning importance in an era of globalization.

In their introduction, Achille, Forsdick, and Moudileno provide a brief and useful overview of the scholarly criticism to date on Nora. For example, they point out that: "the issue of migration and the interplay between immigration and postcolonialism are otherwise largely absent from Nora's seven volumes."[33] They also stress that Nora's volumes have been "attacked for the glaring absence . . . of references to empire, colonial legacy or (post) colonial topography" and his oeuvre "has therefore become emblematic of a certain French incapacity and/or unwillingness to engage with the inherent and increasingly undeniable imbrication of the colonial in the *roman national* [national narrative] (Hargreaves, 2005)."[34] In contrast to Nora then, who was mostly interested in "Hexagonal manifestations," these scholars call for "an investigation of national culture that would consider the territory of the Republic in its broadest geopolitical sense: limiting postcolonial France solely to its hexagonal contours would only reproduce another form of denial that permeates *Les Lieux de mémoire*."[35] They qualify (postcolonial) realms then as: "heterogeneous, some more visible than others, and take a variety of forms. Postcolonial realms of memory, as we (re)conceptualize them, are therefore defined here as spatial/functional or immaterial sites, potentially subject to abstraction and imbued with a symbolic aura that, in the context of the French every day, refers to more or less tangible memory traces linked to the colonial."[36] While these scholars are interested in examining the postcolonial sites of memory both in and beyond the Hexagon, they limit their scope in this particular volume, largely due to space, to the Hexagon as well as its overseas departments, regions, collectivities and territories known as the *Outre-mer*.[37] At the same time, Achille, Forsdick, and Moudileno remain interested in inquiries into the "transcontinental, transcultural, and translingual" and mention how they hope to produce a companion volume that would reconsider the realms of memory "in the wider Francosphère."[38]

In my chapter, I build on their work in postcolonial mythologies and realms of memory. Through an analysis of Taïa's writings, I will illustrate the fact that while queer French-speaking people of color may be drawn to the French Republic and the associated cultural signifiers they first discovered through films and books, individuals like Taïa will sooner or later decolonize them and also propose new "non-blancs" models of belonging in the postcolonial, the French, and the transnational contexts because of their sense of disconnection and disidentification.[39] While Taïa is not a postcolonial French subject creating a new set of cultural myths or realms of memory for all citizens of the Hexagon, he does assemble from a distance to the French metropole a different set of signifiers that are not necessarily always and already linked to colonial memory. In contrast then to the myths that Achille and Moudileno examine in *Mythologies postcoloniales* that emerge in specifically French contexts of the Hexagon and the departments and territories of the *Outre-Mer*—where a tension exists between the two poles of mythmaking—"de l'occultation d'une part, et de l'exploitation racialisante de l'autre" [the concealing on the one hand and the racializing exploitation on the other][40]—we will see that Taïa moves beyond this binary and proposes new disruptive and transfilial paths forward to a more understanding space of belonging for queers of color in the Francosphere and beyond. Indeed, Taïa's work involves global bodies and transfilial signifiers largely due to the desire among queer migratory individuals to seek new forms of queer and neoliberal belonging on a global scale but also to combat forms of isolation, unrealized dreams, and cruel optimism as well as impossible citizenship.[41] Finally, it is important to point out that Taïa himself uses the term "panthéon" [pantheon] at several points in his writing and indeed, this is a conscious effort on his part to construct not only an alternative set of mythologies and realms of memory, but to assemble them as part of an agreed-upon queer grouping of dead and non-dead figures whom he idolizes and honors. In this way, he subverts the French Panthéon in Paris' historic Latin Quarter that includes tombs of reputable national and international figures, and replaces it with his own queer Panthéon, beginning as we will see below with his "salvation army" or army of "angels" and the many other figures he canonizes along the way.

TAÏA'S TRANSGRESSIVE AND TRANSFILIAL MYTHMAKING AND REALMS OF MEMORY

Taïa's writing involves several simultaneous processes of myth and memory making related to postcolonial Francophone space, the French metropole, as well as the transnational and *transfilial* realms. In his early work, the author chronicles an experience of growing up in Salé, a small town in post-independence Morocco, and his protagonist Abdellah's first migration to Rabat to attend university. At the same time, Taïa aspires to a life in Europe where he can become an intellectual, a writer, and a film director. His eventual migrations to Geneva and Paris prompt him to continue romanticizing the French metropole, however as the lived reality in Europe comes into clearer focus for him, this also prompts him to look further afield for new dream-filled places of belonging both symbolically and geographically across the globe. And indeed, all of these experiences affect and shape the way Taïa decides to mythologize and memorialize in his writing. It also determines, as we will see, in this and the following sections, how his characters make sense of their own bodies and place in the world. Moreover, the author initially relies on some dominant postcolonial Francophone (Moroccan) and French myths and realms of memory, however he deconstructs and "decolonizes" many of them as he experiences more fully the quotidian and the real, both in Morocco and in Europe.[42]

Postcolonial Francophone Myth and Memory: Mothers, Fathers, and Royal Prostitutes

First, Taïa's oeuvre includes cultural myths and sites of memory related to growing up in post-independence Morocco and this is what I'm calling "postcolonial Francophone" myth and memory making. This involves allusions, for example, to his "revolutionary" mother, his "transgressive" father, and Moroccan figures such as author Mohamed Choukri and King Hassan II as well as what Taïa himself calls at times "royal prostitutes"—Stellafa and Slima among others—who all can potentially transmit their *baraka* (an Arabic term for "blessings" or "luck") to him. All of these references help to give him a sense of belonging—sometimes normative belonging to the Moroccan tradition—within his homeland while he also plans and writes about his eventual departure for Europe.

Taïa's oeuvre is replete with references to strong female figures like his mother M'Barka and others (Fatéma and Massaouda) from whom he receives a sacred form of *baraka* that helps him on his own revolutionary path. For example, in his letter "L'homosexualité expliquée à ma mère" [Homosexuality Explained to My Mother], Taïa presents M'Barka as the strong, revolutionary, and independent woman of a new Morocco whom he places in stark contrast to an old and "sterile" Morocco.[43] He commemorates and memorializes his mother because of her leading role in the family and ties her to the Moroccan landscape, literally writing her body into the history of the Tadla region in particular. Taïa writes his own scandalous body into existence in relationship to his understanding of M'Barka's role and influence in order to disrupt the status quo in contemporary Morocco. Similarly, in "Le Chaouche" ["The Civil Servant"], the author tries to resurrect the father and memorialize him in epistolary form to his nephew Adnane as Ryan K. Schroth has shown us in this volume.[44] Taïa discusses the rumor surrounding his own father being an "illegitimate" son who was born after his mother supposedly had an affair with another man. This written account of his father allows Taïa to resurrect and memorialize his father as a potentially transgressive outsider. Taïa can also situate his father in relation to Adnane, who was adopted into the family, and hence the author can propose a new queer filial model of belonging in Morocco based on a transgressive genealogy. In both letters, Taïa commits a "scandalous act" by rewriting the memory of his mother and father with new revolutionary female and queer filial figures that help him imagine for himself and his nephew a new Morocco. Indeed, he pulls his nephew, his father, and his mother all into a queer future and away from the ghosts of Morocco's "sterile" past.[45]

As Taïa discovers the world of cinema and literature, he also begins to turn from the "sacred" *baraka* of figures from his Moroccan beginnings to the "secular" *baraka* that many writers, directors and cinematic stars can offer. As he continues his migration first to Rabat and then to Geneva, he dives more deeply into the literary canon, and that of queer, transgressive, and "infidel" writers in particular. In this context, Taïa writes about and memorializes many "sacred" male figures of literature who become his secondary father figures.[46] For example, in the chapter "Un deuxième père" [A second father], of his first novel, *Mon Maroc,* Taïa explains how he discovers Mohamed Chourki's novel *Le Pain nu* [*For Bread Alone*] (1972).[47] He will also include similar stories about Paul Bowles, the *baraka* of Jean Starobinski, and *Le Christ recrucifié* [*Christ Recrucified*] (1948) by Nikos Kazantzaki.[48] And, indeed, as we have seen with the figure of Bruce Lee, Taïa creates tales of secular *baraka* and *transfiliation*, which he then integrates as mythology into his own sense of identity and migratory belonging. By devoting individual chapters to each of these figures, he also places them on equal footing with mythologized familial figures from his homeland as well as the French and transnational figures we will see in the next sections.[49] So while we witness from his very first novel the emergence of postcolonial Francophone myth and memory, we also already notice examples of French and transnational/transfilial references.

If we look more closely at the chapter on his "second father," the reader discovers that Taïa's admiration for Choukri is twofold: he is both Moroccan and a writer like the aspiring young man from Salé. The protagonist admits *Le Pain nu* is the first novel—written in a mix of Arabic and Darija—he discovers as a child in the home where he grew up and reads it despite its scandalous reputation.[50] Even Abdellah's mother knew of Choukri's "mauvaise réputation, ses fréquentations douteuses" [bad reputation, his sketchy friends][51] and he claims the author was infamous both within the family and among the kids in the village who wanted to be like him with his reputation: "baiser les chèvres, les poules, boire du vin" [fucking goats, chickens, drinking wine].[52] Indeed, Choukri earns the status of cultural myth in this chapter and becomes part of Taïa's newly fashioned pantheon: "Choukri est entré dans le panthéon des grands écrivains marocains dès ce premier livre: c'est un mythe" [Choukri entered into the pantheon of great Moroccan writers from this first book: he was a myth].[53] The protagonist admits he devours this novel one summer and is particularly struck by the figure of the prostitute Sellafa. Taïa also states that Choukri and his writing left an impression on him that would endure a lifetime: "Il m'habite depuis ce jour-là. Je pense beaucoup à lui. Il m'a nourri. Il m'a vu naître littérairement" [He has inhabited me since that day. I think about him a lot. He nourished me. He watched me be born literarily].[54] Taïa creates here in Choukri a realm of memory, a degree zero of literature, from which Taïa as a literary figure will emerge. Choukri gives birth to Taïa as a writer because, as the reader knows, "scandalous" bodies play a central role throughout Taïa's oeuvre and the prostitute, for example, will make multiple appearances in his writing, including, among others, in a short story entitled "Sellafa" in the collection *Des nouvelles du maroc* (1999).[55] Taïa memorializes the scandalous Choukri—and, in fact, a whole string of authors he frequented—through his repeated use of disreputable protagonists that also appeared in their oeuvres. Taïa creates a literary genealogy that situates Choukri as part of a group of "outlaw" or "infidel" literary figures because of their own scandalous tales and because they all hung out together, including Genet, Tennessee Williams, Burroughs, Bowles, and others.[56] Taïa's creation here of "second fathers" of literature is not unlike the way he recounts his tales of M'Barka whom he ties to the people and land of Morocco or the transgressive genealogy of the father whom he situates as a transgressive figure in his letter to nephew Adnane. Protagonist Abdellah will catch sight one day of the famous Moroccan author on the Boulevard Mohammed V in Rabat and even will meet Choukri at a literary event during his time as a student at the University in Rabat. Like with many other mythic figures in his life, Abdellah longs to touch Choukri in the hopes that the great author would transmit some of his *baraka* to him. Taïa also mentions a time he walks into a bar in Choukri's hometown of Tangiers and spots a photograph of his master proudly displayed alongside one of King Hassan II. This photo memorializes Taïa's second father in a way that gives him equal importance, at least in this bar in Tangiers, to that of the Moroccan king, whom his protagonist Omar also longs to touch in the later novel *Le jour du Roi* [*The Day of the King*] (2010).

In contrast to King Hassan II however, Taïa gives even more importance to the signs and symbols of Choukri.[57] For, if we turn to consider *Le jour du Roi*, we will understand that instead of building up and mythologizing Hassan II, he actually demystifies and demotes this national figure. In brief terms, *Le jour du Roi* is the tale of two middle-school classmates, Omar and Khalid, who come from two different social classes—poor and affluent respectively—and who await a chance to interact with King Hassan II during the celebration, "le jour du roi," [the day of the king]. Khalid wins a competition at school to kiss the king at the event while Omar is denied this opportunity and his jealousy will determine much of the narrative. In fact, the novel opens with a dream sequence where the protagonist Omar is standing in front of Hassan II, waiting to greet and kiss his royal hand. The dream turns somewhat erotic when Omar witnesses the king undress in front of him and then when the boy also eventually clings to the king, climbs up on him, and finds his way to the king's fragrant neck to deliver several kisses. While the king is initially amused by their conversational exchange, he ultimately rejects Omar because of his many uniformed responses to several of his questions as well as the boy's overbearing and immature behavior. Omar awakens perplexed by this dream and will remain haunted by this "cauchemar éternel" [eternal nightmare][58] throughout the novel.

Unlike the image of Hassan II in *Mon Maroc* where the king is memorialized as an upstanding figure in a photograph at the bar in Tangiers, Taïa decides to devote an entire novel published in 2010 to the deconstruction of the national myth associated with this royal figure. Omar clearly cannot stop thinking about the ceremony, "le jour du roi," especially since Khalid has won the chance in the story to kiss the king's hand. So, while Omar cannot feasibly commit regicide, he will turn violent against Khalid in a scene where he lures his friend away from the ceremony into the forest and eventually will push him from a bridge. Taïa will go further however in demystifying the king, who is also considered the "father" of all Moroccans, and in demystifying Khalid's bourgeois family by tearing down the paternal figures in this novel.

For example, we learn that Omar's mother has decided to leave her husband and return to her hometown of Azemmour and her life as a sex worker. Taïa casts this maternal figure as a character who embodies freedom and revolt and who "dethrones" the father by wearing him down and eventually abandoning him with his male child Omar to become a "pute royale" [royal whore].[59] Omar sees his father destroyed by her departure and he must help his father learn to live a new life as two with his son.[60] At the same time however, Omar internalizes many of the traits and emotions of his mother—including jealousy of men and a desire for resistance[61]—and he harnesses these to take down Khalid, Khalid's family, and the king. Just as his mother dethroned his own father, Omar will tear down Khalid's family and the importance of the king by turning his focus from the royal ceremony to the story of Hadda, the black housekeeper to Khalid's family. In fact, through the voice of Hadda, which becomes increasingly central to the novel's structure, Taïa continues his maneuver to venerate another revolutionary female figure, a "royal prostitute" who wields power[62] like Omar's mother described previously as well as Slima, the "pute-mère" [whore-mother] in *Infidèles* [*Infidels*] (2012).

Like King Hassan II, Hadda will also come to Omar in his dreams but she will play the role of a comforting stand-in mother: "Femme à la place de ma mère" [Woman in place of my mother].[63] As readers, we learn that after serving Khalid's bourgeois family for some time, Hadda has disappeared. She has fled the house of Khalid's family because she is supposedly accused of being a thief and a prostitute.[64] While Khalid condemns Hadda's behaviors, Omar pronounces his solidarity for prostitutes and ultimately glorifies her. In the final chapter, Hadda's quotidian existence becomes clear when we meet the master of the bourgeois house "Sidi" Hamid, Khalid's father, who fantasizes about his maid Hadda. Hamid compares Hadda to the black woman portrayed in Marie-Guillemine Benoist's famous *Portrait d'une négresse* (1800), which depicts a liberated slave following the decree of 1794, that freed slaves in the former colonies and which visitors could see in the Louvre.[65] Taïa resists this legitimated national masterpiece by replacing the image of a liberated black woman with one of Hadda whom Sidi Hamid has unsuccessfully captured in his own amateur and unfinished painting of his maid turned "sex slave." Hadda reacts to Benoist's portrait when she states: "Je ne suis pas cette femme. Je ne suis pas une femme bien. Je suis mauvaise. Une dévergondée. Une putain." [I am not this woman. I am not a good woman. I'm bad. A loose woman. A hooker].[66] Sidi eventually grows tired of Hadda and she will flee their home and change her name in order to start again in a new setting. Hadda states: "Je ne fais que fuir. Depuis toute petite, je suis sur les routes. Dans l'errance. Je me suis habituée à cette vie sans lieu fixe, sans un cœur tendre, sans frère, sans sœur"[67] [I do nothing but flee. Since I was very little, I'm on the road. Wandering. I have gotten used to this life without a fixed abode, without a tender heart, without brothers, without sisters]. Hadda's speech act is an example of the flexible accumulation of language that Taïa adopts from the life of the "royal" and migratory prostitute to make sense of his own diasporic path. In fact, the voice of the wandering and diasporic female child, from a very early age, becomes his own cultural reference and transfilial link as he plans his own departure for Europe. In this novel, he has replaced "le jour du roi" with "le jour de la pute royale" [the day of the royal black whore].[68] In a way, then, Taïa takes the well-known cry of "Le roi est mort, vive le roi!" [The king is dead, long live the king!] and rewrites it through this novel in what would sound like: "Le roi est mort, vive la pute royale!"

[The king is dead, long live the royal whore!]. Taïa ultimately deconstructs the dominant myth of the king and any official national portraits by venerating the life of the working poor especially through the scandalous female sex worker in *Le jour du Roi*. And, in sum then, as we have seen in this section, Taïa memorializes certain scandalous maternal and paternal figures like M'Barka, Mohammed, Choukri, and Hadda, while deconstructing others who are situated on an official national level in the pantheon or national museum. These mothers, fathers, and royal prostitutes ground him through transgressive filiation and flexible language at a moment in his own queer migration when he is most unsure about where it is he is going in Europe.

French Myth and Memory: Saints, Sinners, and Celestial Bodies

In this next section, we examine how Taïa also legitimizes his own literary project by grounding it within an accumulation of French sites of myth and memory. This includes additional sources of secular *baraka* derived from scandalous French literary and cinematic figures. We certainly see an almost inordinate number of mentions of French canonical writers in his oeuvre. These include but are not limited to "Victor Hugo, Rabelais, Molière, Mme de Sévigné, Arthur Rimbaud, Marcel Proust, Jean Genet" and "leurs amis" [their friends][69] as well as Maupassant,[70] Daudet,[71] Gide,[72] Verlaine,[73] and Proust.[74] Of course, Michel Foucault[75] plays an important role, as Thomas Muzart and others have noted in this volume, as the man with the familiar and friendly face working the desk at the entrance of the Salvation Army in Geneva where Abdellah first stays upon his arrival. Interestingly, when Taïa concludes that same novel *L'armée du salut* [*Salvation Army*] (2006), his protagonist Abdellah asks where his set of angels are who could potentially serve as his "army of salvation"[76] to protect him as he enters Europe. I would argue here that this is a clear reference to his desire to construct a queer or nonnormative pantheon of individuals who will guide and ground him as he finds his bearings in an unknown Europe. And arguably, as we will see next, some of the most significant guides and angels of French mythmaking and sites of memory will be author Jean Genet and actress Isabelle Adjani.

Jean Genet is implicitly and explicitly present in Taïa's work and indeed, the Moroccan author devotes an entire chapter to him, "De Jenih à Genet" [From Jenih to Genet][77] in his second novel *Le rouge du tarbouche* [*The Red of the Fez*] (2004). He will also focus other writings and a short film on this saintly second father.[78] In the chapter "De Jenih à Genet,"[79] Abdellah and his cousin Ali, on the recommendation of Abdellah's mother and aunt, visit "la tombe de Jenih" [the tomb of Jenih] in the coastal town of Larache. The female figures in Morocco understand him to be a local saint of sorts, but when the young men arrive to Genet's tomb, Ali explains to Abdellah that Genet is not a saint but an "écrivain français" [French writer] who had much affection for Moroccans such as Mohamed El-Katrani, a native of Larache near whom the French writer insisted on being buried. Ali and Abdellah sit quietly at Genet's tomb to pay homage and then return home to a couscous dinner with mother and aunt in celebration of the saintly figure. As I have argued elsewhere, Taïa takes the figure of Genet and reappropriates him as a cultural myth associated with the coast of Larache and through the Arabization of his name (Sidi Jenih). The writer makes Genet his own and adopts him, like he has with Choukri, as part of his lineage of scandalous second fathers.

Taïa's reliance on transfiliation is evident in this story through Abdellah's insistence on familiarizing himself with this and other French writers, and also assimilating the associated cultural myths like Genet and "Abdallah le funambule" [Abdallah, the tightrope walker] whom Genet loved into his own understanding of the world. By writing them back to life, he resurrects them—through literature and cinema—and memorializes and sanctifies them in new ways.[80] Moreover, the grave of "Jenih-Genet" has made it possible for otherwise unlikely conversations and events as well as new communities and dialogues to form between interlocutors like Abdellah and Ali, as well as between mothers and their sons.[81] In *France and the Maghreb: Performative Encounters* (2005), Mireille Rosello writes: "Not only do the living come to talk to the dead (to their dead), but they also meet other people, individuals, that history forbids them to befriend."[82] The cemetery thus serves as a site of memory where people converge "to establish a connection with the dead person's life" and hence "by describing the place of burial as a beginning" mourners can feel part of a "newly found community."[83] The archetype "Genet" is re-born as a cultural myth belonging both to France and the Maghreb; "Genet" is also indicative of a long-standing "performative encounter" and a source of both "sacred" and "secular" *baraka,* which Taïa will utilize throughout his oeuvre.[84]

I would now like to turn and focus on another saintly figure from France that Taïa venerates in his work, largely due to her role in French cinema. Indeed, for Taïa, Isabelle Adjani guides him both before and after his actual migration to Paris. It is clear that Taïa is looking to migrate to France in search of an intellectual life as a writer and director and indeed, dominant hegemonic myths and sites of memory can sometimes bolster his thinking in order to realize this cinematic dream. While Taïa plans to pursue his literary and cinematic career,[85] he spends a lot of his time narrating his own experience through the lens of characters and scenes from classic movies. One of the most noteworthy is his reference to Alfred Hitchcock's *Rear Window* (1954) when staring out the window of his apartment on rue de Clignancourt looking down as a voyeur on his own cast of urban characters.[86] However, when we look to French references in particular, we see among others Juliette Binoche in *Rendez-vous*,[87] Alain Delon and Jean-Paul Belmondo, and André Téchiné and his film *Alice et Martin* (1998). Notably, in an interview with Antoine Idier from 2019, Taïa speaks explicitly of French actress Isabelle Adjani who "saves him" each time he watches her on the screen.[88] And so if we look now at Taïa's oeuvre, we see maneuvers on his part to mythologize and memorialize this French actress of Algerian descent in dominant ways that position her as part of a national cinematic tradition. At the same time, however, he will turn to counter-images of Adjani that "save him" and these are largely through forms of transgression and *transfiliation*.

One of Taïa's first mentions of Adjani is in *L'armée du salut* when Abdellah is traveling to Ouarzazate with his lover Jean and they are watching the César award ceremony on the television in their hotel room. He is happy to share his admiration for Adjani with Jean where he builds her up in a way that reifies her reputation in France and around the globe: "il m'écoutait racontant mes rêves de films, de stars, parlant encore et encore de celle que j'aimais le plus, Isabelle Adjani, de sa beauté, de son talent, de ses origines, de ses films. À Ouarzazate, le printemps déjà là pour nous envelopper et nous rafraîchir, Isabelle Adjani nous accompagnait" [he listened to me recounting my dreams of films, of stars, talking again and again about the one I loved the most, Isabelle Adjani, of her beauty, of her talent, of her origins, of her films. In Ouarzazate, spring already there to envelop and refresh us, Isabelle Adjani accompanied us].[89] What's interesting in this passage is that while Taïa describes Adjani as a dominant figure of French cinema, he ties her to nature, much like he does with the female figures of his homeland, including M'Barka.

It is not until much later on in Taïa's oeuvre, and much later into his Parisian life, where we see him finally write a longer entry about Adjani and where his reality of the French capital now strongly clashes with the image he had of Paris from literature and cinema. Consequently, Taïa will make new use of Adjani in his myth and memory making to find new ways of being and belonging. In *Un pays pour mourir* [*A Country for Dying*] (2015)—a series of stories that intertwines the lives of Zahira, a Moroccan prostitute, her friend Aziz-Zanouba, an Algerian transexual, and Mojtaba, a gay Iranian revolutionary, Taïa devotes a section of one chapter to Adjani. Given the healing effect Adjani supposedly has on Taïa, it is a little surprising how he has not devoted much attention to her in his writing before this novel. Nevertheless, if we examine the plights of these immigrant outsiders to Paris in *Un pays pour mourir*, we realize that Adjani can provide him and his characters with new forms of transformative strength and transfilial belonging. In this chapter of *Un pays pour mourir*, Taïa constructs an internal conversation between Aziz—an Algerian man who decides to change sexes—and Zanouba who is

Aziz after transitioning from male to female. In this conversation between Zanouba and her former self Aziz, Taïa reappropriates Adjani as a North African figure. Zanouba says to Aziz: "Elle est algérienne. Comme toi et moi." [She is Algerian. Like you and me].[90] As we know however, Adjani is French born to an Algerian father and a German mother. This is similar to the way Taïa flexibly accumulates and disidentifies with Bruce Lee's body in his chapter "Bread and Tea" in order to engender his hero with out-of-this-world qualities. Hence, Taïa proceeds to mythologize Adjani as having superhuman strength that comes from above the Earth. As Zanouba-Aziz admits, Adjani embodies both man and woman, she represents the future, and she speaks all languages. The trans protagonist believes that Adjani is not a goddess, but a spark associated with the Big Bang itself: "Elle n'est pas une déesse. Elle est l'étincelle" [She is not a goddess. She is the spark].[91] The protagonist speaks to her former male self about the actress and reminds him that Adjani's film *L'Histoire d'Adèle H* [*The Story of Adele H*] (1975) transformed them both. In fact, at the beginning of the film, Adjani's character speaks of crossing the Ocean in a flash and walking on water and indeed, these superhuman or divine skills and ways of seeing the world stick with Zanouba-Aziz to the point where she "invents and reinvents" the words of the female star.[92] Zanouba goes on to explain to Aziz that with their sister Zahira (mentioned above), they would spend evenings in "ceremony" lighting candles and watching the actress speak English in the film *Possession* (1981) in order to sanctify her. Zanouba-Aziz and Zahira would replay the film over and over until they would enter into the film with Adjani and would all be on the same level of sanctity: "nous entrons dans la transe éternelle" [we enter into the eternal trance].[93]

This transformative and transfilial story is part of a larger chapter entitled "Paris, août 2010" [Paris, August 2010] where the protagonists have already long been under the impression that Paris was not the city they had originally imagined it to be and calling it "un trou noir" [a black hole]. Zanouba begs her former self Aziz—imagined as a young boy who dances and sings—to stay with her because "Paris est devenu froid, sourd, triste, insensible. Raciste. Paris va me tuer" [Paris has become cold, deaf, sad, insensitive. Racist. Paris is going to kill me].[94] The trans protagonist Zanouba attempts to transcend the city and calls on her former self Aziz and the free- and other-spirited Adjani to help her do so. In order for this image to work, Taïa must simultaneously mythologize Adjani as one of their own (North African) and also of another world in order to help him and his trans characters transition to another place and time. In the same way he draws on the language of Hadda in her migratory tale in *Le jour du Roi*, he galvanizes here the flexible accumulation of language associated with the trans body in order to help communicate his and his characters sense of "double displacement"[95] from both their homeland and adopted country. In sum then, as we see in this section, Taïa memorializes certain scandalous French saintly and celestial bodies like Genet and Adjani in order to ground him through transgressive filiation at a moment when he faces isolation and alienation in his own attempt at integration in the French quotidian.

Transnational and Transfilial Myth and Memory: Divine American Orphans and Black Brothers

Up to this point, we have seen the myths and realms of memory from Morocco and France that constitute parts of Taïa's reimagined "pantheon." In this last section, we will finally see how Taïa creates other significant cultural myths and realms of memory beyond those related to France and the larger Francosphere. After the terrorist attacks associated with Charlie-Hebdo and the Bataclan in France in 2015, Taïa writes an op-ed piece for the *New York Times* asking where in the world he and others can go next to live and feel safe.[96] In my previous work, I have argued that at that moment "Taïa turns away from 'Global Genet' and from global Islam in order to embrace another global cinematic figure, Marilyn Monroe."[97] Moreover, "the fact Taïa waits until much later in his exile in France to begin writing about Monroe suggests that he has somewhat abandoned the symbolic capital of canonical queer French authors like Genet in order to evoke other models of *transfiliation* and martyrdom."[98] We certainly see elements of this in Taïa's later writings including in *Infidèles* (2012), *Celui qui est digne d'être aimé* [*The One Worthy of Love*] (2017), and beyond. For example, from the moment Taïa decides his protagonist Ahmed should "come out of the French language and out of his French lovers" like Emmanuel,[99] his references to a dominant Parisian landscape subside significantly as do his need to memorialize and mythologize dominant figures and sites associated with it. Ahmed writes in a letter to his French lover: "Je t'écris et j'ose enfin passer à l'acte: sortir d'une langue qui me colonise et m'éloigne d'Ahmed à 17 ans." [I write to you and I dare finally to commit the act: come out of a language that colonizes me and distances me from Ahmed [myself] at seventeen years old].[100] Indeed, the more Taïa feels disillusioned with a reified identity and place of belonging in France, the more he turns to transnational myths and memory as well as new forms of language to achieve this. We have seen this in the previous sections related to trans characters who turn to Isabelle Adjani as an "out of this world source."[101] This is also where we can draw a parallel between his French and transnational (American) references that embody new ways of being in the world: Adjani, to whom he devotes a short section of one novel, *Un pays pours mourir* (2015), and Marilyn Monroe, to whom he devotes an entire novel, *Infidèles* (2012).

In *Infidèles*, Taïa relies on the classic American film *Rivière sans retour* [*River of No Return*] (1954) to structure his tale and populate it with recognizable characters that resemble director Otto Preminger's original story involving Kay, Matt, and Mark played respectively on the silver screen by Marilyn Monroe, Robert Mitchum, and Tommy Rettig. Just as Taïa relies on strong female characters including his mother M'Barka in his homeland to create new revolutionary myths on the local Moroccan level, he also turns to transgressive and revolutionary female and queer figures on a global scale to craft new myths and sites of memory.[102] Taïa populates *Infidèles* with Slima, a prostitute mother, who migrates and conducts sex work alongside her son Jallal, as they flee Morocco and look for other places to live both in Egypt and further afield. Slima and Jallal both idolize Marilyn Monroe because the mother teaches her son from a very early age to love Marilyn like a saint, in the same way Abdellah learns to love Sidi Jenih-Genet in *Le rouge du tarbouche*. In parallel to Marilyn's role as Kay in *River of No Return* who bonds with rancher Matt and his son Mark, Slima and Jallal will form a familial tie with a Moroccan soldier who becomes Slima's longtime lover and Jallal's imagined father figure.

At the very beginning of part II of the novel, "Par Amour," [For Love], Taïa constructs a debate among the Egyptian hairdresser and the female clients in the beauty shop about the importance of female stars from the Arab world. Slima refuses however to agree with the hairdresser about the Moroccan singer Samira Said who left for Egypt or admit any admiration for her or other Egyptian stars. Instead, she bravely declares her admiration for Marilyn Monroe and asks the hairdresser to color her hair blond in homage to the American actress. The hairdresser will also try to drag Jallal into the debate but Slima interrupts and speaks on his behalf since he is only ten or so years old at this point. In terms of memory and forgetting Slima states: "Mon fils est à moi. Il aime ce que j'aime. Il est ma mémoire et mon oubli. Il aimera ce que je lui dirai d'aimer. Il sera ce qui je lui dirai d'être." [My son belongs to me. He likes what I like. He is my memory and my forgetting. He will like what I tell him to like. He will be what I tell him to be].[103] Slima says that the reason they fled from Morocco to Egypt was to start again, to have a second life, and to be reborn. Cairo offers a clean slate in a present that remains largely untied to the past for those of an Arab diaspora who choose it.[104] By relying on the wanderings of Monroe as character Kay, Taïa finds additional linguistic elements related to migratory practices with which to write his own tale. Jallal compares his mother through analogy to Marilyn and hence he then ties himself to Marilyn as her son through this association and imagined transfiliation. New memory making then can begin from scratch in Cairo for both mother and son and Marilyn provides this form of transfilial *tabula rasa*.

In *Infidèles*, Slima will remain largely mistreated and marginalized by many of the other men she encounters and Jallal ultimately avenges his mother's death through a suicide bombing with his lover Matthias (Mahmoud). He writes: "Régler enfin mes comptes avec ce monde qui, dès le départ, ne m'avait rien donné et qui, en plus, m'avait pris ma mère, ma Slima" [To even the score with this world, that, from the outset, had given me nothing and that, also, had taken my mother, my Slima].[105] The two men choose to do this in an abandoned movie house and Taïa writes: "Une salle de cinéma abandonnée nous a sauvés. C'est moi qui l'ai repérée. Elle ressemblait exactement à celle de mon enfance, à Salé. Cinéma An-Nasr. Cinéma de la Victoire." [An abandoned movie theater saved us. I was the one who found it. It resembled exactly the one of my childhood, in Salé. Cinema An-Nasr. Cinema of the Victory].[106] Upon blowing themselves up, the two men are greeted at the gates of heaven by Marilyn Monroe, who much like Isabelle Adjani, is a celestial figure that is "out of this world" that saves Taïa. Marilyn, who works at la Porte du Ciel [the Gates of Heaven], states: "Je suis humain. Extraterrestre. Partout. Nulle part. Homme. Femme. Ni l'un ni l'autre. Au-delà de toutes les frontières. Toutes les langues. Vous voyez, je suis comme vous. Dans le malheur puissance. Divine et orpheline. [I am human. Extraterrestrial. Everywhere. Nowhere. Man. Woman. Neither one nor the other. Above all borders. All languages. You see, I am like you. In the malevolent power. Divine and orphan].[107] Similar to Adjani, Monroe serves as a saintly figure who allows Taïa and his characters a myth and site of memory making through which he can craft new forms of being and belonging. Jallal is both his mother's memory and forgetting, and he ultimately helps commemorate his mother's life through a final chapter with the saintly reference to her own transgressive idol. Taïa also transforms heaven into a transgressive space that is welcoming to all different kinds of bodies and this is similar to the way he imagines the role of cinema and Marilyn's resurrection on the screen in *River of No Return* each time he watches the old film again and again on television. Taïa writes: "La résurrection n'est pas une fiction. Le cinéma le démontre. Marilyn Monroe en est convaincue. Ma mère et moi aussi." [Resurrection is not a fiction. Cinema shows this. Marilyn Monroe is convinced of it. My mother and I too].[108] Taïa punctuates his novel with the lyrics from a song "Trouble of the World" by Mahalia Jackson, known to some as the Queen of Gospel.[109] This is an example of language that flexibly accumulates an American divinity and orphan (Marilyn)—who transcends all borders and all languages—and the soundtrack from an American queen of gospel provides Taïa with new meaning that moves him beyond the confines of France and its colonial spaces. In order to achieve this, he and his characters must blow up signifying practices as they have existed within normative social confines. Transnational imagery thanks to cinema and other forms of media allow him to develop transfilial myth and sites of memory that move beyond national realms of myth and memory making. As he concludes: "Le cinéma montrer (sic.) sa véritable puissance. L'impossible deviendra le possible." [The cinema will show its true power. The impossible will become possible].[110]

As I mentioned above, after the attacks in Paris, Taïa asks himself "where do we belong?" and turns his attention more and more to non-French metropolitan references including Marilyn Monroe and others. Indeed, this leads to his sense of frustration whereby he continues to reach even further into other transnational realms and he desires to become more connected intersectionally to other groups. As we have seen, Taïa constructs a transnational and transfilial network of intellectual fathers and brothers even from his earliest novels. However, it has become clear, this transfilially accumulated belonging fall shorts in many respects when trying to find ways to belong in relation to dominant French references. In our final example, Taïa's transnational referencing turns yet again to another American figure but this time it's not a cinematic star of martyrdom but a "scandalous" literary figure. In his letter, "Lettre à James Baldwin 20 juin 2020" [Letter to James Baldwin 20 June 2020], Taïa addresses James Baldwin as "un frère pour nous" [a brother for us] and he proceeds to build a site of memory and counter-memory through this African American literary force.[111] Indeed Baldwin was already creating a new form of belonging and filiation and Taïa is relying on Baldwin's own use of language and counter memory for his new site of memory making. This is essential for Taïa and his readers of the twenty-first century, and especially, I would argue in the context of spring and summer of 2020 with the Black Lives Matter moment that went global following the death of George Floyd on May 25, 2020.

In the first part of the letter, Taïa concentrates on memorializing James Baldwin, first by resurrecting him, like he has done with other maternal and paternal figures in his oeuvre. Taïa writes:

> Tu n'es pas mort. Non. Tu es toujours avec nous dans ce monde qui n'en finit pas de s'enfoncer dans le déni et les mensonges. Ta voix, tes mots et ton regard nous sont plus que jamais nécessaires, absolument indispensables pour oser continuer la révolte, la révolution, sortir du regard colonial et postcolonial.
>
> [You are not dead. No. You are always with us in this world which does not stop sinking into denial and lies. Your voice, your words, and your look are more necessary than ever to us, absolutely indispensable in order to dare to continue the revolt, the revolution, to come out of the colonial and postcolonial gaze.] [112]

In this excerpt, Taïa addresses Baldwin informally with "tu" [you] like a brother and speaks to him in the present tense to remind him that he is still among us. In comparison to the letter "Chaouche" that Taïa writes to his nephew Adnane where he resurrects his father but is unable to speak directly to the father, Taïa boldly engages in direct conversation here with the African American writer whose way of seeing and whose words and writings remain essential to our understanding of the difficulties in the contemporary context related to racism. For Taïa, Baldwin will help us to "come out" of the colonial and postcolonial and this is largely because of his intersectional view as both a Black man and a queer. Taïa continues:

> Tu es un frère pour nous. Mon grand frère James à moi. C'est ce que je ressens pour toi, depuis si longtemps déjà. Et, même si je ne suis pas noir, j'ai l'impression que tu as écrit ta lettre "La prochaine fois, le feu" pour quelqu'un comme moi, un Arabe homosexuel dans la France du 21ème siècle. Je lis tes mots, je les enregistre en moi, j'entre avec toi dans ta radicalité, au passé comme au présent, et je veux propager moi aussi ton message autour de moi, avec mes neveux, mes nièces, mes amis, ceux que je ne connais pas, ceux que je croise dans les rues de Paris et que je reconnais immédiatement comme des frères, comme des sœurs.
>
> [You are a brother for us. My big brother James, mine. That's what I feel for you, for so long already. And, even if I am not black, I have the impression that you wrote your letter "The Fire Next Time" for someone like me, an Arab homosexual in France of the 21st century. I read your words, I record them in me, I enter with you into your radicality, in the past as in the present, I too want to spread too your message around me, with my nephews, my nieces, my friends, those whom I do not know, those whom I cross in the streets of Paris and whom I recognize immediately as brothers, as sisters.][113]

In this excerpt, Taïa claims James as his own brother and wishes to adopt his words and cause. His mention of "in the past as in the present" reminds the reader that this is an exercise in memory making, in that the author ties himself to the important work of the past written by Baldwin and situates himself as part of the same genealogy of radicalism of the present in order to transmit it to his brothers, sisters, nieces, and nephews, known and unknown but immediately recognizable on the street. Similar to how we have seen other disruptive figures throughout this chapter—through Choukri, Hadda, Genet, Adjani, and Monroe—James Baldwin is now at the core of Taïa's project and part of this line of transgressive revolutionary bodies. Each figure, in their own way, helps Taïa rewrite the myths and memories of the postcolonial queer migratory subject.

Next, Taïa turns from an exercise of resurrection to a full-on endorsement of Baldwin's radicality, which will help Taïa construct a new cultural myth and realm of (counter) memory for him, Baldwin, and his like-minded readers. He continues:

> Et puis, comme un petit miracle, je me souviens de tes livres, de tes actions. De ton cri. De comment tu as utilisé la littérature pour dénoncer le racisme envers les Noirs, la littérature pour dire les maux et les espoirs. La littérature pour dire le désenchantement et le dégoût. La littérature pour dire aux Blancs la Vérité sur ce qu'ils ont fait puisqu'ils persistent à nier l'évidence. Dire aux Blancs ce qu'ils font semblant d'ignorer sur eux-mêmes. Oui, c'est cela. Malgré la cruauté et l'indifférence, être dans cette générosité-là: révéler aux Blancs les désastres qu'ils ont infligés à ce monde, à cette Terre.
>
> [And then, like a small miracle, I remember your books, your actions. Your scream. How you used literature to denounce racism toward Blacks, literature to utter those ills and those hopes. Literature to utter disenchantment and disgust. Literature to utter to the Whites the Truth about what they have done since they continue to deny the evidence. To tell the Whites what they pretend to ignore about themselves. Yes, that's right. Despite the cruelty and indifference, to be in that generosity: reveal to the Whites the disasters they inflicted on the world, on this Earth.] [114]

Like Genet, and the other saintly and celestial figures mentioned in this chapter, Baldwin represents another miracle for Taïa, and like M'Barka's screams, Baldwin's screams will galvanize Taïa's own urgent message. He calls on Baldwin in the excerpt above to help him to read the "harmless" culture of the Whites differently, as Achille, Forsdick, and Moudileno have urged us all to do in relation to the everyday. Taïa indexes Baldwin's writing as a site of memory for Blacks and other marginal communities and as a place where they can find a critique of the dominant cultural myths of the United States and France related to slavery, colonialism, and race. Still, Taïa goes one step further to engage an intersectional approach that attempts to unite all of his readers in non-dominant readings of the White western culture we live in. Taïa describes it as: "L'intersectionnalité des combats des minorités, de toutes les minorités." [Intersectionality of the battle of minorities, all of the minorities].[115] By mythologizing and memorializing Baldwin as a transnational and transgressive literary figure, Taïa succeeds in his own project of transfilial memory making for all willing world citizens of the twenty-first century.

Taïa also references directly several of Baldwin's writings including *La prochaine fois, le feu* [*The Fire Next Time*] (1963) and *Giovanni's Room* (1956), as well as the documentary on his life *I am not your negro* (2016).[116] He underscores again how the past and the present are linked in his version of memory making for Baldwin: "'L'histoire n'est pas le passé, c'est le présent. Nous portons notre histoire avec nous. Nous sommes notre histoire. Si nous prétendons le contraire, nous sommes littéralement des criminels,' tu écris dans ton livre 'I am not your negro.'" ["History is not the past, it's the present. We carry our history with us. We are our history. If we pretend the opposite, we are literally criminals" you write in your book "I am not your negro"].[117] He also draws Paris into this site of memory associated with Baldwin when he writes:

> Il y a quelques mois. Dans un café de Belleville fréquenté principalement par des vieux Maghrébins usés par le parcours de combattants d'émigrés, exploités par la France d'hier, rejetés par la France d'aujourd'hui. Ton nom a soudain été prononcé par le patron, un homme d'origine algérienne. Il a dit à un de ses clients: "Mon père m'a dit que l'écrivain James Baldwin venait dans ce café, très régulièrement, dans les années 50. Il vivait ici avec nous."
>
> [A few months ago. In a café in Belleville frequented mainly by old Maghrebi folks worn out by the path of *emigré* combatants, exploited by France of yesterday, rejected by France of today. Your name has suddenly been pronounced by the owner, a man of Algerian descent. He said to one of his customers: "My father told me that the writer James Baldwin came to this café, very regularly, in the 50s. He lived here with us."] [118]

In this excerpt, he takes the Paris neighborhood of Belleville known today as a home to several of France's immigrant communities and he re-memorializes it as site of transnational civil rights movements where Baldwin becomes one of its important (elder/paternal) members living alongside the North African *immigrés* [immigrants] in France in the 1950s.[119] Similarly, Taïa concludes his letter with: "Les combats que tu as initiés sont plus que jamais d'actualité. Nous voyons enfin une lueur d'espoir." [The battles that you started are more than ever timely issues. We finally see a glimpse of hope].[120] Indeed, it is in his act of letter writing that Taïa both re-ignites the memory of Baldwin and mythologizes him and re-memorializes him today for an entire new generation of queers, queers of color, and other marginal community members across the globe who are looking for new forms of language and intersectional models of belonging in the world. As we know, Taïa will also increasingly turn his attention to immigrant populations of Belleville and to the banlieues whom he has long ignored but with whom he has many things in common, especially in trying to re-read the quotidian and all of its colonial blind spots.[121]

For example, in *La vie lente* [*The Slow Life*] (2019), the protagonist Mounir dialogues about belonging with a statue of Turenne Enfant—the historical "patron saint" of this neighborhood—and juxtaposes that neighborhood (the Marais) to the banlieue where he plans to go next.[122] In sum, then, Taïa's original path to Paris to become a French intellectual, writer and director has led him perhaps to a set of more scandalous and transfilial myths and sites of memory that have helped him to find more authentic ways of belonging and connecting in his imagining of a queer migratory world. These queer and *transfilial* bodies provide him a set of flexible linguistics tools and signifying practices that allow him to move beyond the many "troubles of the world."

CONCLUSION

> Tu veux des noms de ces tribus bien françaises? Louis Vuitton. Hermès. Dior. Chanel. Le Louvre. L'École normale supérieure où enseignent mes zozos Jean-Jacques et Pierre. Le Panthéon où ils aiment aller se prosterner devant les Grands. Et après ils osent nous dire qu'ils sont contre l'esclavage, que Dieu n'existe pas ou je ne sais quoi d'autre comme conneries.
>
> Bon. J'arrête là. Je suis en train de faire comme eux. J'analyse trop. Je cite des noms. Des références. Je fais dans les théories. Ce n'est pas moi, ça. Revenons à ma bite. C'est mieux.
>
> [Do you want the names of these really French tribes? Louis Vuitton. Hermès. Dior. Chanel. The Louvre. L'École normale supérieure where my lovies Jean-Jacques and Pierre teach. The Pantheon where they like to go bow in front of the Grand ones. And afterwards, they dare to tell us that they are against slavery, that God doesn't exist or I don't know what other bullshit.
>
> Well. I'll stop there. I'm now behaving like them. I analyze too much. I cite names. References. I do it in the name of theory. That's not me. Let's get back to my cock. It's better.] [123]

While French-speaking queers of color may be drawn to the French Republic and the associated cultural signifiers and realms of memory they first discovered through films and books, individuals like Taïa will either tear down its dominant Paris-based Panthéon or decolonize many of its signifiers, thereby proposing new queer and non-white models of belonging in the postcolonial Francophone (Moroccan), the French, and the transnational contexts because of their own sense of disconnection or disidentification. While Taïa is not a French postcolonial subject creating new cultural myths or realms of memory in the Hexagon, he does assemble from a distance to the French metropole and then from up close from a disillusioned existence in the Hexagon a different set of signifiers that are not necessarily always and already linked to colonial memory. In contrast then to the myths that Achille and Moudileno examine in *Mythologies postcoloniales* that emerge in specifically French contexts of the Hexagon and the departments and territories of the *Outre-Mer*—where a tension exists between the two poles of mythmaking—"de l'occultation d'une part, et de l'exploitation racialisante de l'autre" [the concealing on the one hand and the racializing exploitation on the other][124]—we see that Taïa moves beyond this binary and proposes new transfilial, scandalous, and unfaithful paths forward to a more understanding space of belonging for queers of color in the Francosphère and beyond. Indeed, Taïa's work involves global iconography and transfilial signifiers largely due to a queer migration that ushers in new forms of queer and neoliberal belonging but also because of issues of isolation, unrealized dreams and cruel optimism, and impossible citizenship that queers of color must face in the French metropole.

Like Léopold Senghor who wrote that he wanted to tear down all Banania smiles on all the walls of France,[125] Taïa has attempted to take down many of the established French realms of memory and to give new space and voice to Francophone queers of color in an unwelcoming Hexagon. As we see in the quote above, a turn away from this French-based Pantheon—Vuitton, Hermès, Dior, Chanel, The Louvre, and L'école normale supréri-eur—also requires us to turn to the "trans-" in its broadest sense. Susan Stryker, Paisley Currah and Lisa Jean Moore make the important distinction between the "implied nominalism of 'trans' and the explicit relationality of 'trans-' with a hyphen, which remains open-ended and resists premature foreclosure by attachment to any single suffix."[126] In proposing that scholars learn to "trans" the world and bodies in it the way queer studies and gender studies helped us to "queer" those entities, they argue that we come to new understandings of "embodied difference."[127] These scholars also contend that "trans-" can suggest many different processes that include but are not limited to the following: transformation, transcontinental, transatlantic, transversal, transgressive, translation, and transdisciplinary.[128] In the quote above from Taïa, we see how Aziz, the Algerian male who will become a trans MTF character, Zanouba-Aziz, speaks to Zahira about the sites where they do not belong in France and urges Zahira to return to a discussion of Aziz's "bite" [cock] in order to think differently about belonging because tomorrow he will have his penis removed through sex reassignment surgery. As he states: "Demain je la coupe" [Tomorrow, I'll cut it off"].[129] Hence, like Senghor who tears down the smiles, Taïa, through this trans character Aziz-Zanouba will tear down "ce territoire maudit des hommes" [this cursed territory of men][130] and other forms of normative citizenship in order to find new myths, sites of memory and new forms of belonging in the world.[131] Aziz, with the help of his Swedish (i.e., non-French) doctor Johansson, will replace this site of memory, his penis, with "une ouverture" [an opening].[132]

As we have seen throughout this chapter, Taia's flexible accumulation of language and *transfiliation* rely on new forms of expression in order to make their queer diasporic voices heard in authentic ways. Openings to new ways of being in the world have replaced the former and otherwise color-blind French and Francophone references, but also those references that have kept queers of color in a cage full of other binaries that include but are not limited to issues of gender and sexuality. Arguably, each of the myths and memory we have seen in this chapter, from Choukri and Hadda, to Genet and Adjani, and then Monroe and Baldwin, are not only scandalous transfilial bodies but they are all "trans-bodies" as defined by Stryker, Currah, and Moore. Disloyal bodies that cross boundaries, that transgress, and that seek new communities and ways of being in the world. I do believe that scholarship on postcolonial bodies and postcolonial queer bodies in particular, when coupled with work on myth and memory making, must incorporate the important tools of *trans-filiation* and the flexible accumulation of language, in order to think through and with queer bodies of color and to move us beyond the confines of France and its former colonies. Hopefully, this chapter also has begun to provide a road map for future research on Taïa and in French and Francophone studies related to the scholarship on language and sexuality and the growing field of trans linguistics where "trans practices and subjectivities" are not a rare exception but "central to any understanding of gender,"[133] sexuality, diaspora and migration, among many other intersecting categories.

NOTES

1. I would like to thank Siham Bouamer, Jean-Pierre Boulé, Ralph Heyndels, Daniel Maroun, William Leap, and David Peterson for their critical feedback on an earlier draft of this chapter.

2. Abdellah Taïa, *Mon Maroc* (Biarritz: Séguier, 2000), 65. All translations are my own.

3. Taïa, *Mon Maroc*, 65.

4. Taïa, *Mon Maroc*, 63.

5. It's worth noting that some of the more masculine or macho boys never stayed for the Indian films.

6. Benedict Anderson, *Imagined Communities: Reflections on the Origin and Spread of Nationalism* (New York: Verso, 1983).

7. Abdellah Taïa, originally published this essay on this now defunct link "L'homosexualité expliquée à ma mère." *telquel.com.* Tel Quel, Apr. 2009. Web.

Accessed June 10, 2015. www.telquel-online.com/archives/367/actu_maroc1_367.shtml. Republished at: www.asymptotejournal.com/nonfiction/abdellah-taia-homosexuality-explained-to-my-mother/french/.

8. It is also worth underscoring the association between the symbolism of "bread" and the Arab spring where protests in Europe included slogans related to "freedom" and "bread."

9. Abdellah Taïa, *Mon Maroc*, 66. I deliberately translate the French term "infidèle" as the English term "infidel"—instead of other alternatives—because this parallels the published English translation of Taïa's 2012 novel *Infidèles* as *Infidels*.

10. Abdellah's father was the source of books with his job at the Bibliothèque générale de Rabat (*Mon Maroc*, 13) while Abdellah's brother Abdelkébir largely informed him of the world of music, tv, movies and literature, largely through the French language (*L'armée du salut*, Paris: Seuil, 2006), 34.

11. Denis M. Provencher, *Queer Maghrebi French: Language, Temporalities, Transfiliations* (Liverpool: Liverpool UP, 2017).

12. Provencher, *Queer Maghrebi French*, 47.

13. See Etienne Achille and Lydie Moudileno, *Mythologies postcoloniales: Pour une décolonisation du quotidien* (Paris: Honoré Champion, 2018); and Etienne Achille, Charles Forsdick, and Lydie Moudileno, eds., *Postcolonial Realms of Memory: Sites and Symbols in Modern France* (Liverpool: Liverpool University Press, 2020).

14. Roland Barthes, "Le mythe, aujourd'hui," in *Mythologies* (Paris: Seuil, 1957), 191–247.

15. Ernest Renan, "Qu'est-ce qu'une nation?" 1882. Republished as "What is a nation?," trans. Martin Thom, *Nation and Narration*, edited by Homi Bhabha, 8–22 (New York: Routledge, 1990); Pierre Nora, ed., *Les Lieux de mémoire* (Paris: Gallimard, 1984–1992).

16. Siham Bouamer also points out how Zahira both loves Indian films and is another disruptive character. See Siham Bouamer, "De 'River of no Return' à 'Trouble of the World,': Parcours initiatique musical dans *Infidèles* (2012) d'Abdellah Taïa," *Expressions maghrébines* 19, no. 1 (2020): 107–124.

17. William L. Leap, "Language and Gendered Modernity," in Janet Holmes and Miriam Meyerhoff (eds.), *Handbook of Language and Gender* (Blackwell, 2003), 417. Leap draws on the work of Harvey (1989) and Ong (1999) to develop this notion. In an updated version of his argument, Leap ties flexible linguistic accumulation to disidentification and refusal. See Leap, "Language, Sexuality, History," in *The Oxford Handbook of Language and Sexuality*, edited by Kira Hall and Rusty Barrett, online (Oxford: Oxford University Press, 2020), DOI: 10.1093/oxfordhb/9780190212926.013.12.

18. See also Provencher, *Queer Maghrebi French*, 40–48.

19. Martin F. Manalansan, *Global Divas: Filipino Gay Men in the Diaspora* (Durham: Duke University Pres, 2003), 48.

20. Françoise Lionnet and Shu-mei Shih, eds., *Minor Transnationalism* (Durham: Duke University Press, 2005).

21. I am using the term "queer" throughout this essay as an admittedly awkward cover term to mean "non-conforming," "transgressive," "disidentifying," etc.

22. Astrid Erll also reminds us that "Travelling memory is a process that scholars can describe; but its outcomes cannot be predicted" (16). See Erll, "Travelling memory," *Parallax* 17, no. 4 (2011): 4–18. She continues: "much of the actual semantic shape that travelling memory takes on will be the result of the routes it takes in specific contexts and of the uses made by specific people with specific agendas" (15). Indeed, we see how traveling memory functions here much the same way as the flexible accumulation of language.

23. Following José Estaban Muñoz and other theorists, I am using the term "queers of color" to refer to queers of "non-white" origin and/or queers of immigrant descent. See José Esteban Muñoz, *Disidentifications: Queers of Color and the Performance of Politics* (Minneapolis: University of Minnesota Press, 1999).

24. Abdellah Taïa, *L'armée du salut*, 122.

25. Etienne Achille and Lydie Moudileno, *Mythologies postcoloniales,* 21.

26. Achille and Moudileno, *Mythologies postcoloniales*, 8, emphasis in the original.

27. Achille and Moudileno, *Mythologies postcoloniales*, 12.

28. Achille and Moudileno, *Mythologies postcoloniales*, 7.

29. Achille and Moudileno, *Mythologies postcoloniales*, 7–8.

30. Salim Ayoub talks about how Taïa remains in "an imaginary state of atopia" because he does not belong in either of the hegemonic narratives of Morocco or Europe. See Salim Ayoub, "Abdellah Taïa's Decolonial Trajectory Toward Unbelonging," in *Autour d'Abdellah Taïa: Poétique et politique du désir engagé / Around Abdellah Taïa: Poetics and Politics of Engaged Desire*, edited by Ralph Heyndels and Amine Zidouh (Caen: Editions Passage(s), 2020), 51.

31. Etienne Achille, Charles Forsdick, and Lydie Moudileno, eds., *Postcolonial Realms of Memory*, 1.

32. Achille, Forsdick, and Moudileno, eds., *Postcolonial Realms of Memory*, 1.

33. Achille, Forsdick, and Moudileno, eds., *Postcolonial Realms of Memory*, 4.

34. Achille, Forsdick, and Moudileno, eds., *Postcolonial Realms of Memory*, 5–6.

35. Achille, Forsdick, and Moudileno, eds., *Postcolonial Realms of Memory*, 9.

36. Achille, Forsdick, and Moudileno, eds., *Postcolonial Realms of Memory*, 9.

37. Achille, Forsdick, and Moudileno, eds., *Postcolonial Realms of Memory*, 9.

38. Achille, Forsdick, and Moudileno, eds., *Postcolonial Realms of Memory*, 9 and 14.

39. José Esteban Muñoz, *Disidentifications: Queers of Color and the Performance of Politics*.

40. Achille and Moudileno, *Mythologies postcoloniales*, 21.

41. See Siham Bouamer (in this volume) and Provencher, *Queer Maghrebi French*. For more on these concepts, please see Denis M. Provencher, "Transnational approaches to language and sexuality," in *Transnational French Studies,* edited by Charles Forsdick and Claire Launchbury (Liverpool: Liverpool University Press, forthcoming). In contrast to "les lieux de mémoire," for example, Erll draws on the work of such scholars as Appadurai and Clifford, including the latter's metaphor of "traveling culture," to propose the concept "les voyages ou les mouvements de mémoire" [the trips or the movements of memory] (11), which captures well

the experience of diasporic communities in particular who construct multi-faceted identities as they move through time and space. Other scholars on transnationalism have turned to a multitude of other theoretical concepts that have helped us to conceptualize these temporal-spatial negotiations. These include, for example, "deterritorialization" (Deleuze and Guattari 2009), "liquid modernity" (Bauman 2000), "creolization" (Glissant 1997) and "flexible citizenship"' (Ong 1999). Many of these scholars have recast the idea of "nation and narration" (Bhabha 1990) or an "imagined community" (Anderson 1983) through a transnational frame that now focuses more on "mobile subjectivity" or "multiple mobilities" (Sheller and Urry, 2006, 211–212).

42. It is worth noting here that Taia's collaboration with Frederic Mitterrand looks at French colonial photography (and myths or "mythographies") of Morocco and Taïa reflects on both the colonial gaze and his own relationship to the French colonial "mythographical" past of Morocco. See Abdellah Taïa, and Frédéric Mitterrand, *Maroc, 1900-1960, un certain regard* (Arles/Paris: Actes Sud, 2007).

43. Provencher, *Queer Maghrebi French*, 156; Taia, "L'homosexualité expliquée à ma mère," *telquel.com*. Tel Quel, Apr. 2009. Web. Accessed June 10, 2015. www.telquel-online.com/archives/367/actu_maroc1_367.shtml. Republished at: www.asymptotejournal.com/nonfiction/abdellah-taia-homosexuality-explained-to-my-mother/french/.

44. Taïa, ed., *Lettres à un jeune marocain* (Paris: Seuil, 2009).

45. Provencher, *Queer Maghrebi French*, 170. In this volume, Boulé views these "recapturing and recovery" of the mother and father as part of a reparative process to heal past traumas. Indeed, Boulé and I are approaching similar phenomena from differing perspectives as I argue that not only are these reparative but they are also performative and therefore open up the protagonist, the author, and his readers to new queer possibilities.

46. Provencher, *Queer Maghrebi French*, 172.

47. "Un deuxième père," *Mon Maroc,* 93–97. And later on he explains that it was indeed his brother Abdelkébir who first introduced him to the work of Mohamed Choukri (*L'armée du salut*, 36).

48. See for example in *Mon Maroc,* "A la recherche de Paul Bowles," pp. 105–109; and "La baraka de Starobinksi," pp. 117–121.

49. In *L'armée du salut,* these include among other chapters, entries on his grandfather ("Mon grand-père," pp. 57–60) and M'Barka and her couscous ("Les couscous de M'Barka," pp. 123–125).

50. According to Ralph Heyndels, Taïa first discovers Choukri's *Le Pain nu* in its original Arabic and Darija version and he argues that this mix of languages is what initiates Taïa entry into a literary space. See Ralph Heyndels, Taïa, "'Je suis un Indigène de la République': L'atelier décolonial de l'écriture d'Abdellah Taïa," in *Autour d'Abdellah Taïa: Poétique et politique du désir engagé /Around Abdellah Taïa: Poetics and Politics of Engaged Desire*, edited by Ralph Heyndels and Amine Zidouh, (Caen: Editions Passage(s), 2020): 117–145.

51. Taïa, *Mon maroc*, 93.

52. Taïa, *Mon maroc*, 93.

53. Taïa, *Mon maroc*, 93.
54. Taïa, *Mon maroc*, 94.
55. Choukri, Mohammed, et al. *Des nouvelles du Maroc*, edited by Loïc Barrière (Paris: Paris-Méditerranée, 1999), 73–85. See also Ralph Heyndels, "La prostitution sur la scène de l'écriture chez Abdellah Taïa" *Reveue @nalyse* 11, no. 3 (2016): 9–23.
56. Taïa, *Mon maroc*, 96.
57. See also Abdellah Taïa, "Le roi est mort," in *Le rouge du tarbouche* (Biarritz: Séguier, 2004), 17–20.
58. See also Abdellah Taïa "Un cauchemar éternel," in *Le jour du Roi* (Paris: Seuil, 2010), 24.
59. Taïa, *Le jour du Roi*, 33–35, 51, 56.
60. Omar also adopts a paternal role in place of the father. There is also an exchange between the father and the sorcerer Bouhaydoura who tells the father flatly that he is wrong about the role of women in Moroccan culture. Hence Bouhaydoura assists Taïa in destroying national myths related to gender roles and empowering the author's depiction of women. For more on this topic, please see Daniel Maroun, "Comment échapper à la honte du *zamel*: Vers la construction de la masculinité maghrébine queer," *Revue @nalyse* 11, no. 3 (2016): 135–154.
61. Taïa, *Le jour du Roi*, 91.
62. Taïa, *Le jour du Roi*, 56.
63. Taïa, *Le jour du Roi*, 104.
64. Taïa, *Le jour du Roi*, 115–120. Instead of the Louvre being a site of (inter) national history, memory, and global conquest through its artistic holdings during the day, it becomes a place of imprisonment, abandonment, and death at night in *La vie lente* for protagonist Mounir whose lover Antoine ultimately dumps him. Taïa writes: "Tout est mort. Mort mort." [Everything is dead. Dead dead]. See *La vie lente* (Paris: Seuil, 2015), 193.
65. Taïa, *Le jour du Roi*, 192.
66. Taïa, *Le jour du Roi*, 195.
67. Taïa, *Le jour du Roi*, 199.
68. The fact that she is black is also important as the author wants to bring attention to the invisibility of black people in Morocco and to the racism to which they are subjected. See Jean-Pierre Boulé, *Abdellah Taïa: La mélancolie et le cri* (Lyon: Presses universitaires de Lyon, 2020), pp. 112–114, and especially note 21 on page 113. See also Hicham Mazouz, "Hadda, The Black Mother of Morocco: From the 'Origin' Myth to the Subaltern Abject Rewriting the Nation in Abdellah Taïa's *Le jour du Roi*," in *Autour d'Abdellah Taïa: Poétique et politique du désir engagé / Around Abdellah Taïa: Poetics and Politics of Engaged Desire*, edited by Ralph Heyndels and Amine Zidouh, 161–176. Caen: Editions Passage(s), 2020.
69. Abdellah Taïa, *Celui qui est digne d'être aimé* (Paris: Seuil, 2017), 98.
70. Taïa, *Le rouge du tarbouche*, 53, and Taïa, *Une mélancolie arabe* (Paris: Seuil, 2008), 136.
71. Taïa, *Le jour du Roi*, 85.
72. Taïa, *Celui qui est digne*, 118.

73. Taïa, *Le rouge du tarbouche*, 126.
74. Taïa, *Une mélancolie arabe*, 71.
75. Taïa, *L'armée du salut*, 95–97.
76. Taïa, *L'armée du salut*, 154.
77. Taïa includes discussions of other saints such as Sidi ben Acher, saint of fools, in his writings. See Abdellah Taïa, *Celui qui est digne*, 95.
78. For example, see "La Tombe de Genet" in Jean-Pierre Boulé, *Abdellah Taïa: La mélancolie et le cri*, 179–190. See also Abdellah Taïa, "Genet, Abdallah et moi" in *Les Passions de Jean Genet: Esthétique, Poétique, et Politique du désir,* edited by Ralph Heyndels (Paris: Alain Baudry & Cie., 2010), 11–15; Abdellah Taïa, "Jean Genet et les hommes arabes," in *Archives des mouvements LBGTQ+*, edited by Antoine Idier (Paris: Textuel, 2018), 70–71; and Abdellah Taïa, "Où es-tu. Abdallah? *Europe*, forthcoming.
79. Taïa, *Le rouge du tarbouche*, 45–52.
80. Provencher, *Queer Maghrebi French*, 4–5.
81. Provencher, *Queer Maghrebi French,* 3.
82. Mireille Rosello, *France and the Maghreb: Performative Encounters* (Gainesville: UP of Florida, 2005), 129.
83. Rosello, *France and the Maghreb*, 139.
84. Provencher, *Queer Maghrebi French*, 6. Indeed, Genet has also been the topic of a "distancing" by Taïa, which is already visible implicitly in his introduction to *Jean Genet, un saint marocain,* and more explicitly in *Celui qui est digne* and in his forthcoming "Où es-tu. Abdallah? in *Europe*.
85. Taïa, *Une mélancolie arabe*, 51.
86. See Taïa, "Voyeur à la rue de Clignancourt," in *Le rouge de tarbouche,* 61–66.
87. Taïa, *Le rouge du tarbouche*, 24–29.
88. "Exister aujourd'hui: Abdellah Taïa en conversation avec Antoine Idier" in *Autour d'Abdellah Taïa: Poétique et politique du désir engagé /Around Abdellah Taïa: Poetics and Politics of Engaged Desire*, edited by Ralph Heyndels and Amine Zidouh (Caen: Editions Passage(s), 2020), 20.
89. Taïa, *L'armée du salut*, 134–135.
90. Taïa, *Un pays pour mourir* (Paris: Seuil, 2015), 87–95.
91. Taïa, *Un pays pour mourir,* 89.
92. Taïa, *Un pays pour mourir*, 90.
93. Taïa, *Un pays pour mourir*, 94.
94. Taïa, *Un pays pour mourir*, 95.
95. Salim Ayoub, "Abdellah Taïa's Decolonial Trajectory Toward Unbelonging," in *Autour d'Abdellah Taïa: Poétique et politique du désir engagé /Around Abdellah Taïa: Poetics and Politics of Engaged Desire*, edited by Ralph Heyndels and Amine Zidouh (Caen: Editions Passage(s), 2020), 41.
96. Abdellah Taïa, "Is Any Place Safe?" *New York Times* 18 Nov. 2015.
97. Provencher, *Queer Maghrebi French,* 154.
98. Provencher, *Queer Maghrebi French,* 154.
99. Taïa, *Celui qui est digne*, 81.

100. Taïa, *Celui qui est digne*, 98. Similarly, in an interview with Idier, Taïa states: "Je suis sorti de la période des illusions sur la France" [I've come out of the period of illusions about France] ("Exister aujourd'hui," 19).

101. Taïa, *Un pays pour mourir*, his character Aziz, 34.

102. For more on transgressive filiations in *Infidèles*, see Siham Bouamer, "De 'River of no Return' à 'Trouble of the World,': Parcours initiatique musical dans *Infidèles* (2012) d'Abdellah Taïa."

103. Abdellah Taïa, *Infidèles* (Paris: Seuil, 2012), 83.

104. Taïa, *Infidèles*, 84.

105. Taïa, *Infidèles*, 138–139.

106. Taïa, *Infidèles*, 171.

107. Taïa, *Infidèles*, 186–187.

108. Taïa, *Infidèles*, 74.

109. Taïa, *Infidèles*, 187–188.

110. Taïa, *Infidèles*, 74. I would also like to refer the reader to Boulé's poignant analysis of Taïa's unpublished work on Barbara Stanwick where this star serves a similar transformative function for the author. See Boulé, *Abdellah Taïa: La mélancolie et le cri*, pp. 172–173 and 355–359.

111. Abdellah Taïa, "Lettre à James Baldwin 20 juin 2020," in *Autour d'Abdellah Taïa: Poétique et politique du désir engagé /Around Abdellah Taïa: Poetics and Politics of Engaged Desire*, edited by Ralph Heyndels and Amine Zidouh (Caen: Editions Passage(s), 2020), 9. This letter was originally written for the radio as indicated on page one of the letter, "Lue à la Radio Télévision belge de langue française, RTBF).

112. Taïa, "Lettre à James Baldwin 20 juin 2020," 9.

113. Taïa, "Lettre à James Baldwin 20 juin 2020," 9.

114. Taïa, "Lettre à James Baldwin 20 juin 2020," 10.

115. Taïa, "Lettre à James Baldwin 20 juin 2020," 11.

116. Taïa, "Lettre à James Baldwin 20 juin 2020," 9–10.

117. Taïa, "Lettre à James Baldwin 20 juin 2020," 10.

118. Taïa, "Lettre à James Baldwin 20 juin 2020," 11.

119. Taïa resides (again) in this neighborhood, after a brief stay in the bourgeois avenue de Turenne. The decision to make this neighborhood his "home," where Baldwin appears, adds to the depth of signification associated with this quarter in Taïa's letter.

120. Taïa, "Lettre à James Baldwin 20 juin 2020," 11.

121. Taïa, *La vie lente*, 70 and onward. See also Taïa, *Celui qui est digne*, 107. See also Heyndels this volume where he addresses this shift out of Paris; he also importantly notes that the word "banlieue" appears for the first time in Taïa's oeuvre in *Celui qui est digne*.

122. Taïa, *La vie lente*, 95–126. He wants to leave behind his life on Turenne and go into the banlieue. See pages 70–81.

123. Taïa, *Un pays pour mourir*, 40.

124. Achille and Moudileno, *Mythologies postcoloniales*, 21.

125. Léopold Sédar Senghor, "Poème liminaire" in *Hosties noires* (1948), *Œuvre poétique* (Paris: Seuil, 1990), 55–56.

126. Susan Stryker, Paisley Currah, and Lisa Jean Moore, "Introduction: Trans-, Trans, or Transgender?," *WSQ: Women's Studies Quarterly* 36, no. 3–4 (2008): 11.

127. Stryker, Currah, and Moore, "Introduction: Trans-, Trans, or Transgender?," 14.

128. Stryker, Currah, and Moore, "Introduction: Trans-, Trans, or Transgender?," 18–20.

129. Taïa, *Un pays pour mourir*, 33.

130. Taïa, *Un pays pour mourir*, 34.

131. Stryker, Currah, andMoore, "Introduction: Trans-, Trans, or Transgender?" 11.

132. Taïa, *Un pays pour mourir*, 33.

133. Lal Zimman, "Transgender Language, Transgender Moment: Toward a Trans Linguistics," in *The Oxford Handbook of Language and Sexuality*, edited by Kira Hall and Rusty Barrett, online (Oxford UP, 2020). DOI: 10.1093/oxfordhb/9780190212926.013.4.

BIBLIOGRAPHY

Achille, Etienne, Charles Forsdick, and Lydie Moudileno, eds. *Postcolonial Realms of Memory: Sites and Symbols in Modern France*. Liverpool: Liverpool University Press, 2020.

Achille, Etienne, and Lydie Moudileno. *Mythologies postcoloniales: Pour une décolonisation du quotidien*. Paris: Honoré Champion, 2018.

Anderson, Benedict. *Imagined Communities: Reflections on the Origin and Spread of Nationalism*. New York: Verso, 1983.

Ayoub, Salim. "Abdellah Taïa's Decolonial Trajectory Toward Unbelonging." In *Autour d'Abdellah Taïa: Poétique et politique du désir engagé /Around Abdellah Taïa: Poetics and Politics of Engaged Desire*, edited by Ralph Heyndels and Amine Zidouh, 41–58. Caen: Editions Passage(s), 2020.

Barthes, Roland. *Mythologies*. Paris: Seuil, 1957.

Bauman, Zygmunt. *Liquid Modernity*. Cambridge: Polity, 2000.

Bhabha, Homi. *Nation and Narration*. New York: Routledge, 1990.

Bond, Emma. "Towards a Trans-national Turn in Italian Studies." *Italian Studies* 69, no. 3 (2014): 415–424.

Bouamer, Siham. "De 'River of no Return' à 'Trouble of the World,': Parcours initiatique musical dans *Infidèles* (2012) d'Abdellah Taïa." *Expressions maghrébines* 19, no. 1 (2020): 107–124.

Boulé, Jean-Pierre. *Abdellah Taïa: La mélancolie et le cri*. Lyon: Presses universitaires de Lyon, 2020.

Boym, Svetlana. *The Future of Nostalgia*. New York: Basic Books, 2001.

Choukri, Mohammed, et al. *Des nouvelles du Maroc*, edited by Loïc Barrière, 73–85. Paris: Paris-Méditerranée, 1999.

Decena, Carlos Ulises. *Tacit Subjects: Belonging and Same-Sex Desire among Dominican Immigrant Men*. Durham: Duke University Press, 2011.

Deleuze, Gilles, and Félix Guattari. *Anti-Oedipus: Capitalism and Schizophrenia*. Translated by Robert Hurley. Penguin Classics, 2009.
De Cesari, Chiara, and Ann Rigney, eds. *Transnational Memory: Circulation, Articulation, Scales*. Berlin: De Gruyter, 2014.
Erll, Astrid. "Travelling Memory." *Parallax* 17, no. 4 (2011): 4–18.
Glissant, Edouard. *Poetics of Relation*. Translated by Betsy Wing. Ann Arbor: University of Michigan Press, 1997.
Gröning, Sarah. "Les 'lieux de traumatisme' dans la littérature antillaise contemporaine." *Revue des Sciences Humaines* 321 (2016): 193–209.
Hargreaves, Alec G., Charles Forsdick, and David Murphy. *Transnational French Studies: Postcolonialism and Littérature-monde*. Liverpool: Liverpool University Press, 2010.
Harvey, David. *The Conditions of Postmodernity: An Enquiry into the Origins of Cultural Change*. Oxford: Blackwell, 1989.
Heyndels, Ralph. "'Je suis un Indigène de la République': L'atelier décolonial de l'écriture d'Abdellah Taïa." In *Autour d'Abdellah Taïa: Poétique et politique du désir engagé /Around Abdellah Taïa: Poetics and Politics of Engaged Desire*, edited by Ralph Heyndels and Amine Zidouh, 117–145. Caen: Editions Passage(s), 2020.
———. "La prostitution sur la scène de l'écriture chez Abdellah Taïa." *Revue @nalyse* 11, no. 3 (2016): 9–23.
Leap, William L. "Language and Gendered Modernity." In *The Handbook of Language and Gender*, edited by Janet Holmes and Miriam Meyerhoff, 401–422. Oxford: Blackwell, 2003.
———. "Language, Sexuality, History." In *The Oxford Handbook of Language and Sexuality*, edited by Kira Hall and Rusty Barrett, online. Oxford: Oxford University Press, 2020. DOI: 10.1093/oxfordhb/9780190212926.013.12.
Lionnet, Françoise, and Shu-mei Shih, eds. *Minor Transnationalism*. Durham: Duke University Press, 2005.
Manalansan, Martin F. *Global Divas: Filipino Gay Men in the Diaspora*. Durham: Duke University Press, 2003.
Maroun, Daniel. "Comment échapper à la honte du *zamel*: Vers la construction de la masculinité maghrébine queer." *Revue @nalyse* 11, no. 3 (2016): 135–154.
Mazouz, Hicham. "Hadda, The Black Mother of Morocco: From the 'Origin' Myth to the Subaltern Abject Rewriting the Nation in Abdellah Taïa's *Le jour du Roi*." In *Autour d'Abdellah Taïa: Poétique et politique du désir engagé /Around Abdellah Taïa: Poetics and Politics of Engaged Desire*, edited by Ralph Heyndels and Amine Zidouh, 161–176. Caen: Editions Passage(s), 2020.
McDonald, Christie, and Susan Rubin Suleiman, eds. *French Global: A New Approach to Literary History*. New York: Columbia University Press, 2010.
Muñoz, José Esteban. *Disidentifications: Queers of Color and the Performance of Politics*. Minneapolis: University of Minnesota Press, 1999.
Nora, Pierre, ed. *Les Lieux de mémoire*. Gallimard, 1984–1992.
———, ed. *Realms of Memory: Rethinking the French Past*. Translation directed by David P. Jordan. Chicago: University of Chicago Press, 2001–2010 [1984–1992].

Ong, Aihwa. *Flexible Citizenship: The Cultural Logics of Transnationality*. Durham: Duke University Press, 1999.
Provencher, Denis M. *Queer Maghrebi French: Language, Temporalities, Transfiliations*. Liverpool: Liverpool University Press, 2017.
———. *Queer French: Globalization, Language, and Sexual Citizenship in France*. Burlington/Aldershot: Ashgate Publishing, 2007.
———. ""*Je suis terroriste, pédé et le fils de Marilyn Monroe*": Cinematic Stars and Transfiliaton in Abdellah Taïa's *Infidèles*." In *Paris and the Marginalized Author: Treachery, Alienation, Queerness, and Exile*, edited by Valerie K. Orlando and Pamela A. Pears, 153–166. Lanham: Lexington Books, 2019.
———. "Transnational Approaches to Language and Sexuality." In *Transnational French Studies*, edited by Charles Forsdick and Claire Launchbury. Liverpool: Liverpool University Press, forthcoming.
Provencher, Denis M., and David Peterson. "Diasporic Sexual Citizenship: Queer Language (Im)possible Citizenship and Transfiliation." In *The Oxford Handbook of Language and Sexuality*, edited by Kira Hall and Rusty Barrett, online. Oxford: Oxford University Press, 2020. DOI: 10.1093/oxfordhb/9780190212926.013.36.
Renan, Ernest. "Qu'est-ce qu'une nation?" 1882. Republished as "What is a nation?" Translated by Martin Thom. *Nation and Narration*, edited by Homi Bhabha, 8–22. New York: Routledge, 1990.
Rosello, Mireille. *France and the Maghreb: Performative Encounters*. Gainesville: University Press of Florida, 2005.
Schehr, Lawrence R. *Post-modern Masculinities: From Neuromatrices to Seropositivity*. Liverpool: Liverpool University Press, 2009.
Senghor, Léopold Sédar. "Poème liminaire." In *Hosties noires* (1948). *Œuvre poétique*, 55–56. Paris: Seuil, 1990.
Sheller, Mimi, and John Urry. "The New Mobilities Paradigm." *Environment and Planning A* 38 (2006): 207–226.
Stryker, Susan, Paisley Currah, and Lisa Jean Moore. "Introduction: Trans-, Trans, or Transgender?" *WSQ: Women's Studies Quarterly* 36, no. 3–4 (2008): 11–22.
Taïa, Abdellah. *Mon Maroc*. Biarritz: Séguier, 2000.
———. *Le rouge du tarbouche*. Biarritz: Séguier, 2004.
———. *L'armée du salut*. Paris: Seuil, 2006.
———. *Une mélancolie arabe*. Paris: Seuil, 2008.
———. *Le jour du Roi*. Paris: Seuil, 2010.
———. *Infidèles*. Paris: Seuil, 2012.
———. *Un pays pour mourir*. Paris: Seuil, 2015.
———. *Celui qui est digne d'être aimé*. Paris: Seuil, 2017.
———. *La vie lente*. Paris: Seuil, 2019.
———. "Genet, Abdallah et moi." In *Les Passions de Jean Genet: Esthétique, Poétique, et Politique du désir*, edited by Ralph Heyndels, 11–15. Paris: Alain Baudry & Cie., 2010.
———. "L'homosexualité expliquée à ma mère." *telquel.com*. Tel Quel, Apr. 2009. Web. www.telquel-online.com/archives/367/actu_maroc1_367.shtml. Accessed

February 6, 2021. Re-published at: www.asymptotejournal.com/nonfiction/abdellah-taia-homosexuality-explained-to-my-mother/french/.

———. "Is Any Place Safe?" *New York Times* 18 Nov. 2015. Accessed Feb. 7, 2021. https://www.nytimes.com/2015/11/18/opinion/is-any-place-safe.html.

———. "Lettre à James Baldwin, 20 juin 2020." In *Autour d'Abdellah Taïa: Poétique et politique du désir engagé/Around Abdellah Taïa: Poetics and Politics of Engaged Desire*, edited by Ralph Heyndels and Amine Zidouh, 9–11. Caen: Editions Passage(s), 2020.

———. "Exister aujourd'hui: Abdellah Taïa en conversation avec Antoine Idier." In *Autour d'Abdellah Taïa: Poétique et politique du désir engagé/Around Abdellah Taïa: Poetics and Politics of Engaged Desire*, edited by Ralph Heyndels and Amine Zidouh, 13–27. Caen: Editions Passage, 2020.

———. *Salvation Army.* Translated by Frank Stock. Los Angeles: Semiotexte(e), 2009.

———. "Jean Genet et les hommes arabes." In *Archives des mouvements LBGTQ+*, edited by Antoine Idier, 70–71. Paris: Textuel, 2018.

———. "Où es-tu. Abdallah?" *Europe*, forthcoming.

Taïa, Abdellah, ed. *Lettres à un jeune marocain.* Paris: Seuil, 2009.

———, ed. "Jean Genet un saint marocain." *Nejma, revue littéraire*, Numéro spécial, Winter 2010–2011.

Taïa, Abdellah, and Frédéric Mitterrand. *Maroc, 1900-1960, un certain regard.* Arles/Paris: Actes Sud, 2007.

Vertovec, Stephen. *Transnationalism.* New York: Routledge, 2009.

Zimman Lal. "Transgender Language, Transgender Moment: Toward a Trans Linguistics." In *The Oxford Handbook of Language and Sexuality*, edited by Kira Hall and Rusty Barrett, online. Oxford UP, 2020. DOI: 10.1093/oxfordhb/9780190212926.013.45.

Part IV

NEW DIRECTIONS AND CONCLUSIONS

Chapter 10

The Voices of Reappropriation

Antoine Idier

Washington D.C., March 22, 2019

My dear Abdellah,

When your friend Ralph Heyndels suggested that I take part in the panel organized by Mireille Le Breton at the NEMLA convention in Washington, I joyfully accepted. You had told me about the 2007 colloquium on Jean Genet he organized! Though, beyond the initial enthusiasm, which combined the joy of shared friendship, the celebration of your work, and the discovery of Washington D.C., an anxiety emerged. What could I say?[1]

Friendship should not be chatty, wrote Michel Foucault somewhere. The same Foucault warned against the violence of theoretical discourse that confines an author, one that is nothing more than civil "morality" if it consists in imposing a stability and an identification to those who nevertheless write "in order to have no face." "Do not ask who I am and do not ask me to remain the same";[2] Foucault's injunction has been on my mind for quite some time.

Here, in the intimacy of this friendship, to me the issue appeared even more acute. There was a violence in the public flaying of you and your books, in your absence. A betrayal. We often discussed together the omnipotence of theory when it exacts authority only from itself, about the vain idle talk that it might generate, about the narcissistic and ridiculous satisfaction that it confers upon whomever blissfully discourses on the world while watching it from above; we discussed all of this too much for me not to remember this warning from *Un pays pour mourir* [*A Country for Dying*] (2015) about "these two sissies" who "show off as intellectuals," quoting "Mister Jean-Paul Sartre and Señora Simone de Beauvoir"[3] -- and for me not to otherwise forget the reproach of Ahmed to Emmanuel in *Celui qui est digne d'être aimé*

[*The One Worthy of Being Loved*] (2017), of "corrupting simple beauty" for the fact of "seeing everything in an analytical fashion."[4] Hence the ruse of resorting to this letter.

As I told you a few months ago, your most recent and beautiful novel, *La vie lente* [*The Slow Life*] (2019), is in my eyes "a novel of breaking." Breaking with the past and with your previous novels. As if this one was the form that you had found to raise, in a radical way, many issues that you have been expressing for a long time, including that of your own trajectory, and that you have for example detailed in the interview that we did together for *Fixxion* -- in particular, you were saying, the "déconstruction de toutes les identités dans lesquelles j'ai avancé ou que j'ai volontairement affirmées [deconstruction of all the identities in which I moved forward or that I willingly claimed]," the destruction of "tous les murs [all the walls]," of "toutes les définitions qui m'ont aidé pour arriver jusqu'à Paris et pour me dire 'je suis un être digne de faire telle ou telle chose'" [all the definitions that helped me to arrive in Paris and to tell me 'I am worthy of doing this or that thing'].[5] It seems to me that these words condense and carry, with high intensity, this preoccupation that has troubled you so these past years.

You often joke about the "willful Arab" that you would be in your life. It is certain that you can be like that in literature, if it consists of saying what one should not say, in behaving in a way that no one should. You have a lot of fun in introducing yourself also as a charmer, as an enchanter who knows how to seduce in order to achieve your ends. In this respect, *La vie lente* is a powerful "Trojan Horse," as per Monique Wittig's concept about literature: an object that presents itself under the innocent appearances of a gift but that actually reveals itself as a formidable weapon.

What strikes me is that this novel looks to France as much as it looks to Morocco, and as much toward the future as toward the past. *Celui qui est digne d'être aimé* is itself turned toward the past, by a genealogical shift that seeks to understand how the protagonist Ahmed (who shares many traits with Mounir from *La vie lente*) ended up in this situation. Notwithstanding, *La vie lente* draws the following conclusion: it is Paris that is forevermore the place of the future and it will be necessary to contend with it, for better or for worse. It is also the difference with *Un pays pour mourir*, in which the characters are more transient (Mojtaba, the Iranian emigrant), at the end of their life or otherwise in the margins of a dominant society. There is a geographical displacement that is not insignificant in *La vie lente*: from Belleville (which, like the Goutte d'or, is a place of refuge, one with a protective community, and unlike, for example, the Luxembourg Gardens) to the rue de Turenne—that is, in the heart of French society, or, rather, in the heart of its dominant majority and of the image that its members want to ascribe to this society and to themselves, and in the heart of this power and in the mythologies they seek to preserve.

Precisely, this displacement of the locus of literature seems to me particularly strong and powerful: it is a question of examining France in the depths of itself, its internal roots (its unconscious, its *habitus*)—its dominations, its racism, its islamophobia, its homophobia, its social classes, its exclusions, its history, its lies about its past, and so on. It would be inaccurate to claim that it was one of your first books that dealt as much with France. But France is present in this novel in a new way, one in which Madame Marty embodies a central character who is not an immigrant, which is rare in your books. I was about to write about Madame Marty that she is "truly French," an extremely problematic expression insofar as the book continues to serve as a reminder that the meaning of something "truly French" poses a problem, and poses daily problems, infernal ones, to Mounir, because of his status and his trajectory ("the Arab immigrant well-integrated whom I am supposed to represent in Paris"[6]). Among all your characters, at any rate, Madame Marty is one of the first to embody a French "filiation" in this way (if I may say), and even France itself.

The displacement of the locus of literature and of the place of writing is not the only displacement: the question of "where to go" is everywhere. That is, for example, the imperative solution that appears to Mounir in *La vie lente*: "Saving my skin, a second time. [. . .] Leaving Paris."[7] Movements and geography are vital to him: going to the Défense district, then to Nanterre, and reconnecting with immigrants previously "neglected," "ignored," and "despised."[8] The question is also the one asked by Ahmed in *Celui qui est digne d'être aimé*: "Where to flee?"[9] This question is yours: "Where are we going to live now?," you wrote in the *New York Times* after the terrorist attacks of 2015.[10]

Coming back is also one of the main concerns of the characters in your novels, and, at once, that of fleeing. They are definitely no longer from where they come, this place that they escaped and at the same time from which they were banished. But they can't be from where they are now, where they are not wanted and where they remain considered as foreigners. Moreover, they sway between two borders. They embody this "double absence," discussed by the sociologist Abdelmalek Sayad. Mounir, again, in *La vie lente* explains: "I wanted to become again this little cat that was walking among starved tigers," and "I wanted to come back there where everything had been impossible in the beginning." Again: "It was rather a return to the source," and "It is true that it is not possible to move away too long from our first origin."[11] This expression of "the first origin" is beautiful and intriguing: would there be then a "second origin"? Perhaps even a third, or fourth, and so on? Thus, before coming back, should one know where to come back to? It appears that charting a return may not be as easy to determine.

There is a text of yours that I find very important, my dear Abdellah. It is "Écrire sans mots" ["Writing without Words"], published in 2016. In this text you revisit your relationship to the French language, "a weapon perhaps," and even "the right weapon to see this through to the end," "through this struggle"—the struggle for existence, for life, for love. You write: "Today [. . .] something is collapsing, in my heart, all around me. It is bigger than me, than us. It may be time to return to the Arabic language."[12]

Going back to the Arabic language. Perhaps the point of return lies here. The language of origin, the original origin, before the "departure" and the "betrayal." The language, you explain, of Salé, of poverty, of family—which opposes French, the language of wealthy people, of the bourgeois, of power, of colonizers, of university, of those who are still colonized. The idea is beautiful and powerful. I am very curious to know if that project will come to fruition.

I am wondering also about this project, and about you as well, if I may say so while reading you. This text was published in 2016. Since then, you published two novels written in French; you wrote many texts in French as well—and, to my knowledge, nothing in Arabic. Admittedly, *Celui qui est digne d'être aimé* makes a resounding echo: in the very powerful letter that Ahmed addresses to Emmanuel, Ahmed underscores the alienation of those who, turned into "proper little gay Parisians," pretend that "France saved them." The young man recounts, however, "at 30 years old, I even no longer speak Arabic like before [. . .] I now have a strange accent when I speak this language. My language is no longer my language." Language is then both the sign and the peak of dispossession, of this movement which consists in "integrating forcibly to the French society" and in "making one forget about our skin, our origin"[13] (just like the names Marguerite and Jeanne, chosen for his daughters by Jamal, Ahmed's brother-in-law). Even if Ahmed states: "I want to leave the French language in the way that I practice it since I have known you," a little earlier, he had nonetheless acknowledged: "I will not be able to turn back."[14]

Wanting to leave, not being able to come back . . . To what extent does this impossibility of "coming back" belong to you, my dear Abdellah? And to what extent was *La vie lente* born from the realization of this impossibility? Of the necessity that ensued: for lack of a possibility to return, going even further? As if there were an impossible re-appropriation; or, at least, a return that was not a destination, but a path and an endlessly shape-shifting map, displaced with each attempt of a return, with words and voices expressed within it.

I enjoy the multiplicity of voices in your novels and the power of this polyphony. I think about the arrangement of *Celui qui est digne d'être aimé*: four letters that express four facets of the protagonist's life. But I think also about the many characters and about the way each one of them carries the memory, the story of another. They are haunted by other voices, by other existences; they have a responsibility to make them heard, to carry their voices. It is this shape that results from the interlocking of past and present, betrayal and loyalty, departure and return.

In *Celui qui est digne d'être aimé,* Ahmed voices this very clearly: he remembers the presentation that he gave at the University of Rabat on André Gide's first homosexual experience in Biskra with Oscar Wilde. "Later, I realized that I had made an unforgivable oversight. Tragic. I had regarded the Arab boy offered to André Gide without so much as a mention. I, Emmanuel's Arab queer, I had killed in Rabat, for the umpteenth time, the boy who should be the true hero of that story. I should have been his voice, his lawyer, his friend, his remote brother."[15]

Your novels are populated by those who have been left out, who have been sacrificed, and by those who act as their defenders. Ahmed's father—whose every child, including Ahmed, following their mother in this way, participated in his "second killing" by "forgetting," by "excluding from our memories."[16] Later, Halima, the "servant," "the cook," "the nanny."[17] In *La vie lente*, Samir, who "used to put kohl on his eyes" and "to sing Samira Saïd's songs all the time." Mounir specifies: "I knew that he was paying for me, that he would die instead of me."[18]

In *Celui qui est digne d'être aimé*, Lahbib says to Ahmed: "Don't forget me. You have to seek justice for me. To carry me dead and alive in your heart." Like Samir and Mounir, the characters can save as much as they have killed; Ahmed thus acknowledges: "I stopped talking about Lahbib. I killed him inside me." Ahmed, again, about who he was, himself: "I helped you to kill him."[19]

In *La vie lente*, Madame Marty would like to "resuscitate" her sister Manon so as "not be ashamed anymore." Madame Marty asks Mounir: "Do you accept keeping me alive after my death?"[20]

Among all these voices, there is one that particularly struck me for having little dissonance. It is the voice, in *Celui qui est digne d'être aimé*, of Vincent's Jewish Moroccan father. He refuses to return to Meknes: "It was too late to return. The world was no longer the same. What was the point of coming back and unintentionally destroying precious memories?"[21]

Indeed, what *is* the point of coming back?

There is this wonderful expression by Jean Genet, in his 1970 introduction to prison letters addressed to George Jackson, writing "in the language of the enemy." He immediately specifies that if one has to "accept this language," it is "to corrupt it so skillfully that white people would fall for it"; and he wonders as well to what extent poetry is inconsistent with "the revolutionary project."[22] It remains to be determined, however, who the enemy is. *La vie lente* is also a novel about this uncertainty: between Mounir and Simone, between Antoine and Mounir, who is the friend, who is the enemy? What to do when our friends become our enemies, and vice versa?

A return to the Arabic language, you said. Others did it, thinking about their enemies. Kateb Yacine, for example, after the independence of Algeria. Of course, there is a risk of anachronism when quoting Yacine: the risk of assigning to you a period of time, a context, preoccupations that are not yours. But you are the one who made me discover the Arab-Israeli writer Sayed Kashua, who writes in Hebrew about the life of Arabs in Israel (and who also ended up leaving Israel, feeling hopeless about his own power, or about his own hope). The fact remains I was struck by Kateb Yacine's sentence about the French language, a sentence you would probably endorse: "It is an old love affair with which to settle. Love and hatred are inseparable." Describing "Francophonie" as a "politics of alienation," he adds: "The knowledge of a language is also a weapon. Take, for example, the Algerian War. [. . .] We knew the language of French people, who, on their part, ignored ours. We used the French language to defend our own cause."[23]

His return to Arabic corresponds to the struggle that he led against the politics of "Arabization" in Algeria and the "Arab Islamism," against the "Mandarins" and the "ulemas of literature" who were imposing "a literary Arabic, a formalist and fixed Arabic." Yacine, himself, was defending the "popular Arabic," "despised," "the popular vein of the thugs of literature"—the dialectal Arabic and the Tamazight.[24]

The conclusion that Yacine pushes us to draw is far from anachronistic: language is always strategic, related to a given struggle and context. As he summarizes in 1978:

> jusqu'à l'indépendance nationale, il était important de s'exprimer en français, parce que cela pouvait atteindre le peuple français. [. . .] La situation a changé dans la mesure où il fallait s'exprimer ici. [. . .] La grande masse du peuple comprend deux langues: le berbère et/ou l'arabe parlé. [. . .] Pour l'écrivain, tout dépend alors des personnes qu'il veut toucher.
>
> [up until national independence, it was important to speak in French, because it could reach the French people. . . . The situation changed in the sense that it was necessary to speak here. . . . The great mass of people understands two languages: Berber and/or spoken Arabic. . . . For the writer, everything depends on the people that he wants to reach]."[25]

Precisely, then, what is the fight to lead? It seems to me that it is not your struggle—I mean that it is not the struggle you chose for yourself. This is what moved me when I read *La vie lente*: the break might reside in the designation of the enemy. You precisely delineate a struggle and it is here—or over there, since I am writing from D.C.—in France, that you decided to lead this struggle. The multiplicity of voices I mentioned earlier is so powerful precisely because it is about carrying, here and now, loudly and clearly, these voices, in France in 2019.

A few days ago, we publicly discussed *La vie lente* together in a bookstore. You were asked about writing in Arabic, about the fact of publishing it in Arabic, in Morocco; people often ask you these questions. Well, through *La vie lente*, it seems to me that you answer in advance, that to ask you to write in Arabic would be to send you back toward Morocco, and that would be a form of house arrest, to consider that what you have to say, and even what you are, is about Morocco. However, as you vigorously reminded us—and what an extraordinary vigor!—it is in fact about France. As if the dominations that you were describing, the alienation by language and culture, was definitely settled. To make you quit the French language could be a new sleight of dominant reason.

This discussion about returning is reminiscent of a very beautiful text by Pierre Bourdieu entitled "L'Odyssée de la réappropriation," which is about the Berber writer Mouloud Mammeri. I discovered it thanks to Didier Eribon, for which this text had been crucial to writing *Retour à Reims*. According to Bourdieu:

> l'histoire du rapport de Mouloud Mammeri à sa société et à sa culture originelles peut être décrit comme une Odyssée, avec un premier mouvement d'éloignement vers des rivages inconnus, et pleins de séductions, suivie d'un long retour, lent et semé d'embûches, vers la terre natale. Cette Odyssée, c'est, selon moi, le chemin que doivent parcourir, pour se trouver, ou se retrouver, tous ceux qui sont issus d'une société dominée ou d'une classe ou d'une région dominée des sociétés dominantes.
>
> [the story of the relationship between Mouloud Mammeri and his society and his culture of origin could be described as an odyssey, with an initial movement of fleeing toward unknown shores, and full of seductions, followed by a long return, slow and fraught with many obstacles, toward the native land. This odyssey, is, according to me, the path that all those who come from a dominated society or social class or a dominated region within a dominant society must travel in order to find oneself or to find oneself again].[26]

As Bourdieu describes it, after a moment of appropriation from the dominant culture ("the one which experiences itself as universal"), which was after all only "a movement of repudiation, of renunciation," Mammeri returned toward "paternal culture," "[again starting] to listen to blacksmith-poets, demiurge-poets." But this true return only takes place at the moment when, refusing to dissociate noble western poetry from the ethnology of traditional Berber cultures, Mammeri brought ethnographical research to his poetic language, which means bringing protest and the subversion of hierarchies, domination, and colonization into the very heart of the language of dominant people.

It is this that strikes me in *La vie lente*, where confiscated, imposed, and dispossessed identities are so present: the more you talk about coming back to Morocco, the more you move away from it, geographically at least, and in this way placing France this much at the heart of your novel to make these doubly absent voices heard, between France and Morocco. To bring fire and sword against the society responsible for this "eternal humiliation."[27]

I would have liked to write to you a little more, my dear Abdellah, and to talk to you, among other things, about James Baldwin, whom, as you know, I read intensely at the moment. How omnipresent is the return in his writing! Like Yacine and you, he reminds us how much the displacement and the return, whether they are properly geographical or more metaphorical, never cease to obsess writers from minorities, those who made of their situation of domination (sexual, social, racial, gendered, linguistic) a departure of their work on language. "Every good-bye ain't gone"—writes Baldwin in a 1977 article, one that opens with the memory of his departure from the United States twenty-nine years prior—"my departure, which, especially in my own eyes, stank of betrayal, was my only means of proving, or redeeming, that love, my only hope."[28] I note that, in the French version of the collection where this article can be found, *Retour dans l'œil du cyclone*, the first text of the volume is entitled "Point de non-retour," or point of no return. I also note that Baldwin, even exiled, continued to write in English and that he was able to speak about the vital "necessity" of speaking "Black English."[29]

In his novel *Another Country*, a part of the story is about a return to New York for a gay, white American named Eric who settled in France. The return troubles him, too. This return uncovers "the enormous question he had spent three years avoiding. To accept it was to bring his European sojourn to an end; not to accept it was to transform his sojourn into exile."[30] Visiting or exiled, Baldwin describes here an indecisiveness of departure as much as that of return, of the possibility of their definite and irrevocable nature: "—'People who go to America', said Madame Belet, 'never come back.'—'*Au contraire*,' said Yves, 'they are coming back all the time.'"[31]

I really like a short story from 1960 by James Baldwin, while it leaves me with a feeling of profound indecisiveness and a tremendous confusion where it ends: "This Morning, This Evening, So Soon." The protagonist is African American, a famous singer and actor, who settled in Paris for twelve years with his white Swedish wife and their son. The family is about to return to live in the United States; the protagonist is worried about the brutal confrontation with racism he had left behind. Paris gave him a life he could not have otherwise had. Paris saved his life. However, in this short story, the place itself of the return is displaced: the true confrontation takes place in Paris, before the departure, during an evening that predates the trip to the United States by only a few days. In a bar, the protagonist meets a group of young African Americans travelling in Europe ("it is as though we were all back home"); he also encounters a Tunisian friend, Boona, whom he considers one of his "brothers," much in the same way he regards the "North Africans" he met in Paris (even though their social condition differs, they suffer from French racism).[32] But the encounter between the young Blacks and Boona goes wrong because of a theft. More than merely an encounter, it appears to be the collision of several temporalities and of several social configurations, of several identities and solidarities that are associated: a collision between what it means to be Black in the United States and what it means in France, between a solidarity with African American fellow citizens and a solidarity with Arabs in France, and so on. The protagonist is as much from one country as he is from the other, but he can't seem to be from them both at the same time, simultaneously. And, this, no matter where he is, physically, for the dissonance to manifest between his cleaved identities, his affiliation. To the extent that the "return," if it is the confrontation between the past and the present, if it is an earthquake that causes the several strata of the trajectory of a person to collide, it has no need for a geographical displacement to occur. The trip itself to the United States may not really matter: the tensions are there, violent, perhaps unsurpassable, though they are in any case deep and alive.

Last Friday night, while walking the boulevards of Belleville and la Villette, as I was telling you about my deep disappointment, my anger even, after reading a recent book that, pretending to make a key contribution to postcolonial theory, was actually making a gross caricature of it. You told me that you heard it as if it were a warning addressed to you. You are far from making such a caricature, I was saying to you—quite the contrary. You spoke to me about your next book, of the necessity to proceed with a new displacement. The trip is far from being over, I thought. And more than the next destination—in the sense that each of your books constitutes a new trip in itself, like the one on the RER A in *La vie lente*—I am impatient to know more about the route.

With all my love, my dear Abdellah,
Antoine

NOTES

1. Translation from French by Thomas Muzart and Ramon A. Biel, with the support of the laboratory AGORA, CY Cergy Paris Université.
2. Michel Foucault, *The Archeology of Knowledge and the Discourse on Language* (New York: Pantheon Books, 1972), 17.
3. Abdellah Taïa, *Un pays pour mourir* (Paris: Seuil, 2015), 37. All translations are done by the French-English translators.
4. Abdellah Taïa, *Celui qui est digne d'être aimé* (Paris: Seuil, 2017), 117.
5. Abdellah Taïa and Antoine Idier, "'Sortir de la peur'. Construire une identité homosexuelle arabe dans un monde postcolonial," *Fixxion. Revue critique de fixxion française contemporaine* 12 (2016): 197.
6. Abdellah Taïa, *La vie lente* (Paris: Seuil, 2019), 86.
7. Taïa, *La vie lente*, 125.
8. Taïa, *La vie lente*, 70.
9. Taïa, *Celui qui est digne*, 27 and 62.
10. Abdellah Taïa, "Is Any Place Safe?," *New York Times*, November 18, 2015, https://www.nytimes.com/2015/11/18/opinion/is-any-place-safe.html.
11. Taïa, *La vie lente*, 68–69, 82, and 252.
12. Abdellah Taïa, "Écrire sans mots," in *Voix d'auteurs du Maroc*, ed. Abdellah Baïda, Mamoun Lahbabi and Jean Zaganiaris (Rabat: Éditions Marsam, 2016), 141–144.
13. Taïa, *Celui qui est digne*, 89, 40, 93, and 105.
14. Taïa, *Celui qui est digne*, 106 and 93.
15. Taïa, *Celui qui est digne*, 118.
16. Taïa, *Celui qui est digne*, 13.
17. Taïa, *Celui qui est digne*, 110.
18. Taïa, *La vie lente*, 52.
19. Taïa, *Celui qui est digne*, 135, 100, and 93.
20. Taïa, *La vie lente*, 129 and 173.
21. Taïa, *Celui qui est digne*, 73.
22. Jean Genet, "Introduction à *Les Frères de Soledad*," *L'Ennemi déclaré* (Paris: Gallimard, 1991), 68–69.
23. Kateb Yacine, *Le poète comme un boxeur* (Paris: Seuil, 1994), 99 and 96. Also, 72: "Écrivain, j'ai été, plus que d'autres peut-être, aliéné par la langue française." [As a writer, I have been, more than others maybe, alienated by the French language.] and, 70: "Ma pièce s'adresse à tous ceux qui, en Algérie, ont envie de partir pour la France et qui, une fois en France, souffrent d'y être ou de ne plus pouvoir rentrer." [My play addresses all those who, in Algeria, want to leave for France and who, once in France, suffer from being there or from not being able to go back.]
24. Yacine, *Le poète comme un boxeur*, 80.

25. Yacine, *Le poète comme un boxeur*, 75. I also note that Yacine talked about the difficulty of this return. Asked about a "long silence" in his work during the 1970s, he explained: "J'ai fait plusieurs tentatives de retour en Algérie qui, au début du moins, se sont soldées par des échecs. [. . .] J'avais vécu dix ans d'exil. [. . .] Il fallait reprendre contact avec le pays, avec le peuple, vivre en Algérie à tout prix. Et cela n'a pas été facile." [I attempted several returns to Algeria, which, at least in the beginning, failed. [. . .] I had lived for ten years in exile [. . .] It was a necessity to renew contact with the country, with the people, to live in Algeria at all costs. And it has not been easy] (179).

26. Pierre Bourdieu, "L'Odyssée de la réappropriation," *Awal, Cahiers d'études berbères* 18 (1998), http://www.homme-moderne.org/societe/socio/bourdieu/varia/odyssee.html. See also Didier Eribon, *La Société comme verdict* (Paris: Fayard, 2013), 87–93.

27. Taïa, *La vie lente*, 235.

28. James Baldwin, "Every Good-bye Ain't Gone," *Collected Essays* (New York: The Library of America, 1998), 773.

29. James Baldwin, "If Black English isn't a Language, Then Tell Me, What Is?," *The Black Scholar* 27, no. 1 (1997): 5–6.

30. James Baldwin, *Another Country. Early Novels and Stories* (New York: The Library of America, 1998), 530.

31. Baldwin, *Another Country. Early Novels and Stories,* 556.

32. James Baldwin, "This Morning, This Evening, So Soon," *Early Novels and Stories* (New York: The Library of America, 1998), 894 and 875.

BIBLIOGRAPHY

Baldwin, James. "If Black English isn't a Language, Then Tell Me, What Is?" *The Black Scholar* 27, no. 1 (1997): 5–6.

———. "Every Good-bye Ain't Gone." *Collected Essays.* New York: The Library of America, 1998.

———. *Another Country. Early Novels and Stories.* New York: The Library of America, 1998.

———. *This Morning, This Evening, So Soon. Early Novels and Stories.* New York: The Library of America, 1998.

Bourdieu, Pierre. "L'odyssée de la réappropriation." *Awal, Cahiers d'études berbères* 18, 1998. http://www.homme-moderne.org/societe/socio/bourdieu/varia/odyssee.html.

Eribon, Didier. *La société comme verdict.* Paris: Fayard, 2013.

Foucault, Michel. *The Archeology of Knowledge and the Discourse on Language.* New York: Pantheon Books, 1972.

Genet, Jean. *L'ennemi déclaré.* Paris: Gallimard, 1991.

Taïa, Abdellah. *Un pays pour mourir.* Paris: Seuil, 2015.

———. "Is Any Place Safe?" *New York Times*, November 18, 2015. https://www.nytimes.com/2015/11/18/opinion/is-any-place-safe.html.

———. "Écrire sans mots." In *Voix d'auteurs du Maroc*, edited by Abdellah Baïda, Mamoun Lahbabi, and Jean Zaganiaris, 141–144. Rabat: Éditions Marsam, 2016.
———. *Celui qui est digne d'être aimé*. Paris: Seuil, 2017.
———. *La vie lente*. Paris: Seuil, 2019.
Taïa, Abdellah, and Anotine Idier. "'Sortir de la peur'. Construire une identité homosexuelle arabe dans un monde postcolonial." *Fixxion. Revue critique de fixxion française contemporaine* 12 (2016): 197–207.
Yacine, Kateb. *Le poète comme un boxeur*. Paris: Seuil, 1994.

Chapter 11

Des hommes fatigués

Abdellah Taïa

La guerre avait commencé, bien avant nous, bien avant qu'on ne me fasse entrer dans cette minuscule pièce dont je n'avais jamais deviné l'existence dans ce Grand Magasin parisien.

Une cage. Un sas. Un box. Une petite prison? Un lieu en dehors du temps, en dehors de l'humanité même, peut-être.

J'avais acheté au début de l'été le coffret DVD de la série israélienne "Fauda" qui contenait les deux premières saisons. Et, en rentrant chez moi, je m'étais rendu que la série était entièrement disponible sur Netflix. Il me fallait donc revenir à la FNAC pour retourner le coffret DVD et me faire rembourser. Mais voilà, j'ai tardé à le faire. Paresseux, trop casanier, occupé à ne rien faire, j'ai laissé passer le temps. Et quand, en plein mois d'août, je me suis enfin décidé à y aller, une vague intuition au fond de moi me disait qu'il ne fallait pas le faire. Les 50 euros que tu as payés pour la série, on s'en fout. N'y va pas. N'y va pas. Fais la sieste. Ce n'est pas le moment d'aller affronter le monde.

Je n'ai pas écouté la voix dans ma tête et, bien sûr, je l'ai regretté vite, très vite. Quelque chose de grave aurait pu m'arriver ce jour-là. Basculer dans une autre réalité. Voir la menace virtuelle se réaliser. Un Arabe petit criminel potentiel qu'on soupçonne tout le temps en France, partout où il va, est passé à l'acte. Il a volé. On l'a pris. Quelle joie, quelle joie! On va lui donner une bonne leçon, à ce morveux qui ne respecte pas les lois de la République. On va lui apprendre à sortir de sa peau de sauvage. Et on va lui rappeler d'où il vient.

Au fond, ce n'était même pas du racisme. Ou alors: un racisme qui était en train de muter, de se réinventer et qu'on ne reconnaissait pas encore du premier coup d'œil. C'était juste des scènes rejouées systématiquement chaque jour pour que les hommes, les pauvres hommes fatigués et désorientés, les pauvres mecs vidés et pitoyables, soient un peu divertis. Pour qu'ils fassent semblant d'oublier un petit peu le cercle infernal dans lequel ils sont enfermés. Pour qu'ils continuent ainsi à être dans la solidarité et la lâcheté masculines.

Devant les caisses, il y avait de très longues files d'attente. Cela m'a découragé. Je n'ai pas la force pour ça. Je rentre chez moi. Dormir en plein jour dans mon petit lit.

Au moment de sortir du Grand Magasin, le système de sécurité s'est mis à sonner. Deux agents de sécurité, vigiles noirs, assez jeunes, sont venus vers moi. Je leur ai montré le coffret DVD de FAUDA et aussi la facture. Ils ont regardé cette dernière. Ils ont constaté qu'elle datait d'au moins un mois. Je me suis mis aussitôt à leur expliquer la situation. Mais, déjà, ils ne m'écoutaient pas. Ce que j'avais à dire n'avait déjà aucune valeur. L'un des deux a appelé le chef qui est venu très vite, en moins d'une minute. Il était noir lui aussi et avait sûrement le même âge que moi. Il avait un regard très sérieux. Froid. Qui m'a immédiatement condamné. Tu es un voleur, toi, tu es un petit voleur et tu vas me suivre. J'ai voulu lui dire ce que j'avais essayé de dire aux deux agents, mais je voyais que cela ne servait à rien. La preuve que j'avais entre les mains, la facture, ne le convainquait pas lui non plus. Et je ne comprenais pas pourquoi.

J'ai fait à ce moment-là un geste qui l'a énervé et qui l'a poussé à être plus dur avec moi.

Je ne suis pas un voleur, vous savez, monsieur.

Ces paroles étaient accompagnées de mon index posé sur ma tempe et tourné dans tous les sens, plusieurs fois.

Cela a vexé le chef des vigiles. Énormément.

Vous me traitez de fou, il a dit. Je suis un fou pour vous? C'est ce qu'on va voir. Suivez-moi.

Le suivre où?

Avant, quand je suis arrivé en France en 1998, je passais pour un jeune homme gentil dont la virilité était inoffensive, un petit gars qui en fait un peu trop mais gentil quand même. *The good immigrant*. Qui parle parfaitement le français, qui discute aisément des films de Robert Bresson, ceux de François Truffaut, et qui aime les chansons de Barbara.

Vingt ans plus tard, je suis devenu une menace. Malgré moi une menace. Une menace physique très masculine qui se balade partout dans les rues de Paris et qui, on ne sait jamais, pourrait, vous savez, pourrait vous agresser, violer vos femmes, insulter vos mères, voler votre richesse sans rien foutre de ses journées, exploser devant un café ou bien faire je ne sais quoi de pas très convenable.

Qui a changé? Moi vieilli et désenchanté? Moi, petit garçon devenu homme qui sème le trouble et le danger autour de lui? La France qui a peur, plus qu'avant, de ses objets sexuels comme moi, de ses anciens sujets colonisés qu'il faut de nouveau maîtriser, voire castrer? Peur de quoi exactement, au fond? De qui exactement, au fond?

J'ai suivi le chef des vigiles. Le sas du Grand Magasin. Là où on traite avec les voleurs et autres petits criminels comme moi.

J'avoue que, assez étrangement, j'avais aussi une curiosité pour cet endroit et pour l'homme en face de moi. Il était visiblement fatigué. Fatigué par la canicule du mois d'août. Fatigué par ce boulot ingrat. Fatigué par la vie. Fatigué par tous les *fights* à mener pour avoir une existence digne en France. Fatigué d'attraper des gens comme moi et de leur faire ce qu'il s'apprêtait à me faire.

Il était 17h00. Et cet homme aux traits tirés, las, énervé, en colère (contre moi ? Vraiment contre moi ?), me paraissait très beau. Physiquement très beau. Je me disais qu'il avait raison d'afficher ainsi son état d'esprit, de ne pas retenir en lui ce qui lui faisait mal. La fureur en lui. Les autres doivent payer. Payer. Je dois donc payer moi aussi, en tant qu'arabe. C'est mon tour. Allez-y, dîtes tout, monsieur le chef des vigiles. Je vous écoute. Je veux entendre à quel point vous aussi vous êtes désabusé. Vous n'y croyez plus. Vous en avez marre de faire l'homme bien comme il faut.

C'était tellement petit, tellement étroit, le sas. 4 mètres carrés? 5 mètres carrés? Peut-être que cela était plus grand. Mais moi, à présent que je constatais que le chef me parlait avec un langage qui n'était pas le sien, des mots qui ne lui allaient pas, qu'on lui avait appris, j'étais de plus en plus proche de la crise de panique qui monte, qui monte, et que, je le savais, je ne sais pas calmer.

Pour me protéger alors de ces mots qui accusent et qui veulent me rééduquer, je me mets à regarder le chef avec des yeux méprisants, des yeux qui installent de la distance, des yeux qui vont font tomber sans presque rien faire.

Le chef reçoit le message cinq sur cinq. Je ne me laisserai pas faire. Je n'ai rien volé. Je n'ai rien volé, je vous dis, et si vous voulez, appelez la police.

Je n'ai pas besoin de quelqu'un comme vous, un voleur, pour me dire ce que je dois faire. Compris?

Il s'était levé pour dire ces deux phrases. Il espérait ainsi m'impressionner physiquement. S'imposer. Me faire admettre ce que je ne suis pas. Le voleur que je ne suis pas.

J'ai réussi à lui résister, mais juste quelques secondes. Car, amer, je me rendais compte que tout cela était ridicule, futile et dangereux. Le doute s'est réveillé. Le doute non pas sur le fait d'avoir volé ou pas volé, d'avoir menti ou pas menti. Non. Un doute plus vertigineux. Le doute sur moi tout entier. Ce que je suis. Mon identité, comme on dit. Tout d'un coup, tout cela ne signifiait plus rien et je ne savais plus comment remplir cette enveloppe, mon corps, mon être, comment faire face, l'attitude, comment avoir de la contenance. Comment me protéger. Tout en me posant plusieurs questions: Qui dois-je protéger? Qui? Moi? Uniquement moi? Et pourquoi au juste? Pour gagner contre un homme noir en France qui doit subir bien plus que moi des regards durs et des réflexions d'un autre temps? Gagner et c'est tout?

Dérisoire. Dérisoire. Dérisoire. Et risible destin.

J'ai pensé à ma mère. Au Maroc. A cette femme dans l'espace public et aux nombreuses fois où je l'ai vue s'écraser tout en souriant, s'écraser tout en continuant de remplir son rôle, assumer ses responsabilités de mère, s'oublier pour nous. Ne plus exister. S'effacer alors qu'elle est là, là, devant moi jour et nuit, elle nous nourrit, elle lave nos vêtements, elle nous soigne, elle nous guérit, elle nous pousse à faire des études, à avancer, à aimer, elle prie pour nous, elle fait le sexe avec le père trois fois par semaine et elle éloigne de nous le mal comme elle peut. Comme elle peut et au-delà de ses forces. Là, à côté de moi tant d'années, si présente et si peu visible profondément en moi à l'époque. J'ai éprouvé soudain une immense honte et j'ai compris le prix qu'elle a dû payer, ce que cette chose simple, traverser le quotidien de la vie en tant que femme sans cesse malmenée et réduite à sombrer dans le noir de l'injustice, a dû lui coûter. Donner de l'amour et de la tendresse alors que les conflits ne s'arrêtaient jamais. Jamais. Se sacrifier pour les éviter. Devenir maligne, très maligne, pour savoir en permanence comment négocier avec le monde et les hommes.

Et ces nouvelles questions se sont écrites devant mes yeux, pendant que le chef des vigiles était toujours debout devant moi, silencieux et presque hors de lui: Mais comment elle a fait, ma mère, pour ne pas mourir, pour ne pas tomber? Où a-t-elle trouvé la force pour être à ce point dans l'abnégation et le pardon?

J'ai regardé l'homme noir différemment. J'ai essayé de faire comme ma mère faisait. Profil bas. D'avance déjouer les pièges. Ne pas tomber là où on veut qu'on tombe. Baiser les mains qu'il faut bien baiser pour sauver sa peau.

Mais cela n'a pas marché. Je n'ai pas pu, ou pas su, bien jouer le rôle. Etre une femme qui se sacrifie encore une fois. Ça ne s'invente pas sur commande. Et, au fond, je voulais revenir à la guerre entre hommes. Des hommes qui miment le pouvoir, qui ne leur reste que cela, ce masque de la virilité stérile à porter d'une manière ostentatoire pour prouver que les hommes ce sont eux, les hommes vrais et forts, les hommes qui gagnent et gagneront toujours. Je voulais donner des coups moi aussi et injurier moi aussi, jouer la comédie et entrer un peu plus dans l'affrontement qui ne rapporte rien. Rien. Juste deux hommes, le Noir et moi, qui font les coqs. Deux hommes qui tournent en rond dans un ring de boxe. Qui n'ont déjà plus de pouvoir mais qui s'accrochent quand même. Des hommes qui ne sont plus des hommes, juste des enveloppes vides, des âmes exténuées, des peaux dures, des yeux attirés par l'abîme dans lequel, de notre plein gré, nous sommes en train de nous précipiter tous en ce moment. Des hommes qui sont en train d'être remplacés. C'est sûr. Des cadavres qui bougent encore.

Le chef des vigiles a continué son offensive véhémente contre moi. Sans vraiment le vouloir, j'ai baissé la tête. C'est la défaite?

Pour retourner un produit au Grand Magasin, on n'a que deux semaines pour le faire. Vous dîtes que vous habitez en France depuis 20 ans et vous ne savez pas ça?

Assez étrangement, c'est ce chiffre, cette information que je lui avais donnée de plein gré, qui lui servait de preuve contre moi. En plus, bien sûr, de ce que je suis: petit arabe au crâne rasé. Attention, danger. Même pour un homme noir comme lui.

J'ai 45 ans, vous savez. Et je suis. . . Je suis. . .

J'ai voulu lui dire que j'étais gay. Comme si gay pouvait signifier innocent, gentil, pas dangereux, jamais criminel.

J'ai voulu lui dire aussi que j'avais écrit des livres et qu'ils étaient en vente là, au Grand Magasin. Des livres écrits en français. En très bon français. Je ne l'ai pas fait. J'éprouvais de la honte soudain. Être écrivain, toi, c'est pas crédible. Ça colle pas avec ton physique.

Honte d'être gay et d'être écrivain.

Il fallait prouver cela. Et dans le sas, dans la confusion, devant cet homme noir qui jouait le personnage du noir, avec le masque blanc, je manquais de preuves.

J'étais un voleur. Et j'avais traité le chef des vigiles de fou. C'est au fond pas ça qu'il ne me pardonnait pas. A moins que, noyé dans mes propres obsessions, aveuglé par le point de vue forcément limité que j'ai sur les choses et sur le monde, je n'ai pas pu voir autre chose.

La vérité: cet homme noir était très fatigué, au-delà de la fatigue. Mais pas à cause de moi. Je n'étais que le prétexte pour dire quelque chose au monde, à la France, écraser l'autre, surtout quand il est dans la même barque que vous. La barque des minorités. Des inférieurs. Des faibles. Des indigènes.

La vérité: moi aussi, j'étais exténué, dans le brouillard, je ne savais plus quoi penser, ni de moi ni des autres et encore moins de flux d'actualités tristes qu'est devenue notre réalité humaine.

Constatant que je n'allais pas relever la tête, l'homme noir est revenu à sa place et a appelé quelqu'un. Viens. On tient un voleur.

L'attente. Cinq minutes. Qui m'ont paru une éternité.

Je n'avais rien commis. Et il fallait que je le prouve. Mais comment? J'étais criminel alors que je n'avais rien fait.

Un homme d'une cinquantaine d'années est arrivé. Un homme blanc, grand, maigre, pas vraiment méchant et qui, depuis longtemps déjà, a renoncé. Il ne fait plus l'homme. L'homme hétérosexuel sûr de lui-même et de ce qu'il incarne. Les valeurs masculines, les valeurs de liberté à protéger et, surtout, à léguer aux prochaines générations. Il n'est plus dans tout cela, lui. Il n'en a plus besoin. Parce que tout simplement il ne sait même plus ce que cela veut dire. Être dans cette peau, dans cette fonction. Il est juste un chef. Le deuxième chef. Une incarnation un peu plus grande, un peu plus visible, du pouvoir. Du petit pouvoir qui lui reste encore. Il m'a jeté un regard rapide. Il a constaté très vite la catégorie à laquelle j'appartenais en France. Arabe. Musulman.

L'homme noir lui a expliqué la situation.

J'ai dit ma version des faits.

Mais je n'étais pas du tout convaincant. Je le voyais clairement dans les yeux du deuxième chef.

Je me suis levé. J'ai montré encore une fois l'ancienne facture. Mais, auprès de lui aussi, cela n'était pas suffisant.

Que faire alors? Que va-t-il arriver? On va appeler la police? On va m'emmener au commissariat? Je serai moi fiché? Fiché comme individu dangereux? Jugé, Condamné?

J'avais franchement peur. Très peur.

Je me trouvais dans une situation qui pouvait déraper à n'importe quel moment.

Le livre de Laurent Mauvignier sur l'homme tué à Lyon dans un supermarché par des vigiles parce qu'il avait volé une canette bière m'est revenu à l'esprit. Comment s'appelait-il, cet homme? Comment s'appelle-t-il, ce livre?

J'ai trouvé. "Ce que j'appelle oubli."

Tout est filmé ici. Dites-moi exactement ce que vous avez fait dans le Grand Magasin. Dès que vous y êtes entré. Le chemin. Les rayons. Tout.

L'homme blanc avait donc un autre pouvoir. Le pouvoir de voir ce qu'on ne voit pas. C'est lui qui va me juger. Qui va trouver les preuves dans mon existence captée par les caméras. Captée sans mon accord? Ou bien avec mon accord inconscient?

Je me suis levé. J'ai regardé l'homme blanc d'une manière importante. J'ai parlé. Répondu. Avec un français important. Des mots réfléchis, faussement calmes, des mots précis et qui claquent. Je misais sur cela maintenant. Qu'ils voient que je suis quelqu'un de bien. Vraiment bien. Puisque mon français est très très bien. Mieux que très très bien.

Je reviens.

L'homme noir était sûr de ma culpabilité. Il a repris son discours. J'ai fermé mes oreilles. J'ai fermé mon cœur. Et je me suis dit que si cela est en train de m'arriver, à moi, à moi, c'est que, quelque part, je l'ai bien mérité. J'ai dû faire quelque chose de grave moi aussi. J'ai fauté. Quand? Où? Je paie je ne sais quoi pour l'instant pas présent dans mon esprit. Je paie un passé, mon passé, le passé de la France.

Le passé du monde.

L'homme noir n'était pas le fautif, n'était pas le responsable de cette impasse, de cette fatigue, lassitude, de cette guerre civile qui couve, qui vient.

L'homme blanc est revenu. Il dit la vérité. Rends-lui son coffret DVD.

L'homme noir s'est exécuté immédiatement.

J'ai repris “Fauda.” Je suis sorti du sas sans dire Au-revoir. Un homme effondré. Soulagé. Catastrophé. Amer. Humilié. Et avec un vrai et stupide désir de vengeance.

Chapter 12

Tired Men

Abdellah Taïa translated by Denis M. Provencher

The war had started, long before us, long before they made me enter into this teeny room I had never imagined existed in this Parisian Department Store.[1]

A cage. A sealed security entrance. A box. A little prison? A place out of time, even out of humanity perhaps.

At the beginning of the summer, I had purchased the box set of DVDs for the first two seasons of the Israeli series "Fauda." And, on my way home, I had realized the entire series was available on Netflix. So, I needed to go back to the FNAC to return the DVD set and get reimbursed. But, *voilà*, I was late in doing so. Lazy, too much of a homebody, busy doing nothing, I let time go by. And when the middle of August came, I finally decided to go, a vague intuition deep inside me said I shouldn't do it. The 50 Euros you spent on the series, who cares. Don't go. Don't go. Take a nap. It's not the time, place, or world to go out and confront the world.

I didn't listen to the voice in my head and, of course, I quickly regretted it, very quickly. Something serious could have happened to me that day. Swept into another reality. See the virtual threat come to be. An Arab potential petty criminal they suspect all the time in France, everywhere he goes, has committed the act. He has stolen. They nabbed him. What joy! what joy! They're going to teach him a good lesson, this snotty-nosed kid who doesn't respect the laws of the Republic. They're going to teach him to come out of his savage skin. They're going to remind him where he comes from.

After all, it wasn't even racism. Or maybe: a form of racism that was changing, reinventing itself and one that you wouldn't recognize yet at first glance. They were just scenes replayed systematically each day so that men, the poor, tired, and disoriented men, the poor, empty and pitiful men, would be amused. So that they could pretend to forget a little bit the hellish circle they found themselves stuck in. So that they could thus continue to remain in masculine solidarity and cowardice.

In front of the check-out aisles, there were three long lines. That discouraged me. I don't have the strength for that. I'm going home. To sleep in the middle of the day in my little bed.

When I was leaving the Department Store, the security system started to sound. Two security agents, black security guards, rather young, came toward me. I showed them the DVD set of "Fauda" and also the receipt. They looked at the latter. They noticed it was dated from at least a month ago. I began immediately to explain the situation to them. But, they were already not listening to me. What I had to say already had no value. One of them called the boss who came very quickly, in under a minute. He was also black and was surely the same age as me. He had a very serious look. Cold. That condemned me immediately. You're a thief, you, you're a little thief and you're going to follow me. I wanted to tell him that I had tried to tell the two guards, but I saw it was no use. The proof I had between my two hands, the receipt, didn't convince him either. And I didn't understand why.

At that moment I made a gesture that annoyed him and that prompted him to be tougher with me.

I am not a thief, you know, sir.

These words were accompanied by my index finger pressed up against my temple, which turned in every direction, several times.

This annoyed the head guard. Enormously.

You think I'm a fool, he said. Do you think I'm a fool? That's what we're going to see. Follow me.

Follow him where?

Before, when I arrived in France in 1988, I passed for a nice young man whose virility was non-offensive, a little guy who in fact a little too much so but nice all the same. *Le bon immigrant.* Who speaks French perfectly, who discusses with ease the films of Robert Bresson, and of François Truffaut, and who likes songs by Barbara.

Twenty years later, I've become a menace. Despite myself a menace. A very masculine physical menace who walks everywhere in the streets of Paris and who, you never know, could, you know, could attack you, rape your women, insult your mothers, steal your riches without ever doing a fucking thing with his days, explode in front of a café or do something, I don't even know what, something not very appropriate.

Who's changed? Me, old and disenchanted. Me, small boy become man who sows trouble and danger around him? France who is scared, more than before, of its sexual objects like me, of its old colonial subjects they must master again, even castrate? Afraid of what exactly, deep down? Of who exactly, deep down?

I followed the head guard. The sealed security entrance of the Department Store. There where they deal with the thieves and other petty criminals like me.

I admit that, rather strangely, I also had a curiosity for this place and for the man in front of me. He was visibly tired. Tired from the heatwave in the month of August. Tired from this thankless job. Tired from life. Tired from all the *luttes* needed to have a worthy existence in France. Tired of catching people like me and of doing to them what he was getting ready to do to me.

It was 5 p.m. and this man with drawn features, weary, irritated, upset (with me? Really with me?), seemed very handsome to me. Physically very handsome. I told myself he was correct this way in showing his state of mind, to not withhold what was hurting him. The fury inside him. Others should pay. Pay. I ought to pay too then, as an Arab. It's my turn. Let's go, tell all, mister head of the guards. I'm listening to you. I want to hear to what extent you also feel disillusioned. You no longer believe it. You're fed up with having to be the good guy like you're supposed to.

It was so small, so narrow, the sealed security entrance. 4 square meters? 5 square meters? Perhaps it was bigger. But, at present, I noticed the head guard spoke to me with a language that was not his, words that did not suit him, words that they had taught him, I was closer and closer to a panic attack that was growing, growing, and that I knew I didn't know how to calm.

To protect myself therefore from these words that were accusing me and wanted to reeducate me, I start to look at the head guard with his scornful eyes, eyes that put in place distance, eyes that are going to make you fall without doing almost anything.

The head guard receives the message loud and clear. I will not let myself be pushed around. I didn't steal anything. I didn't steal anything, I'm telling you, and if you want, call the police.

I don't need someone like you, a thief, to tell me what I should do. Understood?

He had gotten up to say these two sentences. He hoped thus to intimidate me physically. To impose himself. To make me admit what I'm not. The thief I'm not.

I succeeded in resisting him, but just for a couple of seconds. For, bitter, I realized all of this was ridiculous, futile, and dangerous. The doubt has awoken. Doubt not about the fact of stealing or not stealing, lying or not lying. No. A more staggering doubt. The doubt about my entire being. What I am. My identity, as they say. All of a sudden, all of it no longer meant anything and I no longer knew how to fill this shell, my body, my being, how to face, the attitude, how to maintain composure. How to protect myself. All of it while asking myself several questions: Who should I protect? Who? Me?

Only me? And why in fact? To win against a black man in France who must be subjected more than I am to hard stares and comments from another era? Win and that's it?

Pathetic. Pathetic. Pathetic. And ridiculous destiny.

I thought about my mother. In Morocco. About this woman in public space and the numerous times where I saw her keep her head down while smiling, keep her head down all the while continuing to fulfill her role, taking on her motherly responsibilities, forgetting herself for us. To no longer exist. To erase herself even though she's there, there, in front of me day and night, she nourishes us, she washes our clothes, takes care of us, cures us, she pushes us to pursue our studies, to keep moving, to love, she prays for us, she has sex with the father three times a week and she keeps us out of harm's way as much as possible. As best she can and above her own strength. There, by my side for so many years, so present and so hardly visible deep inside me at the time. I suddenly experienced an immense shame and I've understood the price she must have paid, what this simple thing, to go through life every day as a woman constantly roughed up and reduced to lapse into the darkness of injustice, must have cost her. To give love and tenderness while the conflicts never ended. Never. To sacrifice yourself to avoid them. To become crafty, very crafty, to forever know how to negotiate with the world and with men.

And these new questions wrote themselves before my eyes, while the head guard was still standing in front of me, silent and practically outside himself: But how did she do it, my mother to not die, to not fall? Where did she find the strength to be at this point in selflessness and in forgiveness?

I looked at this black man differently. I tried to do as my mother did. Low profile. To avoid the traps in advance. To not fall where they want you to. Kiss the hands of those you must kiss to save your own skin.

But it didn't work. I couldn't or I didn't know how to play the role well. To be a woman who sacrifices herself again. It doesn't invent itself on request. And, deep down, I wanted to come back to the war between men. Men who mime power, who having nothing else left but that, this mask of sterile virility to wear in a showy manner to prove they are real men, real strong men, men who win and will always win. I wanted to throw punches too and to injure too, pretend and enter a bit more into the clash that brings about nothing. Nothing. Just two men, the black man and me, who fluff their feathers. Two men who turn in circles in a boxing ring. Who already have no more power but who hang on all the same. Men who are no longer men, just empty shells, worn-out souls, thick skins, eyes stretched by the abyss into which, to our own free will, we are all rushing right now. Men who are being replaced. That's for sure. Cadavers that still move.

The head guard continued his vehement offense against me. Without really wanting to, I lowered my head. Is this defeat?

To return an item to the Department Store, you only have two weeks to do it. You say you've lived in France for twenty years and you don't know that?

Quite strangely, it's this figure, this information I gladly gave him, which he used as proof against me. Moreover, of course, against what I am: little Arab with a shaved head. Attention, danger. Even for a black man like him.

I'm forty-five, you know. And I'm. . . I'm. . .

I wanted to tell him I was gay. As if gay could mean innocent, nice, not dangerous, never criminal.

I wanted to tell him too that I had written books and they were sold there, in the Department Store. Books written in French. In very good French. I didn't do it. I was suddenly experiencing shame. To be a writer, you, it wasn't credible. It doesn't mesh with your physical appearance.

Ashamed of being gay and being a writer.

I had to prove that. And in the sealed security entrance, in the confusion, in front of this black man who was playing the part of the black man, with his white mask, I lacked proof.

I was a thief. And I had treated the head guard like a fool. In truth, it's not for that reason he wouldn't excuse me. Unless, drowned by my own obsessions, blinded by the obviously limited point of view I have on things and the world, I couldn't see anything else.

The truth: this black man was very tired, beyond fatigue. But not because of me. I was not the pretext to say something to the world, to France, to crush the other, especially when he's in the same boat as you. The boat of minorities. The inferiors. Weak ones. Indigenous ones.

The truth: me too, I was exhausted, in the fog, I no longer knew what to think neither of me nor of others and even less of the flood of sad current events that had become our human reality.

Noticing that I wasn't going to raise my head, the black man returned to his spot and called someone. Come.We're holding a thief.

The wait. Five minutes. Which felt like an eternity to me.

I hadn't done anything. And I had to prove it. But how? I was a criminal but I hadn't done anything.

A man around fifty years old arrived. A white man, tall, scrawny, not really mean and who, for a long time now, had given up. He doesn't pretend to be a man anymore. The heterosexual man who is sure of himself and what he embodies. Masculine traits, values of freedom to protect and above all, to bequeath to future generations. This guy, he is no longer part of all that. He no longer needs it. Because quite simply he no longer knows what it all means. To be in these shoes, in this role. He's just a figure head. The second in command. A little larger incarnation, a little more visible, of power. The little power that remains in his grasp. He shot me a quick glance. He quickly surmised the category I belong to in France. Arab. Muslim.

The black man explained the situation to him.

I presented my version of the facts.

But I wasn't at all convincing. I saw it clearly in the eyes of the second in command.

I got up. I showed them one more time the old receipt. But, for him too, it wasn't good enough.

So what to do? What's going to happen? Will they call the police? Will they bring me into the precinct? I'll be flagged. Flagged like a dangerous individual? Judged, Condemned?

Frankly, I was scared. Very scared.

I found myself in a situation that could unravel at any moment.

The book by Laurent Mauvignier about the man killed in Lyon in the supermarket by security guards because he had stolen a can of beer came back into my mind. What was his name, this man? What's the name of this book?

I found it. "What I call forgetting."

Everything is filmed here. Tell me exactly what you did in the Department Store. As soon as you entered. The path you went. The aisles. Everything.

The white man had another kind of power. The power to see what you cannot see. He's the one who is going to judge me. Who is going to find the proof of my existence captured on the cameras? Captured without my agreement? Or perhaps with my unconscious agreement?

I got up. I looked at the white man in an important manner. I spoke. Responded. With an important French. Well-thought-out words, falsely calm, precise words and that strike. I was betting on that now. That they'll see I'm a good person. Really good. Since my French is very very good. Better than very very good.

I'm back.

The black man was sure of my guilt. He started up his spiel again. I closed my ears. I closed my heart. And I told myself that if this was happening to me, to me, to me, it was that, somewhere, I really deserved it. I must have done something wrong too. I sinned. When? Where? I'm paying I don't know what for now not present in my mind. I'm paying for a past, my past, the past of France.

The past of the world.

The black man wasn't the guilty one, wasn't the one responsible for this impasse, for this fatigue, weariness, for this civil war that's brewing, that's coming.

The white man is back. He speaks the truth. Give him back his DVD set.

The black man complied immediately.

I took back "Fauda." I exited the sealed security entrance without an *Au-revoir*. A distraught man. Relieved. Devastated. Bitter. Humiliated. And with a real and stupid desire for vengeance.

NOTE

1. I would like to thank Siham Bouamer and Abdellah Taïa for their invaluable input on the translation.

Conclusion

New Directions for Abdellah Taïa and the Field

Denis M. Provencher and Siham Bouamer

In the spirit of Abdellah Taïa, whose writing is a series of "comings and goings," our edited volume has aimed to offer a non-chronological overview of his work and suggest forms of "non-arrival" in his migration. At the same time, the chapters in our volume have also provided an analysis of the evolution of his work. As Heydnels asks in his opening essay, "is there a next *there* available" to Taïa, Provencher places the "there," in the closing chapter of part III, within transfilial collective mythmaking and unfaithful realms of memory. The other chapters in the volume guide us through this trajectory and identify Taïa's literary movements, which, as our title indicates, go beyond his physical migration. Indeed, the first section (Heyndels, Maroun, and Leblond) questions Taïa's attachment to linear local or transnational migratory structures, be they geographical or narrative, and frames the author's oeuvre around such concepts as liminality and non-places. In part II, Bouamer, Schroth, and Boulé further analyze the author's "unfaithfulness" to fixed social constructs by highlighting Taïa's departure from oppressive affective economies—namely, optimism, shame, and mourning—which, in the words of Sara Ahmed, "align individuals with communities—or bodily space within social space—by the very intensity of their attachment."[1] While these three contributions focus mainly on Taïa's familial structures, the next section, part III, (Muzart, Panizzon, and Provencher) takes the conversion on community (un)building to a macro level in order to discuss processes of political attachment/detachment between the past/present and collectivity/individuality. As the epistolary genre becomes increasingly important in the analysis of the later chapters of our volume, we decided, as editors, to include Idier's letter to Taïa in the last section as an indication of new directions related to Taïa's continued migration.

The Moroccan author's original piece "Des hommes fatigués" serves as a "Terminus" in this journey and confirms the trend that the different chapters ultimately reveal: Taïa's evolution toward "disenchantment" as a queer migrant subject. Reflecting on his transformation as an author in a recent interview with Todd Reeser, Taïa defines the characters of *Un pays pour mourir* [*A Country for Dying*] in similar terms. Despite the fact that he insists, in the same conversation, on his detachment from the character Mojtaba, Taïa's contribution for this volume is tinted with the same "disenchantment," "disillusion," "darkness," and "melancholia" he attributes to the migrant experience, which the author expresses through tiredness.[2] Provencher, in the translation of the text, chooses to stay close to the original piece, the word "tired" to translate "fatigués" in the title where this emotion is first communicated to the reader. The rest of the text leads us to lean toward "fatigue" which evokes a relation between an emotional state and a bodily experience.

The summer heat, laziness, and a bad feeling announce the shift from the author's mental to physical entrapment. The author's pretext for his main character's detainment in the FNAC, the large Parisian department store is his purchase and subsequent refund for the DVD of the first two seasons of the Israeli series "Fauda." It is worth noting that this series chronicles the struggles of protagonist Doron rejoining the Isreali Defense Force. This nod to military activity along the Gaza strip signals to the informed reader the protagonist's own interest in (peaceful) cohabitation of different populations in a geographically limited space. The "sas," or sealed security entrance to the department store, serves as an experiment in close proximity for the protagonist as he negotiates conflict, referred to in the opening of the text as "war," with the white and black guards with whom he comes into close contact.

The "sas" also serves here as a confessional box, a space which, despite its narrowness, allows self-examination. Indeed, Taïa's original new piece can be read as a sort of letter of confession and reflection between himself, his past self, and the reader—three important interlocutors, as Maroun notes, to consider when trying to understand Taïa's liminality. More specifically, this new text expands on his letters from *Lettres à un jeune marocain* and other epistolary narratives—a genre to which Schroth and Boulé attribute a confessional mode——into a sort of "lettre à un jeune français d'origine maghrébine/noire" [letter to a young French citizen of Maghrebi of black origin]. Taïa provides his readers the story of "tired men" or "three tired men"—the alternate title he proposed to us for his piece—and their conflict with each other but also their internal and personal conflicts. Despite the tensions that arise, Taïa attempts to find the commonalities between them. An answer that Taïa gives in his recent interview with Reeser in relation to his other work is, "All [these] characters are disillusioned about Paris."[3]

At first glance, it seems that the three "poor, tired, disoriented, empty, pitiful" men occupy different temporal and social spaces, however, their shared temporality in the "sas," a sealed space that is out of synch with French normative time of the real and unsealed world, comes into clearer focus. Several chapters in the volume identify similar spaces of shared oppression: the banlieue (Maroun), resistance (Muzart), otherness (Panizzon), trans- language (Provencher). Returning to the epistolary genre dear to the Moroccan author, Idier's contribution offers an overview of those imagined solidarities through his oeuvre. We chose to put this letter in conversation with Taïa's piece in this last section not only because of the exchanges between the two shared in the letter, but also because of the reference to Baldwin's novel *Another Country* and the incident involving Boona, a Tunisian immigrant, wrongly accused of theft.

In Taïa's earlier work, he would perhaps have been excited about his queer protagonist being transformed into a "petty Arab criminal." This turn would have allowed the writer to be part of a series of other canonical queer French writers like Genet, where their miraculous characters remain on the margins of society in celebratory fashion. However, in Taïa's later writings, the material conditions of everyday life and marginal communities become more of the world he describes, and in this context, being identified as a criminal could leave him "fiché" [flagged, but also "screwed"]. Taïa's more recent protagonists realize the "cruel optimism" Bouamer writes about in our volume and the inability to remain a "good immigrant," a "good French speaker," "a gay man," and "a writer" who is protected from the real-life experience of racism or hatred that other tired men in France, including the guards working in the FNAC, have also grown tired of. They all belong, as he writes, to: "The boat of minorities. The inferiors. Weak ones. Indigenous ones." And yet, it is the guard who speaks French like an integrated citizen that destabilizes Taïa's protagonist as he realizes they must all wear masks in order to survive in this system.

What ends ups saving the protagonist in the end however occurs in true Taïa style. It is not the understanding, compassion, or complicity from the guards or other citizens of color in this story that forgive the protagonist. While the white guard "speaks the truth" it is not due to some form of authentic understanding or compassion on his part that finally frees the protagonist. It is the camera's eye of surveillance that frees his character. At once the panopticon of Foucault, and yet the miraculous and disruptive cinematic force of Taïa that allows freedom to be reimagined but always at a price of disillusionment. In the end, his protagonist leaves the store: "A distraught man. Relieved. Devastated. Bitter. Humiliated. And with a real and stupid desire for vengeance."

So where does Abdellah Taïa and where does the field actually go next? Indeed, Abdellah Taïa punctuates much of his recent work with several of the elements discussed above related to disenchantment, disillusion, and continued isolation. And the author continues to juxtapose the poverty of Morocco and the wealth of France, its people, and its language. As we have also discussed, it is not until several years into Taïa's oeuvre where he begins to consider the disenfranchised communities of Africans and North Africans in France, and it is during this same timeframe that he considers returning to similar elements and communities in his homeland and where he finds perhaps a renewed sense of belonging and radicalism.

As an indication of this, we want to consider one of Taïa's latest pieces, "Un jardin, en attendant" [A garden, while waiting . . .], which punctuates Heydnels and Zidouh's edited volume. In this original essay, Taïa writes of a garden he stumbles upon in Morocco, and how he and other marginal citizens initially remain skeptical about this communal space, but where he and others eventually discovers a sense of belonging if not common purpose. Taïa writes:

> Et un jour: le miracle arrive. De notre côté, sans nous demander notre avis, on construit un jardin. Pour tout le monde. Avec des bancs, du gazon, quelques arbres et même un terrain pour jouer au basket ball [...]
>
> Un soir, je suis seul dans le jardin, je m'attarde. La nuit. Le noir. Des gens arrivent. Ils ont des bouteilles de vin bon marché entre les mains. Je les suis du regard. Ils sont loin. Dans la radicalité. Des ivrognes. Des clochards. Des prostituées. Je n'ai pas peur. Je vais vers eux.
>
> Je résiste à côté d'eux. Simplement. Naïvement. Amoureusement.
>
> [And one day: a miracle arrives. On our side, without asking our advice, they construct a garden. For everyone. With benches, grass, some trees and even a court to play basketball.
>
> One evening, I'm alone in the garden, I linger. The night. The dark. People arrive. They have bottles of cheap wine in their hands. My gaze follows them. They're far. In radicalism. Drunkards. Bums. Prostitutes. I'm not afraid. I go toward them.
>
> I resist next to them. Simply. Naively. Lovingly.][4]

In some ways, Taïa comes full circle here: he began writing about poverty and denizens in his very first novels, including characters on the margins such as sex initiators, sex workers, queers, and terrorists. Two decades later, he returns to several of the same characters in order to find a continued sense of radicalism and community. On one level, the garden, described as a "miracle" can be read in parallel to his arrival at the gates of heaven in *Infidèles,* a space guarded by Marilyn who embodies all languages, all people, all backgrounds. Taïa's protagonist in "Un jardin, en attendant . . ." enters another miraculous heterotopic space—the garden being a archetype of this material form of utopia—where all are welcome. He carries the torch, in a similar fashion as the Foucault lookalike character in *L'armée du salut*, to welcome all outcasts in his newfound shelter, a reimagined "Nef des fous" [Ship of Fools].

At the same time, when we read "Un jardin, en attendant" alongside his later works like *Celui qui est digne d'être aimé, Un pays pour mourir*, and *La vie lente*, or "Lettre à James Balwin," we cannot help but think about the way Taïa has taken both an intersectional and trans turn. In these later works, he reaches toward other characters of embodied difference—refugees, trans men and women, drunkards, bums, and sex workers—similar and yet different from the experiences of his gay male protagonists like Abdellah or Jallal of his earlier works. He finds new meaning related to freedom through shared communities and shared experiences on the margins. As Taïa states in his recent interview with Reeser: "My novel gives them the space in which to invent something else." He continues: "Disenchanted, they understand that they have to invent another space where they can live and, one day in the future, die."[5] The garden, in this short piece cited above, allows author Abdellah Taïa to continue to reimagine new verdant if not celestial places of queer belonging in the world. In conclusion, the editors of this volume hope that future scholarship on Taïa will turn toward the intersectional and trans-broadly defined in his current and expanding oeuvre.

NOTES

1. Sarah Ahmed, *The Cultural Politics of Emotion* (Edinburgh: Edinburgh University Press, 2004), 119.
2. Todd Reeser, "Abdellah Taïa on Illuminating the Immigrant Experience," *Lambda Literary,* November 27, 2020, https://www.lambdaliterary.org/2020/11/abdellah-taia/.
3. Reeser, "Abdellah Taïa on Illuminating the Immigrant Experience."
4. Abdellah Taïa, "Un jardin en attendant," in *Autour d'Abdellah Taïa: Poétique et politique du désir engagé/Around Abdellah Taïa: Poetics and Politics of Engaged Desire*, edited by Ralph Heyndels and Amine Zidouh (Caen: Editions Passage(s), 2020): 352, 354.
5. Reeser, "Abdellah Taïa on Illuminating the Immigrant Experience."

BIBLIOGRAPHY

Ahmed, Sara. *The Cultural Politics of Emotion*. Edinburgh: Edinburgh University Press, 2004.

Reeser, Todd. "Abdellah Taïa on Illuminating the Immigrant Experience." *Lambda Literary,* November 27, 2020. https://www.lambdaliterary.org/2020/11/abdellah-taia/.

Taïa, Abdellah. "Un jardin, en attendant..." In *Autour d'Abdellah Taïa: Poétique et politique du désir engagé/Around Abdellah Taïa: Poetics and Politics of Engaged Desire*, edited by Ralph Heyndels and Amine Zidouh, 351–354. Caen: Editions Passage(s), 2020.

Index

About the Contributors

Siham Bouamer is assistant professor of French and Francophone Studies at Sam Houston State University. Her research focuses on travel writing and transnational movements from/to the Maghreb in literature and film. Her work on Abdellah Taïa specifically concerns transcultural and transtemporal intermediality. She is currently working on her first monograph tentatively titled *The Mariannes of the Protectorate: Women's Travel Writing on Morocco (1906–1956)* and on a co-edited volume on the artistic, cinematic, and literary representation of women at work in contemporary France. Her work has been published in *Expressions Maghrébines, Études Francophones, French Studies, Francosphères, Intertexts: A Journal of Comparative and Theoretical Reflection, Transitions: Journal of Franco-Iberian Studies, I-LanD: Identity, Language and Diversity Journal*, and *Linguistics and Education*. Recently, she co-founded the *Diversity, Decolonization, and the French curriculum* collective.

Jean-Pierre Boulé is Emeritus professor of Contemporary French Studies at the Nottingham Trent University (United Kingdom). A specialist in contemporary French literature, he has published six monographs on Sartre, Guibert, and HIV Literature, and edited or co-edited four volumes on Beauvoir, Guibert, and Sartre. He has published approximately twenty-seven articles in journals such *as Contemporary French Civilization, L'Esprit créateur, Essays in French Literature, French Cultural Studies, French Review, La Règle du Jeu, Revue Critique De Fixxion Française Contemporaine, Roman 20-50, Sartre Studies International*, and *Simone de Beauvoir Studies*, building an expertise on *autofiction*, notably on Serge Doubrovsky and on Abdellah Taïa on which he has already published two articles. His monograph—*Abdellah Taïa: La Mélancolie et le cri* published by Presses universitaires de Lyon in

2020—is the first comprehensive study of Taïa's works, including his cinematic and political writings.

Ralph Heyndels is professor of French and Comparative Literature at the University of Miami where he also teaches Queer and Franco-Arabic Studies. He has been Chair of the Modern Languages and Literatures Department at the University of Miami; Director of the Center for Sociology of Literature at the University of Brussels; Director of the Comparative Literature Program and Center for Critical Studies at the University of Maryland, College Park; and Visiting Professor at the Ecole Normale, Paris, and the University of Cape Town, among other appointments. His fields of published scholarship do include classical, modern, and contemporary French literature from Pascal and Racine to Diderot and Sade, to Flaubert, Aragon, Duras, Beckett, and Zahia Rahmani; and theory (Goldmann, Adorno, Blanchot, Lévinas, Derrida). He is the author and editor of several volumes including *La Pensée fragmentée*, *Ecrire dit-elle: les imaginaires de Marguerite Duras*, *Les Afriques de Rimbaud*, *Les Ecrivains français et le monde arabe*, and *Les Passions de Jean Genet.* He has recently published numerous articles on Flaubert, Sade, Rimbaud, Jean Genet, Roland Barthes, René de Ceccaty, François-Marie Banier, Rachid O., and Abdellah Taïa, among many other writers, and on topics related to decolonial and immigration studies. He is currently completing *Nuit politique du désir. L'engagement amoureux de Jean Genet.*

Antoine Idier holds a PhD in Social Science from the University of Amiens and is the author of several publications on sexuality, politics, and the history of ideas as well as contributions about contemporary visual art and literature. His books include: *Les Alinéas au placard. L'abrogation du délit d'homosexualité 1977–1982* (Cartouche, 2013); *Les Vies de Guy Hocquenghem. Politique, sexualité, culture* (Fayard, 2017); *Archives des mouvements LGBT+* (Textuel, 2018); and *Pureté et impureté de l'art. Michel Journiac et le sida* (Sombres torrents, 2019). He also has edited a collection of press articles written by Guy Hocquenghem: *Un journal de rêve. Articles de presse (1971–1987)* (Éditions Verticales, 2017). He is currently Head of research at the school of arts of Caen/Cherbourg (ésam Caen/Cherbourg).

Olivier Le Blond is assistant professor of French at the University of North Georgia (UNG). A graduate of SUNY Buffalo, his dissertation explored the emergence of a queer Moroccan literature through the works of Rachid O., Abdellah Taïa, and Bahaa Trabelsi. His research interests include but are not limited to gender studies, same-sex representation in French and Francophone literature, and porn studies. Dr. Le Blond has published in *The French Review*, *Nouvelles Études Francophone*, and *Women's Studies*

International Forum. His most recent publication includes a chapter in the upcoming volume of collected works entitled *Éduquer en pays dominé* that explores the use of the Arab male body in French ethnic pornography, and sees it as a locus of resistance against colonialism. In addition to his research, he co-authored the textbook used in the second semester elementary French courses of his current institution. He is also the senior co-director of the university's Gender Studies Council, created to promote gender-related events as well as the Gender Studies minor to the student community.

Daniel Maroun holds a PhD in French and teaches at the University of Illinois where he is also the director of Undergraduate Studies. His work focuses on queer expressions of masculinity in two diverse axes: North African cultural productions and HIV/AIDS narratives in French literature. Recent publications include, "Comment échapper à la honte du *zamel*" in *@nalyses: Revue de Critique et de Théorie Littéraire* (2016) and forthcoming publications "Contact Tracing: Forty years of HIV/AIDS Narratives in French Literature. What's Next?" (2021) for *Contemporary French Civilization* as well as a large translation project of Guillaume Dustan's works published through Semiotexte (2021).

Thomas Muzart completed his PhD in 2020 in French at the Graduate Center of the City University of New York. He is currently a Postdoctoral Associate in French Studies at Duke University. His research focuses on the relationship between geographical movements (migration, nomadism, and tourism) and minority politics in the works of Jean Genet, Guy Hocquenghem, Virginie Despentes, and Abdellah Taïa. His work on Taïa has been published in an edited volume by the Canadian journal *@nalyses*. Thomas also collaborates with the gender studies section of the online magazine *non.fiction* and is a board member and editor of the American Society of Geolinguistics.

Philippe Panizzon completed his PhD, entitled "Out in Morocco: Male Homosexuality and Transnationalism in Late 20th and Early 21st Century Moroccan Literature," in 2020 at the University of Oxford. He is currently preparing a project entitled "The Gender Politics of Anticolonialism" for the Swiss National Science Foundation. His research focuses on French and Francophone literatures and cultures, the Global South, queer theory and human rights. His work has been published by the *International Journal of Francophone Studies*, *Francosphères*, *French Studies,* and the *French Studies Bulletin.*

Denis M. Provencher is professor of French & Francophone Studies and is head of the department of French & Italian at the University of Arizona. His scholarship is intersectional and cuts across traditional disciplinary boundaries through an exploration of the transnational flow of languages, peoples, and ideas—related to gender, sexuality, class, race, and religion—across North America, Europe, and North Africa. Dr Provencher is the author of *Queer French: Globalization, Language, and Sexual Citizenship in France* (Ashgate/Routledge, 2007) and the companion volume *Queer Maghrebi French: Language, Temporalities, Transfiliations* (Liverpool UP, 2017). He is also the editor-in-chief of the journal *Contemporary French Civilization* (Liverpool UP), co-editor of the book series *Modern & Contemporary France* (Liverpool UP), and a member of the editorial board of the *Journal of Language and Sexuality* (John Benjamins Publishing).

Ryan K. Schroth, PhD, is assistant professor of French Studies at Wake Forest University. He specializes in North African queer cultural production, especially the work of Abdellah Taïa. His research employs affect theory and ideas of migration in order to better understand the place of the queer body in post- and neo-colonial contexts. He is currently at work on his first manuscript, tentatively titled *Queer Feelings: Affect, Migration, and the Body in Queer Francophone Literature.*

Abdellah Taïa was born in Rabat, Morocco, in 1973. He is the first Arab writer/filmmaker to publicly declare his homosexuality. He is the author of nine novels written in French, including *Salvation Army* (2006), *An Arab Melancholia* (2008), both translated into English by Semiotext(e), and *Infidels* (2012) published by Seven Stories Press. His novel *Le jour du Roi* was awarded the prestigious French Prix de Flore in 2010. *Salvation Army*, his first movie as a director, is adapted from his eponymous novel. The film was selected for the Venice Film Festival 2013, TIFF 2013, New Directors 2014, and won many international prizes. His novel *A Country for Dying*, translated into English by Emma Ramadan for Seven Stories Press, was published in the United States in 2020, and won the Pen America Translation Prize in 2021.

Lightning Source UK Ltd.
Milton Keynes UK
UKHW042139150721
387236UK00001B/14